Correspondences:
Medievalism in
Scholarship and the Arts

Studies in Medievalism XIV

2005

Studies in Medievalism

Founded by Leslie J. Workman

Volume I
1   Medievalism in England. Edited by Leslie J. Workman. Spring 1979.
2. Medievalism in America. Edited by Leslie J. Workman. Spring 1982.

Volume II
1. Twentieth-Century Medievalism. Edited by Jane Chance. Fall 1982.
2. Medievalism in France. Edited by Heather Arden. Spring 1983.
3. Dante in the Modern World. Edited by Kathleen Verduin. Summer 1983.
4. Modern Arthurian Literature. Edited by Veronica M.S. Kennedy and Kathleen Verduin. Fall 1983.

Volume III
1. Medievalism in France 1500–1750. Edited by Heather Arden. Fall 1987.
2. Architecture and Design. Edited by John R. Zukowsky. Fall 1990.
3. Inklings and Others. Edited by Jane Chance. Winter 1991.
4. German Medievalism. Edited by Francis G. Gentry. Spring 1991.
    Note: Volume III, Numbers 3 and 4, are bound together.

IV.   Medievalism in England. Edited by Leslie Workman. 1992.
V.   Medievalism in Europe. Edited by Leslie Workman. 1993.
VI.   Medievalism in North America. Edited by Kathleen Verduin. 1994.
VII. Medievalism in England II. Edited by Leslie J. Workman and Kathleen Verduin. 1995.
VIII. Medievalism in Europe II. Edited by Leslie J. Workman and Kathleen Verduin. 1996.
IX.   Medievalism and the Academy I. Edited by Leslie J. Workman, Kathleen Verduin, and David D. Metzger. 1997.
X.   Medievalism and the Academy II. Edited by David Metzger. 1998.
XI.   Appropriating the Middle Ages: Scholarship, Politics, Fraud. Edited by Tom Shippey and Martin Arnold. 2001.
XII. Film and Fiction: Reviewing the Middle Ages. Edited by Tom Shippey and Martin Arnold. 2002.
XIII. Postmodern Medievalisms. Edited by Richard Utz and Jesse G. Swan. 2004.

Correspondences: Medievalism in Scholarship and the Arts

Edited by
Tom Shippey
with
Martin Arnold
(Associate Editor)

Studies in Medievalism XIV 2005

Cambridge
D. S. Brewer

© Studies in Medievalism 2005

All Rights Reserved. Except as permitted under current legislation no part of this work may be photocopied, stored in a retrieval system, published, performed in public, adapted, broadcast, transmitted, recorded or reproduced in any form or by any means, without the prior permission of the copyright owner

First published 2005
D. S. Brewer, Cambridge

D. S. Brewer is an imprint of Boydell & Brewer Ltd
PO Box 9, Woodbridge, Suffolk IP12 3DF, UK
and of Boydell & Brewer Inc.
668 Mt Hope Avenue, Rochester, NY 14620, USA
website: www.boydellandbrewer.com

ISBN 1 84384 063 4

ISSN 0738–7614

PN
671
.C67
2005

A catalogue record for this book is available
from the British Library

This publication is printed on acid-free paper

Printed in Great Britain by
Antony Rowe Ltd, Chippenham, Wiltshire

Studies in Medievalism

Founding Editor	Leslie J. Workman
Editor	Tom Shippey (Saint Louis)
Associate Editor	Martin Arnold (Hull)
Advisory Board	Geraldine Barnes (Sydney)
	Rolf H. Bremmer, Jr. (Leiden)
	William Calin (Florida)
	Philip Cardew (King Alfred's College, Winchester)
	David Matthews (Newcastle, Australia)
	Gwendolyn Morgan (Montana State)
	Ulrich Müller (Salzburg)
	Richard Osberg (Santa Clara)
	Nils Holger Petersen (Copenhagen)
	Clare A. Simmons (Ohio State)
	John Simons (Edgehill College, Ormskirk)
	Paul Szarmach (Western Michigan)
	Toshiyuki Takamiya (Keio)
	Kathleen Verduin (Hope College, Michigan)
	Andrew Wawn (Leeds)

Studies in Medievalism provides an interdisciplinary medium of exchange for scholars in all fields, including the visual and other arts, concerned with any aspect of the post-medieval idea and study of the Middle Ages and the influence, both scholarly and popular, of this study on Western society after 1500.

Studies in Medievalism is published by Boydell & Brewer, Ltd., P.O. Box 9, Woodbridge, Suffolk IP12 3DF, UK; Boydell & Brewer, Inc., 668 Mt Hope Avenue, Rochester, NY 14620, USA. Orders and inquiries about back issues should be addressed to Boydell & Brewer at the appropriate office.

Submissions and inquiries regarding future volumes should be addressed to the Editor, **Studies in Medievalism**, English Dept., Saint Louis University, 221 N. Grand Blvd., St. Louis, MO 63103, USA, tel. 314–977–7196, fax 314–977–1514, e-mail <shippey@slu.edu>. Contributors should submit the original manuscript and one copy with an abstract: unsolicited manuscripts should be accompanied by a stamped self-addressed envelope. When a manuscript is accepted for publication, copy on an IBM-compatible disk will be required.

Acknowledgments

The Editors make grateful acknowledgment for technical and other assistance to Saint Louis University.

The device on the title page comes from the title page of **Des Knaben Wunderhorn: Alte deutsche Lieder**, edited by L. Achim von Arnim and Clemens Brentano (Heidelberg and Frankfurt, 1806).

The epigraph is from an unpublished paper by Lord Acton written about 1859, printed in Herbert Butterfield, **Man On His Past** (Cambridge University Press, 1955), 212.

Studies in Medievalism

Editorial Note	Tom Shippey	1
Long-lost Letters: Francisque Michel's Contribution to the Invention of French Medieval Literary Studies	Mark Burde	5
A Lot of Learning is a Dang'rous Thing: The Ruthwell Cross Runes and their Icelandic Interpreters	Magnús Fjalldal	30
Joast Halbertsma, Jacob Grimm, and Count Carlo Ottavio Castiglioni: Nineteenth-Century Sensitivities concerning a Gothic Bible Translation	Alpita de Jong	51
Imagining Medieval Music: a Short History	Annette Kreutziger-Herr	81
The Medievalism of Carl Maria von Weber's *Euryanthe*	Nils Holger Petersen	110
"Those effigies which belonged to the English Nation": Antiquarianism, Nationalism, and Charles Alfred Stothard's *Monumental Effigies of Great Britain*	Rachel Dressler	143
Commedia Images in the Neo-Gothic Age(s)	Karl Fugelso	175
Harriet Monroe as Queen-Critic of Chaucer and Langland (*viz.* Ezra Pound)	William Quinn	200
Zoë Oldenbourg, the Albigensian Crusade, and Terrorist Repression	Peter Christensen	217
Notes on Contributors		241

Two great principles divide the world, and contend for the mastery, antiquity and the middle ages. These are the two civilizations that have preceded us, the two elements of which ours is composed. All political as well as religious questions reduce themselves practically to this. This is the great dualism that runs through our society.

Lord Acton

Editorial Note

As has been remarked in the "Editorial Notes" to earlier volumes, diversity is intrinsic to medievalism. Not only are there very different "Middle Ages" to confront, they are also confronted differently in different periods, and by different disciplines. One of the rewards of editing such divergent materials, however, is to find pieces of a very complex jigsaw puzzle at last beginning to fit together. We have one such case in Rachel Dressler's piece on Charles Alfred Stothard, son of the illustrator Thomas Stothard whose work was considered by Betsy Bowden in *Studies in Medievalism* 11, and deserving at least of pre-eminence here as a genuine martyr to medievalism: in 1821 he "died as he had lived," as the result of a fall suffered while trying to preserve and bring to general knowledge an aspect of the medieval world which, in England, had never quite gone away, the large corpus of medieval effigies and representations in cathedrals and parish churches. Studying stone, in the field, bears more significant risks than the "armchair scholarship" of critics and historians.

Another aspect of the diversity phenomenon is to find familiar names cropping up in unfamiliar contexts, and making unexpected connections. To Anglicists (such as the current editors) Francisque Michel is known primarily for his *Bibliothèque anglo-saxonne* of 1837, with its preface by J. M. Kemble, though his editing of the Oxford MS of the *Chanson de Roland* is also a part of philological history. Here Mark Burde's piece shows us Michel figuring, in France, at "a crucial early moment of constitution of the discipline," negotiating cautiously between the demands of literary and historical scholars, and using tricks of "manipulation . . . exaggeration and hyperbole" not unfamiliar to the modern world of "grantsmanship" to get what he wanted.

Michel's trip of 1833 represented a genuine breakthrough. Magnús Fjalldal's piece, by contrast, studies a failed breakthrough. The runic inscription on the Ruthwell Cross, again according to philological legend, was triumphantly explained first by J. M. Kemble in 1840, a reading which swept aside the pre-scientific nonsense of earlier antiquarians like the Icelanders Thorleifr Repp and Finnur Magnússon. Magnús Fjalldal shows, however, that Kemble probably learned more from his predecessors than he was prepared to admit, and furthermore that the Icelanders were misled less by ignorance than by knowledge: they saw, in brief, what they might well have expected to see. Only after this had been brought into focus could the unexpected be revealed. Alpita de Jong meanwhile considers a more wide-ranging scholarly dispute, which however also involves the sensitivities of major and minor European language groups. Why should Joast Hiddes Halbertsma, "the Frisian Grimm," dedicate the two volumes of his *Letterkundige Naoogst* or "Philological Aftermath" to the Italian scholars Count Castiglioni and Bernardino Biondelli? De Jong's answer shows Halbertsma carefully "positioning himself" amid the tensions between German comparative philologists, full of the confidence of their new discipline, and Italian scholars, who whatever their methodological deficiencies still controlled many manuscript resources. In a situation where the very word "Gothic," or *gotisch*, or *gotisk*, was liable to be bitterly disputed, the editing of Gothic manuscripts roused unusual passions, not without political significance, as Grimm, his followers and his competitors, all groped for the boundaries of *deutsch* and *germanisch*.

The three essays so far mentioned all deal with aspects of the philological scholarship of the 1830s and 1840s. Annette Kreutziger-Herr's essay on medieval music reminds us, however, that at that period, while Victor Hugo might well be able to imagine the bells ringing out over medieval Paris, virtually nothing at all was known about medieval music. Moreover, while medieval literature can only be appreciated through some form or other of mediating scholarship, medieval music (once rediscovered and reinterpreted) can and does make a much more direct appeal to the senses, requiring no special knowledge or mental adjustment before it can be enjoyed. This is another salutary reminder for literary scholars and historians, as showing a much more direct route from the medieval world to the modern popular consciousness. Nils Holger Petersen's article on Weber's *Euryanthe*, based on *Le Roman de la Violette*, and first performed in 1833, takes a detailed look at an early example of what (remembering Werner Wunderlich's article in *Studies in Medievalism* 11) was to be one of the most powerful and influential forms of medievalist transmission during the 19th and 20th centuries, the medievalist opera. It is amusing to see, on the one hand, the modern opinion that "more abuse has been heaped on [the libretto of *Euryanthe*] than on any other in the history of opera," and on the other, Francisque Michel (once more) in 1834 praising its music (though admittedly not its libretto) as "very beautiful, full of originality, of charm, of strength throughout, and [having] a very pronounced medieval colour."

When it comes to the visual arts, Rachel Dressler (as mentioned above) reminds us again of the direct nature of some medieval continuities in the "medieval effigies of England" studied and reproduced by Charles Stothard, though she notes also Stothard's attempt at a take-over bid of French effigies in the ruins of Fontevraud, interestingly parallel, if antithetic, to Michel's more successful capture of the Oxford *Roland* for the self-image of France. Dressler further notes the attraction, for the English propertied classes in a time of European unrest, of the effigies' apparent demonstration of stability, continuity, aristocracy, and military virtue. This attraction, of course, could hardly be felt in the United States of America, a nation without medieval churches and indeed without a Middle Ages of its own, a nation furthermore committed to non-aristocratic ideals. The question of how Americans could receive the Middle Ages has been aired in previous volumes of this series, as in William Calin's account of Longfellow's Chaucer and Paul Hardwick's of Florence Converse's Langland, both in *Studies in Medievalism* 12. The two poets are confronted here in William Quinn's account of Harriet Monroe, influential editor and proprietress of *Modern Poetry* in the 1920s, and the champion of Langland against Chaucer (and against Ezra Pound) as the more "formally vital and politically significant" poet. Like Converse's, her support does not seem to have borne fruit; yet it was a strand in the development of modernist poetry, which deserves to be recognized and remembered.

Finally, two contributions here address the traumas of the recent and the remoter past. Karl Fugelso, once again studying the visual arts, shows how Dante's *Inferno* has provided continuing impetus for illustrators both to reach out for the sublime, and to mirror the increasingly terrible experiences of their own times: "Inferno" as a permanent state, a state permanently renewed, an inevitable but developing part of the human condition. In this sense the medieval world remains terribly present. Peter Christensen's study of the "Albigensian" works of Zoë Oldenbourg continues our sequence of studies of historical novels (see Carl and Jóna Hammer's articles in issue 12), but also takes up a topic which continues to have modern resonances. Christensen's survey of the scholarship on the Albigensian Crusades shows how deeply polarized it has remained, especially in France, between supporters of orthodoxy and tolerators of heresy, while his account of the novels argues for Oldenbourg's attempt to get through the issues to a "sense of lived experience." The issues, however, remain, and no modern reader can quite escape a sense, once again, that the medieval world with all its cruelty and fanaticism has not been entirely buried, is all too capable of returning to haunt us. Medievalisms remain dangerous, and dangerously vital: that is one reason why they require careful and dispassionate study, of the kind they too rarely receive inside or outside the academy.

Tom Shippey
Saint Louis University
April 2005

Long-lost Letters:
Francisque Michel's Contribution to the Invention of French Medieval Literary Studies[1]

Mark Burde

In June of 1833 a precocious and ambitious 24-year-old paleographer named Francisque Michel wrote an unsolicited letter to France's Minister of Public Education, François Guizot, requesting governmental funding to travel to England so as to transcribe rare and unpublished manuscript copies of several early medieval vernacular works deemed crucial to a proper understanding of French history and letters. After convening a committee of prominent scholars, the minister, an eminent medieval historian himself, agreed to send Michel on what became a pioneering research mission for the fledgling speciality. Over the course of the following several years, Michel would do for French medieval literary studies something akin to what the Louisiana Purchase did for early American territorial expansion, vastly increasing the stock of foundational Anglo-Norman works available in print for the first time. Because of the sheer quantity of the works transcribed and published, because he epitomised the fervour of the first generation of specialist scholars to be trained in medieval vernacular paleography and codicology at the newly-founded *Ecole des chartes*, and especially because his most famous transcription, the long-lost and oldest surviving manuscript copy of what would soon become known as the *Song of Roland*, would provide France with a national epic and moment of poetic origin, Michel's first "mission" to England, as it is referred to, is often viewed as an important early paradigmatic breakthrough in the modern discipline of French medieval literary studies.[2]

Oddly, however, Michel's letter of solicitation, though regularly referred to in general terms, has never to my knowledge been quoted or even accurately paraphrased in medievalist criticism. I believe this fact to be attributable to its having been archivally misfiled for at least the better part of the past century, and hence unavailable to the one or two scholars whose detailed research into the Michel mission has served as a foundation for all subsequent discussion of its importance.[3] This article reproduces the letter for the first time and argues that it affords important insights into French medieval literary studies at a pivotal but understudied juncture. Although on a superficial level this document does little to dispel a conventional assessment of Michel as a manipulative and personally flawed scholar, its subtleties reveal a tale of the complex negotiations by which medieval literary studies – specifically those pertaining to *Roland* research – inserted themselves into the official projects of a nation in search of its origins and illustrate how a brash young scholar presumed to invent a moment of origin for his discipline.

For most scholars writing the history of French medieval literary studies, the year 1833 has never been considered a serious rival to the early 1870s. Not only does the term "medievalist" date from this momentous later period (Michel and his contemporaries having been known variously as "*littérateurs*," "*archéologues*," "*bibliothécaires*" or, pejoratively, "*fouilleurs de chartes*"), but so do the discipline-defining journals and publishing endeavours such as *Romania* and the *Société des anciens textes français*.[4] Most earlier milestones, including Michel's mission, have tended to be viewed as preparatory steps leading to the imposing academic manor house built by Gaston Paris and Paul Meyer.[5] It is true that comprehensive official support for medieval literary (as opposed to historical) research and publishing was practically non-existent prior to the 1850s. Yet the advent of parliamentary and constitutional monarchy in France in 1830 had made urgent the need for a unifying and celebratory narrative of a rich national past, for which archival research would provide the raw material. The Middle Ages were a natural locus of memory, seen as having devised the systems and institutions of government and as having fostered the rise of the all-important bourgeoisie.[6] If the bulk of the documents of primary interest to Guizot were resolutely prosaic and non-narrative, he did nonetheless sanction the publication of texts of a more poetic nature deemed to be historically significant. Michel's transcription of Benoît de Sainte-Maure's *Chronique des ducs de Normandie*, for example, would be published in 1836 under the very prestigious auspices of Guizot's new "*Collection des documents inédits sur l'histoire de France*" series, the publishing arm of his state-sponsored *Comité des travaux historiques et scientifiques*.[7]

It has long been assumed that Michel's avowed interest in this and another contemporary verse chronicle, while genuine, served to camouflage his true and more purely literary ambition, believed to have been withheld from his letter of request for pragmatic reasons – namely, the recovery of the enigmatic *Roland* manuscript.[8] In fact, however, Michel's request explicitly mentions the manuscript that, since his 1837 edition of it, has been known as the *Song of Roland* (referring to it as the version of the "Romance of Roncevaux" composed at the beginning of the twelfth century). What is more, the "*Song of Roland*" as the term was understood in 1833 – that is, the quasi-mythical epic many medieval chroniclers asserted and many early modern scholars believed to have been chanted by Norman warriors or by their jongleur Taillefer at the Battle of Hastings – is also everywhere evident in Michel's letter.[9] Of the four specific works Michel names whose declared historical, literary, or philological value underlie his request, two are chronicles recounting the Norman invasion that mention Taillefer, one had been proposed by a predecessor of Michel as a (wildly inappropriate) candidate for Taillefer's performance, and one – Oxford Bodleian MS Digby 23(2) – would eventually win the designation of "Song of Roland."[10] Evidence suggests that Michel could not wait to get his hands on these documents, especially since his enthusiastic participation in the conundrum that had preoccupied numerous early nineteenth-century Romantics, taking on the allure of a literary Loch Ness Monster quest ("What had Taillefer sung?"), has long been established.[11] What has until now been unknown is the precise manner in which he accommodated his predominantly literary interests to the tastes and expectations of a camp of historians, equally committed to recovering foundational vernacular documents of France's formative centuries, for whom tall tales concerning the exploits of Charlemagne's mythical nephew were of no particular documentary interest.[12]

It is my contention in this article that the "hidden agenda" trope heretofore commonly attributed to Michel's 1833 mission (according to which Michel concealed his real, *Roland*-centered intentions) need not be discarded entirely, but can, rather, be reformulated. That is to say, the ghostly presence in Michel's letter of Roland's heroism as remembered by invading Normans and their later chroniclers serves as an apt metaphor for the ghostly presence of the literary in official, state-sponsored medieval-studies projects in the 1830s. Michel's letter, in other words, deepens our understanding of the degree to which not just the paradigmatic French literary epic but medieval literature itself was absently present at a crucial early moment of constitution of the discipline.

I say "constitution of the discipline" because Michel did not simply compose a letter but organised a veritable petition, creating a visually forceful piece of epistolary theater that brings to bear on his project the signatures and testimonials of over a third of the fifty full-time members of the pre-eminent scholarly institution of his day, the *Académie des Inscriptions et Belles-Lettres*. One of the five constituent bodies (along with the *Académie française*) of the *Institut de France*, the *Académie des Inscriptions et Belles-Lettres* had long since outgrown its original seventeenth-century mission of supplying Latin inscriptions for royal monuments and medallions and had been charged since the reign of Louis XIV with studying the antiquities of the nation.[13] By 1833 it not only housed the country's most prominent classicists, archaeologists, paleographers and men of letters, but also actively promoted the advancement of learning – predominantly classical and orientalist – through a series of publications it oversaw and training institutes, such as the *Ecole des chartes*, that it sponsored.[14] Since Guizot took up his post at the same time as oversight of the *Académie*, thanks to a recent governmental reorganisation, came under his jurisdiction, and since the *Académie* for a number of reasons was the institution that best embodied the promise of bridging the gap between pre- and post-Revolutionary institutional culture by creating a national memory, its members' signatures carry indisputable weight.[15]

Although it contains no date of composition, the letter bears a ministerial stamp indicating receipt on 10 June 1833. The signers include not just the two most prominent literary medievalists of the day – François-Just-Marie Raynouard and Claude Fauriel – but also prominent academics from a variety of disciplines, as well as manuscript library curators, politicians, and the director of the *Ecole des chartes*. A space initially provided for the date within the signers' group statement has been left blank, presumably because the document circulated among the signers, the last of whom neglected to fill it in. At the top of the first page, the letter bears a note from Guizot, the minister of Public Education, directing an aide on the next step to be taken – that is, soliciting a preliminary evaluation from Fauriel. After a few intervening bureaucratic steps, including a personal interview, Michel received an official governmental decree six weeks later charging him with research travel to England and allocating one thousand francs for initial expenses, with the possibility of renewal.

The letter (the French version of which can be found in on pp. 19–21 below), reads as follows:

> *Dear Sir: Scholars devoted to the study of medieval philology, history, and French literature often bemoan their incapacity to bring their research to a satisfactory conclusion, for they lack access to essential works whose loss, however, we need not mourn. Thus they cannot study in all its detail the history of the Anglo-Saxon kings and of the Dukes of Normandy, because the precious poems that Geoffroy Gaimar and Benoît of Sainte-Maure, Anglo-Norman trouvères of the twelfth century, devoted to chronicling their lives are housed only in the public libraries of England.*

Likewise, Sir, the mythical history of Charlemagne and the state of Old French [langue romane d'oil] *in the eleventh and twelfth centuries have not yet been sufficiently determined, given that the Anglo-Norman poem composed around the middle of the eleventh century on the travels of Charlemagne to Constantinople and that the Romance of Roncevaux written in the early years of the first half of the twelfth century are also to be found only in England.*

The learned men of this country have often tried to publish portions of these works separately, but they have done so with such a lack of expertise that their extracts turned out to be even more unreadable in print than in the original manuscripts, and that even they themselves realised their inability to undertake such work.

I am thus honoured to be able to propose, Sir, that you might send me to England so as to take copies there [crossed out: *for the Royal Library*] *of the manuscripts that you should choose to request of me. The medieval chronicles, romances, and poems that I have edited, the copies of long thirteenth-century works that I have made for my own use and that, if you should so desire, I would be honoured to submit to your inspection, testify to my qualifications for the work that I am offering to undertake.*

But I shall not limit myself, Sir, solely to this demanding task. I shall also carry out any learned research that you should care to charge me with; in particular, I shall devote myself to examining English archives and historical publications so as to locate charters and titles, both published and unpublished, for the volume that the Académie des Inscriptions et Belles-Lettres *has requested I continue, along with three students of the Royal* Ecole des chartes. *My knowledge of English will make this work easy for me.*

I sincerely hope that you will give my request every consideration, and I beseech you, with the deepest respect, Sir, to consider me your very humble and very obedient servant, [signed] *Francisque Michel, rue Jacob no. 26.*

Group Statement:
    The members of the *Académie des Inscriptions et Belles-Lettres*, undersigned, entreat the Minister of Public Education to give due consideration to the request of Mr. Francisque [sic], with whose work and aptitude for all types of research related to medieval literature and history they are familiar. In Paris, this day of [space for date left blank], 1833.
Individual testimonials:
    Louis-Jean-Nicolas Monmerqué [(1780–1860), politician and man of letters]: I join my learned colleagues in entreating the Minister of Public

Education kindly to look favourably upon the request made by Mr. Francisque Michel. This young scholar's breadth of learning would permit him while in England to recover medieval works that are lacking in our rich French libraries, and I know so well the care with which he carries out his work that I am certain of the full confidence one can have in the results of his research.

Carl-Benedikt Hase [(1780–1864), Hellenist, paleographer, and manuscript curator at the *Bibliothèque royale*]: I hasten to add my remarks to those of my learned colleagues. What I know of the work of Mr. Michel has elicited true admiration for his expertise, and I often have occasion to note the assiduousness he applies to the study of medieval manuscripts, languages, and history.

Individual Signatures, top left to bottom right, of sixteen other members of the *Académie des Inscriptions et Belles-Lettres* (including that of Claude Fauriel, elected in 1836) – that is, approximately one-third of the total number of full-time members in 1833, with signed portion of name underlined:

François-Just-Marie Raynouard [(1761–1836), comparative grammarian and pioneering specialist of troubadour poetry] / Jean-Baptiste Dugas-Montbel [(1776–1834), hellenist and translator of Homer] / Eugène Burnouf [(1801–52), professor of Sanscrit at the *Collège de France*] / Pierre-Claude-François Daunou [(1761–1840), former professor of history at the *Collège de France*, guardian of the National Archives beginning in 1808, and driving force behind reconstituting the Institut after the Revolution] / le Marquis de Fortia d'Urban [(1756–1843), mathematician and historian] / Benjamin-Edme-Charles Guérard [(1797–1854), professor at the *Ecole des chartes* and assistant manuscript librarian at the *Bibliothèque royale*] / Joseph-Toussaint Reinaud [(1795–1867), Arabist and assistant manuscript librarian at the *Bibliothèque royale*] / Antoine-Jean Letronne [(1787–1848), classical archaeologist, professor at the *Collège de France*, and director of the *Ecole des chartes*] / Charles-Alexandre Amaury-Duval [(1760–1838), lawyer and man of letters] / Count Alexandre-Louis-Joseph de Laborde [(1773–1842), politician and man of letters] / Alexis-François Artaud de Montor [(1772–1849), Italianist] / Laurent-François Feuillet [(1771–1843), head librarian at the *Institut de France*] / Aignan-Stanilas Julien [(1799–1873), professor of Chinese at the *Collège de France* and assistant librarian at the *Institut de France*] / Désiré-Raoul Rochette [(1789–1854), professor of history at the Sorbonne and conservator of medals and antiques at the *Bibliothèque royale*] / Claude-Charles Fauriel [(1772–1844), named first professor of medieval literature ("littérature étrangère") in France in 1830, and specialist of troubadours and modern Greek oral poetry] / Joseph-

Basile-Bernard Van Praët [(1754–1837), librarian in charge of printed books at the *Bibliothèque royale*].¹⁶
Marginal ministerial note at top left corner of first page, in Guizot's hand, addressed to his aide Hippolyte Royer-Collard: "Request that Mr. Fauriel give me the detailed information on this subject that he promised me." Fauriel's response was printed by Joseph Bédier in 1937.¹⁷

As a man who for a time fancied himself a Romantic novelist and frequented Charles Nodier's salon, Michel had a propensity for dramatic and showy self-affirmation. The presumptuously messianic tone of this letter fits into a larger pattern of self-aggrandisement, and it is important not to over-romanticise Michel. The main rhetorical strategies here, in addition to the unrestrained and ritualistic boasting of the funding supplicant, are manipulation (offering to copy whatever he is directed to after having proposed a list of four particularly important works), picturesque exaggeration, and bald-faced hyperbole. The last paragraph, for example, alludes to a proto-nationalist Enlightenment-era project to inventory and classify disparate historical documents in order to facilitate research into the national past; the *Table chronologique des diplômes, chartes, titres et actes imprimés concernant l'histoire de France*, entrusted to Louis-Georges-Oudard Feudrix de Bréquigny in 1763 and subsequently interrupted by the Revolution, would be reentrusted to students of the *Ecole des chartes* in 1829, of which team Michel was a member at the time of this letter.¹⁸ Michel evokes the Bréquigny project so as to call attention to his experience and trustworthiness, but also to allude to a separate project carried out by Bréquigny in copying an immense cache of French charters and other historical documents during a three-year state-sponsored mission to London in the 1760s.¹⁹ Michel thus invokes a highly successful precedent for his request; even more cannily, he also gives himself justification, on grounds of double employment, for requesting several months later that his comfortable Paris salary accompany him to England as a complement to the episodic and irregular pay schedule to which he would soon be shifted.²⁰

Likewise, the first three paragraphs also need to be taken with a grain of salt. As Michel would have it, medieval studies are at an impasse; with foundational works languishing barely touched in far-away archives, the best academic minds are throwing up their hands in frustration at the state of affairs. Attempts to rectify the situation by a few well-meaning souls have supposedly only made matters worse. In actuality, although some historians had recently lamented a lack of available documents, they were not as categorical as Michel makes them sound.²¹ Furthermore, Michel's immediate editorial predecessors, despite being self-taught, had proven themselves to be relatively competent paleographic interpreters of the works mentioned, and in any event not disposed, as Michel would have it, to regarding their best efforts as embarrassing collections of bloopers and howlers for which any self-respecting scholar could only beg forgiveness with an apologetic smile. It is true that in June of 1833, only fifty-five lines of the Oxford *Roland* manuscript's 4002 verses had been published, and the figures for the three other works Michel mentions were similarly paltry (forty-two of 870 for the *Voyage de Charlemagne à Jérusalem et à Constantinople*, sixty-five of 6500 for Geoffroy Gaimar's *Estoire des Engleis*, and approximately 1500 of almost 45,000 lines for Benoît de Sainte-Maure's chronicle).[22] But whereas quantitatively the portions were tiny, qualitatively the extracts furnished workable transcriptions of what, in more than one case, are now acknowledged to be notoriously difficult manuscripts.[23] To be sure, Michel's predecessors adhered to vestiges of an outmoded eighteenth-century convention of simplifying and regularising spelling in order to accommodate a readership easily repelled by the unfamiliar case system and spelling conventions of Old French and its dialectical variants (substituting, for example, "Charles" for *Carles*, "le" for *li*, and "emperere magne" for *emperere magnes*). Such interventions may have been heretical by the standards of the nascent paleographical and philological sciences, but true misreadings – as opposed to willful interventions to "clean up" the text without altering its essential meaning – were not as common in published extracts of the four works Michel was proposing to transcribe as he claims.[24]

Readers of early medievalist scholarship will recognise Michel's technique here to be to some extent conventional, embellishing as it does on the Incompetent Predecessor topos, whereby a long line of early medievalists regretted the lamentable state of affairs in their profession. Typically, these scholars deplored a perceived lack of technical skills afflicting their predecessors or even peers, thereby rendering their own efforts all the more urgently needed. Seventy years previously, the major medievalist of the *Ancien Régime*, La Curne de Sainte-Palaye, had complained that critical historical works in the vernacular, such as William the Conqueror's law code, were unintelligible in published editions.[25] Michel's contemporary Paulin Paris had also in 1833 indulged in scathing criticism of the older Claude Fauriel, acerbically mocking the authority and competence of a scholar who would admit in print to finding epic manuscripts difficult to decipher and boring.[26] Taking a more nuanced tack, Raynouard in the same year pointed out a number of inaccuracies in a recent installment of the *Histoire littéraire de la France*, thereby implicitly calling into question the authority of the source critic, the octogenarian abbé de La Rue.[27] La Rue, for his part, soldiered through his career with his God-given light of reason always in service of his sharp tongue in the papers he published in the British antiquarian journal *Archaeologia*.[28]

As for Michel, his correspondence reveals he had no qualms about deriding Paulin Paris and Claude Fauriel in deferential – even fawning – correspondence with La Rue, who was fifty-eight years his senior, while simultaneously dismissing La Rue as a doddering old man in correspondence with Guizot.[29] The prefaces to his editions, moreover, return with mechanical predictability to the error-strewn path the (recently deceased) abbé de La Rue bequeathed to his successors (Michel refutes six separate La Rue fallacies in the introduction to the landmark 1837 edition of the *Roland*); at one point Michel even informed Guizot that he considered it his civic duty to devote an entire book to refuting what he deemed the abbé de La Rue's supposed scholarship.[30] Later, Paul Meyer would return the favour to Michel, becoming the principal detractor of a scholar who, as Meyer damningly opined in his obituary of Michel, "atteignit du premier coup le degré de perfection jusqu'auquel il lui fut donné de s'élever" [attained from the outset the degree of accomplishment to which he would be capable of rising].[31] The circular vituperation that characterised the times is perhaps most amusingly recorded by Paulin Paris's mid-century sketch of the acrimonious critical genealogy of *Chanson de Roland* scholarship.[32]

And yet something *is* new here. Michel can rightly claim the mantle of a new breed of medievalist insofar as his training, his omnidirectional enthusiasm, and the unique historical juncture at which he found himself all combine to create an opening of greater significance than has generally been recognised. Reading between the lines of Michel's ingenious grant proposal (complete with built-in letters of recommendation), one can detect the signs of the growing professionalisation of the discipline, with all that such evolution entails. The disdain for the seeming artlessness and barbarity of medieval literature that had led almost all eighteenth-century medievalists to doctor their editions of texts (usually only extracts anyway) is clearly giving way to the proto-scientific insistence on exact replication that, as I have just suggested, underlies much of Michel's dissatisfaction with his predecessors. If Michel could not bear to read La Rue's doctored transcriptions of passages from Benoît de Sainte-Maure, it is also in part because of the unusual degree of appreciation he held for the literary value of medieval imaginative works in their pure state, as the prefaces to his early editions attest.[33] Michel was in fact one of the most vocal of a small minority of pre-twentieth-century critics for whom literary value always trumped documentary interest in medieval works.[34] By contrast, the antiquarian scholars whose productive period overlapped with Michel's often promoted the instrumentalisation of medieval literature in the service of parochial and provincial concerns. Frédéric Pluquet, for example, the professional pharmacist and amateur medievalist from Bayeux who had edited the first full edition of Wace's *Roman de Rou*, devoted part of the preface of this 1827 edition to pointing out the importance of the work to "our Norman history" [*notre histoire normande*].³⁵

Pluquet was not alone. The entire career of the abbé de La Rue, also from Normandy, had been premised in part on the need to sing the praises of medieval Anglo-Norman literary production. Claude Fauriel, for his part, insisted on the pre-eminence of the Provençal tradition, even – infamously – crediting it with originating the Arthurian material. Even scholars temperamentally inclined to cast their net more broadly than the regionally chauvinistic specialists had to rely more on the rhetorical and argumentative skills of the antiquarian than on any formal or technical training. Jean-Baptiste-Bonaventure de Roquefort, a colorful character with a murky background, had begun his career as a piano teacher, launching himself into the study of medieval manuscripts as a consequence of his musicological research. Eventually he would compile an important early glossary of Old French (*Glossaire de la langue romane*) and win an 1813 prize from the *Académie des Inscriptions et Belles-Lettres* for an essay on "la poésie françoise" of the twelfth and thirteenth centuries, an important early work to which Michel would later occasionally refer.³⁶ First or very early editions of Eustache Deschamps and the Châtelain de Coucy romance were published, very conscientiously and even lovingly, by the eminent printer Georges-Adrien Crapelet, who, nonetheless, despite his dedication and assiduousness, revealed his philological limits in admitting that the recent deaths of two manuscript librarians had left him to fend for himself in preparing his translations.³⁷ Fauriel started out in politics and Monmerqué and Raynouard were lawyers by trade, although Raynouard in particular later showed a brilliant propensity for inventing structures of grammatical analysis from scratch, and the great admiration that the highly judgmental Michel frequently professed for Monmerqué appears to have been genuine.³⁸ Even the great Paulin Paris, only nine years Michel's senior, had taken a classical education in Reims and gone to Paris to make a name for himself as a man of letters before eventually being offered a post as a Royal Library manuscript librarian at, by Michel's standards, the somewhat advanced age of 28.

Michel's strong implication that his *chartiste* training put him in a new category of scholar is thus not hyperbolic when taken in a general sense (as opposed to the specific and overblown critique he presumes to make of previous copyists of the four named Anglo-Norman works). Although he was never formally admitted to the *Ecole des chartes*, having narrowly failed to rank highly enough on the competitive entrance exam, he somehow managed to pick up enough skills as a course auditor to be able to command the same respect as his peers Adrien-Jean-Victor Leroux de Lincy and Achille Jubinal, both of whom had in fact graduated from the *Ecole*. Perhaps in compensation for this early defeat, Michel flaunted his considerable linguistic abilities in his publications, frequently quoting sources not just in English and Latin but in many other modern European languages and even, on occasion, quoting Maimonides in Hebrew.[39] For Michel, the past was a rich and vast foreign country that only polyglots could profitably visit, and he stubbornly refused to accommodate non-specialist readers in the prefaces to his early editions. It is entirely possible, in fact, that Michel saw himself doing for French medieval studies what Jean-François Champollion was in the process of doing for Egyptology in the wake of the latter's deciphering of the trilingual Rosetta Stone in 1821 and his momentous 1828–30 expedition to Egypt. Like Michel, Champollion had successfully petitioned a minister of the king (Charles X at the time) for governmental funding to retrieve a vast historical treasure imperfectly understood and even derided by some of his contemporaries, and Champollion's proposal, entitled "*Mémoire sur un projet de voyage littéraire en Egypte*" had been published in a collection of his letters posthumously appearing, coincidentally enough, in 1833.[40] To the degree that Michel presents himself in his petition as uniquely-competent interpreter and decoder of ancient artifacts, he may well be fashioning himself implicitly as the Champollion of a vast and understudied national – rather than exotically foreign – heritage in urgent need of repatriation.

Furthermore, as I have suggested, the unique historical moment also lends credence to the presumptuousness of Michel's brash claims. For one thing, his letter arrived at a juncture – almost to the week – when the state was deciding it was particularly in need of the skills he was proposing. As Laurent Theis points out, Louis Philippe's experiment in constitutional monarchy having denied itself most of the conventional means of monarchic self-legitimation (including hereditary transmission and coronation ceremonies, to say nothing of elections), it found itself all the more urgently committed to constructing a historical narrative that celebrated a shared national heritage. As noted above, the Middle Ages were deemed a natural locus of memory for having laid the groundwork for the systems and institutions of the civil state.[41] Not surprisingly, one of the first texts published in Guizot's *Documents inédits sur l'histoire de France* series was *Le journal des Etats-Généraux de France tenus à Tours en 1489*.[42] Michel's repeated evocation of the archives of England, moreover, subtly taps into the nationalistic imperatives underlying Guizot's publishing project by casting his proposal as a bid to reclaim national treasures from a country intimately acquainted with France's storied past. Second, the advent of archival science was coinciding with a revival in historical interest throughout French society, inspired in part by the Romantic vogue for Walter Scott and also, no doubt, by rapid development of the North African French colonial empire. As one of Guizot's biographers notes, "[p]ublishers began to vie with each other in producing 'Histoires Universelles,' 'résumés' and short histories, memoirs and recollections, editions of chronicles, correspondence, translations and histories of foreign countries. All the reviews carried numerous historical articles."[43] Third, the specific topic of the medieval Norman invasions of both France and England had seen important recent developments in 1833. Aside from Depping's prize-winning *Histoire des expéditions maritimes des Normands* of 1826 (which reproduced extracts of Benoît de Sainte-Maure's *Chronique*) and Pluquet's 1827 edition of the *Roman de Rou*, both already mentioned, two manuscript copies of (what is still) the earliest known detailed account of the Battle of Hastings had been unearthed in Brussels by the archivist to the king of Hanover in 1826, and the eminent historian Augustin Thierry had recently devoted a four-volume study to the Norman invasion of England.[44]

Michel's letter thus clearly plays on both the general historical and nationalistic imperatives of the day and on recent interest in the Norman conquest in particular. Evidence suggests in fact that Michel's evocation of the "*ducs de Normandie*" functioned at least in part as something of a modish and fashionable topic calculated to appeal to his readership: summarising the most promising points of Michel's project in the draft of a letter to the *secrétaire perpetuel* of the *Académie*, Guizot, following Michel, mentioned the Anglo-Saxon kings and Norman dukes, but then, as though having taken Michel's bait, added to the list of desirable dividends information on William the Conqueror specifically.[45] Just as important is Guizot's complete omission in the same letter of any mention of the two Charlemagne works Michel was also proposing to copy, and to the extent that Guizot was clearly far more excited about the prospect of learning facts about the Battle of Hastings than myths about the Battle of Roncevaux, the *Roland* project was relegated to secondary if not tertiary importance from the outset.[46] To this extent, the conventional wisdom that, since Bédier's 1937 treatment of the topic, has viewed Michel's intention to retrieve the *Roland* manuscript as a covert agenda or subliminal urge is not entirely false: Michel had to resign himself to the fact that the *Roland* project would indeed never be accorded official sanction by his government.

This is not to imply that Guizot had a narrow-minded or exclusive idea of what constituted legitimate historical documentation. On the contrary, his *doctrinaire* school of historians stressed the value of original documents, and he had participated avidly, through his thirty-one volume *Collection des mémoires relatifs à l'histoire de France*, in the promulgation and vulgarisation of a new approach to history, less wedded to charters and dry annalistic analyses, inclusive of the narrative element inherent to chronicles and even poetic treatments of historical events.[47] He was not even averse to proposing a literary account of an actual event as a national historical treasure, and he had in fact already done so in an 1825 volume of his Mémoires series, which offered a French prose translation of *La Philippide*, Guillaume le Breton's thirteenth-century Latin verse epic on the life of Philip Augustus (1165–1223). For Guizot the value of this work lay not in its compositional merits, which he pronounced to be meager to non-existent, but in its remarkable depictions of novel historical realities, and in particular Guillaume's depiction of a coalescing sense of national unity stimulated by Philippe's victory in the battle of Bouvines.[48] All of this in spite of what Guizot cautioned in his introduction to the work were its slight literary value and an unfortunate medieval tolerance of great amounts of subjectivity in historical narration.

This contextual detail suggests two practical implications for Michel, one discouraging and the other encouraging. The first is that Guizot had allotted a mental category to accommodate a foundational national epic, and that the *Philippide* came much closer to occupying it than any hypothetical *Song of Roland* would.[49] The second is that Michel could profit from enhancing the attractiveness of his requests by couching them in terms of their historical value. Hence Michel's justification of his interest in the two non-chronicle manuscripts – the *Voyage of Charlemagne* and the Oxford *Roland* – as important documents for determining "*l'histoire fabuleuse de Charlemagne*" (paragraph 2 of his letter) should be interpreted as more than just a recourse to a conventional formula.[50] Equated here with the study of philology as something admitting of systematic investigation and determination, this mythical "history," in Michel's formulation, lays claim to a category implicitly parallel in legitimacy to that occupied by the two works for which he would be accorded his grant, Benoît's *Chroniques* and Gaimar's *Estoire*. Not, of course, that Michel believed either the Oxford *Roland* or the *Voyage of Charlemagne* could compete for referential validity with the two verse chronicles. Rather, the unspoken logic of Michel's request recognises the powerful fictional truth that the Charlemagne legend held for medieval authors – poets and chroniclers alike.[51] Long before the *Song of Roland* would be proclaimed France's *Iliad* in the 1850s, the exploits of Charlemagne, Roland, Olivier, and the twelve peers at Roncevaux held pride of place in the medieval French poetic imagination, elements of an ur-epic as fundamental to their culture as the immortal deeds of Hector, Achilles, Agamemnon, and Aeneas at Troy had been to classical civilisation. When Guillaume le Breton needed to describe an anxious monarch flying to the aid of his endangered warriors in his thirteenth-century poem, he found it natural to compare Philip Augustus to Charlemagne on his return to Spain to avenge the death of Roland.[52]

Granted, the Taillefer-at-Hastings scene by which Wace inserts the Roland legend into yet another epic medieval battle functions as more than the simple literary comparison one finds in the *Philippide*. Guillaume makes the reference himself in a poetic recourse to epic simile, whereas Wace attributes it to a performer present at the climactic scene of battle. Taillefer's "Chanson de Roland" thereby becomes a historical artifact of supposedly independent existence, and the interest of what Michel calls "*l'histoire fabuleuse de Charlemagne*" thereby gains an even greater degree of referentiality: if on one occasion performance of this "*histoire fabuleuse*" inspired real warriors to feats of real valor, then fable finds itself ennobled in the process, woven into the regal fabric of historical facticity as a defining moment in performance history.

Needless to say, belief in the literal reliability of Wace's Taillefer account has evaporated since Michel's day, when it was common currency among many literary scholars (if not always historians). Debate may continue over the appropriateness of the title Michel selected for the work, but no current-day scholar is likely to dispute the fact that lending credence to Wace's account of Taillefer's performance in the twenty-first century would smack of a quaintly dated if not naïvely literal understanding of the nature of medieval historical narration.[53] It would be unfair to Michel, however, to end the story here, with this foundational figure saddled with a host of now-questionable beliefs in the factual reliability of premodern historical exposition and in the fighting minstrel-jongleur as early repository of historical memory. As I suggested at the outset of this essay, what is remarkable is not any independently verifiable confirmation that the memory of Roland and the twelve peers was invoked at the Battle of Hastings but, rather, the authenticity of Michel's *belief* that it was. It was this belief that underlay the insertion in his request of the two forms of the "Song of Roland" I mentioned in my introduction, one the contents of a specific manuscript and the other the convention of medieval historiography – Taillefer's supposed performance – that made the more specific designation possible. That the evaluators of Michel's proposal overlooked mention of the first and showed little sign of believing in the second had no ultimate effect on the outcome of Michel's mission, but it did have symbolic importance. The long-lost *Song of Roland* manuscript thereby becomes to the history of official sponsorship of French letters what the Taillefer legend is to the historiography of the Battle of Hastings: a shadowy poetic presence that bears a tenuous, unconfirmable relationship to historical truth.

Roland specialists can take satisfaction, then, from the revelation that their object of study played an even more fundamental and symbolically appropriate role than has been suspected in a foundational moment of the study of medieval French letters. Historians of the discipline of medieval studies, already cognizant of the ascendancy of the manuscript librarian and the archivist as important new figures in the 1830s, will, for their part, smile at the degree to which a skillful young scholar could turn to his advantage the trope of the archive as a locus of acts of scholarly prowess and heroism.[54] Finally, scholars intrigued by the interpenetrations of history and literature – those cohabitants of the same richly referential narrative territory now eying each other with suspicion, now conjoined in a marriage of convenience – will appreciate the degree to which Michel took advantage of a unique moment in French national historiography to win backing for a multifaceted research project of more than just historical import to a French state in search of a past.

Original French Text of Letter: Francisque Michel to François Guizot

Transcription in Full

Note: here as throughout the body of my article I retain the idiosyncrasies of the spelling and use of accents in the original document.

Monsieur le Ministre,
Les savans qui se livrent à l'étude de la philologie, de l'histoire et de la littérature françoise du moyen âge, gémissent souvent de ne pouvoir tirer un résultat satisfaisant de leurs investigations, et cela faute de monumens dont on n'a pas néanmoins à déplorer la perte. Ainsi ils ne peuvent étudier dans tous leurs détails l'histoire des rois Anglo-Saxons et des ducs de Normandie, parce que les précieux poëmes qui ont été composés sur leur vie par Geoffroi Gaimar et par Benoît de Sainte-More, trouverres Anglo-Normands du XIIe siècle, ne se trouvent que dans les bibliothèques publiques de l'Angleterre.

De même, Monsieur le Ministre, l'histoire fabuleuse de Charlemagne et l'état de la langue romane d'oil au 11e et 12e siècles n'ont pu encore être suffisamment déterminés, attendu que le poëme anglo-Normand composé vers le milieu de l'XIe se sur le voyage de Charlemagne à Constantinople et que le roman de Roncevaux rédigé dans les prémieres années de la première moitié du XIIe siècle n'existent pareillement qu'en Angleterre.

Les savans de ce pays ont tenté bien souvent de publier des parties séparées de ces ouvrages; mais ils l'ont fait avec une telle impéritie que leurs extraits ont paru encore plus illisibles que dans les manuscrits originaux, et qu'ils ont senti eux-mêmes leur incapacité pour un pareil travail.

J'ai donc l'honneur de vous proposer, Monsieur le Ministre, de vouloir bien m'envoyer en Angleterre, afin d'y prendre [*crossed out*: pour la bibliothèque du Roi,] copie des manuscrits qu'il vous plaira de me désigner. Les publications de chroniques, de romans et de poésies du moyen-âge dont je suis l'éditeur, les copies de longs ouvrages du XIIIe siècle que j'ai faites moi-même pour mon usage particulier et que, si vous le désirez, j'aurai l'honneur de mettre sous vos yeux, vous sont garants de mon aptitude au travail que je vous offre d'entreprendre.

Mais, Monsieur le Ministre, je ne me bornerai pas à cette seule besogne. Je ferai en outre toutes les recherches scientifiques que vous voudrez bien m'ordonner; je m'attacherai surtout à compulser les archives et les publications historiques de l'Angleterre afin d'y trouver des chartes et des titres imprimés ou inédits, pour le recueil que l'académie des Inscriptions et Belles-Lettres m'a chargé de continuer avec trois élèves de l'école royale des chartes. Ma connoissance de l'anglois me rendra ce travail facile.

J'espère que vous voudrez bien prendre ma demande en considération et vous prie de me croire, avec un profond respect, Monsieur le Ministre, votre très humble et très obéissant serviteur, [*signed*] Francisque Michel, rue Jacob N°. 26.

Group Statement [in different hand from above]:
    Les membres de l'Académie des Inscriptions et belles-lettres, soussignés, prient Monsieur le Ministre de l'Instruction publique de vouloir bien prendre en considération la demande de M^r. Francisque [sic] dont ils connaissent les travaux, et l'aptitude à toutes les recherches relatives à la littérature et à l'histoire du moyen âge. A Paris le [*space for date left blank*] 1833.
Individual testimonials:
    Louis-Jean-Nicolas Monmerqué [(1780–1860), politician and man of letters]: Je me joins à mes savans confrères pour prier Monsieur le ministre de l'Instruction public de vouloir bien accueillir favourablement la demande formulée par M. Francisque Michel. Les connoissances étendues de ce jeune savant le mettroient à portée de recueillir en Angleterre des ouvrages du moyen âge qui manquent dans nos riches bibliothèques de France, et le soin qu'il apporte à ses travaux est si connu de moi, que je suis persuadé de la pleine confiance qu'inspireront les résultats de ses recherches.
    Carl-Benedikt Hase [(1780–1864), Hellenist, paleographer, and manuscript curator at the Bibliothèque royale]: J'ajoute avec empressement mon témoignage à ceux de mes savans confrères. Ce que je connais des travaux de M. Francisque Michel m'a inspiré pour ses connaissances une estime véritable, et j'ai souvent occasion d'apprécier l'application avec laquelle il se livre à l'étude des manuscrits, des langues et de l'histoire du moyen âge.

[Signatures, arranged in a rectangle on lower left-hand side of sheet, of eleven other members of the *Académie des Inscriptions et Belles-Lettres*]

[Signatures, at lower edge of sheet, beneath Hase and Monmerqué testimonials, of five additional members of the *Académie des Inscriptions et Belles-Lettres*]

[Added upon receipt:
In the hand of Guizot, addressed to his aide Hippolyte Royer-Collard, top left corner of first page: "Prier M. Fauriel de me donner à ce sujet les renseignements détaillés qu'il m'a promis."

Oval ministerial stamp, top center of first page: "INSTR<u>on</u> PUBL<u>que</u> 10 juin 1833]

NOTES

1. I thank the Griswold Fund Committee at Yale for providing research assistance that helped make this article possible.

2. This idea is most clearly developed in William Roach, "Francisque Michel: A Pioneer in Medieval Studies," *Proceedings of the American Philosophical Society* 114.3 (June 1970): 168–78. For a laudatory consideration of Michel as a methodological pioneer over the course of his whole career, see Michel Espagne, *De l'archive au texte: Recherches d'histoire génétique* (Paris: Presses Universitaires de France, 1998), ch. 7.

3. By far the most detailed conventional treatment of Michel's mission to England is found in Joseph Bédier's "Premier Article" of the three-part series entitled "De l'édition princeps de la *Chanson de Roland* aux éditions les plus récentes: nouvelles remarques sur l'art d'établir les anciens textes," *Romania* 63 (1937): 433–69, continued in *Romania* 64 (1938): 145–244 and *ibid.*, 489–521. See also Claudine I. Wilson, "A Frenchman in England: Francisque Michel," *Revue de littérature comparée* 17 (1937): 734–49. For a presentation and assessment of Bédier's claims, see my "Francisque Michel, Joseph Bédier, and the Epic History of the First Edition of the Song of Roland (1837)," *Exemplaria* 16.1 (Spring 2004): 1–42. In 2002, I came across Michel's letter of solicitation in the papers of a certain "Magnoncourt," another nineteenth-century scholar who had corresponded with the Ministry of Public Education, in Paris, *Archives Nationales de France*, F17 3295; the document has since been returned to Michel's file, *Archives Nationales*, F17 3296, "*Recherches Philologiques en Angleterre*" dossier. The current files having been constituted between 1906 and 1935, the misfiling presumably dates from at least seventy years ago.

4. For details, see Charles Ridoux, *Evolution des études médiévales en France de 1860 à 1914* (Paris: Honoré Champion, 2001), and Michael Glencross, *Reconstructing Camelot: French Romantic Medievalism and the Arthurian Tradition* (Cambridge, England: D. S. Brewer, 1995), 63–64.

5. A sample of these earlier milestones would include Napoleon's resuscitation of the *Histoire littéraire de la France*, which the Revolution had forced the

Benedictines to abandon, entrusting it to the *Académie des Inscriptions et Belles-Lettres* in 1807; the *Académie*'s choice of medieval French literature ("*l'état de la Poésie françoise dans les XIIe et XIIIe siècles*") as its essay contest topic for 1811; the reconstitution of the *Ecole des chartes* in 1821; Claude Fauriel's appointment as professor of "*littérature étrangère*" at the Sorbonne in 1830; Paulin Paris' appointment to the first chair of medieval literature at the *Collège de France* in 1853; the mammoth early 1850s project undertaken by Hippolyte Fortoul whereby the state endeavored to publish all medieval vernacular verse composed prior to 1328. For details, see Ridoux, *Evolution*, and Glencross, *Reconstructing Camelot* (as in note 4).

6. Laurent Theis, "Guizot et les institutions de mémoire," *Les lieux de mémoire*, ed. Pierre Nora, 3 vols. (Paris: Gallimard, 1986), 2b:569–92.

7. I believe Michel's edition of the *Chronique* to be the first full-length medieval French vernacular work to have been published by the French state press. Of the approximately 325 scholarly works issued by the Royal Press between 1800 and 1835, works devoted to Arabic, Chinese, and Turkish language and literature collectively outnumbered those devoted to Old (and modern) French. For treatment of Guizot's historical projects, see Pim Den Boer, *History as a Profession: The Study of History in France, 1818–1914*, trans. Arnold J. Pomerans (Princeton: Princeton University Press, 1987), ch. 2. See also the references at notes 41 and 42 below.

8. Until now, scholars have devined Michel's intentions from an evaluative synopsis of his project – which now can be shown to have been incomplete – that Claude Fauriel furnished at Guizot's request and that was published by Joseph Bédier in 1937. See Bédier's "Premier article" 458–59, and my "Francisque Michel" (both as in note 3), 20–21.

9. For accounts of this preoccupation, see Harry Redman, Jr., *The Roland Legend in Nineteenth-Century French Literature* (Lexington: University Press of Kentucky, 1991), and Andrew Taylor, "Was There a Song of Roland?," *Speculum* 76.1 (January 2001): 28–65. For a review of medieval accounts of Taillefer's performance, see Frank Barlow, ed. and trans., *The Carmen de Hastingae proelio of Guy Bishop of Amiens* (Oxford: Clarendon Press, 1999), xxxiii–xxxiv.

10. The two verse chronicles, both composed in the twelfth century for the Angevin court of Henry II, were, as mentioned above, the *Chronique des ducs de Normandie* by Benoît de Sainte-Maure, and Geffroy Gaimar's history of the Anglo-Saxon kings entitled the *Estoire des Engleis*; the inappropriate "Chanson de Roland" candidate was the burlesque *Voyage-* or *Pèlerinage de Charlemagne à Jérusalem et à Constantinople*. La Rue had speculated that the *Voyage de Charlemagne* could be the elusive *Song of Roland* in a presentation before a learned society to which he belonged, a claim repeated in print both in the academy's proceedings and, several years later, in a survey study of Old French literature. See P.-F.-T. Delarivière, *Rapport général sur les travaux de l'académie des sciences, arts et belles-lettres de la ville de Caen*, 2 vols. (Caen: P. Chalopin, 1811), 1:199–201; and Jean-Baptiste-Bonaventure de Roquefort in *De l'état de la poésie françoise dans les XIIe et XIIIe siècles* (Paris: Audin, 1821), 206. La Rue later retracted his assertion in his *Essais historiques sur les bardes, les jongleurs et les trouvères normands et anglo-normands* 3 vols. (Caen: Mancel, 1834), 1:133.

11. From the ecstatic letter Michel wrote his Parisian mentor and collaborator

Louis-Jean-Nicolas Monmerqué, it is clear that initially he felt sure he had found the Normans' performance piece; see Gerard J. Brault, " 'C'est presque la quadrature du cercle': Francisque Michel's Letter Announcing his Discovery of the Oxford Manuscript of the *Chanson de Roland* (1835)," *Olifant* 5.4 (May 1978): 271–75. He later tempered his enthusiasm, asserting in the introduction of his edition that the limited available evidence merely suggested a match; see Francisque Michel, *La Chanson de Roland ou de Roncevaux du XIIe siècle* (Paris: Silvestre, 1837), xi–xiii. The medieval works depicting the Battle of Hastings are presented by William Sayers in "The Jongleur Taillefer at Hastings: Antecedents and Literary Fate," *Viator* 14 (1983): 77–88.

12. As the pre-eminent historian of his day, Guizot embodied these official historical interests. His writings from the period, which are almost completely silent on the Roland manuscript, reveal that he considered the momentous manuscript find of the mid-1830s to have been a copy of Abelard's *Sic et Non*, unearthed in 1834 at the Avranches library in Normandy. See Xavier Charmes, *Le comité des travaux historiques et scientifiques (histoire et documents)*, 3 vols. (Paris: Imprimerie nationale, 1886), 2:21.

13. Geoffrey J. Wilson, *A Medievalist in the Eighteenth Century: Le Grand d'Aussy and the Fabliaux ou contes* (The Hague: Nijhoff, 1975), 75. By the early nineteenth century, however, the vast majority of the work published by *académiciens* treated classical antiquity and the Middle and Far East, not France; see next note.

14. Among the publications of the Académie were the *Journal des Savants*, the *Mémoires de l'Institut royal de France*, and the *Notices et extraits des manuscrits de la Bibliothèque du roi* (or *de la Bibliothèque impériale*, as the circumstances dictated). Most important of all was the *Histoire littéraire de la France, ouvrage commencé par des religieux bénédictins de la congrégation de Saint-Maur, et continué par des membres de l'Institut (Académie royale des inscriptions et belles-lettres)* (as in note 5). For more on these publications, see Ridoux, *Evolution* (as in note 4), 249–56. The 1833 issue of the *Mémoires de l'Institut impérial de France* (volume 10) contained eleven articles on Middle-Eastern, East Asian and classical subjects, but only two on medieval French history; clearly the founding of the *Ecole des chartes* played an important part in the later upturn in research into domestic topics.

15. On this point, see the highly informative essay by Laurent Theis, as in note 6, 1579.

16. Short biographies of all these men are available in Le Comte de Franqueville, *Le Premier siècle de l'Institut de France*, 2 vols. (Paris: J. Rothschild, 1896), vol. 1. For several signers, a more judgmental portrayal of their foibles and penchant for factionalism is provided in passing by Jean Lacouture, *Champollion. Une vie de lumières* (Paris: Grasset, 1988).

17. "Premier article" (as in note 3), 458–59.

18. This despite the fact that he had never been officially admitted to the Ecole. On this complicated point, see Bédier, "Premier article" (as in note 3), 457. Further details of Michel's involvement in this project are contained in a letter from Guizot to Michel of 23 September 1833, *Archives Nationales*, F17 3296.

19. Details are spelled out in Lionel Gossman, *Medievalism and the Ideologies*

of the Enlightenment: The World and Work of La Curne de Sainte-Palaye (Baltimore: Johns Hopkins University Press, 1968), 212–15.

20. There was nothing untoward in this impulse itself, given the exorbitant cost of living in England at the time, but Michel asked Guizot to overrule the head of the *Chartes* commission when the latter was temporarily absent from his post; Guizot, showing some irritation at the ruse, denied the request (letter of Michel to Guizot of 10 September 1833, *Archives Nationales* F17 3296).

21. Michel was probably alluding most directly to a remark made by one of the many scholars with whom he collaborated, Georges-Bernard (also Georg Bernhard) Depping. In the preface to his recent treatment of the Viking invasions, Depping, as an afterthought appended to his version of the modesty topos, had written, "Les monumens ne sont pas d'ailleurs assez nombreux, pour qu'ils puissent suffire à tout éclaircir . . ." [the monumental works are not in any case numerous enough to shed sufficient light on all points]. See his *Histoire des expéditions maritimes des Normands et de leur établissement en France au dixième siècle*, 2 vols. (Paris: Ponthieu, 1826), 1:ii. Michel and Depping jointly published *Véland le Forgeron, dissertation sur une tradition du moyen âge* (Paris: Didot, 1833).

22. I extrapolate these figures largely from the publishing history Michel retraces for each work in the prefaces of his editions; complete references to these editions can be found in Roach, "Francisque Michel" (as in note 2). With few exceptions, Michel had only two predecessors in each case: the authors of the multi-volume *Histoire littéraire de la France* and the abbé de La Rue, who, in the thirty years leading up to his death in 1835, had published extracts of these works in the English journal *Archaeologia* and in his *Essais historiques sur les bardes* (as in note 10). The main omission in Michel's lists is the extended passages of the *Chronique des ducs de Normandie* published by the Danish classical archaeologist Peter-Oluf Brøndsted as an appendix to volume 2 of Depping's *Histoire des expéditions maritimes* (as in note 21).

23. Michel's complaint describes much more accurately the history of work on Wace's *Roman de Rou* than it does the four works he cites; the eighteenth-century scholar La Curne de Sainte-Palaye, who had transcribed (not published) one of the medieval manuscripts of the work, had admitted to having frequently guessed at the meaning of certain passages, and his overall transcription was notoriously faulty. The main justifications Michel gives for his project (faulty transcriptions, best manuscript housed in England, self-exculpatory previous editor, and so on) in fact collectively applied best to the *Rou*, a work that had finally seen a complete edition in 1827. See Frédéric Pluquet, ed., *Le Roman de Rou et des ducs de Normandie* (Rouen: Frère, 1827), pp. xvi–xviii and xxi, and A. J. Holden, ed., *Le roman de Rou de Wace*, 3 vols. (Paris: Picard, 1971), 3:23.

24. Examples can, however, be cited: a Spanish nobleman named Andrés Bello had reproduced a couple of dozen lines from the *Voyage de Charlemagne* in an article devoted to assonanced poetry and rendered the word <u>dous</u> ("soft") as <u>bons</u> ("good"). The forty-six Oxford Roland lines published by the abbé de La Rue in 1834 contained, by my count, approximately a dozen transcription or punctuation errors of varying severity – far from a perfect performance, but also not exactly the situation Michel describes, either. See Dom Andrés Bello, "Uso antiguo de la rima asonante en

la poesía latina de la media edad i en la francesa; i observaciones sobre su uso moderno," *El Repertorio americano* 2 (Jan. 1827): 21–33 (29), compared to the diplomatic edition in Paul Aebischer, ed., *Le Voyage de Charlemagne à Jérusalem et à Constantinople* (Geneva: Droz, 1965), 56; and La Rue, *Essais historiques sur les bardes* (as in note 10), 2:60–62, compared to portions of laisses 1, 94, 290, and 291 appearing in Joseph Bédier, ed. and trans., *La Chanson de Roland* (Paris: L'Edition d'Art, H. Piazza, 1944) and the photo-facsimile of the Oxford manuscript in Alexandre de Laborde, ed., *La Chanson de Roland* (Paris: Société des anciens textes français, 1933).

25. "J'ai leu à dix fois les loix de Guillaume, et il y a un bon tiers où je crois qu'il est impossible de rien entendre, parce que l'éditeur lui mesme n'a pas scu les lire et n'avoit pas d'idée du langage," quoted in Gossman, *Medievalism* (as in note 19), 177, n. 6. [Countless times I have read the William the Conqueror law codes, and there is a good third where I believe comprehension impossible because the editor himself was incapable of reading them and had no notion of the language.]

26. Quoting Fauriel's "*Origine de l'épopée chevaleresque du Moyen Age*" from the *Revue des deux mondes* of the previous year, Paris wrote, "il aura toujours mauvaise grace à nous dire que les beaux manuscrits qui les [i.e. chansons de geste] contiennent 'sont difficiles à déchiffrer, et semblent braver la patience et la curiosité des littérateurs.' Car, pour moi, je ne demande pas qu'on me sache le moindre gré de les avoir déchiffrés. En effet, combien d'heures ai-je vu passer rapidement en poursuivant cette lecture!" (emphasis in original). [it will always be bad faith on his part to tell us that the wonderful manuscripts that contain them (i.e. chansons de geste) 'are difficult to decipher, and seem to try the patience and the curiosity of men of letters.' For I do not expect the least amount of gratitude for having deciphered them. On the contrary, how many hours have I seen pass swiftly while I pursued this reading!] Paulin Paris, *Li Romans de Garin le Loherain* (Paris: Techener, 1833), iii.

27. François-Just-Marie Raynouard, review of vol. 17 of the *Histoire littéraire de France* in *Journal des savants* Feb. 1833: 65–74.

28. See, for example, La Rue's survey of the writings of Wace in his "A Letter Concerning the Lives and Writings of Various Anglo-Norman Poets of the 12th Century," *Archaeologia* 12 (1796): 297–326 (298).

29. A letter from Michel to La Rue of 17 March 1833 maligned Paulin Paris's latest edition, the *Garin le Loherain*, for being as disappointing as Paris's earlier *Berte aus grans piés* ("je pense que c'est un travail aussi mal fait que le précédent"); Michel, in the same missive, casually noting the ascension of Monmerqué to the *Académie des Inscriptions*, also remarked, "C'est un travailleur. Il est tout disposé a [sic] recevoir l'impulsion de gens habiles comme vous et non à forger des systèmes ridicules et inadmissibles comme M. Fauriel." [He is diligent and is very inclined to benefit from the lead provided by skillful people like you, rather than to concoct ridiculous, untenable systems like Mr. Fauriel.] On the other hand, Michel dryly reported to Guizot from England on 2 December 1834 that an archival tip provided by La Rue had proven to be false ("nous n'avons découvert aucune trace de ce chroniqueur, qui, au reste, paroît n'exister que sur la foi de M. l'abbé de la Rue dont les souvenirs, nous le savons, sont parfois fort infidèles" [we discovered not a trace of this chronicler, who, moreover, seems not to exist but on the testimony of the abbé de la Rue, whose recollections, we know, are sometimes very unreliable"). For sources, see Caen,

Bibliothèque du Musée des Beaux Arts, Collection Mancel, ms. 113, fol. 268, and *Archives Nationales*, F17 3296, Francisque Michel, "*Recherches philologiques en Angleterre.*"

30. At the end of his first year in England, Michel had addressed a progress report to Guizot; dated 1 October 1834 from London, it announced, among many others, the following projected volume: "une réfutation de l'ouvrage de M. l'abbé de la Rue [i.e. the *Essais historiques sur les bardes, les jongleurs et les trouvères normands et anglo-normands* of 1834], en société avec Sir Frederick Madden, garde des mss. du Musée Britannique. Nous regardons ce livre, pour lequel nous avons fait un traité avec le libraire Silvestre, comme l'accomplissement d'un devoir; car les textes cités par M de la Rue sont presque tous altérés de manière à changer le sens, et la plupart des indications sont fausses. En outre, la plus grande partie des assertions de cet auteur sont inadmissibles. Laisser un pareil ouvrage sans réponse seroit favoriser l'erreur et lui permettre de s'établir dans l'histoire littéraire de la France, où elle prend un caractère officiel" (underlining in original) [a refutation of Monsieur abbé de la Rue's study, in collaboration with Sir Frederick Madden, manuscript librarian at the British Museum. We consider this book, for which we have made an agreement with the Silvestre bookseller, as a duty: the texts quoted by Monsieur de la Rue have almost all been distorted so as to change their meaning, and the majority of the references are incorrect. Furthermore, most of this author's assertions are baseless. To let such a work pass without a response would be to sanction error and to allow it entry into the *Histoire littéraire de la France* series, where it takes on an official character.] *Archives Nationales*, F17 3296.

31. *Romania* 16 (1887): 166–67 (166).

32. Writing on the publication of the second edition of the *Roland* in 1851, Paris summarised three decades of scholarship on the Oxford manuscript this way: "Voulez-vous juger du sentiment d'urbanité qui préside assez naturellement aux travaux d'érudition? M. l'abbé de La Rue avait le premier découvert la vieille chanson de geste dans la bibliothèque d'Oxford; il fut aussitôt pris à partie par son jeune élève M. Francisque Michel; celui-ci, premier éditeur, fut rudement gourmandé par M. Bourdillon, second éditeur; et MM. Michel et Bourdillon, en récompense du zèle qu'ils avaient montré pour nous faire connaître le même poëme, n'ont obtenu du troisième éditeur, M. Génin, qu'une suite non interrompue d'injustes dédains ou d'insolents quolibets." [Would you like a sense of the feeling of decorum that attends naturally to the work of scholarship? The abbé de La Rue was the first to have discovered the old *chanson de geste* in the Oxford Library; he was immediately taken to task by his young student Francisque Michel; Michel, the work's first editor, was then severely berated by Monsieur Bourdillon, the second editor; and Messrs Michel and Bourdillon, as a reward for the zealousness that they had shown in making the same poem known to us, obtained from the third editor nothing but an uninterrupted stream of insolent invective and undeserved disdain.] Paulin Paris, "La Chanson de Roland (Edition de M. F. Génin)," *Bibliothèque de l'Ecole des chartes* 2 (2nd series) (March–April 1851): 297–338 (297).

33. For example, the preface to his 1830 edition of the *Chronique de Duguesclin* begins with this sentence: "Aujourd'hui que la littérature française, libre du cercle étroit où les pédants l'avaient emprisonnée si long-temps, a pris son vol

vers sa source, pour y retremper son langage; aujourd'hui que les arts et l'histoire de concert avec elle jettent un regard d'admiration et d'étude sur nos anciens monuments, insultés par le dédain de quatre siècles; aujourd'hui enfin que l'épithète de gothique, ajoutée à un édifice ou à un livre, n'est plus une expression de mépris, c'est rendre service au public que de mettre à sa portée quelques-unes de nos vieilles richesses littéraires dont la rareté, le prix commercial et les vénérables caractères sont des obstacles insurmontables pour quiconque n'a pas grande provision de patience et d'argent." [Now that French literature, freed from the confines in which pedants had imprisoned it for so long, has returned to its source to reinvigorate its language; now that the arts and history have joined literature in turning their admiring scholarly gaze toward our ancient monuments, disparaged by four centuries' worth of disdain; now, finally, that the designation of gothic, appended to a building or a book, is no longer a term of reproach, it can be only beneficial to put at the public's disposal some of our old literary riches, whose rarity, cost, and ancient writing forms are insurmountable obstacles to whoever lacks large reserves of patience and money.] Francisque Michel, ed., *Chronique de Duguesclin* (Paris: Bureau de la Bibliothèque choisie, 1830), 1–2.

34. Another member of this small group was Etienne Barbazan, an eighteenth-century scholar who insisted on presenting the texts in their original form, unaccompanied by a modern French translation; his paean to the beauties of Old French is reproduced in Gossman, *Medievalism* (as in note 19), p. 259. On the predominance of the documentary over the esthetic strain in medieval studies prior to the late nineteenth century, see Ridoux, *Evolution* (as in note 4), esp. 123–30.

35. He also wrote, in a passage that may have inspired Michel, the following wish: "Puisse cette entreprise, *exécutée dans l'unique but de contribuer à l'illustration de notre belle Normandie*, offrir quelque intérêt à mes compatriotes, et inspirer à quelques uns d'entre eux l'idée de publier l'ouvrage de Benoît de Sainte-More, rival et contemporain de Wace, dont M. Depping vient d'imprimer des fragmens si curieux" (emphasis added). [May this undertaking, *carried out with the sole intention of increasing the renown of our fair Normandy*, be of interest to my fellow countrymen and inspire some of them to publish the work by Benoît de Sainte-More, a rival and contemporary of Wace, curious fragments of whose work have just been published by Mr. Depping.] Pluquet, *Le roman de Rou* (as in note 23), xx. The quotation reproduced in the body of my article is located on page xviii of this edition.

36. Roquefort, *De l'état de la poésie françoise dans les XIIe et XIIIe siècles* (Paris: Fournier, 1815), and *Glossaire de la langue romane* (Paris: Warée, 1808). Pluquet and Roquefort biographical details are taken from the *Index biographique français*, 2nd ed. (Munich: Saur, 1998), compiled by Tommaso Nappo.

37. Georges-Adrien Crapelet, ed., *L'histoire du Châtelain de Coucy et de la Dame de Fayel* (Paris: Crapelet, 1829), ix.

38. Raynouard advanced the study of Old French immensely by proposing the dual case (sujet/régime) system.

39. In the introduction to his edition of the *Voyage de Charlemagne*; see his *Charlemagne: An Anglo-Norman Poem of the Twelfth Century* (London: Pickering, 1836), ii.

40. See Jean-François Champollion, *Lettres écrites d'Egypte et de Nubie, en*

1828 et 1829 (1833; repr. Geneva: Slatkine, 1973). Extracts of the "Mémoire" are reproduced in Lacouture, *Champollion* (as in note 16), 396–97.

41. Theis, "Guizot et les institutions de mémoire" (as in note 6).

42. Charles-Olivier Carbonell, "Guizot, homme d'Etat, et le mouvement historiographique français du XIXe siècle," in *Actes du Colloque François Guizot (Paris, 22–25 octobre 1974)* (Paris: Société de l'Histoire du Protestantisme français, 1976), 219–37 (224).

43. Douglas Johnson, *Guizot: Aspects of French History, 1787–1874* (London: Routledge, 1963), 324.

44. See G. H. Pertz, *Archiv der Gesellschaft für ältere deutsche Geschichtskunde*, vol. 7 (Hanover: Hahn, 1839), 1006–07, and Augustin Thierry, *Histoire de la conquête d'Angleterre par les Normands*, 3rd ed. (Paris: Jovet, 1830). For the early account of the Battle of Hastings, see Barlow, ed., *The Carmen de Hastingae proelio* (as in note 9).

45. "Plusieurs ouvrages précieux, relatifs à l'histoire des rois anglosaxons ou des Ducs de Normandie, et de Guillaume le Conquérant dans la Grande Bretagne, ne se trouvent que dans les Bibliothèques publiques de l'Angleterre. Ces ouvrages me paraissent offrir un puissant intérêt historique, et pourraient être copiés, en totalité ou en partie." [Several precious works relating to the history of the Anglo-Saxon kings or of the dukes of Normandy, as well as of William the Conquerer in Great Britain, are found only in English public libraries. These works seem to me to offer a strong historical interest and could be copied in part or in whole.] Draft of Guizot letter to Antoine-Isaac Sylvestre de Sacy, 22 July 1833, *Archives Nationales* F17 3296.

46. The prevailing critical opinion that Guizot was *totally* indifferent to Michel's success at retrieving the Roland manuscript needs to be nuanced, however. Upon being informed by Monmerqué in July of 1835 of Michel's recent discovery at the Bodleian, Guizot had a response drawn up by an aide. In an undated second draft of it, the tepid prose apparently penned by the aide ("je la [= la découverte] crois d'un assez grand intérêt" [I find it (the discovery) to be of fairly substantial interest]) has been crossed out and replaced by an expression of genuine enthusiasm in what appears to be Guizot's hand ("Je vous serai fort obligé si vous voulez bien témoigner à M. Fr. Michel toute ma satisfaction de son zèle et de ses efforts" [I will be much obliged if you would kindly communicate to Mr. Michel my considerable satisfaction at his zeal and his efforts]). *Archives Nationales* F17 3296.

47. This was typical of the 1820s, when collections of "mémoires," as they were called, proliferated. Claude-Bernard Petitot, in the preface to the first volume of his *Collection (complète) des mémoires relatifs à l'histoire de France* (Paris: Foucault, 1819), had regretted the dryness of French historical writing; he faulted historical narrative based solely on charters and proclamations for failing to illuminate causes and passions, "ces puissans mobiles des actions humaines" [these powerful motives of human action] (v).

48. François Guizot, ed. and trans., *La Philippide*, Collection des mémoires relatifs à l'histoire de France 12 (Paris: Brière, 1825), ix. Medieval literary works also had their place in Guizot's research paradigm, but as documents of historical and linguistic – rather than aesthetic – interest.

49. Another medieval work that interested Guizot greatly for its philological,

historical, and literary value (exactly the three primary interests Michel lists in his letter) was the *Chanson de la Croisade Albigeoise* (or *Chanson de la Croisade contre les Albigeois*), written around 1210 by the Navarran cleric Guilhem of Tudela. See Charmes, *Le Comité* (as in note 12), 2:18–19.

50. The abbé de La Rue refers to Arthurian romance ("les Romans de la Table Ronde") as "l'histoire fabuleuse du roi Artur" [the mythical history of king Arthur] and to a branch of what we now call epic (which he dubs "les Romans de Charlemagne") as "l'histoire fabuleuse de ce prince et de chacun de ses paladins" [the mythical history of this prince and of all of his paladins]. Such works treating the "histoire fabuleuse de Charlemagne" include, by his classification, the Pseudo-Turpin Chronicle and *Ogier le Danois*. See La Rue, *Bardes* (as in note 10), 1:127–28.

51. The very first argumentative point made by Michel in the preface to his 1837 edition is the universality of the Roland legend in the Middle Ages: quoting a passage from *La complainte d'outremer*, Michel writes, "Ce passage, qui, sans aucun doute, fait allusion au Roman de Roncevaux, tel que nous le publions, nous montre assez combien il étoit répandu au moyen-âge, et combien la lecture en étoit attachante pour nos aïeux." [This passage, which clearly alludes to the Romance of Roncevaux as published here, demonstrates how widely this work was known in the Middle Ages, and how much our ancestors enjoyed reading it.] Francisque Michel, *La Chanson de Roland ou de Roncevaux du XIIe siècle* (Paris: Silvestre, 1837), i.

52. "Une semblable ardeur animait Charles se rendant sur les terres d'Espagne, alors que séduit par les présens du roi Marsilius, le misérable Ganélon avait trahi les escadrons français, car Charles désirait vivement tirer vengeance de cette horrible scène de carnage dans laquelle le prince Rolland, à la suite de brillans combats, et ces douze chevaliers dont la valeur faisait l'honneur de la France, succombèrent sous les mains sanglantes des Sarrasins, et anoblirent de leur sang généreux la vallée de Roncevaux." [Such was the ardor driving Charles as he returned to Spain, when the miserable Ganelon, seduced by gifts from king Marsilius, betrayed the French squadrons. For Charles longed to wreak vengeance for the horrible scene of carnage in which prince Roland, after having fought brilliantly, and the twelve knights whose valor was the honor of France, were overcome at the bloody hands of the Sarrasins and ennobled with their generous blood the valley of Roncevaux.] Guizot, *La Philippide* (as in note 48), 80–81. For a more recent edition of the work and this passage, see Henri-François Delaborde, *Oeuvres de Rigord et de Guillaume le Breton* (Paris: Renouard, 1882–85), II, 80, II, 389–96.

53. Useful reflections on the complexities of twelfth-century historical writing can be found in Jean Blacker, *The Faces of Time: Portrayal of the Past in Old French and Latin Historical Narrative of the Anglo-Norman Regnum* (Austin: University of Texas Press, 1994), and Barbara N. Sargent-Baur, "Veraces Historiae aut Fallaces Fabulae?" in *Text and Intertext in Medieval Arthurian Literature*, ed. Norris J. Lacy (New York: Garland, 1996), 25–39. For treatment of the varying medieval attitudes concerning the veracity of the Taillefer performance in particular, see Barlow, ed., *The Carmen de Hastingae proelio* (as in note 9), and Sayers, "The Jongleur Taillefer at Hastings" (as in note 11), esp. 87–88.

54. For previous thought on this point, see Glencross, *Reconstructing Camelot* (as in note 4), 64.

A Lot of Learning is a Dang'rous Thing: The Ruthwell Cross Runes and their Icelandic Interpreters

Magnús Fjalldal

In the minds of modern day students of Old English, the Ruthwell Cross, located in Dumfriesshire in Scotland, is inevitably linked with "The Dream of the Rood," of which it preserves parts, carved as a runic inscription. Less familiar is the fate of the inscription before the connection between the Anglo-Saxon poem and the cross was established. That fate involved two badly mistaken attempts to decipher the runes, which, however, eventually led to their correct interpretation. It is these failures and their authors, Þorleifur Repp and Finnur Magnússon, that will be the main subject of my discussion. Their efforts – on the few occasions that these have attracted any scholarly attention – have most commonly been mentioned in order to make fun of the Icelandic pair for being as spectacularly wrong, as they indeed were, in their interpretation of the Ruthwell runes. Far less attention has been paid to the probable causes of their failure and the role of their work in actually solving the puzzle. It is on these aspects of the story that I would like to dwell in the pages that follow. First, however, a brief description of the celebrated cross and its history is required.

The cross which today stands inside the church in the village of Ruthwell near Gretna was until 1887 located in the churchyard.[1] It is about five meters tall, rectangular in shape and made of local sandstone. The cross is ornamented on all four sides with a number of Biblical images showing the role of Christ in the world, both historically and eternally as mankind's benefactor, judge and savior. In addition, there are inscriptions both in Latin and in runes, but unfortunately, time, destruction and neglect have left the ornamentation scarred and incomplete. The runic inscription is to be found on the front and back upper panels and on the front and back edges of the upright beam, arranged in clusters of two to four characters. The inscription records material that corresponds closely with lines 39 to 64 of the "Dream of the Rood," composed in the Northumbrian dialect of Old English. The Ruthwell Cross is believed to date from the mid-eighth century,[2] and thought by some to be a "preaching cross" associated with a carefully planned theological program.[3]

The earliest scholarly reference to the cross and its runic inscription dates back to the beginning of the 17th century and is based on notes and a drawing by one Reginald Bainbrigg, compiled for a new edition of Camden's *Brittania*. It is clear from Bainbrigg's observations that he was more interested in the runes than the religious iconography of the cross, and the same can be said of most subsequent visitors. But soon afterwards the cross was to attract attention of an altogether different kind. In an age of Calvinist fervour in Scotland and in the wake of the Kirk's hostility to "idolatrous monuments," a special Act for the Kirk of Ruthwell ordered the cross to be broken after the local parish minister had resisted a similar order of two years earlier. But even after the demolition of the cross, out of sight was by no means out of mind. The 17th century was the dawn of antiquarian fascination with all things ruined, strange and mysterious, and what object could fit that description better than the Ruthwell Cross? A steady trickle of visitors continued to record their impressions of the mysterious artifact for all that they were unable to make the slightest sense of its runic text.

Gradually, the initial sketches that Bainbrigg had made of the cross and its inscription were supplemented by others. In 1703, William Nicolson's transcription of the runes was published in Hickes's *Thesaurus*. Nicolson also sent copies of his transcription to antiquarian friends in England and Sweden in the hope that someone might be able to interpret it, but to no avail. Two decades later, Alexander Gordon provided two plates of the cross in his *Itinerarium Septentrionale* (1726). Gordon's volume, which remained the authoritative work on the Ruthwell Cross for more than a century, was, however, flawed. Although he attempted to record the marks inscribed as faithfully as possible, his transcription of the runes was not entirely trustworthy. As for the art work, Gordon's reproduction did not include all the fragments of the cross, and the images that he did sketch were more often than not what he expected to see rather than what was actually there. In 1789, Gordon's prints were partly utilised as models for engravings by Adam de Cardonell, which were commissioned to accompany Richard Gough's *Vetusta Monumenta* in 1789. Like others before him, Gough was primarily interested in the runic inscription, and like Nicolson, he sent off prints to learned friends. Whether he had any more luck than Nicolson in this enterprise is debatable, but one of his prints was eventually to end up in the hands of Finnur Magnússon, probably through Grímur Thorkelín. The final and decisive effort in making the cross known to a wider audience and getting the runes deciphered was made by the Rev. Henry Duncan who had the cross reconstructed in the garden of his vicarage in 1802 and three decades later published a descriptive essay on the cross, accompanied by accurate engravings of its images and inscriptions – including Þorleifur Repp's (1833) partial and quite mistaken reading of them.[4] This publication and Finnur Magnússon's equally misguided attempt (1837)[5] were the immediate catalyst that prompted John Kemble's more correct reading of the runic text in 1840, as I shall try to explain later in this essay.

And now to the mysterious inscription that had for so long frustrated antiquarian curiosity. A reproduction of it may be presented as follows, bearing in mind of course the actual location of the runes in clusters on the edges of the cross. [Runes which have been collated from various drawings are indicated, for technical reasons, by square brackets round the matching letters on the lower line transcription only, while missing characters (one or more) are indicated by three dots (. . .).[6] It should also be noted that the Ruthwell inscription distinguishes "hard" and "soft" values of both g and k, represented in the lower line transcription by G / g and K / k respectively. This distinction is not marked in the reconstruction immediately following. Ed.]

I. Front – upper panel:

ᚷᛖᚱᛖ
g e r e

Front – right panel (north-east):

ᛗᚫ ᚾᛁ ᛏᚱ ᚷᚠ ᛗᚫ ᛚᛗ ᛗᛇ ᛏᛏᛁ ᚷᚦ ᚠᚾ ᛗᚦ ᚠᛚ ᛗᛗ ᚠᛁ ᚷᚠ ᛚᚷ
dæ hi næ Go da l m eȝ tti gþ ah ew al d e on Ga lG

ᚢᚷ ᛁᛋᛏ ᛁᚷᚠ ᛗᚠᛗ ᛁᚷᚠ ᚠᚱᛗ ᚠᛚᛚᚠ ᛗᛗᛁ ᛒᚢᚷ
ug ist iGa mod igf [o r e] [allæ] men [buG] ...

II. Front – left panel (south-east):

ᚠᛁᛗ   ᚾᚠᚠ ᛁᚻᚱ ᛁᛁᚻᛏ ᚠᚷᛗ ᛏᛁᚷ ᚻᚾᛏ ᚠᚾᛁ ᚠᚻᚾ ᛚᚠᚠ ᚠᚱᛗ
[+onm] ... [hof] i c r iicn æKy ni ŋ chêa fun æsh [l]af ard

ᚾᚠᛚ ᛗᚠᛁᚻ ᛏᛁᛗᚠ ᚱᚻᛏᚠ ᛒᛁᚻᛗ ᚠᚱᚠᛗ ᚾᚾᚷ ᛉᛗᛏ ᛗᛗᛁ ᛒᚠᚠᛏ
hæl daic nido rstæ [b]ism ær[ad] uuŋ Ket men bæt

ᚷᚠᛗ   ᛗᛁᚻ   ᛗᛁᚦᛒ ᛚᚠᛗᛁ ᛒᛁᚻᛏ ᛗᛗᛁ ᛗᛒᛁ   ᚠᛏ
[G]ad ... [e i]c ... [m]iþþ lod[i] bist [e]mi [d]bi ... [ot]

ᛗᛁᚠᚠ...
[enof] ...

III. Back – upper panel:

ᚲᚱᛁᛋ ᛏ ᚹᚫᛋᚩᚾ
[+]k r i s [t] wæson

Back – right panel (south-west):

ᚱᚠ ᛖᛁ ᚾᚦ ᛗᚦ ᚱᚠ ᚦᛖ ᚱᚠ ᚻᛋᚠ ᚠᛏᚱ ᚱᚠᚾ ᛄᛈ ᚠ ᛗᚢ ᚠ
ro di hw eþ ræ þe rf us[æ] fêar ran kw[o] mu[æ]

ᚦᚦᛁᛚ ᚠᛏᛁᛚ ᚠᚾᚢ ᛗᛁᚳ ᚦᚫᛏᚠ ᛚᛒᛁᚾ ᛏᛚ   ᛋᚫᚱ   ᛁᚳᚹ ᚠ
þþil ætil anu mic þæta lbi[h] [êal] ... sa[r] ... icw[æ]

ᛋᛗᛁ ᛋᚫᚱ ᚷᚢᛖ ᚷᛁᛗ ᚱᚫᛈᛁ ᛖᚾ ᚠᚷ
smi ... s[or] Gu[m] gid rœ[fi] dh ... aG ...

IV. Back – left panel (north-west):

ᛖᛁ ᚦᛋ ᛏᚱᛖ ᛚᚢ ᛗᚷ ᛁᚹ ᚢᚾ ᚻᚫᚻ ᚠᛚᛖ ᚷᚻᚢ ᚾᚾᛁᚫ ᚾᛁᚾᚫ
[m]i þs [t]re [l]u mg iw un dad ale gdu nhiæ hinæ

ᛚᛁᛗᚹ ᚱᚱᛁᚷ ᚾᚫᚷᛁ ᛋᛏᚠ ᚦᚦᚢ ᚾ ᚾᛁᛖ ᚾ ᛚᛁ ᚻᚫᛋ   ᚫᚠ
limw ærig nægi sto ddu [n]him ... h ... [li] cæs ... [êa]f ...

ᛖ ᚾᛏ ᚻᚢ ᚾᛁ ᚦᛖ ᛏ
h ... [h]êa ... [d]u ... [h]i ... [þ]e ... [êa]

Reconstructed and translated the text reads:

I. Front – upper panel and right panel (north-east):
    + ondgeredæ hinæ god alme3ttig. Þa he walde on galgu gistiga
                            modig fore allæ men
                            buga ic ni dorstæ
                            ac scêalde fæstæ standa.

II. Front – left panel (south-east):
                            ahof ic riicnæ kyniŋc.
                    hêafunæs hlafard   hælda ic ni dorstæ.
            bismæradu uŋket men ba ætgadre;   ic wæs miþ blodi bistemid,
            bigoten of þæs guman sida   siþþan he his gastæ sendæ.

III. Back – upper panel and right panel (south-west):
                            + krist wæs on rodi.
                    hweþræ þer fusæ   fêarran kwomu

æþþilæ til anum: ic þæt al bihêald.
saræ ic wæs miþ sorgum gidrœfid;   hnag ic þam secgum til handa.

IV. Back – left panel (north-west):
       miþ strelum giwundad
alegdun hiæ hinæ limwœrignæ;   gistoddun him æt his licæs hêafdum;
bihêaldun hiæ þer hêafunæs dryctin;   ond he hinæ þer hwilæ restæ.

[I. God Almighty stripped Himself. When he wished to ascend on to the gallows, brave before all men, I dared not bow down, but had to stand fast.

II. I raised up a powerful King, I dared not tilt the Lord of Heaven. Men mocked us both together. I was drenched with blood issued from the Man's side after He sent forth His spirit.

III. Christ was on the Cross. But hastening nobles came together there from afar. I beheld it all. Sorely was I with sorrows afflicted. I bent to the men, to their hands.

IV. Wounded with arrows they laid Him down weary in limb. They stood for him at the head of His corpse. They beheld there Heaven's Lord. And He rested Himself there for a time.][7]

  It is easy to be wise in hindsight and to ask whether the inscription should not have been deciphered long before John Kemble turned his attention to it? He certainly thought so, for in the article in which he presented his reading, Kemble could not resist taking a swipe at fellow laborers past and present: "it is . . . very strange that none of our philologists and antiquaries have so much as attempted to give any thing like a reasonable account of the few lines we have [i.e. the runic inscription]." And then Kemble proceeded to brand English antiquaries as a "degenerate" lot.[8] Kemble's criticism was not entirely unjustified; two manuscripts, Domitian A IX and Titus D XVIII, which both contain runic futharks with Latin glosses on the characters, had been known since the late 16th century and would hence have been available to antiquarians since the days of Camden.

  But there was also much which served to distract scholars from producing a correct solution. Despite a fairly large number of surviving inscriptions, Anglo-Saxon runes, as such, had never been a subject of study in Britain. To compound the problem, no one knew in what language the Ruthwell inscription might be written: Old Norse, Old English, a mixture of the two, a special Runic language or something equally mysterious? Although Wilhelm Carl Grimm had in 1821 declared the runes to be Anglo-Saxon,[9] his verdict was of little consequence in the absence of a reading of the inscription. A further difficulty was presented by the fact that the characters were only partly legible in places and, as we now know, the equally significant fact that the words of the inscription are run together in such a way as to give no clue to where one word ends and another begins. Local legends were of no help either. They favored an exotic provenance for the cross; it had been shipwrecked when being transported to some distant place, or brought to Ruthwell by angels.[10] In short, Þorleifur Repp and Finnur Magnússon had no more to aid them than their "degenerate" British counterparts when they were confronted by the Ruthwell inscription.

The two Icelanders came to the Ruthwell mystery with many impressive credentials. Some of Repp's contemporaries at Copenhagen University considered him to be one of the most talented and learned young men of his generation. Equally conversant in science and the humanities, his university education ranged from studies in medicine, chemistry and physics to ancient and modern languages and literature. Eventually, however, Repp became fascinated by the new philology that Rasmus Rask was pioneering in the 1810s, and Rask became Repp's friend and mentor.[11] Although Repp failed to obtain his M.A. from the university (for what was seen as scandalous behavior at his disputation ceremony), he had – before moving to Edinburgh and becoming involved with Duncan – already worked on an edition of *Laxdæla saga* and other projects for the Arnamagnæan Institute in Copenhagen and had thus become well acquainted with Norse texts. His knowledge of Old English – mostly acquired through his revision of the 1830 translation of Rasmus Rask's *Anglo-Saxon Grammar* – was, according to his biographer Prof. Andrew Wawn, "by no means negligible."[12] As for his knowledge of Scandinavian runology, the University of Copenhagen appointed him – on at least one occasion – to assist in the defence of a thesis on that subject.[13] And once in Edinburgh, runology was among the courses that Repp taught privately to augment his meager income as a librarian.[14] If some of Repp's contemporaries also found him rash and arrogant, nothing of the kind could be said of Finnur Magnússon, although both had a tendency to show off their immense learning – a trait that is not entirely unknown in Norse studies today.

Repp's biography has recently been written, but Finnur Magnússon has had no such honors and is seldom remembered today. In recent years, only two Icelandic scholars, Jón Helgason and Aðalgeir Kristjánsson, have attempted to describe his life and career in any detail. He was born in 1781 into a prominent intellectual family in Iceland. At the age of 16, he was sent to Copenhagen to study law, but apparently Magnússon was more interested in poetry than jurisprudence. Four years later he was back in Iceland without any academic qualifications and working as a clerk for the Danish governor of the country. But whether it was out of guilt or interest, it is known that he read extremely widely as he languished in the Danish hamlet of Reykjavik.

The Napoleonic Wars largely disrupted Danish administration of Iceland, and in 1809, a Danish-born adventurer named Jorgen Jorgensen seized the opportunity to usurp power and proclaimed himself as the new king of the country. Magnússon was offered a senior post in the new administration, and when he refused to accept it, he was briefly jailed. Ironically, that jail sentence was to turn out to be one of the luckiest breaks of his life. Jorgensen's reign in Iceland was short-lived, and for decades to come, the Danish authorities would have a particularly friendly attitude to those who had stayed loyal during the coup.

In 1812 Finnur Magnússon returned to Copenhagen, at a time when learned Icelanders were in great demand. Scholarly editions of Icelandic manuscripts, which had begun four decades earlier, had virtually come to a halt for lack of funds and qualified editors. Magnússon was immediately offered work for the Arnamagnæan Institute and given the task of seeing through the last two volumes of the handsome three volume edition of the Codex Regius manuscript of Eddic poetry which had been begun in 1787. It took him six years to complete this monumental work, which included, among other things, the first Lexicon of Northern Mythology.

Next, Magnússon turned to comparative mythology and produced a four volume study of the origins of Norse mythology which he traced to Asia. Unfortunately, this work has all the characteristics of Magnússon's weaknesses as a scholar: gullibility, lack of common sense and unbridled flights of fancy, which, despite his great learning, would mar many of his later publications. Still, he gradually rose through the ranks to become Professor of Nordic Antiquities at Copenhagen University where his scholarly output – regardless of its shortcomings – was nothing less than prodigious.

However, it must also be said that when Magnússon could keep his scholarly imagination in check, he was capable of producing first rate work. One such example is his part in a three volume study on the history of the Icelandic colony in Greenland, completed in 1845 and a standard authority on the subject for more than a century. But long before that publication appeared, Magnússon had, unfortunately, become absorbed in the study of runic inscriptions; an interest that would lead him from one disaster to the next. Being a kind and generous man was of no help as he gradually came under increasing criticism for his scholarly blunders. Later, his countrymen would mostly remember Magnússon for these and curse him for having sold his collection of Icelandic manuscripts to Britain.

The most notorious of Magnússon's mistakes occurred around the time that he was contemplating the Ruthwell Cross runes. This was the so-called Runamo "inscription" (discovered in the district of Blekinge, Sweden). This "inscription" Magnússon would eventually declare to be nothing less than one of the oldest heroic poems of Scandinavia and thus one of the most remarkable discoveries ever made in the field of runology. The instant European fame that followed the publication of his findings in 1841 must have been gratifying, and such was Magnússon's temperament, that it caused him no qualms that he had to read the runic letters backwards (i.e. from right to left) to obtain the desired results. In 1844, however, it was established beyond a shadow of a doubt that the Runamo "inscription" was not runic at all but merely a collection of glacial marks. So it was that Magnússon had to endure this humiliation in addition to Kemble's scathing attack from four years earlier which was now coming to the attention of his Scandinavian critics, and they were more than happy to rub a little salt into the wounds.[15] But Magnússon was by all accounts a good-natured man, and these defeats, which might have broken a lesser soul, do not appear to have dampened his spirits much.[16]

Whatever character flaws Þorleifur Repp and Finnur Magnússon may have had in common, there is little doubt that the worst handicap that the two shared, as they attempted to solve the Ruthwell mystery, lay, paradoxically, in their great familiarity with the traditions of Scandinavian runology. In Denmark, the study of runic inscriptions began in earnest with the pioneering work of Ole Worm as early as the 17th century. His efforts culminated in a six-volume study: *Danicorum Monumentorum*, published in 1643. Worm collaborated closely with learned Icelanders of his day – among them Arngrímur Jónsson, Þorlákur Skúlason and Magnús Ólafsson. The Icelandic contribution was mostly in the form of material for a dictionary of the "old language" – which Worm saw as essential for progress in the field – and had published in 1650.[17] After Worm's day, his work was continued by several antiquarians in Scandinavia. In Denmark more finds were reported in Erik Pontoppidan's two volume *Marmora Danica*, published in 1739, and by the middle of the century, an official position of a royal archivist responsible for accurately drawing and describing runic monuments had been created. In 1750 a thorough description of the then known Swedish runic monuments was published by Johan Göransson,[18] and by the end of the 18th century, German scholars (e.g. J. C. Jürgensen and J. M. Schultz) had begun to show interest in new finds in southern Jutland (Slesvig). In short, by the time that Repp and Magnússon attempted to read the Ruthwell runes, a large quantity of data had already been collected and interpreted, and the subject of Scandinavian runology already had something of an international flavour.

From early on, many of the Danish, Swedish and Norwegian monuments displayed certain characteristics with which every Scandinavian runologist would have been familiar at the beginning of the 19th century. First of all, it was well understood that most commonly the purpose of the monuments was to convey someone's name to posterity and thus honor his or her memory.[19] But how this aim was carried out varied, and the majority of such inscriptions fell into three distinct categories. In the first place, there was a very large number of monuments that only recorded the name of the deceased, together perhaps with that of the individual who had had the stone erected. Secondly, there were numerous monuments that also included a place name – usually that of the foreign location where the person had died. Finally, a few longer inscriptions, containing not only names and places but also some historical information, had been discovered by the beginning of the 19th century.

Let us now proceed to look at a few examples from these three categories:

A *Personal names*:
    1. **The Hune Stone** (known since 1627): Hofi, Þorkil [and] Þorbiorn erected this stone in memory of their father Runnolf the Wise.[20]
    2. **The Second Gunderup Stone** (known since ca. 1627): Østen erected this stone in memory of his father Asulv.[21]
    3. **The Nørre Nærå Stone** (known since 1684): Thormund, enjoy your grave-mound and monument.[22]
    4. **The Rønninge Stone** (known since ca. 1627): Sote erected this stone in memory of his brother Elev, the son of Asgot of the red shield.[23]

B *Personal names and place names*:
    1. **The First Haddeby Stone** (known since 1796): Thorulv, Sven's retainer, erected this stone in memory of his companion Erik who met his death when brave men laid siege to Hedeby (in southern Jutland). He commanded a boat and was a most noble man.[24]
    2. **The Sønder Kirkeby Stone** (known since 1802): [Azz]er erected this stone in memory of his brother Ask[a] who died in Got[land]. May Thor consecrate these runes.[25]
    3. **The Tirsted Stone** (known since 1627): Asråd and Hildung erected this stone in memory of [their uncle?] Frede [who terrified other warriors?]. He met his death in Sweden . . .[26]
    4. **The Sjörup Stone** (known since ca. 1640): Saxe erected this stone in memory of Esbern, the son of Toke. He did not flee from battle at Uppsala, but fought while he could wield his weapons.[27]

C *Personal names, place names and legend*:
    1. **The Second Jelling Stone** (known since ca. 1591): King Harold ordered this grave-mound and stone to be made in memory of his

father, Gorm, and his mother, Thyre. This Harold conquered all of Denmark and made the Danes adopt Christianity.[28]

2. **The Glavendrup Stone** (known since 1806): Ragnhildr erected this stone in memory of Alle the Pale (?), the guardian of the temple and an honorable retainer. The sons of Alle made this grave-mound and monument in memory of their father and his widow did so in memory of her husband. Sote carved these runes in memory of his master. May Thor consecrate these runes. May he be called an evil-doer (?) who destroys this stone or has it carried away to erect it as a monument for someone else.[29]

3. **The Karlevi Stone** (known since 1634): This stone is erected in memory of Sibbe the Good, the son of Foldar. His retainers . . . made a monument in his honor on the island. [Here follows a stanza:] Now he lies hidden in this grave-mound; he, the warrior who accomplished great achievements, as most people knew. Never will a more perfect and powerful ocean-god come to rule over Denmark.[30]

4. **The Rök Stone** (known since 1624): For Væmod stand these runes. And Varin wrote them, the father for his dead son. I tell the ancient tale which the two war-booties were, twelve times taken as war-booty, both together from man to man. This I tell second who nine generations ago . . . with the Reidgoths; and he died with them, because of his guilt.

>Theodoric the bold
>king of sea warriors,
>ruled over
>Reid-sea shores.
>Now sits he armed
>on his Gothic horse,
>shield strapped,
>protector of Mærings.

This I tell in the twelfth instance where the horse of the Valkyrie sees food on the battle-field, where twenty kings lie. This I tell in the thirteenth instance, which twenty kings sat on Sjaelland for four years, with four names, sons of four brothers: five called Valke, sons of Radulv, five Reidlulvs, sons of Rugulv, five Haisls, sons of Harud, five Gunnmunds, sons of Björn . . . I tell the tale which of the Ingvaldings was revenged through a wife's sacrifice. I tell the ancient tale to what young warrior a kinsman is born. Vilin it is. He could slay a giant . . . I tell the ancient tale: Thor. Sibbi, guardian of the sanctuary, ninety years of age, begot a descendant.[31]

5. **The Sparlösa Stone** (known since 1750): Eyvísl(?), Eiríkr's son gave, Alríkr gave . . . . . . gave . . . as payment. Then (?) the father sat (?) (in) Uppsala (?), the father that . . . . . . nights and days. Alríkr . . . feared (?) not Eyvísl (?) . . . that Eiríkr's boy is called Sigmarr, celebrated for victories. Mighty battle (?) . . . in memory of Eyvísl (?). And interpret the runes of divine origin there . . ., that Alríkr . . . colored . . . . Gísli made this monument in memory of Gunnarr, (his) brother.[32]

Let us now consider the solutions that Þorleifur Repp and Finnur Magnússon offered in respect to the mysterious Ruthwell runes with the above-mentioned texts in mind.

Repp (in the words of the Rev. Henry Duncan who announced his discovery in 1833) could not produce a coherent reading of the inscription, which is hardly surprising as he was getting all his word-divisions wrong. Still, he offered the following observations, according to the enthusiastic clergyman:

> On the left hand column of the left face he reads the word *Ashlafardhal*, i.e. *The vale or dale of Ashlafr* (cf. hêafunæs **hlafard hæl**da), *Ashlafr* being the genitive of a common female name, as Asleifr is that of a man, among northern nations. On the same column occurs likewise the word *Menboat* (cf. **men ba æt**gadre), i.e. *The expiation for an injury*.
> On the right-hand column of the left face no intelligible word has yet been made out; but on the left-hand column of the right face, Mr Repp finds the following sentence, – *Cristpason* (cf. **krist wæs on**) *mith siretum* (cf. **miþ strelum**) *XI. punda male* (cf. **giwundad ale**gdun hiæ) i.e. *The vessel of Christ* [or baptismal font], *of eleven pounds of weight, with ornaments;* while on the right-hand column of the same face this sentence is found – *Radith phedra* [for *fedra*] (cf. on **rodi** . . . **hweþræ**) . . . *Therfusa aqrran*, i.e. *By the authority of the Therfusian fathers* [or Monks of Therfuse] (cf. **þer fusæ fêarran**), *for the devastation of the fields*.
> And afterwards the words *Kua XIII*. (cf. **kwomu**); the former being the genitive plural of *Ku*, Norse and Anglo-Saxon for a *Cow*; the latter being probably numeral.[33]

It is quite clear that the two place names Ashlafardhal and Therfuse formed the core of Repp's tantalising but incomplete solution. Duncan had, in all likelihood, hoped for more, but as he explained apologetically in his article, "important avocations [had] not permitted Mr Repp to prosecute his investigation further." Hence, it fell to the Rev. Duncan himself to piece the clues that Repp had unearthed into something of a coherent legend:

> Upon considering so much of the inscription as has been deciphered, it may be conjectured that the monument owed its origin to the following circumstances. Some powerful chief having ravaged the lands of the church in a particular district, and having afterwards become penitent, had procured a reconciliation with the monks by various gifts, including a rich baptismal font, and perhaps an annual payment of cattle. All this was probably recorded by the holy fathers of Therfuse upon what is supposed to have been the original column . . . It is obvious that, in future inquiries on this subject, it will be of considerable importance to fix the locality of *Ashlafardhal* and *Therfuse*, more particularly in connection with the tradition of the Monument having been brought by sea from some distant country.[34]

In retrospect, it can be said that the two mysterious localities that Repp postulated look rather suspect, and Duncan's hypothesis that the monks at a particular – albeit wholly unknown – monastery had felt the need to erect a five meter tall monument and carve it with runes and Biblical images to record amends for a minor raid on their place is less than convincing. (Still, one of Repp's biographers – writing in 1971, but blissfully ignorant of Kemble's article – gives him full credit for correctly interpreting the Ruthwell inscription.)[35] Repp would later complain that Duncan had rushed him in his examination of the drawings of the runes (Repp never visited Ruthwell in person), and that the enthusiastic clergyman had over-interpreted his findings.[36] But such excuses carried little weight against the Kembles of this world.

Three years after Repp and Duncan had announced their solution, Finnur Magnússon (using the Adam de Cardonell engraving, which he quite mistakenly believed to be much older than those of Hickes and Gordon)[37] offered a completely different solution, which was not only much more extensive than that of Repp and Duncan, but came complete with a detailed description of a hitherto unknown language and a mysterious civilisation. Magnússon also obliged his readers by furnishing the history of this forgotten tribe in "105 stupendous pages," as Kemble was later to characterise his work.[38]

It did not help Magnússon in his efforts that the engraving that he was using was not very accurate. Furthermore, it is clear from his transcription that he did not have a clue in what order to read the runes – although I rather expect that his enemies would have been quick to point out that in his case, hitting upon the correct order would not have made much difference. But let us now look at Magnússon's actual transcription:

Front – upper panel:
Offa Vodo khon med . . .
Mag Isgo gere   (these lines are not on the actual cross)

Front – left panel (south-east):
icr iicn
akr iing   (cf. ic riicnæ kyniŋc)
khifum Ashlof
ord holda ic niðarsta bism   (cf. hêafunæs hlafard hælda ic ni dorstæ)
or(ink)e ung   (cf. bismæradu uŋket)
het men bool god   (cf. men ba ætgadre)
ic (v)id bodi
bist imili   (cf. ic wæs miþ blodi bistemid)

Front – upper panel and right panel (north-east):
Ða hi no
hold ol mellti   (cf. hinæ god almeʒttig)
gev ok e valde
on halhu gist   (cf. Þa he walde on galgu gistiga)
ih a moþ
ig före men   (cf. modig fore allæ men)

Back upper panel:
In Erincr(ed)
Ver bu iii   (these lines are not on the actual cross)

Back upper panel:
Krist vas on   (cf. krist wæs on [rodi])

Back – left panel (north-west):
miþs
ir elum givun   (cf. miþ strelum giwundad)
ðad al egdun hio   (cf. alegdun hiæ)
hina aimvö
rigja gistod   (cf. hinæ limwœrignæ)
dunhim ——   (cf. gistoddun him)

Back – right upper panel (south-west):
Radi hved
rad er fusa   (cf. hweþræ þer fusæ)
atr rau

yv a mulþ	(the runes for "atr rau yv" are unidentified)
vil atil	
a nu mic	(cf. **æþþilæ til anum**)
þótat b i i	(cf. **ic þæt**)
Back left panel (north-west):	
Sa ik us mi son	(cf. **saræ ic wæs**)
hva gin radh.	(cf. **miþ sorgum gidrœfid**)

In his study, Magnússon interpreted the runic inscription as follows:

> I, Offa, Voden's kinsman
> Transfer to Eska's descendant . . .
> To you two the property,
> Field, meadow
> Give we Ashlof!
> The words of the noble I below make known.
> To Erinc young
> Promised *she* riches, estates good,
> I for the *marriage* feast[39]
> Prepare in the mean time.
>
> "Received he now" –
> The noble spoke, –
> "The gift, and aye preside
> In the hall *over* the guests!
> I have magnanimity,
> I bring rings (riches)
> . . .
> . . .
>
> These three estates
> Erinc(red) possesses.
>
> Christ was among –
> When to all we gave
> All that they owned –   [i.e. what they were entitled to receive]
> The married pair [i.e Offa and his wife]
> At their home,
> The rich women's, you were a guest,
> *Their* town dwelling –
>
> Give every –
> The advice is willing (willingly given)
> Back spoilation
> If yet living on earth!

> Well the Etheling
> Possesses now me
> This property.
> Saw I us my son!
> Every where again rule.[40]

To some this might appear to be a suspiciously cryptic concoction, and it certainly did to Kemble. But the undeterred and erudite Magnússon – fifty pages or so later – had succeeded in making perfect sense of the whole scenario, to his own satisfaction at least. And whereas Repp's interpretation had centered on place names, Magnússon saw the personal names that he read into the inscription as the key to the entire puzzle:

> Four persons are named in the inscription. *Offa*, the relation or descendant of *Voda*, gives to his daughter *Aslof* (or Oslof, or Oslafa, or Oslava) and to her betrothed or husband *Ermen* . . . (or Erincred) one or more landed estates. If we succeed in identifying these as historical persons, we also ascertain the age of the Inscription.[41]

Needless to say, Magnússon had few problems in identifying this cast of characters, their background and circumstances, and the language and the age of the inscription. It was clearly the two individuals, Voda and Offa – seemingly mentioned in the runes of de Cardonell's engraving, but nowhere to be found on the cross – that gave him the clue to solving the whole puzzle. Voda was Óðinn, whom the Jutish royal family of Kent claimed as their forefather, and Offa, the son of Edelfrid, King of Bernica. Basically, the inscription celebrated a marriage ceremony that united the royal houses of Kent and Northumbria. The groom was Erinc, Prince of Kent (b. ca. 613, according to Magnússon) and his bride Ashlof (b. 635–6), the daughter of Offa, who by then had come to power in Northumbria by marrying Ashlof's unidentified mother, of whom Magnússon could all the same inform his readers that she was the daughter of a Pictish prince and had brought Dumfriesshire into the marriage as her special property. He also recognised the parents of bride and groom in two pictures on the cross.

With all this information, the date of the monument was easily fixed around 650. But the language of the inscription gave Magnússon a slight problem, because it consisted of nothing less than a mixture of Old Norse, Old Saxon, Old English, Frisian and Dutch, including dialectal variations in some of these languages. So how could such a hotchpotch of a language have come about? The answer, Magnússon argued, had to be that a colony of nationals from Scandinavia, the low countries and probably Scotland had come about in Cumbria even before the invasion of the Angles, the Saxons and the Jutes. Old English had then understandably colored the indigenous language of the region.

As we have already seen, the two Icelandic scholars found in the Ruthwell inscription the place names and the personal names that their familiarity with Scandinavian runes had taught them to expect. But now to Kemble's more correct solution of 1840. How could these rather sadly mistaken previous efforts have helped him? Understandably, Kemble was not about to give Repp and Magnússon much credit in his article, but he did admit that they "read the mere letters with reasonable accuracy: it is only when they come to divide them into words, that their good star deserts them."[42] Prof. Wawn notes this comment in his biography of Repp and adds that "as Kemble would be only too aware, it is often easier to be right after someone else has been wrong."[43] While I entirely agree with Prof. Wawn's observation, I also think that Kemble was not prepared to admit that he owed more than a reasonable reading of the runic letters to the Icelandic pair. In the first place, although they assumed that the inscription was written in or influenced by Old Norse, they had both noted a reference to Christ, and it could hardly have taken a leap of the imagination to realise that this could point to a Christian reading rather than the secular ones that Repp and Magnússon had favored.[44] Secondly, it was the sheer improbability of their solutions: unknown localities and monasteries (Repp) and equally unknown individuals and nations (Magnússon) – that must have inspired Kemble to look for a wholly different reading. At the heart of one interpretation was, as we have seen, place names, and the other, personal names, and Kemble rejected both these ideas with scorn. It is thus my contention – although we shall never know the full story – that in 1840 Kemble set out to decipher a Christian text (or a poem) in Old English and in the process deliberately avoided looking for personal or place names of any kind. After all this approach had already been tried and failed to produce credible results. If this is indeed how John Kemble worked, he owes more to the mistakes of Repp and Magnússon than he was prepared to admit in his article on the Ruthwell inscription. For all the ridicule that Kemble exposed Repp and Magnússon to, their attempted readings had, in the first place, shown that the language of the Ruthwell inscription could not be Old Norse, and hence it was only logical to explore the possibility that it might be Old English. Secondly, the Icelandic pair had detected a Christian element in the inscription, and thirdly, it was by now abundantly clear that Scandinavian expectations as to what message the text of the Ruthwell inscription might contain were out of place in this context.

In his 1840 article, John Kemble was on the right track concerning the reading of the Ruthwell runes, and he knew it. But had he also known how imperfect his own solution was, he might have been less arrogant in his condemnation of the failed attempts of Repp and Magnússon. In the first place, Kemble had no more idea than they in which order to read the text. He reads the four narrative sections II, I, IV and III with little attempt to make them hang together. Secondly, Kemble is not above bad misreadings of the runes either. In section II, for example, the line: "ic wæs miþ blodi bistemid" ("I was drenched with blood") becomes: "Ik (n)iðbædi bist(e)me(d)," which Kemble renders as "I stained with the pledge of crime." In section I, he reads "god almeʒttig" ("god almighty") as "gamælde estig" which he takes to mean "he spake benignantly." But Kemble's most blatant errors are reserved for section III where he reads "til anum" ("to him") as "ti lænum" and translates it to mean "in misery" and then crowns his efforts by turning "sorrows" into "gallows."

It should also be noted that Kemble was unable to read substantial parts of the inscription: in section II, the last line; in section I, the last two lines; in section IV, the last line and in section III, much of the last line.[45] It is therefore quite clear that although Kemble's interpretation was a great improvement upon the attempts of Repp and Magnússon, it was still far from being a comprehensive reading of the runic text. That was not achieved until Kemble discovered the relationship between the Ruthwell Cross inscription and "The Dream of the Rood" in 1844.

In discussing Repp's failure in the Ruthwell affair, Prof. Wawn ascribes it in part to the nature of runology as a "slydynge science,"[46] a phrase fittingly borrowed from Chaucer's description of his frustrated alchemist.[47] As we have seen, both Repp and Magnússon were made to experience first-hand how fickle a mistress this subject indeed is, and yet, perhaps their only sin was to be wrong for the right reasons. It is therefore a touch of poetic justice that one of Britain's foremost modern runologists should – after, of course, giving credit where credit is due – choose to remember John Kemble by relating what he calls "the sad case of the Chertsey bowl." This was a copper dish with an inscription which Kemble triumphantly claimed to have deciphered in 1844. He came to the conclusion that the text was a mixture of runes and uncials; it was later found to be in modern Greek.[48]

It is important to remember that the whole subject of "runology" was a deeply contested issue during the 19th century, especially between Scandinavian and German scholars and their respective British partisans. George Stephens, for instance, regarded the very existence of Anglo-Saxon and Old Norse runes as proof that England had been part of the Scandinavian cultural world, and, indeed, that English was a Scandinavian language rather than a West Germanic one.[49] By contrast, John Kemble was an equally passionate advocate of the "Germanness" or "Saxonness" of England. The one group, accordingly, saw only similarity in runes, the other only difference. And, of course, the "Scottishness" of the Ruthwell Cross further compounded the problem. In the most elementary way, reading even the letters of this short text was affected by issues of national sentiment and national self-definition.

NOTES

1. General information concerning the Ruthwell Cross and its history is mostly derived from Brendan Cassidy (ed.), *The Ruthwell Cross* . . . (Princeton: Index of Christian Art . . ., 1992).

2. Douglas Mac Lean: "The Date of the Ruthwell Cross," in Cassidy, *The Ruthwell Cross*, 69–70.

3. See Michael Swanton, ed., *The Dream of the Rood* (Manchester: Manchester University Press, 1970), 13. It should be noted that there is no general consensus on what precisely the cross means or stands for.

4. See Henry Duncan, *Account of the Remarkable Monument in the Shape of a Cross Inscribed with Roman and Runic Letters, Preserved in the Garden of Ruthwell Manse, Dumfriesshire and a Letter from Mr Thorleif Gudmundsson Repp, A. M., F. S. A. Scot. to the Honourable Mountstewart Elphinstone Regarding the Runic Inscription on the Monument at Ruthwell* (Edinburgh: Printed by Thomas Allan junior and Co., 1833), 9–11 and 15–24.

5. See Finnur Magnússon, "Om obelisken i Ruthwell og om de angel-saxiske runner," in *Annaler for nordisk oldkyndighed*, 1836–1837, 243–337. This very long essay was instantly translated into English (where it became even longer) by George G. Macdougall and John McCaul. It appeared in *Report Adressed by the Royal Society of Northern Antiquaries to its British and American Members* under the title of "A dissertation on the Ruthwell Obelisk and the Anglo-Saxon Runes" (Copenhagen: J. D. Quist, 1836), 81–188. John Kemble was clearly only familiar with this English translation so all further references to Magnússon's ideas will be based on it.

6. Adapted from David Howlett: "Inscriptions and Design of the Ruthwell Cross," in Cassidy, *The Ruthwell Cross*, 83.

7. Reconstruction and translation quoted from Howlett's essay in Cassidy, *The Ruthwell Cross*, 88.

8. John Kemble, "On Anglo-Saxon Runes," *Archæologia*, 28 (1840): 350.

9. For further discussion, see Brendan Cassidy, "The Latter Life of the Ruthwell Cross: From the Seventeenth Century to the Present," in Cassidy, *The Ruthwell Cross*, 12 and note 43.

10. Cassidy, *The Ruthwell Cross*, 6–7.

11. For further discussion, see Andrew Wawn, *The Anglo Man: Þorleifur Repp, Philology and Nineteenth-Century Britain* [Studia Islandica 49] (Reykjavik: Bókaútgáfa menningarsjóðs), 28–41.

12. See Wawn, *The Anglo Man*, 130–31.

13. See Aðalgeir Kristjánsson, *Nú heilsar þér á Hafnarslóð, ævir og örlög í höfuðborg Íslands 1800–1850* (Reykjavik: Nýja bókafélagið, 1999), 109.

14. See Wawn, *The Anglo Man*, 92.

15. See e.g. P. A. Munch, "Bemærkninger ved det i Danmark stiftede kongel. nordiske Oldskriftselskabs virksomhed med hensyn til gammel nordisk literatur og historiographie," in *Literaturtidende* 1, 1845–1846: 1–48.

16. For further discussion of Finnur Magnússon's life and career, see Aðalgeir Kristjánsson, *Nú heilsar þér á Hafnarslóð*, 35–59 and Jón Helgason, "Finnur Magnússon," in *Ritgerðakorn og ræðustúfar* (Reykjavik: Félag íslenzkra stúdenta í Kaupmannahöfn, 1959), 171–96.

17. See Ludvig Wimmer, *Om undersøgelsen og tolkningen av vore runemindesmærker* (Copenhagen: Thieles Bogtrykkeri, 1895), 16–21.

18. See Johan Göransson, *Bautil, Det är: Alle Swea og Götha Rikens Runstenar* (Stockholm: Lars Salvius, 1750).

19. For further discussion, see e.g. Ludvig Wimmer, *De danske runemindesmærker* (Copenhagen: Gyldendalske boghandel, 1914), 10–11.

20. Translation mine. For further discussion, see Wimmer, *De danske runemindesmærker*, 64 and Niels Åge Nielsen, *Danske Runeindskrifter* (Copenhagen: Hernovs Forlag, 1983), 129–30.

21. Translation mine. For further discussion, see Nielsen, *Danske Runeindskrifter*, 65.

22. Translation mine. For further discussion, see Nielsen, *Danske Runeindskrifter*, 75.

23. Translation mine. For further discussion, see Nielsen, *Danske Runeindskrifter*, 93–95.

24. Translation mine. For further discussion, see Nielsen, *Danske Runeindskrifter*, 138–39 and Wimmer, *De danske runemindesmærker*, 97.

25. Translation mine. For further discussion, see Nielsen, *Danske Runeindskrifter*, 184–85 and Wimmer, *De danske runemindesmærker*, 111.

26. Translation mine. For further discussion, see Nielsen, *Danske Runeindskrifter*, 130–32 and Wimmer, *De danske runemindesmærker*, 112–13. I have left out the end of this inscription, as there is no agreement on how to interpret it.

27. Translation mine. For further discussion, see Nielsen, *Danske Runeindskrifter*, 193–94 and Wimmer, *De danske runemindesmærker*, 127–28.

28. Translation mine. For further discussion, see Nielsen, *Danske Runeindskrifter*, 110–14 and Wimmer, *De danske runemindesmærker*, 53–56.

29. Translation mine. For further discussion, see Nielsen, *Danske Runeindskrifter*, 78–92 and Wimmer, *De danske runemindesmærker*, 103–106. This text of 50 words in the original is the longest inscription preserved on Danish runestones. It is closely related to the Tryggevælde inscription that presumably commemorates another dead husband (Gunulf) of the same Ragnhildr.

30. Translation mine. For further discussion, see Nielsen, *Danske Runeindskrifter*, 212–13.

31. Translation Sven B. F. Jansson, *The Runes of Sweden* (Stockholm: Norstedt & söners förlag, 1962), 13–14. The Rök Stone inscription contains more than 750 characters and is by far the longest text preserved on a runic monument. For further discussion, see Ingrid Sanness Johnsen, *Stuttruner i vikingtidens innskrifter* (Oslo: Universitetsforlaget, 1968), 140–51.

32. Translation Henrik Karlsson, www.algonet.se/hkkbs/sparlosa. For further discussion see Johnsen, *Stuttruner,* 153–61.

33. Duncan, *Account of the Remarkable Monument in the Shape of a Cross,* 10.

34. Duncan, *Account of the Remarkable Monument in the Shape of a Cross,* 11.

35. See Tómas Guðmundsson, "Hrekkvís hamingja," in *Sagnaþættir Tómasar Guðmundssonar* (Reykjavik: Mál og menning, 1999), 281. Guðmundsson, whose article was originally published in 1971, has this to say about Repp's achivement: "He became famous for being the first scholar to interpret correctly the ancient runic inscription of the Ruthwell monument in Britain, and it is clear from his papers that an enormous amount of work went into this." Translation mine. The Icelandic text reads: "hafði hann getið sér frægðarorð fyrir að ráða, fyrstur vísindamanna, hið forna rúnaletur á steini þeim hinum mikla, sem kenndur er við Ruthwell, Bretlandi. Hefur hann lagt í það óhemjumikla vinnu eins og sjá má af plöggum hans."

36. Wawn, *The Anglo Man,* 128. Repp would eventually expand and revise many of his initial interpretations, although he chose not to publish any further on the subject. In these later readings he abandons the idea of the Therefusian fathers, but the locality of Ashlof's dale is still at the center of his interpretation. For further discussion, see Wawn, 129–31.

37. See Magnússon, "A Dissertation on the Ruthwell Obelisk," 89. Kemble would later wrongly insinuate that Magnússon's engraving was a spurious document ("no one here has ever heard of such an engraving"). Kemble, "On Anglo-Saxon Runes," 371.

38. See Kemble, "On Anglo-Saxon Runes," 351.

39. Magnússon uses italics in his transcription where he feels the need to add something that he does not find in the runic text. Here he reads *bode* which he takes to mean a feast and further interprets it to be a marriage feast: Magnússon, "A Dissertation on the Ruthwell Obelisk," 124. With his usual acerbity Kemble referred to Magnússon's italics as an indication of the "scrupulous accuracy with which the translation has been made": Kemble, "On Anglo-Saxon Runes," 351–52.

40. Magnússon, "A Dissertation on the Ruthwell Obelisk," 136–38.

41. Magnússon, "A Dissertation on the Ruthwell Obelisk," 145.

42. Kemble, "On Anglo-Saxon Runes," 352.

43. See Wawn, *The Anglo Man,* 129 and 131.

44. It seems quite probable that Kemble knew "The Dream of the Rood" before he turned his attention to the Ruthwell inscription. Although he published his discovery of the relationship between the two as late as 1844 (for details, see Brendan, *The Ruthwell Cross,* 13–14), one of his biographers reports that in 1835 "he was working . . . on the *Vercelli Book* religious poetry." See Raymond A. Wiley, "Anglo-Saxon Kemble: The Life and Works of John Mitchell Kemble 1807–1857, Philologist, Historian, Archaeologist," in S. C. Hawkes, D. Brown and J. Campbell (eds.), *Anglo-Saxon Studies in Archaeology and History* I, B A R British Series 72 (Oxford: B.A.R., 1979), 203.

45. Kemble, "On Anglo-Saxon Runes," 353–359.

46. See Wawn, *The Anglo Man,* 129.

47. Chaucer's *Canterbury Tales*, "The Canon Yeoman's Tale," l. 732.
48. See R. I. Page, *An Introduction to English Runes*, 2nd ed. (Woodbridge, England: The Boydell Press, 1999), 6.
49. See Andrew Wawn, *The Vikings and The Victorians* (Cambridge: D. S. Brewer, 2000), 63–64 and 236–41.

Joast Halbertsma, Jacob Grimm, and Count Carlo Ottavio Castiglioni: Nineteenth-century Sensitivities Concerning a Gothic Bible Translation[1]

Alpita de Jong

The name of Joast Hiddes Halbertsma (1789–1869) – linguist, antiquarian, dialectologist, author of Frisian stories and poems, and in addition to all this also an anabaptist minister – will not immediately meet with widespread recognition. Like many scholars from the first half of the nineteenth century, he has been relegated to the background by colleagues from the succeeding generation. Nevertheless, Halbertsma appears to have withstood the ravages of time to some extent. At one point or another, theologians, lexicographers, Anglists, Germanists, literary scholars or ethnologists, are bound to come across Joast Halbertsma at one point or another, through one of his remarkable publications, through one of the nineteenth-century scientific, scholarly or societal debates, or through one or other of his text editions. Especially his publications on old and modern languages and dialects – ranging from Gothic, Germanic, and Anglo-Saxon to Dutch, Frisian, and the dialect of the Frisian town of Hindelopen – have lent Halbertsma some fame, within but also across the Dutch borders. These publications were often the result of an extensive intellectual interaction with foreign scholars.

With regard to Halbertsma's contribution to English studies, for instance, his contacts with Joseph Bosworth have been of great importance. Thus, Bosworth provided Halbertsma with copies of Benjamin Thorpe's edition of the Caedmon poems (1832) and John Kemble's *Beowulf* (1833), which as a fellow of the Society of Antiquaries he was able to obtain at a discount. Bosworth also regularly sent him *The Gentleman's Magazine*, as well as several of his own publications.[2] In turn, Halbertsma contributed the chapter "Friesic, Ancient and Modern Friesic Compared with Anglo-Saxon" to Bosworth's *The Origin of the German and Scandinavian Languages and Nations* . . ., the latter serving as an introduction to his *Anglo-Saxon Dictionary*.[3] Scholars such as Bosworth, Sharon Turner, Robert Southey, and John Bowring, but also Jacob Grimm and Rasmus Rask – to name some striking nineteenth-century personalities with whom Halbertsma maintained a personal correspondence – informed him of important publications in the fields of linguistics, history, and archaeology in several European countries. In return, Halbertsma shared his own knowledge with them. At the same time, he built up a vast private library and contributed to other European scholars' libraries himself. At the end of his life, Halbertsma donated his library to the Provincial Library of Friesland (called Tresoar) in Leeuwarden. Some of Halbertsma's holdings, which can be recognised by the stamp "Bibliothecae Frisiae J. H. Halbertsma," provide valuable information regarding Halbertsma's scholarly activities – as well as regarding his sympathies. John M. Kemble's *The Saxons in England*,[4] for instance, he must have read with interest, witness the many exclamation marks and "bravo's" which appear in the copy now in the possession of Tresoar. Kemble's lecture "On names, surnames, and nicnames of the Anglosaxons," delivered in September 1845 before the Archaeological Institute of Great Britain in London, likewise met with Halbertsma's approval: Halbertsma refers to the *skrandere Kemble* ["smart Kemble"] and his lecture in a footnote to a story in the *Rimen en Teltsjes* ["Rhymes and Tales"].[5] These *Rimen en Teltsjes* are a collection of Frisian poems and tales, which he wrote and published in collaboration with his brothers, in much the same manner as the Grimm brothers. Just as the Grimm brothers' *Kinder- und Hausmärchen* proved crucial to German popular literature, so did the Halbertsma brothers' *Rimen en Teltsjes* to Frisian culture.

Joast Halbertsma, as a nineteenth-century personality,[6] belonged to a society which was in the process of inventing a national culture. This process usually took the form of writing literary studies, delivering lectures before learned societies and at scholarly conferences, erecting statues, and establishing archaeological collections. Halbertsma, as a linguist, antiquarian, dialectologist, and writer of Frisian poems and stories, actively participated on all fronts within the cultural circuit. Halbertsma was both a Frisian and a Dutchman, and he moved within both "national" environments – or, to be more precise: in what was in the process of definitively becoming a regional environment (Friesland) as well as in a national environment (The Netherlands). His correspondence with foreign scholars concerns the regional, national, and international heritage, namely linguistic monuments (or fragments thereof) which were considered to be of great cultural value. What interests me are the international channels through which the knowledge regarding such linguistic monuments was exchanged, the manner in which this exchange took place, and the way in which a specific value was subsequently assigned to those linguistic monuments within the framework of a national culture. This article will address several details of these research questions in relation to the involvement of a number of European scholars in the study of Ulfila's Gothic Bible translation.

Scholarly flirtations

When Joast Hiddes Halbertsma, in 1840 and 1845, respectively, published the two volumes of his *Letterkundige Naoogst* [Philological Aftermath], he decided to dedicate these publications to two Italian philologists, Count Carlo Ottavio Castiglioni and Bernardino Biondelli.[7] This dedication is remarkable. The work contains a multiplicity of texts: editions of previously unpublished texts of the eighteenth-century philosopher Frans Hemsterhuis, an exhaustive philological commentary on the 1838 edition of the Middle Dutch romance *Ferguut*, a fragment of the Middle Low German version of Wolfram von Eschenbach's *Parcival* with annotations, two poems by the seventeenth-century Frisian poet Gysbert Japiks with an extensive philological commentary and elaborations on Frisian antiquities, and an essay concerning a manuscript written by Franciscus Junius (1591–1677), to name but a few. The essays were not just concerned with widely diverging topics, they were also written in different languages: in Dutch, French, Frisian, German, and Latin. Each time, Halbertsma adapted the language of his comments to that of his subject.[8] The work being unmistakably philological in character, it was only natural for Halbertsma to choose philologists for his dedications. But it is far from clear why he selected *Italian* philologists for this purpose. Italian scholars were not quite the most authoritative participants in the philological debate at the time. Through his membership of several learned societies, amongst other ways, Halbertsma maintained relations with so many European scholars of distinction – why, then, would he choose two relatively unknown Italians, who moreover were not uncontroversial? Count Carlo Ottavio Castiglioni had done very useful work in deciphering Gothic texts, but was severely criticised for it by the established German philologists. Opinions on Bernardino Biondelli and his many linguistic studies were also divided.[9] Halbertsma could well have decided to play it safe by opting for Teutonic thoroughness. Why, then, did he not do so?

According to himself, his actions were inspired by purely scholarly appreciation, and not by any form of flattery. In the dedication to Count Castiglioni Halbertsma wrotes, in a manner as modest as it is self-confident, that he knews but all too well his gift was exceedingly humble, but that it also needed to be considered as completely pure, coming as it did from someone who was entirely disinterested and who aspired to nothing more than a small place in the highly esteemed scholar's heart.[10] But what does this actually mean? Many factors must be taken into account in order to assess why Halbertsma dedicated the first volume of his *Letterkundige Naoogst* to Count Castiglioni. In an attempt at arriving at a tentative answer, I have come across some interesting details concerning the recent discovery and publication of a Gothic Bible text in Italy, and the sometimes bizarre reactions this provoked from other European scholars.

A spectacular discovery

In 1817, the Italian clergyman Angelo Mai, S.J.,[11] ordered the circulation of a pamphlet in which he announced that he had found fragments of a Gothic Bible translation and a Gothic homily[12] from the fourth century in the Ambrosian Library in Milan. This pamphlet was reprinted in several newspapers, including the internationally oriented Genevan scholarly journal *Bibliotèque universelle*.[13] The announcement emphasised the momentous significance of this discovery: two bulky volumes containing St. Paul's thirteen pastoral letters, in addition to twenty pages containing parts of the Gospels missing from the famous Codex Argenteus, a large excerpt from the homily, and – most surprisingly – part of the Old Testament books of Ezra and Nehemiah. An exceptionally knowledgable and generous Milanese sponsor, who took great interest in the publication of the text, had expressed his willingness to arrange the manufacturing of a full Gothic typeface in different sizes in order to enable such a publication.

The announcement in the *Bibliotèque universelle* was published on 15 September 1817 and the swiftness with which Jacob Grimm sent a copy to the general secretary of the Koninklijk Instituut [Royal Dutch Institute] in Amsterdam is illustrative of the value attached to this discovery within the international world of learning. Jacob Grimm's accompanying letter to the secretary is dated 21 October 1817.[14] Assuming that Grimm first set eyes on the announcement in late September at the earliest, he must therefore have contacted not only Mai but also several other European scholars and learned societies in a matter of only a few weeks. To the chairman of the Maatschappij van Nederlandse Letterkunde [Society for Dutch Letters], the Leiden professor of Law H. W. Tydeman, Grimm wrote 7 November 1817:

> You have undoubtedly already heard about Angelo Mai's most felicitous discovery, my highly esteemed friend? He has brought to light several palimpsest manuscripts of the Ulfilas, which do not only allow the completion and emendation of the hitherto known fragments, but actually bring to light Paul's thirteen canonical letters in Gothic, and even parts of the Old Testament (from Ezra

and Nehemiah), and who knows what else. This discovery is of the utmost importance with respect to language and Biblical exegesis, and it will shed so much light on matters of etymology and grammar.[15]

How eagerly the philological world was looking forward to the moment when the texts would appear in print is also apparent from a remark by the learned Slavist and custodian of the manuscripts at the Imperial Library of Vienna, Jernej (Bartholomäus) Kopitar. In an 1818 review, Kopitar, who by then had been corresponding with Mai (and Castiglioni) for quite some time, made it known that he hoped to see the manuscript in print shortly.[16] This impatience among foreign scholars, and particularly among those from Germany, only grew when Mai and Castiglioni published a sampler containing fragments of all the codices in 1819.

Castiglioni's "honourable" task

It was Count Carlo Ottavio Castiglioni who was entrusted with the task of transcribing, editing, and annotating the Gothic texts.[17] A tremendously tall order, since the Gothic texts were hidden under Latin texts, which had been written over it as the parchment was being re-used. The text was exceedingly difficult to read. Castiglioni had proved an expert in the field of classical, oriental, and modern languages. At the time Mai asked him to start working on the palimpsests, Castiglioni was busy finishing a monumental catalogue of Arabian coins from the Brera coin cabinet. On the basis of the research that preceded this publication, he had already made a name on account of his insights concerning the Arabic and European world at the time of the Arabic expansion. However, Castiglioni was apparently not born for good fortune. Firstly, the glory of his widely praised coin catalogue was tarnished when it was plagiarised soon after its publication. Secondly, the honour of being assigned the task of deciphering the Gothic manuscripts, apart from nearly costing him his vision, also exposed him to highly disagreeable insinuations from the German side.[18]

Things had looked promising at first. The sampler of 1819,[19] mentioned above, was published by the royal printing office, using type that had been manufactured especially for the edition of the texts.[20] The introduction in turn discussed the Gothic version of the Bible in general, the "Codices Ambrosiani" and the fragments of the Gothic Bible contained therein, and finally the history of the Goths up to the time when they ruled over Italy. It was followed by printed fragments of all the codices, with a Latin translation running alongside, as well as the Greek text for the Biblical passages. Facsimiles of parts of all five palimpsests completed the work. In

1829, Castiglioni published Paul's second letter to the Corinthians, together with a translation in Latin, notes, a glossary, and additions and emendations to the specimen of 1819. In 1834, 1835, and 1839, the remaining parts of Paul's letters followed, without a Latin translation and glossary, but with extensive philological notes in each edition. To the last edition Castiglioni appended a list with emendations and additions to the previous editions.[21] He did not get around to publishing the texts from the Old Testament. By that time, several German and Danish scholars, who had long since firmly established themselves in the fields of historical linguistics and the study of Gothic, had also claimed the Ambrosian texts for themselves. According to the Italian scholar Ceriani, it was Castiglioni himself who had handed the text of Ezra over to Hans C. de Gabelentz and Julius Löbe, who published in 1843 a complete edition of Gothic texts from the Old and New Testaments, *Ulfila, Veteris et Novi Testamenti versionae Gothicae fragmenta quae supersunt ad fidem codd.* (Leipzig, 1843).[22]

Joast Hiddes Halbertsma and Carlo Ottavio Castiglioni

It is not possible to establish exactly when Halbertsma began keeping track of Castiglioni's publications. Halbertsma started to publish in the field of linguistics, especially historical linguistics, in 1822, and from this year onwards he gradually established his name within the scholarly world. As early as the mid-1820s, he kept in close contact with the aforementioned Professor H. W. Tydeman, who was later to recommend him to Jacob Grimm.[23] In 1830, Halbertsma became a corresponding member (and, a few years later, a full member) of the prestigious royal society for the sciences, letters, and arts, the Koninklijk Instituut, in particular of the department concerned with Dutch literature and history. Grimm was a member of this society as well, and the two scholars corresponded with some regularity between 1830 and 1856.[24] Halbertsma's correspondence with Castiglioni started in 1835. Halbertsma greatly admired Castiglioni's editions of the Gothic texts. They made an important contribution to the body of learning concerning Germanic languages, he emphasised in the dedication in the first volume of *Letterkundige Naoogst*.[25] It had been the Dutchman Franciscus Junius who in 1665 had enabled a great leap forward in the development of Germanic studies by publishing the Gospels of the famous Codex Argenteus, a richly decorated manuscript containing large portions of the Bishop Ulfila's Bible translation. Little hope was left of ever finding more Gothic material by the time Angelo Mai announced his discovery of several palimpsests in 1817. All praise therefore should go to Junius, Mai, and Castiglioni, and – according to Halbertsma – through them to the Dutch and the Italians in general.[26] This remark appears to have an element of provocation to it.

Halbertsma makes it appear as if no other European or non-European country had ever made a contribution of any importance to Germanic philology. This suggestion must have been especially embarrassing to the Germans, who were extremely active in this field. Scandinavia and Central Europe, too, were naturally very much involved with Gothic, as these areas were considered to be the original Gothic heartlands. The level of Italian philological practice at the beginning of the nineteenth century only adds to the impression that it was indeed rather provocative for Halbertsma to ascribe the greatest scholarly contribution to Germanic linguistics to Italy of all places.

Goths and clergymen

Interest in Gothic in Italy at the beginning of the nineteenth century was fairly marginal. In a collection of essays dedicated to Angelo Mai of 1954, several scholars confirm, each from their own perspective, that Italy hardly counted for anything internationally in the field of literary studies.[27] Whereas Germany, "as the fortunate heir to Italy's magnificent humanism,"[28] developed a convincingly new philological method, Italian philology remained firmly rooted in the formalism of the sixteenth-century. In this way, Italian scholarship became sidelined internationally, but it still held a trump card: Italian monasteries were the repositories for material of which foreign scholars could only dream. Notes written by the founder of the Biblioteca Ambrosiana most likely inspired Angelo Mai to go searching among the codices from the Bobbio monasteries which were being kept in Milan.[29] Mai had joined the Jesuit Order while he was still young. His education had of course included Latin, Greek, and Hebrew, but more noteworthy was his knowledge of methods to treat parchments, of which the original script had been more or less erased and subsequently written over, with a certain kind of acid in order to render the underlying script visible.[30] On the basis of his specific knowledge of paleography, Mai had been appointed as librarian of the Biblioteca Ambrosiana, which is most likely where he met Count Castiglioni.

As a librarian, Mai had unrestricted access to the enormous collection of manuscripts in the Biblioteca Ambrosiana. It is not surprising, therefore, that he made one discovery after the other. His activities earned him a great reputation, if not completely uncontested. His discoveries, and through them his name, rapidly became well-known throughout Europe. However, his tight watch over the manuscripts seriously frustrated some scholars: it depended completely on Mai whether and when the texts would be made accessible to others. Moreover, it was rumoured that Mai was unacquainted with the latest developments in the field of historical and comparative linguistics, and that he was somewhat negligent in editing the texts brought to light by his good fortune as an investigator. It is remarkable how jubilantly Mai's discoveries were discussed both within Italy and elsewhere, and how much criticism he invited at the same time.[31] Abroad, annoyance about Mai's doings became especially apparent with regard to his involvement with the Gothic Bible texts. This response does not come as a surprise, as the discovery was different from the others in many ways.

In 1819, very soon after his spectacular discovery, Mai had been appointed custos of the Vatican library. This promotion can be taken as a token of appreciation for his investigative activities, but possibly also as a means to bind Mai more closely to the hierarchy of the Roman Catholic Church. For Angelo Mai's recent discovery must also have been a source of anxiety for the Church authorities. Rome generally was not favourable to Biblical texts in the vernacular – and in a way this was exactly what this Gothic Bible represented. A letter written in January 1818 by Cardinal Litta to Count Mellerio, vice-president of the Kingdom of Lombardo-Veneto, of which Milan formed the administrative and intellectual centre, and the man who provided Mai with the material he needed to facilitate a printed edition of the manuscript, is especially interesting in this respect:

> I again ask you to convey my regards to Father Mai. I would be most pleased if he, when publishing the Ulfila version of the Bible, could dedicate some words, either in the introduction or in the notes, to the expediency of the Index regulations, to Quesnel's propositions concerning reading the Bible in the vernacular, which is starting to become common practice, concerning unbelief and the way Heretics are abusing many versions of the Bible, concerning the dangers of translations into vernacular languages and of allowing anyone access to Holy Writ while its great and profound meanings are not accessible to just any reader, as is apparent from the fact that the overwhelming majority of heresies has sprung from a misunderstanding of Holy Writ – for it is not so straightforward to properly interpret Holy Writ, as the Protestants seem to think: even such a great mind as St Augustine has had great difficulty in doing so, as he admits himself –, and, finally, concerning the danger which for all these reasons emanates from Bible societies . . .[32]

In Rome's view, Gothic studies had from its earliest days been linked to the Reformation. Ulfila's Bible translation was regarded as the Germanic popular Bible and had chiefly been studied closely by Protestant humanists.[33] Moreover, scholars and Church officials disagreed as to whether or not this Bible translation contained traces of the Arian heresy. At the Council of Nicaea in 325, the bishops had condemned Arius' doctrine as heresy. However, Arianism and related forms of Christian religious doctrine had persisted for a long time, especially in those regions which had been settled by the Goths: Thrace, Italy, Africa, Spain, and Gaul.[34]

Germans versus Italians

As custos of the Vatican Library, Angelo Mai apparently made it quite hard for foreign scholars to study manuscripts in Rome for scholarly purposes.[35] Protection of orthodox dogmas may have played a role in this defensive attitude, but in addition to this religiously motivated attitude, it is possible that frictions and irritations caused by the nationalistic tendencies which had stealthily infiltrated philological scholarship also contributed to it. After Napoleon's fall a small intellectual avant-garde in an otherwise rather inert Italy began, just like many intellectuals in other European countries, to orient itself on its past.[36] The Italian intellectuals increasingly no longer regarded themselves as the heirs of classical Rome, but rather of the barbarians who had destroyed the great Roman Empire. A problem for the Italians was that the barbaric peoples – Goths, Vandals, and Longobards, who under the common denominator of "Germanic peoples" had invaded the Roman Empire from North-Eastern Europe – had managed to establish unity and independence in Gaul, Spain, and Britain, whereas their counterparts in Italy had not. Unity and independence were important topics in the European discourse of the first half of the nineteenth century. The new national orientation forced Italian intellectuals to give up a substantial part of their glorious past. The great Roman Empire could in this respect no longer function as a positive point of reference. Italian intellectuals tried to present the Italians as the heirs to the Germanic barbarians. However, as it was difficult to give a proper definition of the notion *Germanic*, German intellectuals could present the Germans as the heirs of the Germanic tribes as well.[37] Nationally oriented German men of letters appropriated the Germanic attack on the Roman Empire as part of their national history. According to them, the Germanic peoples had restored the unity which had been eroded during the last decades of the Roman Empire. Moreover, the unity was more durable this time round, as it had been purged of the decadent features which had so much characterised the Roman Empire. The Germanic-style unity was thus regarded as purer than its Roman counterpart. In addition to this, the foundations for an enlightened version of Christianity were supposed to have been laid with the arrival of the Germanic tribes. In this respect, Georg Niebuhr had already set the tone with his *Römische Geschichte*, published in several volumes from 1811 onwards. *Römische Geschichte* is an account of the Roman Empire according to the new insights, a new interpretation of its history which would possibly be not very agreeable to the Italians. To speak of a general animosity between Italians and Germans in the first half of the nineteenth century would be stretching the case too far, but several sources do bear witness to a certain amount of mutual irritation among scholars, to say the least.[38]

"Storms from the North"

While deciphering the Gothic texts, Count Castiglioni accordingly experienced the restraints imposed on him by the church on the one hand, and the obstructions caused by the nationalistic ideologies of his fellow scholars on the other. For instance, Castiglioni needed permission from Rome to keep the palimpsests in his house. When one of the foremost scholars in the field of Gothic studies, H. F. Massmann, pointed out the semi-Arianist nature of one of the texts which Castiglioni had given him on loan, Castiglioni was forced to request an extended license from Rome for the possession and study of banned books. A letter, dated 22 June 1835, in which Castiglioni asked Angelo Mai to help him obtain this extension to his license, at the same time gives an indication of the awkward relations between the German philologists and the Italian scholar.

> Now that I have buried myself in my work over the past six or seven months (which I am forced to do due to the incessant and often discourteous exhortations from the German philologists, who have threatened to set the powers of earth against me if I do not finish within the year), I yet again find myself in circumstances which press me to call on your friendship. As you know, Massmann has published the fragments of the Gothic homilies from Rome and Milan, and it was I who provided him with the latter, albeit with great displeasure as I was intently studying this matter myself at precisely that time. When he had returned to Munich, he wrote me that he had discovered that this text was "semi-Arian," and that he therefore congratulated me on having managed to save myself the trouble of publishing the text of a heretic. I did not reply to this remark, as I am quite outraged by the fact that he would so cowardly mock something which could be disagreeable to me...
> As I would therefore not want this Ulfila, which has unleashed the storms from the North against me, to also cause me disquiet from the South, which for me would be considerably more, I should say

incomparably more, painful, I ask of you to check my notes (leaving aside the prudence which for many years already has led me to consult with a friend like you in my affairs), and to have them checked to this end by whomever you deem appropriate and in as far as you deem it necessary to do so within the framework of the clerical hierarchy, so that I can rest my mind about this matter.[39]

H. F. Massmann's scholarly status was considerable at that time.[40] In the early 1830s, Maximilian, crown-prince of Bavaria, commissioned him to study the Gothic homily, a large part of which was kept in Milan, while another part was kept in the Vatican Library.[41] In the introduction to his edition of several of the Gothic texts, to which the letter quoted refers, Massmann related some of the circumstances in which he had performed this task.[42] The controversialist manner in which he did this is striking. According to Massmann the Italians who discovered the palimpsests, Angelo Mai and Count Castiglioni, had held back the full announcement of their discovery for more than fifteen years deliberately, while German historical linguists were yearning for it. The fact that German philologists now had access to the Gothic manuscripts, which were of such great importance not only for Germanic philology, but also for theology and ecclesiastical history, should solely be attributed to the Bavarian crown-prince, who had personally undertaken a journey to Italy to liberate the manuscripts from their exile. Maximilian had provided Massmann with the intercession needed to gain access to the institutions concerned. However, as Massmann pointed out in his introduction, he had still encountered much resistance in Rome. Massmann then went on to blast Angelo Mai: according to him, Mai had deliberately thwarted foreign scholars, in addition to producing botched work as a scholar and not knowing the first thing about Gothic – something which Mai himself had told Massmann on two occasions. Massmann himself modestly opined that four eyes would see more clearly than two, "und besonders zwey deutsche mehr als die eines Römers" [and definitely two German [eyes] more than those of a Roman].[43]

Massmann's opinion on Castiglioni was more favourable. He commended his scholarly work and noble character. Castiglioni had also confessed his scant command of Gothic, but Massmann thought that this was a sign of "modesty."[44] Massmann's introduction also dealt with the supposed Arianism of the Goths. He reasoned that the Goths should not be accused of Arianism, or of semi-Arianism, because they essentially practiced a purer form of Christianity. Ulfila had obviously attempted to provide a literal translation of the original Greek text, and had wished to stay well clear of the intellectualistic debates of the time. The Germanic people were concerned with "Sittenkraft" [moral fiber], something which the "entartete

Romanen" [degenerate Romans] no longer possessed very much. Thus, Ulfila's only concern was the needs of his people:

> . . . to salvage the clear fountainhead of the already very turbid doctrine in Holy Writ by transposing it completely faithfully into his native language and to save the original gospel of life and love from the confused contradictions of opinions, denunciations and persecutions; and he thought that it would not be harmful to either the inner or the outer well-being of his people to turn to a form of belief which – as it perhaps seemed to him – in its basic form yielded more simplicity and retained more originality than the more cultivated Nicaean doctrine of the Trinity and than the form of the orthodox church, which had in his time already gone through many liturgical multiplications.[45]

Halbertsma's position

In one of his letters to Joast Halbertsma (dated February 1835), Castiglioni discussed Massmann's publication.[46] The letter is exceedingly difficult to read, due to the eye condition from which the author was suffering. However, from the passage in which he discussed Massmann's book, it can roughly be deduced that Castiglioni's opinion was positive, from a philological as well as from a historical and theological point of view. He added that he was very much disturbed by the grievous remarks directed at his friend Angelo Mai and Massmann's rage towards those Italians who had called the Gothic words "barbaric."

Halbertsma, of course, was well acquainted with Massmann's work. The Tresoar contains a copy of the *Skeireins* which used to belong to Halbertsma's library and the titles of a few more of Massmann's works that formed part of Halbertsma's library. Moreover, Halbertsma and Massmann exchanged books. Halbertsma had sent Massmann one or more books through the secretary of the Royal Library of Munich, J. A. Schmeller.[47] In a letter to Grimm, dated 20 November 1837, Halbertsma appears to have complained about the failure of a parcel from Massmann, very likely containing books, to arrive.[48]

There is no doubt that Halbertsma was interested in Massmann's work. Because Massmann enjoyed a fine reputation in the field of Gothic studies with which Halbertsma had great affinity, his work was of great interest to him. This did not keep him from commenting on this great German philologist in a slightly ironic fashion, though. In the *Algemeene Konst- en Letterbode* [General Messenger of Arts and Letters] of 1837, one of the most important Dutch journals for the dissemination of scholarly knowledge to which Halbertsma contributed on more than one occasion, he remarked that

Massmann must clearly have a great knowledge of Gothic, considering how he had been able to present an alliterative poem in Gothic at the latest jubilee of Göttingen University. He added: "Men moet zeer geoefend in het Gothisch zijn, om er een paar ergelijke gebreken in op te merken" [One has to be well-versed in Gothic in order to be able to notice a few annoying shortcomings].[49] A letter to Grimm, dated 7 April 1835, makes it clear that Halbertsma also seriously disliked Massmann's controversialism.

> Professor Massmann's Skeireins is currently lying before me. Is the lashing he delivers to Mai, for which he raises his arm higher and higher, compatible with the rules of true humanity?
>   die grammatici
>   Sind streitbare ziegenböcke.
>   Hagedorn.[50]

Halbertsma appears to also have corresponded with Mai about Massmann. In a reply to Halbertsma, dated December 1838, Mai at least wrote that he had noticed the attack of a certain German scholar, about which Halbertsma had written him, but that he was not very impressed by it, since the anger of the man in question appeared to have been incited solely by the fact that it had been Mai who had discovered those Gothic texts and had had them transcribed.[51]

In two of the four letters addressed to Halbertsma, dated February 1835 and May 1838, respectively, Castiglioni discussed Jacob Grimm's reactions to his editions of the Gothic manuscripts.[52] Incidentally, Castiglioni had already in 1831 broken off his correspondence with Grimm, due to the latter's discouraging criticisms.[53] Grimm had publicly complained about the delay with which the manuscripts became accessible in print. Halbertsma indirectly referred to these complaints in his announcement in de *Algemeene Konst- en Letterbode* of 1834. In this announcement, he explained the reason for the delay in Castiglioni's work on the manuscripts. The Germans had complained "hoogelijk over de traagheid des uitgevers" [vociferously about the editor's tardiness], but Castiglioni had recently informed Halbertsma that the death of his father and a "zwaar ongemak aan de oogen" [severe ailment of the eyes] had kept him from working.[54] In the February 1835 letter, Castiglioni explicitly thanked Halbertsma, who had probably informed him of his announcement in the *Algemeene Konst- en Letterbode*: "You, who did not stop here, but went on to act as my advocate vis-à-vis the learned Germans in literary periodicals."[55] Castiglioni frankly admitted to having made mistakes in his edition of Paul's letter to the Corinthians, and to having learned a great deal from Grimm's intelligent comments.

But if *filautheía* [amour-propre] does not deceive me, Cl[arissime]

V[ir], he was unable to cope very well with the fact that his conjectures in a partly debased language are not always very successful, causing him to lash out rather more viciously than to me would seem appropriate when dealing with a man of foreign stock who has dedicated many years of studies to researching the antiquities of his people.[56]

Relations between Grimm and Castiglioni were less than cordial. Those between Castiglioni and Halbertsma appear to have been very good. Those between Grimm and Halbertsma were by no means bad, although their opinions as scholars diverged and the German scholar's stern and thorough personality was a little too stiff for Halbertsma's liking.[57]

In context

One should not discard the possibility that personal frictions played their part. But there are sufficient indications that, more generally, serious agitation was rife between several German philologists on the one hand, and the Italian scholars Mai and Castiglioni on the other. This agitation appears to combine both differences in scholarly views as well as sensitivities of the national-ideological type. The question is whether Halbertsma, by dedicating the first volume of his *Letterkundige Naoogst* to Castiglioni, was responding to this agitation and, if so, what kind of signal he was sending out in doing so. The fact that Halbertsma dedicated both volumes to *Italians* in particular appears meaningful, especially in view of the fact that the other Italian scholar whom Halbertsma addressed in his *Letterkundige Naoogst*, Bernardino Biondelli, voiced harsh criticism with regard to Grimm's work. In an extensive study of the Germanic languages, in which he had paid much attention to Grimm's *Deutsche Grammatik*, Biondelli condemned repression of diversity in favour of a linguistic system devised by Grimm. In this respect, the following lines of an unnamed "corrispondente olandese" quoted by Biondelli to reinforce his criticism, is remarkable.

> It is well known that Grimm and others greatly value vowels, even more than they do consonants; and as I, my dear Sir, am asking you to provide an explanation for this phenomenon, I will provide you with my own opinion on this matter. The Germans pride themselves on being the real *Germani* of Tacitus, and thereby brothers of the Goths, of the Chauci, of the Frisians, of the Anglo-Saxons, etc.; but they realise quite well that the consonants do not allow them to claim this status; on the contrary, these consonants relegate them to the status of illegitimate cousins. The development, or rather the hardening, of the consonants is an

irrefutable sign of the age of languages and dialects. *Frater, dens* are older than *brothar, thunthus*, which are in turn older than the German *prouder, zand*. With regard to vowels, however, the Germans resemble the Goths more than we do. This, then, is the reason why these gentlemen, in order to more closely approximate the pure blood of the *Germani* to their advantage, give pride of place to the vowels.[58]

Biondelli did not mention his source, but his letters to Halbertsma suggest that he was quoting from Halbertsma's correspondence. In a letter dated 10 June 1840, Biondelli wrote to Halbertsma:

> Within the next few days, I will also publish the critical review of doctor J. Grimm's grammar, in which I have managed to cite your name and publications. In this article you will undoubtedly find observations which match the principles which you have expounded to me in your kind letters.[59]

A passage in a letter from Biondelli to Halbertsma, dated 26 April 1840, strengthens our supposition to identify Halbertsma as his "corrispondente olandese." In this letter, Biondelli gave early notice of his upcoming article on Grimm's *Deutsche Grammatik* by way of the following remark:

> I am still saving my strengths somewhat in order to discuss doctor J. Grimm's system, in a review of his *Deutsche Grammatik* on which I have already started to work. It is a long and difficult article, in which I want to put forward a good many completely original observations that are at odds with the system of this eminent linguist; Count Castiglioni has provided me with several more, so I hope that this will be a truly interesting article, albeit one received with suspicion by the Germans, with the exception of Mr. Bopp, who has provided me, in his *Vocalismus* etc., with interesting material.[60]

Is Biondelli perhaps responding to an invitation by Halbertsma to give his opinion on the phenomenon that "Grimm and others greatly value vowels, even more than they do consonants"? Did Biondelli directly seek the confrontation into which Castiglioni did not dare or did not want to enter, and into which Halbertsma implicitly entered by not dedicating his *Letterkundige Naoogst* to the famous and eminent Grimm or to Massmann, but rather to two much less famous and less undisputed *Italian* linguists? It would go too far to speak of a Frisian-Italian connection which wanted to counterbalance the German hegemony within the field of Germanic historical linguistics, on the basis of the available evidence. However, Halbertsma does appear to be responding to frictions between German and Italian scholars by dedicating his *Letterkundige Naoogst* to two Italians.

The dedication to Count Castiglioni in the first volume of *Letterkundige Naoogst* shows Halbertsma positioning himself. For example, he specified the word "Germanic" by following it with the bracketed qualification "ce mot pris dans l'acception de Tacite."[61] Furthermore, his remark that the manuscripts studied and edited by Castiglioni proved that the Gothic idiom consisted of a conglomerate of dialects is important with respect to his position within the linguistic debate. Halbertsma, just like Biondelli, attached great importance to the fundamental diversity of languages and dialects. Halbertsma's attachment to a dialogue between the peoples of the North and the peoples of the South, to which he professed further on in his dedication, could equally well be a sincere opinion or a commonplace. His remark about Dutch and Frisian as the least contaminated contemporary remains of the primitive language of the Germanic people also seems somewhat clichéd. The ensuing explanation of his choice to comment on each separate piece using the language of that piece itself, finally, provides an indication as to the way in which Halbertsma's signal of dedicating his work to Castiglione could be interpreted:

> Because those who study the languages of the North using the great methods of our times can understand Latin and Greek with equal ease, as well as all variants of the Germanic language, it should suffice to say that it is mainly for such people that I have written. However, as I may occasionally reach a reader who is unable to undertake the study of so many languages because he focuses his strengths on one particular point only, and who is therefore interested in one piece only, I have conformed the language of my commentary to that of the piece itself; for whoever is able to understand the piece, will also be able to understand my comments, which would not have been the case had I used the same language throughout . . . I have, therefore, yielded to the readers in every respect as far as the pieces of my collection are concerned, without in the least striving for elegance in those languages in which I do not think. To be clear and precise, or intelligible at the very least, this is the goal I have set myself. Still, the static mind of one or other dignitary of Dutch letters, who, for fear of falling or of getting tired, prefers to walk the beaten track, will not be able to accommodate my ideas. This is unfortunate for me, or rather for my publisher. For to tell you the whole truth, dear Sir, it is not to such people that I have addressed myself. I am

speaking for men of letters from the North who satisfy or, like me, are trying to satisfy the demands of this century, assuming that they are indeed listening to me . . . In any case I am certain that I have spoken in accordance with the nature of your spirit. For you, dear Sir, know that a linguist cannot listen to one of the Germanic languages without hearing all of them: you reconcile these extremes, which to this day seemed as far apart as the heavens and the earth . . . So to whom could I have better dedicated my book, even if gratitude in me had been in the first place mute, than to you, dear Sir, who sees this colourful mixture of three or four languages for what it really is: the more or less different branches of the same stem, which has its roots right beside the cradle of humanity?[62]

Halbertsma appears to have dedicated the first volume of his *Letterkundige Naoogst* to Castiglioni because he admired in him the *homo universalis*. Halbertsma appreciated the new German-developed scientific method, but he was skeptical about the often inordinate degree of importance attached to it. The professionalisation of academic scholarship appeared to entail a contraction of its field of activity. He was apprehensive that as a result the *homo universalis* scholar would shrink into a specialised scientist, knowledgeable in one particular specialty, but heedless of the fullness of life. It was not nostalgia for eighteenth-century erudition from which Halbertsma suffered; he was far too sympathetic to the new academic developments for this. Rather, he mistrusted the positivism which would set the pace in the second half of the nineteenth century. This critical attitude may have made him reach across the Alps. But there is also the possibility that Halbertsma's penchant for originality and independence was ultimately the deciding factor in his choice to dedicate the first volume of his *Letterkundige Naoogst* to Count Castiglioni. Castiglioni, an erudite but taunted man, perfectly fitted the bill as a paragon of the original and independent scholar that Halbertsma wanted to be himself.

Appendix

Letter from J. Grimm to the president of the Koninklijk-Nederlandsche Instituut van Wetenschappen, Letteren en Schoone Kunsten [Royal Dutch Institute of Sciences, Letters and Arts] accompanying his handwritten copy of the announcement of the spectacular discovery of the Ambrosian Gothic palimpsests in the *Bibliothèque universelle* (September 1817).

Cassel ce 21 Octobre 1817

Monsieur,

venant de recevoir de l'Italie l'avis ci-joint en copie, il m'a paru meriter l'attention générale du monde savant et je m'empresse de vous l'adresser pour vouloir bien le soumettre à la 2e classe de l'Institut des paysbas,[64] auquel j'ai l'honneur d'appartenir. La decouverte en question est de la dernière importance et sans contredit une des plus inattendues et des plus fécondes, qui aient eté jamais faites. Je me trouve precisement dans le cas de savoir l'apprecier dans toute son etendue, m'occupant depuis quelques ans d'une grammaire moesogothique, où il y a tant d'erreurs à combattre et tant de faux systèmes à detruire. Aussi n'ai je pas tardé à me mettre en communication avec M^r. l'abbé Mai et je me reserve de rapporter à la Classe les nouvelles ulterieures sur ces palimpsestes, aussitôt qu'elles me parviendront.

Je viens d'apprendre en même tems, que le même savant milanais, si heureux et si riche en decouvertes, a egalement trouvé une histoire d'Alexandre le grand, inconnue jusqu'à present et datant de l'époque de la literature classique.

Sous peu de tems j'aurai l'honneur de vous adresser un rapport relatif à l'edition d'un poème latin du douzième siecle, que je me propose de publier. Il contient la fable de Reinardus et d' Isangrin et a echappé à la connaissance de tous les literateurs.

Agréez Monsieur le Sécretaire l'assurance de la parfaite consideration avec laquelle je suis

votre très humble et très ob.sant
Jacob Grimm.

Avis concernant une nouvelle decouverte d'Ulphilas dans la bibliothèque Ambrosienne à Milan.
Tandis que la basse Italie fournit en abondance d'anciens monumens, qu'elle tire du sein de ses ruines pour l'etude des beaux arts, la partie septentrionale de cette belle et celebre contrée ouvre un nouveau champ à la literature en

publiant un nombre d'ecrits classiques précieux, que la barbarie et le temps avaient ensevelis dans l'oubli.

Monsieur l'abbé Ange Mai, un des bibliothécaires de la bibliothèque ambrosienne à Milan s'appercut en examinant quelques manuscrits très anciens, qu'il y avait sous l'ecriture latine une autre écriture d'une epoque plus reculée, de forme differente et présentant un sujet entierement interessant. Cette vaste matière masquée pour ainsi dire par la seconde ecriture et remplissant deux manuscrits volumineux, est la traduction moesogothique des treize epitres protocanoniques de S. Paul, faite dans le quatrième siècle par l'evêque Ulphilas et dont on a regretté la perte jusquà ce jour.

Il est reconnu d'après le temoignage unanime des anciens historiens, qu'Ulphilas, appelé le Moyse de son temps a traduit toute la bible à cette même epoque, excepté peutêtre les livres des rois. Tout cet ouvrage ayant eté égaré, il parut enfin au 17. siècle le codex argenteus d'Upsal, qui renfermait une partie considerable des quatres evangiles, qui a eté publié par François Junius l'an 1665. Cette edition, ainsi que les suivantes, qui eurent lieu successivement jusqu'en 1805 eurent le plus grand succes à cause de leur utilité. Le savant Knittel ayant aussi examiné dans la bibl. de Wolfenbuttel un manuscrit palimpseste, il y trouva dans huit pages plusieurs versets de cinq chapitres de la traduction ulphilanienne de l'epitre de S. Paul aux romains. En 1762 il publia ces fragmens avec beaucoup d'erudition. Mais la matière, que renferment les manuscrits dont il s'agit ici, surpasse par son etendue tout ce qui a eté publié jusqu'à ce jour d'après ceux d'Upsal et de Wolfenbuttel et peut fournir une vaste carrière où la critique des saintes ecritures et l'etude des antiquités germaniques peuvent s'exercer pendant plus d'un siècle. Ils offrent une main differente et ils paraissent avoir eté ecrits entre le 5e et le 6e siècle de l'ere chretienne. Ce qui manque des epitres sacrées dans un des manuscrits est renfermé dans l'autre; mais ils ne constituent pas un seul corps. C'est pourquoi on trouve huit epîtres (au moins en partie) ecrites dans les deux manuscrits, de sorte qu'on a l'avantage de la comparaison de la repetition d'un trésor si precieux. Les caracteres sont grands et beaux. On voit les titres des epîtres à la tête des manuscrits et des apostilles aux marges en la même langue. Une des pages contient un sujet extremement curieux.

La langue d'Ulphilas est appelée moesogothique par la raison suivante. Les Goths, nation très nombreuse etant sortis anciennement de la Scandinavie occupèrent les pays situés à l'est de la mer baltique, la Pomeranie, la Prusse et les rives de la Vistule. S'étant aussi emparés de la sarmatie, ensuite de la Dace, ils poussèrent leurs conquêtes jusqu'aux bords du pont euxin. C'est pourcela que la nation se partagea en Ostrogoths, c'est à dire, goths orientaux et en goths septentrionaux. Dans le 4e siècle du christianisme une grande partie des goths, ne pouvant endurer le mauvais traitement, que leur faisaient essayer les Huns, sortis de regions septentrionales de l'Asie, ils demandèrent à l'empereur Valens la permission de passer dans ses provinces. L'ayant obtenue, deux cents mille hommes capables de porter les armes passerent le Danube et s'établirent dans la Moesie, d'où ils furent nommés Moesogoths. plusieurs d'entre les tribus gothiques avaient embrassé depuis quelque tems le Christianisme, et Théophile un de leurs evêques avait paru au premier concil de Nicée.[65] L'an 325 les Moesogoths avaient pour pasteur un homme d'un génie fort rare, nommé Ulphilas, dont tous les anciens ecrivains ont faits l'éloge. La nation elle même n'etait pas tout à fait barbare. Jornandes assure, quil y avait deja quelque tems qu'elle cultivait les études. La lettre de S. Jerome à Sunnia et à Fretila goths, est aussi un temoignage de l'etude de l'ecriture sainte si florissante au moins peu de tems après chez cette nation là. Ulphilas dejà famuex par ses missions et par sa presence à des conciles voulut faire connaître la bible à son peuple en sa propre langue. Il reussit parfaitement, comme le prouve la haute reputation dont sa memoire jouit depuis quinze siècles.

Telle est la decouverte, que M[r] l'abbé Mai vient de faire dans la bibliotheque ambrosienne et dont il donnera sous peu un essai fort etendu dans une dissertation préliminaire. Un personnage milanais éstimable pour ses connaissances et ses liberalités et rempli de zèle pour la publication d'Ulphilas, vient de faire fondre par un habile ouvrier un assortiment complet de caracteres ulphilaniens de differentes grandeurs tant pour le texte que pour les notes et les apostilles. Il est inutile de parler aux savans de la lumière que va repandre sur l'ecriture sainte une version faite dans le quatrième siècle d'apres des exemplaires d'une date probablement plus reculée. Au reste l'estime unique dont le codex argenteus d'Upsal a joui jusqu'à present, peut être la mesure du prix des manuscrits de la bibliotèque ambrosienne.

Outre la decouverte de ces deux manuscrits M[r] l'abbé Mai a recueilli 20 autres pages en langue moesogothique tirés de plusieurs autres manuscrits palimpsestes de la mème bibliotheque. Cest dans ces mèmes pages qu'on trouve des pièces ulphilaniennes evangeliques qui manquent à l'edition mutilées du cod.argenteus et une grande partie d'homélie ou commentaire, et ce qui interesse le plus un morceau du livre d'Esdras et de celui de Nehemie, decouverte de la plus grande importance, puisque jusqu'à présent on n'a vu nulle part la plus petite partie de la version ulphilanienne de l'ancien testament.

Avec cette vaste partie d'Ulphilas on va rediger aussi un nouveau lexique moesogothique, qui augmentera prodigieusement le nombre des mots de la langue. Quel présent surtout pour les allemands, qui verront retablir en grande partie le corps de la langue mère des idiômes septentrionaux. Ils vont entendre tant de nouveaux termes de leurs glorieux ancêtres, de cette nation immense, qui occupa par ses conquètes les plus belles et les plus grandes provinces du monde.

Il ne nous est pas permis d'en dire davantage dans un avis qui exige la breveté, mais nous croyons en avoir dit assez pour que les savans se rejouissent de cette decouverte et que le public soit dans la plus vive et la plus juste attente de la publication d'un ouvrage qu'on ne pourrait différer sans porter un grand préjudice à la literature sacrée et ancienne.

Milan le 15 Septembre 1817

NOTES

1. I wish to thank my colleague Floris van Nierop for translating my Dutch text into English. A special note of thanks should go to Joep Leerssen and Rolf Bremmer for their corrections and support.

2. S. Sybrandy, "J. H. Halbertsma en syn biblitheek," [J. H. H. and his library] in *Joast Hiddes Halbertsma (1789–1869) Brekker en bouwer: Stúdzjes fan ûnderskate skriuwers oer syn persoan, syn libben en syn wurk, útjown ta gelegenheit fan de betinking fan syn hûndertste stjerdei* [J. H. H. (1789–1869), breaker and builder: essays by various authors on his person, his life and his work, published on the occasion of the commemoration of his 100th day of death], ed. Hylke Halbertsma *et al.* (Drachten: Laverman, 1969), 264–84, at 274.

3. J. Bosworth, *The Origin of the Germanic and Scandinavian languages, and nations: with a sketch of their literature* . . . (London: Longman, Rees, Orme, Brown, and Green, 1836) and *A Dictionary of the Anglo-Saxon Language* (London: Longman, Rees, Orme, Green, and Longman, 1838). See also: E. G. Stanley, "J. Bosworth's Interest in 'Friesic' for his *Dictionary of the Anglo-Saxon Language* (1838): 'The Friesic is far the most important language for my purpose'," in *Aspects of Old Frisian Philology*, ed. Rolf H. Bremmer Jr, Geart van der Meer and Oebele Vries (Amsterdam and Atlanta, GA: Rodopi, 1990), 428–52, at 443–52.

4. John M. Kemble, *The Saxons in England: A History of the English Commonwealth till the Period of the Norman Conquest* (London: Longman, Brown, Green, and Longmans, 1849). Tresoar call-number 1219 G.

5. Bruorren Halbertsma, *Rimen en Teltsjes* [Rhymes and tales], 11th ed. rev. Ph. H. Breuker (Leeuwarden: A. J. Osinga, 1994), 369. (*Bruorren* – Frisian for "brothers" – refers to the brothers Joast, Eeltsje and Tsjalling Halbertsma.)

6. A comprehensive biography of Joast Hiddes Halbertsma is wanting. Biographical information can be found in many articles in various Dutch and Frisian periodicals. For a useful introduction, see the collected essays in *Joast Hiddes Halbertsma (1789–1869) Brekker en bouwer.*

7. J. H. Halbertsma, *Letterkundige Naoogst* [Philological Aftermath], 2 vols. (Deventer: J. de Lange, 1840–1845), the dedications at V–X and V–XV, respectively.

8. Halbertsma wrote his comments in French, German, Dutch and Latin. Strikingly, Halbertsma's commentary to Gysbert Japiks' Frisian poems is written in Dutch. It is abundantly clear that Halbertsma wrote his *Letterkundige Naoogst* for an international readership. Apparently, he did not regard the Frisian language as fit to serve this purpose. Although he worked on the assumption that philologists who practiced their trade according to the latest insights would understand all linguistic variants within the Germanic language family with equal ease (Halbertsma, *Letterkundige Naoogst* 1, IX), he apparently regarded the Frisian language as either too difficult or too unknown for this purpose. The reason he did not restrict himself to one single language for his commentaries is, as he explained on this same page of the introduction, that he also wished to accommodate readers with a limited field of interest. (See also the last paragraph of this article).

9. For criticism on Castiglioni and the various opinions on Biondelli and his work, see *Dizionario Biografico degli Italiani* [Biographical dictionary of the Italians], vols. 10 and 22 (Rome: Instituto della Encyclopedia Italiana, 1968 and 1978), 521–23 and 137–38, respectively.

10. Halbertsma, *Letterkundige Naoogst* 1, VIII.

11. For biographical information on Angelo Mai, see *New Catholic Encyclopedia* (1967; repr. Washington, DC: The Catholic University of America, 1981), or the more comprehensive first edition to be consulted at http://www.newadvent.org/cathen. See also the contributions of A. Mainetti, B. Riposati, and A. Galletti in *Bergomum: Bollettino della Civica Biblioteca e dell'Ateneo di Scienze, Lettere ed Arti in Bergamo. Numero speciale dedicato alle celebrazioni in onore del Card. Angelo Mai nel centenario della morte* [Bergomum: Bulletin of the Municipal Library and the Athenaeum of Sciences, Letters, and Arts in Bergamo. Special issue to commemorate the centenary of Cardinal Angelo Mai's death], vol. 28 (Nuova serie settembre-dicembre) no. 4 (Bergamo, 1954), 119–35, 45–69, 141–54, respectively. In the following, I will refer to the contributions in *Bergomum* more in detail.

12. On further consideration, the homily in question turned out to be an exegesis of the Gospel of St. John. The complete manuscript, which comprised eight leaves, five of which were located in Milan and three in Rome, was eventually published, with comments, by H. F. Massmann. I will return to this issue below. The text was henceforth often referred to by the Gothic name which Massmann had given it: "skeireins." However, I will continue to refer to the Gothic manuscript as to a homily, since this is the term Castiglioni and Mai used for it; the name "skeireins" I will use for Massmann's edition of the text only.

13. "Avis concernant une nouvelle découverte d'Ulphilas dans la Bibliothèque ambroisienne à Milan" in *Bibliotèque universelle* 6 (September, 1817), 99–102. The announcement is unsigned, but Mainetti, who has studied Angelo Mai's correspondence with several scholars, points out that it was Marc Auguste Pictet who undertook the announcement of the discovery. See A. Mainetti, "Il Cardinale Mai e i frammenti della bibbia di Wulfila nei Codices Ambrosiani," [Cardinal Mai and the fragments of the Wulfila Bible in the Ambrosian codices] in *Bergomum*, 124. For general information on the announcements see also M. E. Ceriani, "Nota sui lavorici gotici di Mai e Castiglioni," [A note on the Gothic studies of Mai and

Castiglioni] in *Rendiconti del I. Istituto Lombardo di scienze e lettere* [Reports of the Royal Lombardic Institute of Science and Letters] 3 (1866) serie 2, 23–34, at 26.

14. For the letter and the copy of the announcement mentioned here, both from the hand of Jacob Grimm, see the appendix. Letter and handwritten announcement are kept in the archives of the Koninklijk-Nederlandsche Instituut van Wetenschappen, Letteren en Schoone Kunsten, as the institute is officially named in these days. The Koninklijk Instituut is a society for the advancement of science, literature, history, and the arts inspired by the French example of the Académie Royale des Sciences. Its archives are lodged in the State Archives of the Province of North Holland in Haarlem, accession number 175. The record is numbered 86, file 186, letter no. 3.

15. *Briefe von Jakob Grimm an Hendrik Willem Tydeman*, ed. A. Reifferscheid (Heilbronn: Verlag von Gebr. Henninger, 1883), 65: "Sie haben, wehrtgeschätzter Freund, ohne Zweifel von des Angelo Majo allerglücklichstem Fund schon gehört? Er hat mehrere Codices palimpsestos des Ulfilas heraus gebracht, wodurch nicht blos die bisherigen Fragmente ergänzt und berichtigt werden können, sondern überhaupt die dreizehn canon. Briefe des Paulus in gothischer Sprache ans Licht kommen, selbst Stücke aus dem alten Test. aus Esdras u. Nehm. und wer weiss, was noch alles. Die Entdeckung ist von der grössten Wichtichkeit für Sprache u. bibl. Exegese, und welches Licht wird uns über Wortforschung und Grammatik aufgehen."

16. A. Mainetti, "Il Cardinale Mai," in *Bergomum*, 128. Mainetti mentions a review of von Arndt's *Ueber den Ursprung und die verschiedenartige Verwandtschaft der europaeischen Sprachen* by Kopitar, occasioned by the publication of Joh. Ludw. Klüber's edition in 1818, but fails to mention where this review was published. The review can be found in the Viennese *Jahrbücher der Literatur*, vol. 2 (April, May, Juny 1818), 258–60. For further reading on Kopitar, see J. Pogacnik, *Bartholomäus Kopitar: Leben und Werk* (Munich: Trofenik, 1978).

17. Biographical information on Carlo Ottavio Castiglioni is scant, mostly dating from the nineteenth century, and not very reliable. Most elaborate and correct is B. Biondelli, "Della vita e degli scritti del conte Carlo Ottavio Castiglioni," [On the life and publications of Count Carlo Ottavio Castiglioni] in *Studii linguistici* [Linguistic studies] (Milan, 1856). More recent, equally correct, but somewhat concise is the *Dizionario Biografico*. In a very recent article on the discovery and edition of the Ambrosian Gothic Palimpsests Giancarlo Bolognesi corrects many biographical errors on Castiglioni that are spread through various publications. See G. Bolognesi, "La scoperta e l'edizione dei Palinsesti Gotici Ambrosiani," [The discovery and edition of the Ambrosian Gothic Palimpsests] in *II Seminario avanzato in Filologia Germanica – Antichità Germaniche* [Second Advanced Seminar in Germanic Philology – Germanic Antiquities] ed. V. D. Corazza and R. Gendre ([Alessandria:] Edizioni dell'Orso, [2002], 129–72).

18. *Dizionario Biografico*, vol. 22, 137–38.

19. *Ulphilae partium ineditarum in Ambrosianis Palimpsestis ab Angelo MAIO repertarum specimen conjunctis curis ejusdem MAII et Caroli Octavii CASTILLIONAEI* – Mediolani, 1819, regiis Typis.

20. The term "royal" is slightly confusing. Although since 1815 Milan had

belonged to the Kingdom of Lombardo-Veneto, it in fact was administered directly by the Austrian Empire, of which Lombardo-Veneto formed a part. Especially in those early years after 1815, Austria pursued a deliberate policy to control the intellectual infrastructure as well. (See for instance *Storia di Milano* [History of Milan], vol. 16: *Principio di secolo (1901–1915)*, [Beginning of the century] ([Milan:] Fondazione Trecciani degli Alfieri per la storia di Milano, 1962), 260–78). The royal printing office, mentioned throughout in the editions themselves as well as in publications concerning editions of Gothic texts, thus rather paradoxically represents imperial interference.

21. *Ulphilae gothica versio epistolae divi Pauli ad Corinthios secundae, quam ex Ambrosianae bibliothecae palimpsestis depromptam cum interpretatione adnotationibus glossario edidit Carolus Octavius CASTILLIONAEUS* – Mediolani, 1829, Regiis typis; *Gothicae versionis epistolarum Divi Pauli ad Romanos, ad Corinthios primae, ad Ephesios quae supersunt ex Ambrosianae Bibliothecae palimpsestis deprompta cum adnotationibus edidit Carolus Octavius CASTILLIONAEUS* – Mediolani, 1834, Regiis typis; *Gothicae Versionis Epistolarum Divi Pauli ad Galatas, ad Philippenses, ad Colossenses, ad Thessalonicenses primae quae supersunt ex Ambrosianae Bibliothecae palimpsestis deprompta cum adnotationibus edidit Carolus Octavius CASTILLIONAEUS* – Mediolani, 1835, Regiis typis; *Gothicae Versionis Epistolarum Divi Pauli ad Thessalonicenses secundae, ad Timotheum, ad Titum, ad Philemonem quae supersunt ex Ambrosianae Bibliothecae palimpsestis deprompta cum adnotationibus edidit Carolus Octavius CASTILLIONAEUS* – Mediolani, 1839, Regiis typis.

22. M. E. Ceriani, "Nota sui lavorici gotici," in *Rendiconti*, 29.

23. The aforementioned *Briefe von Jakob Grimm* contain only Grimm's letters, not those of H. W. Tydeman. However, in the introduction to the correspondence between Grimm and Halbertsma, published in *Briefe von Jakob Grimm* as an appendix, reference is made to a letter by Tydeman dated 26 December, 1830, in which he wrote to Grimm: "De beste taalkundigen, die wij nu nog hebben zullen zijn Halbertsma, Predikant te Deventer en Lulofs, Professor te Groningen." [The best linguists we still have at present would be Halbertsma, minister in Deventer, and Lulofs, professor at Groningen University], *Briefe von Jakob Grimm*, ed. A. Reifferscheid, 260.

24. The correspondence between J. Grimm and Halbertsma has been published not only as an appendix to *Briefe von Jakob Grimm* but also in *Zeitschrift für deutsche Philologie*, vol. 17 (Halle a. S.: Verlag der Buchhandlung des Waisenhauses, 1885), 1–36. In both cases, the correspondence between Halbertsma and Grimm has been edited and commented by B. Symons.

25. Halbertsma, *Letterkundige Naoogst* 1, V and VI.

26. The remarkable fact that Halbertsma did not mention any famous editor of Gothic texts between 1665 and 1817 was also noted by an anonymous reviewer of *Letterkundige Naoogst* in *De Gids. Nieuwe Vaderlandsche Letteroefeningen* [The Guide. New National Exercises in Letters] (1841), an important Dutch journal for literary criticism in the nineteenth century. However, in previous publications – as, for instance, in an article in another authoritative literary journal, the *Vaderlandsche Letteroefeningen* [National Exercises in Letters] of 1835, (pages 165–78), written at the occasion of Castiglioni's publication of a part of the Gothic manuscript –

Halbertsma had shown himself to be well acquainted with the important landmarks in the development of knowledge concerning Gothic. Halbertsma was something of an authority in this field, as illustrated by the fact that he was charged with providing announcements of publications in the field of Germanic Languages and Literature, including Gothic, in several Dutch scholarly journals and monthly literary reviews. Moreover, the many important editions of Gothic texts, complete with his own notes, critical remarks, and additions, in his personal library bear witness to thorough study. The fact that in *Letterkundige Naoogst* he mentions only Junius, Mai, and Castiglioni, seems to be inspired by rhetorical considerations.

27. See for instance the contributions by Mainetti, Riposati, and Galletti in *Bergomum*.

28. B. Riposati, "Angelo Mai nella storia della cultura," [Angelo Mai in cultural history] in *Bergomum*, 48.

29. The Biblioteca Ambrosiana was founded in 1609 by Federico Borromeo, a highly esteemed, learned, and relatively enlightened cardinal. As such, the Biblioteca Ambrosiana was one of the first public libraries in Europe and, like the Bodleian, it came to serve as an example for other European libraries. Ceriani mentions that among the Biblioteca's manuscripts was a file card with a note in Cardinal Borremeo's handwriting, containing the clue that whoever was to find a fragment of the Ulfila Bible among the Biblioteca's manuscripts was to consult the Church Fathers as well as all that had been written concerning the Codex Argenteus. See: A. Mainetti, "Il Cardinale Mai," in *Bergomum*, 122 and M. E. Ceriani, "Nota sui lavorici gotici," in *Rendiconti*, 25. For more information on the manuscripts from the Bobbio monasteries see *Codices Latini Antiquiores. A Paleographical Guide to Latin Manuscripts Prior to the Ninth Century*, ed. E. A. Lowe, vol. 3: Italy: Ancona-Novara (Oxford: Clarendon Press, 1938).

30. A. G. Roncalli, "Discorso inaugurale," [Keynote address] in *Bergomum*, 29–40, at 33. Incidentally, by using this method Mai incurred many reproaches, as it seriously damaged the parchment. See for instance Massmann's introduction to his edition of the Gothic homily *Skeireins . . . Auslegung des Evangelii Johannis in Gothischer Sprache. Aus römischer und maylandischer Handschriften nebst lateinischer Uebersetzung, belegenden Anmerkungen, geschichtlicher Untersuchung, gothisch-lateinischen Wörterbuche und Schriftproben* [Skeireins . . . Explication of St. John's Gospel in Gothic. From Roman and Milanese manuscripts with a translation into Latin, supporting comments, historical research, Gothic-Latin glossaries, and script sample] (Munich: George Jaquet, 1834), IX–XVII, at XI. See also *Catholic Encyclopedia*, http://www.newadvent.org/cathen, s.v. Arius.

31. Foreign criticism of Angelo Mai will be discussed further below. The reactions from within Italy itself give the impression that a younger generation of philologists was of the opinion that Mai was unequal to his task. His stale erudition and well-established position also provoked a more general aversion among young romantics. The way in which Angelo Mai and "his" journal *Biblioteca Italiana* were characterised in Pietro Borsiero's romantic manifesto *Avventure letterarie di un giorno o consigli di un galantuomo a vari scrittori* (Milan, 1816) is revealing in this respect.

32. Cited in A. Mainetti, "Il Cardinale Mai," in *Bergomum*, 125. "Vi prego di rinnovare i miei saluti all'egregio Abbate Mai. Mi piacerebbe che nel pubblicare la

versione dell'Ulfila dicesse nella prefazione, o nelle note qualche parola sull'opportunità delle regole dell'Indice, sulle proposizioni di Quesnello intorno al render comune la lettura della Bibbia nelle lingue volgari, intorno all'infedeltà e l'abuso di molte versioni fatte dagli Eretici, intorno al pericolo delle traduzioni nelle lingue volgari, del dar a tutti in mano la S. Scrittura, i sensi altissimi, e profondi della quale non sono per tutti i lettori, avendo l'esperienza dimostrato che la maggior parte delle eresie sono nate dell'intendere male la S. Scrittura, la quale non è cosi facile come sognano i Protestanti, ma difficilissima riusciva alla gran mente di S. Agostino, come egli confessa; e finalmente intorno al pericolo che per tutte queste ragioni può derivare dalle Società bibliche . . ."

33. R. G. van de Velde, *De studie van het Gotisch in de Nederlanden* [Gothic Studies in the Low Countries] (Gent: Koninklijke Vlaamse Academie voor Taal- en Letterkunde, 1966), 16 and 17. See also K. Dekker, *The Origins of Old Germanic Studies in the Low Countries* (Leiden, Boston, Cologne: Brill, 1999), 29–36.

34. Massmann, in his introduction to *Skeireins*, spent considerable attention to Arianism. See also the on-line edition of the *Catholic Encyclopedia*.

35. On this issue, see F. Weigle, "Rapporti tra Angelo Mai e i *Monumenta Germaniae Historica*," [Relations between Angelo Mai and the *Monumenta Germaniae Historica*] in *Bergomum*, 81–84, and Massmann's introduction to *Skeireins*.

36. The following depends largely on A. Galletti's discussion "Filologia e poesia," in *Bergomum*, 141–54.

37. See for instance H. D. Meijering, *Oudere Germaanse literatuur als nationaal erfdeel. Nationale motieven bij de bestudering van de gotische bijbelvertaling, de oudsaksische Heliand en Genesis, en de oudfriese rechtsliteratuur* [Older Germanic literature as national heritage. National motives in the study of the Gothic Bible translation, the Old-Saxon Heliand and Genesis, and the Old-Frisian legal texts] (Amsterdam: Vrije Universiteit, 1978), 12–14.

38. To illustrate this point: the astute Italian poet Giacomo Leopardi ended one of his poems, in which he provides an ironic commentary on the systematism and scholarly skepticism of German philologists, in the following lines:
    Pur manifesto si conosce in tutto
    Che di seme tedesco il mondo è frutto.
Freely translated: One thing however is certain – the whole world is of German origin. Cited by A. Galletti, "Filologia e poesia," in *Bergomum*, 150.

39. Cited by A. Mainetti in "Il Cardinale Mai," in *Bergomum*, 131. "Rimessomi da 6 in 7 mesi al mio lavoro (al quale sono continuamente spinto dalle incessanti e spesso inurbane istanze dei letterati tedeschi che mi hanno minacciato di muovere la podestà della terra contro di me se non finisco entro l'anno) mi trovo in una nuova circonstanza che mi obbliga ad aver ricorso nella di Lei amicizia. Ella saprà che Massmann ha pubblicato i frammenti delle omelie gotiche di Roma e Milano e che io gli ho ceduti questi ultimi, quantunque con molto dispiacere, perchè appunto nel tempo in cui col maggior impegno mi occupavo in questi studi. Ritornato egli a Monaco mi scrisse avere ritrovato che quest'opera era "semi ariana" e che perciò mi felicitava di avermi liberato dall'imbarazzo di pubblicare l'opera di un eretico. Io non risposi sopra questo argomento, perchè mi moveva la bile che volesse

fare il lepido così male a proposito sopra un argomento che poteva essermi spiacevole . . .
Siccome però non vorrei che questo Ulfila che mi ha suscitato contro le burrasche del Nord mi procurasse inquietudine il che sarebbe a me assai anzi senza paragone più doloroso, anche da codesta parte del Mezzogiorno, così io La prego di esaminare (messo da parte quella prevenzione con la quale di Lei antica amicizia le fa vedere le cose mie) le mie note e all'uopo di farle esaminare da chi crede e sino a quel punto che Ella crede necessario nella Gerarchia ecclesiastica, affinchè io possa essere tranquillo intorno a questo punto."

40. The *Allgemeine Deutsche Biographie* (Leipzig: Verlag von Dunker & Humblot, 1884) contains both positive and negative qualifications of Massmann: Heinrich Heine appears to have derisively called him Marcus Tullius Massmannus because of his "ausgesuchtesten Bosheiten" [extraordinary malices], whereas Alexander von Humboldt commended his thoroughness and the clarity of his ideas. It was to Massmann, among others, that Grimm dedicated the fourth volume of his *Deutsche Grammatik*.

41. After Angelo Mai had been appointed custos of the Vatican Library in 1819, he discovered in this library three more leaves of the manuscript he had found in Milan, and which he thought to be a homily. He published it several times, in parts and with emendations, and in 1833 he finally published the whole text (eight leaves) in facsimile edition in the eight volume of the *Scriptorum veterum nova collectio e Vaticanis codicibus*. As it turned out, this text contained quite a few mistakes. See also note 12 above, as well as Ceriani, "Nota sui lavorici gotici," in *Rendiconti*, at 28.

42. Massmann's introduction to *Skeireins*, V–XVI.

43. *Ibid*. XI.

44. *Ibid*. XII.

45. *Skeireins*, 103 ". . . den klaren Urquell der schon viel getrübten Lehre in der heiligen Schrift urgetreu in seiner Muttersprache und das ursprüngliche Evangelium des Lebens und der Liebe aus dem wirren Widerstreite der Meinungen, Verketzerungen und Verfolgungen zu retten; und hielt es für seines Volkes inneres wie ausseres Wohl nicht für schädlich, einer Glaubensform sich zuzuwenden, welche ihm in ihrer Grundlage vielleicht mehr Einfachheit zu offenbaren, mehr Ursprünglichkeit bewahrt zu haben scheinen mochte, als die mehr ausgebildete nicäische Dreyeinichkeitslehre und die zu seiner Zeit schon mannigfaltig liturgisch vervielfachte Form der rechtglaubigen Kirche."

46. Castiglioni's letters to Halbertsma have not yet been published, and Halbertsma's letters to Castiglioni have not even been traced yet. In a forth-coming book, I will include a transcription of the Latin text and a translation of Castiglioni's letters, if possible supplemented by a transcription and translation of Halbertsma's letters. Castiglioni's original letters are located in J. Halbertsma's collection of scholarly correspondence in the Tresoar. The collection's accession number is 6185 Hs. The letter by Castiglioni quoted here is numbered 30/2.

47. S. Sybrandy, "J. H. Halbertsma en syn bibliotheek," in *Joast Hiddes Halbertsma (1789–1869). Brekker en bouwer*, 275.

48. Halbertsma's letters to Grimm, in B. Symons's edition (see note 23 above),

have not been printed in their entirety. Precisely the discussion with Grimm on the derivation of Gothic words in relation to Castiglioni's and Massmann's publications has been omitted. The original letters have unfortunately been lost. The remark about the failure of a parcel of books from Massmann to arrive is made by the editor, Symons, while summarising a part of a letter by Halbertsma. For this, see *Briefe von J. Grimm*, ed. Reifferscheid, 277.

49. J. H. Halbertsma, *Algemeene Konst- en Letterbode* [General Messenger of Arts and Letters] [in the section: Untitled short comments on works published abroad] (1837), part 2, 406–07, at 406. In a letter to Halbertsma from 4 November 1837, Grimm expressed himself in a similar fashion. See *Briefe von J. Grimm*, ed. Reifferscheid, 277.

50. *Briefe von J. Grimm*, ed. Reifferscheid, 271. "De Skeireins von Prof. Massmann ligt thands voor mij. Is die gezeling, welke hij met telkens hoger opgeheven arm aan Majus geeft, overeen te brengen met de regelen der ware humaniteit?" The quotation from the eighteenth-century German fabulist Hagedorn translates as: "the masters of grammar are pugnacious billygoats."

51. The collection of Halbertsma's scholarly correspondence, accession number 6185 Hs, contains only one letter from Angelo Mai to Halbertsma. The letter is numbered 95/1. So far there is no trace of a letter (or letters?) from Halbertsma to Angelo Mai.

52. The letters concerned here are 6185 Hs, nos. 30/2 and 30/4.

53. Mainetti, "Il Cardinale Mai," in *Bergomum*, 130: "Il Grimm gli rimprovera la grande lentezza (nè sapremmo, in verità, dargli gran torto!) ed il Castiglioni rompe col filologo ogni rapporto epistolare" [Grimm reproaches him with his extreme tardiness (and, to be honest, we cannot fully blame him for doing so!) and Castiglioni breaks off all correspondence with the philologist]. Grimm reviewed Castiglioni's text editions in *Jahrbücher der Literatur* and the *Göttingische gelehrte Anzeigen*, amongst others. The tone taken in the reviews is not explicitly negative, but not very generous or sympathetic, either. Besides, there is a letter from Grimm to Professor Tydeman of 12 May 1824, that gives an impression of Grimm's rather negative opinion on his Italian colleagues: "und gehe mit dem Gedanken um – noch dies jahr nach Mailand zu reisen und den Ulphilas dort zu heben. Einleitungen sind gemacht, können aber am eigensinn der faulen, neidischen Italiener scheitern" [and I am entertaining the thought of traveling to Milan before the year is through, and picking up the Ulfila there. Preparations have already been made, but these could still founder due to the capriciousness of those lazy, envious Italians], *Briefe von Jakob Grimm*, ed. Reifferscheid, 78.

54. J. H. Halbertsma, *Algemeene Konst- en Letterbode* (1834), 323–24, at 323.

55. Letter from C. O. Castiglioni to J. Halbertsma: 6185 Hs, no. 30/2. "nec hic tamen contentus, et defensorum meum egisti in ephemeribus literariis adversus doctos Germaniae viros."

56. "Sed ni [xxx] me φιλαυθεια [φιλαυτεια] fallit Cl[arissime] V[ir] male ferens divinationes suas in lingua partim deperdita non semper felicem exitum habuisse, acrius invectus est, quam mihi par videbatur in virum exterae gentis, qui multorum annorum studia in antiquitatum suae gentis studium contulerat."

57. In my opinion, Halbertsma's and Grimm's letters bear out a clear

difference in character between the two scholars. Halbertsma was very strongly inclined to mock the human, and in particular scholarly, endeavour. He did not suppress this inclination vis-à-vis Grimm. Grimm, however, did not respond to this mockery in any way. Another indication for their diverging dispositions can be found in an essay by Halbertsma on the differences between the Dutch poet and philologist Willem Bilderdijk and Grimm, in as far as their linguistic studies are concerned: although Halbertsma is quite critical of Bilderdijk's philological works, he appreciates his imagination, linguistic instinct, and poetic genius. In comparison with Bilderdijk's universal mind, Halbertsma seems to find Grimm's scholarly work somewhat limited. Grimm was active within a well-defined field, and surveyed this field in a calm, precise, and methodical manner. Halbertsma's review *Het onderscheid tusschen de taalstudie van Willem Bilderdijk en Jacob Grimm* [The difference between Willem Bilderdijk's and Jacob Grimm's linguistic studies], which exists in at least two slightly different manuscript versions, kept in Tresoar and the archives of the Koninklijk-Nederlandsche Instituut van Wetenschappen, Letteren en Schoone Kunsten, respectively, has been published by Lida Zutt in *Voortgang. Jaarboek voor Neerlandistiek* [Progress. Yearbook for Dutch Studies] 17 (1997/98), 207–27. On the differences in scholarly views between Halbertsma and Grimm, see for instance A. Feitsma, "Oardielen oer J. H. Halbertsma as etymolooch," [Opinions on J. H. Halbertsma as an etymologist], *De Vrije Fries* [The Free Frisian] 77 (1997), 139–51.

58. B. Biondelli, "Delle lingue Germaniche e della loro grammatica," [On the Germanic languages and their grammar] in *Studii linguistici*, 331–56, at 345: "On sait que Grimm et autres font autant et plus de cas des voyelles que des consonnes; en vous demandant, Monsieur, l'explication de ce phénomène, je vous débite mon opinion. Les Allemands se piquent d'être les vrais *Germani* de Tacite, et par conséquent frères des Goths, des Chauces, des Frisons, des Anglo-Saxons, etc.; mais ils voient fort bien que leurs consonnes ne leur accordent pas cette place; au contraire elles leur destinent celle de neveux abâtardis. Le développement, ou plutôt l'endurcissement des consonnes, est une marque irrécusable de l'âge des langues et des dialectes. *Frater, dens*, sont plus anciens que *brothar, thunthus*, qui à leur tour sont plus anciens que l'allemand *pruoder, zand*. Dans les voyelles au contraire les Allemands ressemblent autant que nous aux Goths, et voilà pourquoi ces messieurs, pour se rapprocher d'avantage au vrai sang des *Germani*, mettent les voyelles au premier rang." This article had been published earlier as "Grammatica di tutte le lingue germaniche, del dott. Jacopo Grimm," [Grammar of all the Germanic languages, by doctor Jacob Grimm], *Politecnico*, vol. 3 (1841), 250–78.

59. The six letters in French from Biondelli to Halbertsma, which are kept in Tresoar under accession number 6185 Hs, nos. 12/1–12/6, will also be published in my book. The quotation given here is from letter no. 12/5: "Dans quelques jours je publierai encore la revue critique de la grammaire du Dr. J. Grimm, où j'ai eu occasion de citer votre nom et vos ouvrages. Dans cet article vous trouverez sans doute des observations conformes aux principes que vous m'avez manifestés dans vos aimables lettres . . ."

60. Quoted from letter 6185 Hs, no. 12/4: "Je me réserve à parler du systhème du Dr. J. Grimm, dans une Revue, que j'ai déja commencée, de sa

Deutsche Grammatik. C'est un article long et pénible, dans lequel je présenterai une quantité d'observations tout-à-fait originales, contraires au systhème de ce celebre linguiste; monsieur le comte Castiglioni m'en a procuré d'autres, ainsi j'espère que cet article sera beaucoup intéressant, quoique mal vu des Allemands, excepté mr. Bopp, qui dans son *Vocalismus* etc. m'a fourni d'intéressans matériaux."

    61. Halbertsma, *Letterkundige Naoogst* 1, V.

    62. *Ibid.* VIII–X: "Comme ceux, qui etudient les langues du Nord d'après la grande méthode de nos jours, entendent également le Latin et le Grec et tous les idiomes Germaniques, il suffit de dire que c'est surtout pour eux que j'ai écrit. Mais puisque je trouve peut-être çà et là un lecteur, qui concentrant ses forces sur un seul point ne réunisse pas l'étude de tant de langues, et qui s'interesse pourtant un peu á une seul pièce, j'ai conformé la langue de mon commentaire à celle de la pièce; ainsi celui qui comprend la pièce comprendra mon commentaire, ce qui ne serait pas le cas, si je m'etais toujours servi de la même langue . . . Je me suis donc accomodé en tout aux lecteurs respectifs des diverses pièces de mon recueil, sans prétendre à aucune élégance de style dans des langues, dans les quelles je ne pense pas. Etre clair et précis, être intelligible pour le moins, voilà le but que je me suis proposé. Cependant l'esprit stationnaire de tel ou tel chef de la littérature Hollandaise, qui de peur de tomber ou de se fatiguer préfère parcourir le chemin battu, ne lui permettra pas de donner dans mes idées. C'est bien malheureux pour moi, ou plutôt pour mon libraire. Car à vous dire toute la verité, Monseigneur, ce n'est pas aux gens de cette trempe là proprement, que j'ai adressé la parole. Je parle aux literatuers du Nord, qui sont ou qui comme moi aspirent à la hauteur du siècle, si tant est qu'ils m'écoutent . . . En tout cas je suis sûr d'avoir parlé sur la composition de votre tête. Car vous savez, Monseigneur, qu'il est impossible d'entendre une des langues Germaniques en linguiste sans les entendre toutes; vous réunissez ces extrêmités, qui jusqu'à nos jours paraissaient séparées autant que le ciel l'est de la terre . . . A qui donc, quand même la reconnaissance se tairait en moi, dédierois-je mon livre plutôt qu'à vous, Monseigneur, qui dans ce melange bigarré de trois ou quatre langages ne regardez, que les branches plus ou moins divergentes de la même tige, qui prit racine à côté du berceau de l'humanité?"

    63. Grimm is somewhat inconsistent in his use of capital letters and orthography, both in his letter and in his copy of the "Avis." Also in other respects Grimm's copy of the "Avis" and the text in the *Bibliothèque universelle* show some minor differences. The single occasion in which Grimm deviates meaningfully (however still accidentally) will be pointed out below.

    64. In the *Bibliothèque universelle* this sentence ends with "au premier concil de Nicée l'an 325." Then a new sentence begins: "Les Moesogoths . . ."

Imagining Medieval Music: a Short History[1]

Annette Kreutziger-Herr

C'est vers le Moyen Âge enorme et delicat qu'il faudrait que mon coeur en panne naviguât, Loin de nos jours d'esprit charnel et de chair triste. (Verlaine)

In the third book of his novel *Notre-Dame de Paris*, published in 1832, Victor Hugo evokes the image of "gothic Paris," which culminates in the festive peal of bells at Easter or Pentecost:

> Behold, at a signal given from heaven, for it is the sun which gives it, all those churches quiver simultaneously. First come scattered strokes, running from one church to another, as when musicians give warning that they are about to begin. Then, all at once, behold! – for it seems at times as though the ear also possessed a sight of its own, – behold, rising from each bell tower, something like a column of sound, a cloud of harmony. First, the vibration of each bell mounts straight upwards, pure and, so to speak, isolated from the others, into the splendid morning sky; then, little by little, as they swell they melt together, mingle, are lost in each other, and amalgamate in a magnificent concert. It is no longer anything but a mass of sonorous vibrations incessantly sent forth from the numerous belfries; floats, undulates, bounds, whirls over the city, and prolongs far beyond the horizon the deafening circle of its oscillations.
> Nevertheless, this sea of harmony is not a chaos; great and profound as it is, it has not lost its transparency; you behold the windings of each group of notes which escapes from the belfries. You can follow the dialogue, by turns grave and shrill, of the treble and the bass; you can see the octaves leap from one tower to another; you watch them spring forth, winged, light, and whistling,

from the silver bell, to fall, broken and limping from the bell of wood; you admire in their midst the rich gamut which incessantly ascends and re-ascends the seven bells of Saint-Eustache; you see light and rapid notes running across it, executing three or four luminous zigzags, and vanishing like flashes of lightning . . . Assuredly, this is an opera which it is worth the trouble of listening to.[2]

Victor Hugo outlines a "soundscape" of unsurpassed splendour and opulence, in which the description of music is central – be it from bells or produced by human voices. It is as if Victor Hugo had known about the central importance of listening in the Middle Ages, the capacity to listen as the most important quality of man. Hildegard von Bingen and others have repeatedly underlined how important it is to listen to divine intuitions and how singing corresponds, answers, to this supreme sense. Listening is central and runs from the dove of the Holy Ghost whispering liturgical chant melodies in Pope St. Gregory's ear, through the masses of ecclesiastical sound accompanying the mass, and it seems that the tragic figure of the deaf hunchback is put into the centre of Hugo's novel in order to hint already here at the decline of the medieval world. In the light of the importance of eye and ear for medieval society at large, the memory of the body being extremely important, the construction of a deaf hunchback working in a Gothic cathedral is an unsurpassed hint to medieval living and thinking.

Victor Hugo's novel, though billowed with life, sensuous and filled with lush images, is not medieval, but a masterpiece of French Romanticism, conveying sights and sounds for our imagination. At the same time there is a punch line: Around 1830, while Hugo was giving a soundscape to medieval tones, medieval music itself was almost unknown. Being the only reconstructable aspect of medieval soundscapes, be they either urban or rural, music could at least open a door to historic reconstruction of medieval life. But medieval music was in the 19th century absent as a historic fact, and when looked upon in detail it is more colour and atmosphere than reconstruction. When minstrels or chant recitations are described, they lend the description a soft and fictional effect of depth in this literarisation of history. No other effect is aimed at when Matthew G. Lewis, in his 1796 novel *The Monk*, describes the abbot of the Milan Capuchin Monastery, Ambrosio, who in his colossal introductory sermon portrays the pangs of eternal damnation, while his voice turns into "a heavenly melody," carrying the listeners above the abyss of ultimate destruction into the realm of blessed peacefulness.

With no oral tradition alive and the interest in medieval music gone, which had died around 1500 completely, the sources for a revival of medieval music lay in monasteries waiting to be rediscovered. And polyphony, notated with a notation and harmonic system so different from the notation of modern times, the revival of medieval music had to wait for the transcription of the music first before it could become alive again in sound. This transcription though had to be a reconstruction – and a reinvention, with so many parameters of medieval music lost and gone forever.

Music as an Object of Research and Study

Music as a sounding attribute is at the same time a cultural asset and an object of research. But unlike all other historic artifacts and remnants of material culture, music is irretrievably lost when history progresses. Notations and notes do not convey the essence of sound itself, they cannot by their very nature supply the fullness of information of the resounding, they do not transmit the information in order to comprehend a performance – notations are mere hints and permit only a slight idea of the liveliness and beauty with which time had been formed into sound. Likewise, it is a basic philosophical and musical problem that a musical artifact is only present when it is completely gone. Music is able, like no other art, to illustrate the fleetingness of time and mortality through its very nature, while music is for many philosophers – like Schopenhauer or Bloch – the mediator that, if any, can convincingly reach transcendence. The realisation and manifestation of music is inseparable from the possibilities of the present and is to the highest degree dependent on empathy and knowledge, on emotional understanding, experience, theoretical exploration and penetration. Music is a fleeting something, that only acquires duration through sound and loses this duration immediately in order to *be*.

So music lives in a hidden, invisible space, in what Ernst Bloch once called "the secret territory of the highest good" ("die Geheimlandschaft des höchsten Guts"). Its reconstruction and its sounding belong to the area of tension between the preservation of music, kept like objects of art in a museum – music as sounding history – and on the other hand emotional identification – music as sounding presence, where historical distance has no meaning and the question of any historic context is not asked. The preservation of a musical past for the sake of preserving it – like paintings of court and castle kept in museums without the context that could convey meaning – and without any expectation that ancient music could still have any emotional meaning, stays in contrast to an emotional approach to the music of the past, in which music could mean anything as long as it touches the heart. Most people today do not realise that the classical music they admire and love was composed for specific contexts (church, court, salon) and conceptualised in circumstances totally different from ours today, the same being even more true for the music of ancient times. So the moments in which "the real meaning" of music unfolds clearly cannot be put down on paper or parchment and they are developed only within the dialogue of composer and interpreter. The ability to see a connection between the deviations from notated music – the small variants that define the character of the individual performance – and musical meaning, are rooted within the conviction that music is eloquent, while at the same time it is not definite or unambiguous what music is saying. It is an expressive language without clearly outlined content and object.

The problem and the opportunity of a realisation of notated music in a concert – the transformation of script to sound – are evident, they culminate in the dilemma of historic reconstruction of musical history and they gain in explosive force when eye and ear are geared towards a musical culture that is removed farther away.

Medievalism and Medieval Music

Medievalism organises, one could argue, forms of recollection and memory of the Middle Ages in a new, creative way, bringing to the surface those aspects of medieval culture which the present is interested in. These can be divided into four forms: the productive, creative medievalism, in which topics, themes, forms, works of art and authors of the Middle Ages are formed into a new work of art; the reproductive medievalism in which medieval works are reconstructed in a way which the present regards as "authentic," through a musical performance or renovation (of a painting or a building); the scientific medievalism, in which medieval authors, works, events or facts are studied and explained with the methods of each participating discipline; political and ideological medievalism, in which works, themes, ideas or persons from the Middle Ages are exploited for political reasons in the widest sense and used to legitimise actions. These forms of medievalism are rarely separated from each other. The most explosive forces are the second and third ones, for they shake the foundation of the humanities at large. For if artistic, that is intrinsically subjective approaches are accepted into the "objective" humanities, the "pure" foundations of the disciplines are in question.[3]

Generally the medievalist seems to be in charge of the first two categories, though medievalists work in a network, in which all four categories are mixed. Here, one can already perceive that the reconstruction and performance of medieval music is something between creative, reproductive and scientific medievalism, and the mix of those three approaches is guided by imagination: medieval music is an especially convincing dream of the Middle Ages.

For the music history of Europe, medieval culture is the phenomenon farthest away from the present. From antiquity there are no musical testimonies, and the few which have prevailed are mostly disputable and subject to speculation. Medieval music, therefore, is Europe's oldest music, the earliest music to which access seems to be possible. But this musical culture cannot be accessed by searching and finding – you need first an inner access, which opens ears and eyes for this stunningly new art. As long as thought ignored the Middle Ages as an interesting epoch, no substantial research was done, and the hundreds of sources remained undiscovered in the ecclesiastical and secular archives. So before medieval music was rediscovered in full, starting around 1900, and before it was possible to find a sound for the mysterious manuscripts in the 20th century, a full history of ideas had to develop. The Middle Ages themselves had to become interesting enough for the music to become interesting too, and the reconstruction of medieval music – rediscovery and invention alike – is embedded in the history of medievalism in modernity.

While in the 18th century the Middle Ages were mostly regarded as a dark, retarded time, and while the Middle Ages in history books were often dealt with mostly in one sentence, as an epoch which should be dealt with as quickly as possible, around 1800 the Middle Ages blossom out into an object of longing of first range, away from the rhapsodic prelude of historical observation and towards the monumental importance of medieval culture. Harbingers had been the English *gothic novels* and the leaning towards medieval architecture – *Strawberry Hill* by Horace Walpole and his early attempts to translate the Middle Ages in his novel *The Castle of Otranto* – to be followed by the *Waverley Novels* by Sir Walter Scott, to which also Victor Hugo's *Notre-Dame de Paris* would be indebted.

Goethe's praise of the Dome of Strassbourg – his article *Von deutscher Baukunst*[4] – from 1772 is an early testimony, in which in seemingly modest and unspectacular ways, the foundations of a new aesthetic of art are proposed. Generally, the Middle Ages in England, France and Germany would be rediscovered first on the architectural and literary level, later also on the historical, music historical and political level, to be regarded as an ideal epoch. The traces of this redirecting can be followed through treatises, novels, remarks and speeches published from the late 18th century and into the middle of the 19th, when the Middle Ages were established as an important European epoch and when more could be said about them than one sentence.

In the late 18th century, a specific history of ideas began which prepared the way for concepts of medieval music. To name just one, the English and later on German theories of "gothic forests" and "domes of plants"[5] flourished in an attempt to explain Gothic architecture through analogies to organic growth. This idea, for example, would take root in concepts of medieval polyphony – concepts of the music of the Middle Ages as an organic art following rules like organic growth. This concept would contribute to a high degree to the elaborated concept of progress in music history, the individual expressions of musical concepts as growing from the meagre to the more elaborated, from the simple to the complex – a concept which permeated all writing on music and was, for many decades, as prevailing as it was misleading.

A first attempt, on a more precise level, to come to grips with medieval music can be found in a glossary of middle and late Latin compiled by the Frenchman Charles de Fresne, Sieur Du Cange (1610–1688). He defined terms like "cantus," "discantus," "musica," "organum," and gave the etymological meaning of those terms.[6] About a century later, the Benedictine Carpentier added a supplement, comprised of four volumes, that was incorporated into later editions of the "Glossarium." This supplement added more information, but also added misconceptions, such as the notion that there existed in France, before "the Guidonian hand," a kind of "new singing" based on staff notation – that is neumes notated on lines.[7]

The *Glossarium novum*, other collections of medieval treatises on musical topics, and other small booklets on music history stand only as modest predecessors to the monumental work *De cantu et musica sacra*, in which Martin Gerbert undertook, in 1774, to write the history of medieval ecclesiastical music.[8] This historic text already shows a deep knowledge of the theoretical sources and led ultimately to his famous collection of medieval treatises called *Scriptores ecclesiastici de musica sacra potissimu*. It was the first critically compiled work that would make musical medieval studies possible in a philologically oriented – that is, modern – way. But this work, as well as its successors – including Coussemaker's supplemental *Scriptores* collection of the 19th century – turned interest in the Middle Ages almost exclusively toward the theorists of music.

Apart from this early systematic approach to medieval music theory, there prevailed a general sort of charming disregard for medieval music, as it surfaces in the writings of Charles Burney, for example, especially in his *General History of Music* of 1776.[9] This book, based on Burney's readings in libraries in Paris, Rome, Milan, Florence and Venice, tries to do justice to what he calls "the dark ages of ignorance and superstition."[10] Yet he sees no real beauty and greatness in the music he finds. For example, commenting on a piece of Gregorian chant, written in undiastematic neumes (that is neumes notated without lines and not conveying the general melodic flux), he says that "the history of barbarians can furnish but small pleasure or profit to an enlightened and polished people . . . these chants bear nearly the same proportion to a marked and elegant melody, as a discourse drawn from Swift's *Laputan Mill* would do with one written by a Locke or a Johnson."[11]

"Gothic" for Burney is – like for Goethe – a pejorative word: "Melody was so gothic and devoid of grace, that good poets disdained its company or assistance."[12] At the same time, it is here that interest in a history of earlier music than the present started to develop, again in England. The large collections of medieval manuscripts from John Stow, Robert Cotton and Robert Harley were handed over to the British Library, and they enabled the most important music historians of the Age of Enlightenment, Charles Burney and Sir John Hawkins, to catch a glimpse of medieval music history.

The 19th century and historic imagination

A pioneer of research in the 19th century was the French music historian François-Louis Perne, who, as a lone rider in 1814, attempted a complete transcription of a polyphonic mass for the first time – the mass of Guillaume de Machaut of the 14th century. The first extensive studies on the Middle Ages were by Raphael Georg Kiesewetter (1773–1850) and by François-Joseph Fétis (1784–1871), both trying to understand neumes – the notation of chant – and to start from there to attempt transcriptions of modal and mensural notation – the notation of polyphony. Their individual contributions prepared the way for many later 19th-century medievalists,[13] the most important one being the Belgian lawyer and music historian Edmond-Charles de Coussemaker, who published the first musicological mongraphy, dedicated in the title to the music of the Middle Ages: his *Histoire de l'harmonie au Moyen Âge* (1852).

While the 19th century saw the evolution of historicism, it also combined the romantic movement and the Gothic Revival, the latter having been supported by the powerful force of nationalism. The seemingly "stable" Middle Ages seemed to be a paradise of political unity and fixed harmony in times of the political unrest, following the French Revolution and eventually reaching all other parts of Continental Europe. At the same time, it is important to see that latter waves of medievalism tried to interpret early testimonies of longing for the Middle Ages as nationalist upheaval, while they spoke out for a general interest in history, in culture and in the roots of thought.[14] This Gothic Revival changed the approach to the Middle Ages from indifference to curiosity, and medieval music, still unheard, was envisioned as the embodiment of the natural, the innocent, and the divine. While a tidal wave of the so-called Gothic Revival swept across Continental Europe and Great Britain, and while a few individuals made important contributions to a budding historiography of medieval music,[15] most important manuscripts still remained unknown and untranscribed. Music histories written at the time continued to display an ignorance of medieval music, which, at least in light of the theory available already, can be explained only by the fact that eras in general know no more than they are interested in knowing. Only Gregorian chant, revived after 1830 in the monastery of Solesmes, began to live again, conveyed by the intense Cecilian movement – a similar construction to medieval polyphonic music in the 20th century, as Katherine Bergeron has shown.[16] Through the knowledge of Gregorian chant and its "aura," the rest of medieval music, "the art in its earliest stages" as Carl von Winterfeld described it, would become something of an unreal ideal – more a product of the romantic mind than a tangible presence.[17] Romantic poetry filled the imagination of the general public with "blessed" images, while at the same time, historiography seemed to go beyond mere anti-rationalist feelings, while adding to the essence of the romantic cult of the Middle Ages. Just as the romantics would avoid the study of mathematical proportions and see Gothic cathedrals as having resulted from "an earth-fleeing yearning for the hereafter or the result of ecstatic mysticism,"[18] so too, medieval music would first be studied without looking for principles of organisation – certainly not expecting to find any.

Prominent in all 19th-century writing on medieval music is the word "harmony" – a fashionable term that designated the texture of polyphonic music and implies even more: "Harmony" was viewed as a unifying quality in a political sense, as an aesthetic as well as a political ideal, exemplifying "unity" and even "peace." Montesquieu and Voltaire had already shown that there is something like a specific European tradition of ideals, which had no universal meaning. It seemed important to link 19th-century history to all of European history and to distinguish Europe's destiny from the rest of the world. In this regard "harmony" could function as a uniquely European ideal (like "beauty"); it was, for the romantic mind, evident in the important stylistic changes that occurred during the 18th-century and that brought about a musical language preferring homophony and harmony to elaborate counterpoint and polyphony. The specifically romantic definition of "harmony" broadened the meaning of the word, which now carried political, aesthetic, and musical connotations that resulted, eventually, in methodological misunderstanding when applied to medieval music.

In his analysis of the polyphonic compositions of Adam de la Halle, for example, Kiesewetter describes the sonorities, the chords, while not having enough material at hand to analyse the polyphonic peculiarities typical of the medieval motet and the medieval chanson.[19] He was looking for the 19th-century ideal in a 13th-century piece.

But there is more to the concept of harmony: In Germany during the 19th century, the Berlin *Singakademie* and the Heidelberger Singverein were founded – the Heidelberg Association formed between 1811 and 1814 by the author of a widely read pamphlet *Über Reinheit der Tonkunst*, Anton Friedrich Thibaut. His choir would be active until the year of this death in

1840. These institutions took up the English idea of an *Academy of Ancient Music*, which had been formed in London in 1710. For the Heidelberg formation, Thibaut found his repertoire in earlier sacred vocal music, which had been published since 1806 by Alexandre Choron in Paris – who was forming a conservatory himself in 1817, the *Institution royale de musique classique et religieuse*. Its aim was to educate choirmasters, but also to install an appreciation for a *musique sacrée et classique* – an undertaking to be elaborated on by the succeeding institution of Louis Niedermeyer, the *Ecole de Musique Religieuse et Classique*. All these efforts were united by a voiced historic attitude. They were all, with different, nationally-patriotically coloured ways, dedicated to the care of early music, to bringing it closer to the educated and interested audience and to lay the basis for a historic performance practice. Although no medieval music was known or performed here, these efforts prefigure historic thought about medieval music, and especially the attempt by Thibaut in Germany, to unite the interest in early sacred music with concepts of harmony and moral purity, has a promising future for music historical concepts of medieval music.

While between 1800 and 1820 the foundations were laid for historicism and historic thought, and while historicism became the dominating stream of thought in Europe, the aim in music was also the empirical appropriation of historic traditions. There is a feeling of responsibility towards history. There is respectful feeling towards history, a European interest in history is evident. To pick out just the most famous example – the attempt by Felix Mendelssohn Bartholdy and others to prepare the re-entry of the music of Johann Sebastian Bach into concert life in the 1820s – and this was done, among other attempts, by connecting Bach to Gothic Architecture, by then regarded as national German historic style, and connected to German importance. At the same time, first attempts were made to take up the study of German Minnesang – through Karl Lachmann and others – in a philological way, that was able to attract artistic interest, too.

In the 19th century in France and Germany, "medieval music" meant mostly minstrel songs, the songs of the trouvères and troubadours, the Minnesang. But the romantic interest in Minnesang culminated not only in the theory of the medieval Kunstlied – as formulated by many music historians and most eloquently by Hugo Riemann, the most famous and active music historian and one of the founding fathers of modern musicology – in which concepts of Minnesang and trouvères melody are derived from the Lieder of Robert Schumann and Johannes Brahms, but also leads to an overwhelming mass of artificial Minnesang by composers in the wake of Ludwig Tieck's famous edition *Minnelieder aus dem Schwäbischen Zeitalter*, published for the first time in 1803. Composers like Joseph Wölfl, Simon Sechter, Wilhelm Taubert, Adolf Jensen and many others "invented" minstrel songs of their own, which were performed and sung in the salons and concert halls of 19th century Germany. At the same time, a countless number of popularised text editions reached the public, from *Hesperische Nachklänge in Deutschen Weisen*, edited in 1824 by Friedrich Rassmann, to the collection *Altes Gold* from 1878, edited by Karl Ströse.[20]

It was Richard Wagner's turning to the German Middle Ages and his interest in the Minne- and Meistersänger that lead to an unsurpassed boom in 19th century medievalism. Here, Minnesang as a concept reaches the centre of interest, and stories stemming from medieval literature, such as the *Nibelungenlied, Parzival, Lohengrin, Tristan and Isolde*, are presented to a large audience in a very effective way. Even today, the interest in the Middle Ages is often triggered through the music-theatrical works of Wagner, which in one way or another are all connected to the Middle Ages, and from *Tannhäuser* onwards, exclusively to the German literature of the Middle Ages. They convey an influential image, against which the parallel to its evolvement, developed specialised humanities, look like pale excavation of facts. Philogical studies and history in their early stages in the 19th century could not defend themselves effectively against Wagner's influence, not only the popularised image of the Middle Ages, but also on the discourse within the disciplines themselves. Wagner's artistic ideas of Minnesang were taken up by the early writings on music history as "sources" and not as what they most certainly are: a fantasy idea of the Middle Ages. The dovetailing of music historiography, contemporary music history and historic imagination in the 19th century is evident here – and the connection is "imagination," a concept which had been introduced to medieval studies in 1978 by George Duby in his *Les Trois Ordres ou l'imaginaire du Féodalisme*. This term is central to the whole rediscovery of medieval music – imagination being related to the dream and stemming from the dialogue between *imaginatio* und *memoria*. Imagination fills the empty position within historic reconstruction.

Again, in the 19th century it was not medieval music itself, be it monophony or polyphony, which was the centre of interest; only about 50 examples were known – and even then only mentioned or published untranscribed in facsimiles, hidden in highly specialised literature and mostly mysterious in their meaning and musical adaptability – far too few to understand the notation and to come to grips with an image of music history from the 8th to the 15th century.[21] It is a fiction without a material base. What was known about the music of the Middle Ages at the end of the 19th century came mainly from medieval treatises on music, the group of theoretical writings that had been systematically collected, edited, and interpreted by Gerbert and Coussemaker. The music itself was still presented in a casual way, as it had been since the 17th century; it was most often looked at at random, as the individual scholar came across a particular manuscript source, almost by chance. It followed that during the Gothic Revival medieval music became something magically "natural" and "harmonic," the embodiment of the real and the truthful. At the same time we observe the increasing importance of the work of the monks of Solesmes and the Cecilian movement, which swept across Europe and reached into the 20th century. And we see the pioneering efforts of a budding musicology, preparing itself to discover a musical world that still lay hidden in the shadows of castle and cathedral.

The 20th century and the developing image of medieval music

Around 1900 there was a breakthrough in musicological medieval studies in Germany and France, and the historic method which had been developed in the 19th century found a fruitful field of application. While in all only about 50 examples of medieval music were known before 1900, the mass of sources now searched for and rediscovered made transcription not as impossible and cryptic anymore, while several people regarding themselves as musicologists entered the stage of the humanities, putting heart and mind into the transcription of medieval music. So notation of polyphonic music from the 12th to the 15th century became understandable and transcription was possible. Sources were discovered by the hundreds, to an extent that had been previously unthinkable. They were copied, studied, transcribed, edited – medieval music developed into an object of study. The interpretation of musical monuments in connection with the theoretical writings, which had been known since the late 18th century, helped people to understand the treatises, and they lead to a coherent concept of medieval music history. The institutionalisation of musicology started with a mass of publications, institutions, *Denkmälerausgaben*, organisations and musicological societies. They carried the discourse on medieval music.

It was now public opinion that helped to construct medieval music history. The zeal with which early medievalists took up their work followed from their pioneering role – which is often described and underlined – but also derived from the public interest in something new. After the world fairs of 1889 and 1900 in Paris, testimonies of foreign, non-European peoples and cultures had been presented to the public, and there was the desire to improve knowledge of the origins of European culture itself – back to the roots. The rediscovery of medieval music in the 20th century is a complex phenomenon. It emerges from several sources: Post-Romanticism and the increasing social and political unrest culminated in World War I and were accompanied by similar unrest and tension in the musical realm, as manifested by various radical experiments. These led to a desire for something "stable," "whole," and "meaningful" – words with which medieval music would soon be described. Wagner's influence and popularity, only hinted at, continued to rise in the 20th century among European musicians and it continued to trigger the interest in the Middle Ages on the level of research and literary imagination. Also, the continuing growth of musical styles that employed significant elements borrowed from national folk idioms had the general effect of opening listeners' ears to all kinds of music. At the same time, the movement of neo-Classicism specifically aimed to incorporate new discoveries from early music into musical styles, which had more or less overt connection with principles, forms, and techniques of the past. This contributed to the study and reconstruction of medieval music. Finally, the early music movement can be seen and studied as a reaction to the twelve-tone approaches of Schönberg, Berg, and Webern, culminating in the desire for more audience-pleasing, eclectic, simpler idioms. The musicological research in the Middle Ages also had the special position within the cultural dialogue as mediatrix. It opened the way for early music, which, in German publications, started to be written as *Alte Musik* from around 1920, with capitalised adjective for with added emphasis, becoming a term in itself. Early music became as exclusive and as geared against the classical-romantic repertoire as the exploding musical avantgarde.

In a special "rezeptionsästhetische Konvergenz" ("convergence of reception") – to use Hans Robert Jauss's concept – in Germany, the interest in medieval research and the Jugendmusikbewegung merged. With the publication of sheet music and the scope for reconstructing medieval music – which was at first thought of as complex music, but was in fact performed more easily than music from the 1920s composed by the musical avantgarde, such as the second Viennese school – the recorder, the main instrument of the Jugendmusikbewegung and charged with special meaning, featured in the realisation of early music. Both interest groups formed their concerts and activities in opposition to what they felt was the pathos of an out-dated ideal of art and artist, seeming even more senseless and empty after World War I, and set out to fight for the authentic old ideal.[22]

Finally, the argumentative arms race must be mentioned, which inflamed the study of medieval music in France and Germany towards the end of the 19th century, and again after the first world war. In France, the focus was exclusively on an archeology of French national music history, especially on the history of the French *chanson*. However for the German-speaking musicologists, the development of a "German music history" was not such a priority, as the 19th century was automatically seen as "the German century." The musical line of Bach-Beethoven-Brahms or Bach-Beethoven-Wagner was seen as an obvious "fact," just as it was normal in music historical literature to speak of the "old German" and "new German" schools, and of national schools. With the talk of "national schools," the "natural state of German music" was retrospectively established. But developing parallel to this continuing feeling was a more urgent search for German identity against the background of the first world war. The longing for German unity from 1871, the demoralisation that followed the first world war, the development of a theory of the racial superiority of the Germans and the mission to spread German culture to all parts of the globe all leave clear traces in the writings of supposedly apolitical music historians. Some musicologists, but not all, react with argumentational patterns idealising German identity, which had been proliferated in the past and outside of musicology – in Nordic legend and art history, for example. The possible extremes are the presentation of alternatives to the existing picture of music history, deliberate internationalisation, or recognition of the massive devaluation of the foreign, which either questions all independent musical developments outside of the German-speaking world, or attributes an influence from German composers, music theorists or musicologists to all developments showing a progressive character.

These factors support, strengthen and justify musicological medieval studies. They facilitate a process of interaction between historic research and musical artistic approaches within academic circles and the interested public. It is the musicology of the "founding-fathers" who prepare the concepts, the sheet-music, and the basic theories for 20th century medievalism in music: for the movement of historical performance practice, for the study of medieval music, and for the stylistic development of 20th century music in giving controlled access to composers who take up the interest in early music.

The first public performance of medieval music occurred in Paris, in 1900, when a little concert – about which we know almost nothing – took place during the meeting of the musicological society of Paris. Twenty years later, a more important concert series in Germany built upon this first modest attempt: between 1922 and 1924, concerts in Karlsruhe and Hamburg presented medieval music to the public. The concert "Music of the Middle Ages in the Hamburg Music Hall" in 1924, for example, was a "systematic presentation" of medieval music. The first evening was dedicated to the Proper of the Mass, to *Gregorian chant*. The choir, invisible to the audience, sang an Easter mass unaccompanied, followed by pieces which included the *Alma redemptoris mater* by the 11th-century Hermannus Contractus (died 1054) and an anonymous 11th-century *Salve regina*. The second evening featured *musica composta*: one could hear organa from the Parisian Notre Dame School, a variety of motets from the Montpellier and Bamberg manuscripts, vocal and instrumental music of the Italian Trecento, and works by Machaut, Dufay, Ockeghem and Josquin. On the third evening, dedicated to *musica*

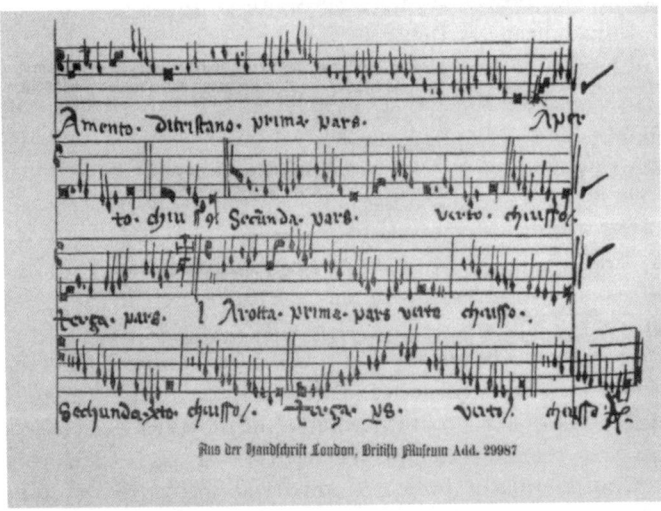

Musik des Mittelalters, Concert Series in Hamburg (1924),
Title page and illustrated page of the programme notes (Sample).

vulgaris, one could hear music by the troubadours and trouvères, instrumental dances, a Spielmannslied, and examples of 14th and 15th century accompanied monody.[23] Although this event could not make medieval music popular, it did help to form a small community of interested *Liebhaber*.

These first performances were made possible through the concerted efforts of medievalists, who dedicated themselves to the rediscovery of medieval music. At the end of the 19th century, scholars such as Peter Wagner, Friedrich Ludwig, Heinrich Besseler, Willibald Gurlitt, Wilhelm Mayer, and Jacques Handschin began to study medieval sources, aided greatly by the secularisation of monastic libraries. Suddenly, sources were more accessible than ever, and this availability coincided with the development of a keen interest. The interest in them made them visible.

These early medievalists, the "founding fathers of modern musicology," paved the way for the rebirth of medieval music. Preparation of monographs on medieval chant, a first modern musicologically systematic work on Gregorian chant,[24] the Editio Vaticana Chant books, the first history of notation – Johannes Wolf's *Geschichte des Mensuralnotation von 1250–1460*[25] – and thousands of transcriptions and editions of medieval modal and mensural music all gave the phantom of medieval music a real face.[26] When Guido Adler's extensive *Handbuch der Musikgeschichte* came out in 1924, the chapters on early music largely exceeded the rest, having by then, at least in theory, somehow reversed certain 20th-century musicological notions about music history. Whereas in 19th-century historiography of music, early music seemed to be a blank, now early music seemed to be the very focus of scholarly interest, exceeding all other areas of music history.[27]

The enthusiasm as well the ideology of these scholars can be felt in their writing: One example from the 1930s may stand for many: It is from Rudolf von Ficker, another early champion of medieval music through his performances, editions and writings. His article "Die Musik des Mittelalters" was written in 1929 and appeared in 1930 in the series *Wissenschaft und Kultur*:

> We are placed now in the time of the crusades, the movement which would shake and reshape the thinking and feeling of the western world. The first crusaders returned, filled with religious zeal, but also with the unimagined wonders of the sensuous oriental world. The fantastical art of the Gothic is the towering symbol of this new, exuberant world-feeling. In the mystical half-light of the roman cathedral the beholder is enveloped by a feeling of a clear, powerful, spatial presence. Massive wall surfaces, barely pierced by little window niches, accost him on all sides with oppressive force. A mood – as mysterious as it is oppressive – makes itself apparent throughout the entire room and communicates itself to the mind of the believer. Totally different is the impression upon entering a gothic cathedral. The massive walls seem to have burst; in its place glows colorful shimmering glass. Slim columns stream from the earth's floor to the heights, at one pull running up to the ribs of the pointed arch, pushing out into seemingly infinite distances. All the burdening aspects of con-

struction have been removed. The whole structure breathes movement . . .

As the enormous moving power of the gothic cathedral structure is the expression of an inner excitement and tension of those people who built these structures, so too is the literature of this time, with the excitement of the crisp metrics of the poet's language, yes even in the rhymed reports of Christian chronicles. In music it is the concept of rhythm, which shows forth and organises the movement's powers. We see therefore, that rhythmic principles rule all the music of the so-called gothic era . . .

It is in the organum of Perotinus that the northern impulse (sic!), to increase enormously the simple meaning of the choral and lift it to gigantic heights, has found its highest fulfillment. For example the short choral phrase of the "descendit de coelis" becomes in its arrangement as an organum an earth-shaking, exalted, and visionary expression: we seem to see, descending slowly from distant heights, the brilliant figure of the Saviour bringing redemption to sinful humanity. This movement grows stronger and stronger, the vision grows clearer, until finally a last stroke declares the beginning of the mysterium of God's own son being manifested in the flesh. And there is nothing more powerful in the whole of music literature, a jubilee going beyond all limits, and these are the Alleluias of this great master from Paris.[28]

The expression "northern impulse" is noteworthy. In Von Ficker's, Ludwig's and Besseler's writings, this term means a contrast of northern or Nordic music history to Mediterranean music history, eventually trying to show the superiority of the former and eliminating the focus on the French origin of the gothic style and of polyphony in music. This ideology, in Besseler's case, helped make him an ardent supporter of Nazi ideology in the following years, as precise as his observation on other kinds of music may be. Also, the concept of "northern music" will lead to the notion of the superiority of counterpoint over homophony, and harmony over melody. The Gothic Revival seems to have continued, on a different level, with different masks and with different results – more hidden, but still tangible.

Adaptation, invention, separation

Medieval music was old and new at the same time, so much so that, in order to be understood, it had to be adapted for the scholar/student and listener of the 20th century. I'd like to present just one example, Rudolf von Ficker's edition of Perotinus's *Sederunt Principes* from the early 12th century. Von

Ficker published his edition in 1929, and made it look not like a piece written more than 700 years ago, but like a piece from the romantic era. This he did by casting it into C minor, and by adding various performance instructions such as "langsam, schwebend," crescendi and decrescendi, and so on. In the introduction, von Ficker explains what was necessary to turn this work into "music." He describes the conflicts between a "critical-scientific" and a "musical-artistic" task, proceeds to offer an arrangement for piano, and at the end submits a scientific transcription with comment – a critical edition. In his text he poses an important question: "How can we today, with entirely different musical conditions, even think of finding an appropriate substitute for those performing institutions which were present 700 years ago?"[29]

At the beginning of his text, von Ficker quotes Goethe – who himself is quoting Aristoxenos: "What good is the string and all its mechanical divisions, compared to the ear of the musician?" By quoting Goethe, that great monument of German literature, he somehow "enlarged" Pérotin, connecting him to a certain mainstream scholarship culminating in the idea of an *Abendland*, this highly ideological term meaning Europe in contrast to the rest of the world, and at the same time bolstering his argument for the importance of medieval music, justifying his own version of *Sederunt principes*, and backing up his own fight for the acceptance of medieval music.

Under the heading "Our changing attitude," one of the most knowledgeable advocates of medieval music, Robert Donington, wrote in 1977 that ". . . it still seemed very necessary . . . to make out a case, and to buttress it with argument and evidence, for interpreting early music on its own merits as mature art: as an art not requiring to be patronisingly adapted to our modern habits of performance; but on the contrary, requiring us a very considerable effort of adaptation in order to avoid the gross inadvertent modernisation which our prevailing habits must otherwise entail."[30]

Donington, who started to study the performance practice of early music in 1948 and published his study in 1963, underlines the necessity of interpreting "early music on its own terms rather than on ours": this was the credo of the early music movement. The intention was "separation," not "adaptation," not adapting or altering the music, but rather broadening our ears.

Regardless of their different approaches to performance practice, the early music makers were united in their effort to represent medieval music first and foremost as historically correctly as possible and, only as a second priority, to have medieval music come *alive* in the ears of the listener. The second point is especially difficult to realise without some kind of adaptation to listening traditions. As Donington put it: "music of whatever generation

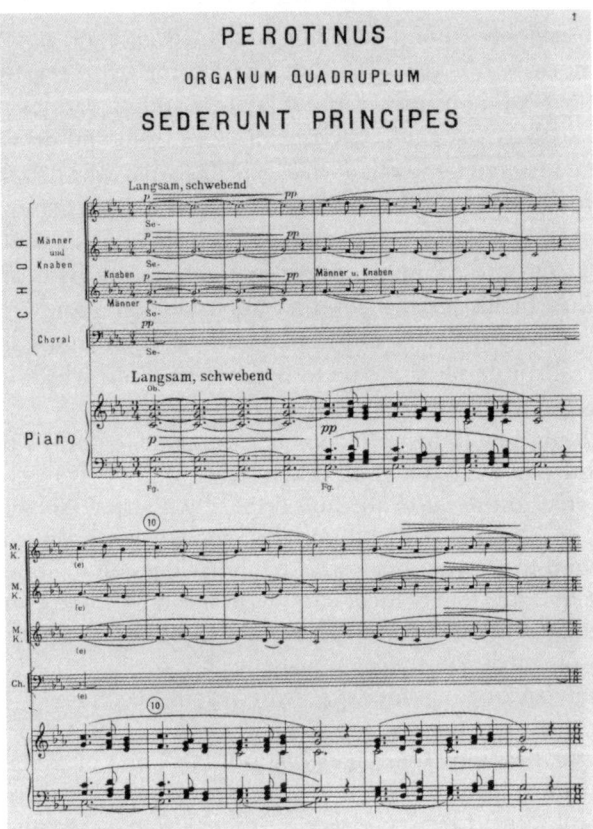

Rudolf von Ficker, *Sederunt Principes* (1929), Beginning

will sound more effective and more moving when we make every reasonable attempt to present it under its original conditions of performance. If we want to share in a composer's experience, we have to carry out his intentions. If we find his experience somewhat strange, we have to remember that it may be more rewarding to come to terms with an unfamiliar experience than to recapitulate a familiar one in a less telling form."[31]

The appearance of the long playing record in 1948 greatly helped the early music movement to find its audience. It fostered the idea – now that recordings could be preserved, like critical editions – of presenting an authentic "soundscape" of the Middle Ages. Here, for example, Safford Cape's interest in historical authenticity coincided with his forming of his *Pro Musica Antiqua* and with Deutsche Grammophone's *Archivproduktion*, designed to preserve those "works whose beauty and vitality can still exert an immediate appeal on the music-lover of the present day," by offering works "in their complete authentic form," and by using "historical instruments, in 'living' interpretations by highly qualified specialist performers."[32] And in order to give this "archival effort" even greater scientific meaning, *Archivproduktion* was subdivided into twelve "research periods," corresponding to the successive phases of musical history: The sounding equivalent of the *Musik in Geschichte und Gegenwart*.

The early music movement gained influence and import from such artists as David Munrow and his *Early Music Consort of London*,[33] as well as Michael Morrow and John Beckett and their the London *Musica Reservata*. In the U.S., the scholar/performer Thomas Binkley organised his *Studio der Frühen Musik* in the late 50s together with Andrea von Ramm; they gave over a hundred concerts a year and recorded many items from the early music repertoire.[34] Soon the publication of specialised Journals would become an integral part of the early music movement,[35] and the first edition of Early Music in 1973 opens with these words:

> Ten years earlier, a journal such as this would have been impossible: there were, at that stage, no early music consorts such as those whose reputation now begins to reverberate beyond these shores. There were relatively few instrument makers, and those interested in early music tended to be divided into members of the various separate societies for recorder, lute or gamba, or were readers of specialist journals. Now all has mysteriously changed. The contents of this first issue make our aims and directions clear. We want those who play or listen to early music to feel that there is an international forum where diverse issues and interests can be debated and discussed. We want to provide a link between the finest scholarship of our day and the amateur and professional listener and performer.[36]

In 1981, again in England, *Early Music History* was founded and edited by Ian Fenlon and published by Cambridge University Press, adding to *Early Music*'s approach to fostering and promoting research on medieval, renaissance, and baroque music.[37] These are but a few of the most prominent examples of writing about medieval music. Another important one is *Plainsong and Medieval Music*, a magazine founded in 1992 and currently edited by John Caldwell and Christopher Page.[38]

This separation of early music from the rest of music history introduced a new and different meaning of "separation," which kept medieval music from entering the canon of concert repertoire. For this, I see essentially two reasons: the early music movement argued that the conditions for performance of medieval music are so different from those of the 19th-century orchestra and choir – on which our concert life still depends – that its integration into the canon would be impossible even if it were desired. Secondly, the separation of medieval music has been so successful that the desire to adapt it to the classical concert repertoire is simply non-existent.

Dreaming and Othering the Middle Ages

In 1988, the German label ECM, guided by its well-known producer Manfred Eicher, brought out a CD featuring the music of Perotinus as performed by the Hilliard Ensemble, a group specialising in early music. The novel sound of this recording is due not only to a different technical approach to sound itself, but also to an innovative handling of "musica ficta"[39] and an entirely new approach to medieval music.[40]

One of the pieces presented is again the organum *Sederunt Principes*, and for his recording, Paul Hillier has chosen to omit the B-flat at the end of the very first melodic phrase. The evidence from the manuscripts is questionable, but I would argue that Hillier's reason has not so much to do with the manuscript evidence as with the strongly archaic feeling that is produced when the upper leading tone is omitted.

This supposition is supported by Paul Hillier's introductory text to the CD.[41] Starting with a quotation from Alexandra David-Neel's *Tibetan Journey*, which says that "each atom perpetually sings its song, and the sound, at every moment, creates dense and subtle forms," Hillier goes on to describe the long journey that is required to actually hear Perotinus' music. After a description, he compares it to 20th-century minimalist music and says: "Pérotin speaks to the 20th-century listener quite naturally as a composer of minimalist music, nor is he alone in this amongst the composers of both the Ars Antiqua and the Ars Nova. The concept of minimalism is of course a modern phenomenon"; but "the attitudes and purposes that stimulate minimalism (in its various guises) occur frequently throughout history and in both Western and non-Western cultures."[42] The association with minimalist music is especially interesting here because Steve Reich, one of the fathers of minimalism, had earlier recorded his "Music for 18 Musicians" for the same label, ECM. ECM is mainly known for its fine recordings of Meredith Monk, John Adams, European Jazz, and world music. As John Levin recently noted, "the early music of the Hilliard Ensemble seems a logical extension of the ECM catalogue – a music of emotion and integrity suffused with an underlying sense of tonality."[43]

Comparing a recording like "Perotin" by the Hilliard Ensemble with the early approaches to medieval music, one sees that medievalism has traveled a long road. But there are also many threads which can be shown in detail when looking at strategies of argumentation or concepts for concerts and performances. The idea, for example, to present medieval music together with other kinds of music, to mix it with other styles, to present medieval music within art galleries or churches with medieval art, is as fashionable as it had been already in the first half of the 20th century. And what about the mix? Medieval music still avantgarde? Or mainstream?

In a concert that took place in July 1995, the Hilliard Ensemble and Jan Gabarek performed most of the pieces of the "Officium" CD in a tour leading them through all the important concert halls and churches of Europe. The concert I attended took place in Hamburg, in the main church of St. Michael's, which was filled with mostly young people, holding hands and full of excitement, as if some popular music idol were about to appear. There was a feeling of expectancy in the air, very different from the "feel" of the traditional early music concert. It was not a scholarly expectancy, the expectancy to *learn* something, but rather a sensuous expectancy, the expectancy to *experience* something. Nobody noticed that the pieces were not performed in the order of their appearance on the program. This simply did not matter. What mattered was sound. The performers themselves, wearing black trousers and brightly colored shirts, were scattered across the church. One by one they stood up and walked and sang their way across the church, down from the balcony, towards the altar, with their heads bent like monks who were absorbed in some kind of secret vision.

The concert, like the recording, was somewhere between the secular and the sacred. It was a kind of religious experience, but one that permitted either participation or uninvolved observation. As Katherine Bergeron has written of a similar occasion, "This was a concert that treated the church as a meaningful, functional space, rather than ignoring its meaning. This concert presented a virtual liturgy. It is the condition of being between two realities, both of which are offered and both of which are denied, that creates the desired effect of this music." Bergeron goes on to argue that her concert, like the one I am describing, strained the limits "of 'authenticity' at the same time that it opened a new arena on which the 'authentic' might be reimagined: in the virtual space of a neither/nor."[44] In thinking about "my" concert, I wondered, why the "in-between" could be so attractive, since both the following realities were indeed denied: (1) The musical reality, which could provide a maximum of penetration and musical experience, and (2) the religious reality, which could provide a maximum of realisation and enlightenment. John Potter, the Hilliard Ensemble's tenor, alludes to this mixture of musical and religious experience, perhaps unwittingly, when he describes the recording experience as being "shut away (sic!) in the monastery of St. Gerold," where "the saxophone became an extension of our own voices."[45]

The interest in the Middle Ages suggests a desire for meaning, for purpose, for renewed guidance and worth. What has fueled this interest is not the feudal political system of the Middle Ages nor its lack of everything that would later be regained in the Renaissance, but rather more general notions about the Middle Ages, squeezing with the framework of inventive reception hundreds of medieval years together to a few stereo- types, of which I might enumerate four in particular: The Middle Ages serve us as a reservoir for emotions and feelings; they are regarded as the era of the witch and the wizard, the knight and the princess, a magic kingdom of secret knowledge and secret understanding and secret wisdom of a sort which the men of the Renaissance, the enlightenment, the industrial era, and the 20th Century, have lost. One can enter into this "kingdom" not by research or knowledge, but only by *feeling*; they are perceived to be a time when man was in harmony with the universe, dedicating his thoughts and feelings, the rational and the sensual, to *one* centre of supremacy. It is perceived to be time without time, an era in which the narration of its own historicity (unlike the self-conscious eras of antiquity and the renaissance) was stopped. Thinking about the Middle Ages, listening to medieval music, pondering medieval issues thus presents not a loss but rather a gain of time, of timeless possibilities, an encounter with "timelessness," an exploration of "eternity"; finally the Middle Ages are looked upon by composers of the 20th century (whom I have not mentioned here for reasons of space) as a desirable musical period *before* major-minor tonality, *before* the bar line, before "four-four time." The impact of the discovery of medieval music on composers like Stravinsky Krenek, Hindemith, Nono, Ligeti and many others has been profound.

As in the Gothic Revival, where medieval music was regarded as something wonderfully natural and innocent, this notion persisted somehow in the writings of the first medievalists of the 20th century, tainted, as had been the romantic Gothic Revival as a whole, with nationalist feelings. The current revival of medieval music for meditative purposes depends upon the construction of the Middle Ages as a desired *beyond* or *other* before our eyes. One can even go as far as to say that the Middle Ages seem to occupy a space formerly reserved for concepts of a *Jenseits* (a world beyond). When people developed concepts such as heaven and hell to shape their present, there can be suggested a "virtual" beyond, creating for ourselves the vivid image of a lost world, which in turn has started to shape our present. It is in this sense that the Middle Ages have become postmodern. Their strangeness and diversity can be both puzzling and frightening. To accept strangeness seems extremely difficult, especially in the postmodern era, which tries to incorporate everything into itself without realising its constructive nature, while sometimes playfully displaying a deepening consciousness of itself, being increasingly able to differentiate between the many levels of adaption and separation.[46]

So medieval music, which does not exist without us, is a dramatic way of Othering the Middle Ages, and it can be applied what the musicologist Leo Treitler has described in another context: "What we regard as the opposite traits of the Other show through as the trait of a surrogate, underground – we may as well say unconscious – Self. The Other is, in effect, a projection of the Self, or rather of an unacknowledged aspect of the Self that is suppressed as unacceptable to that identity that is the speaker for the Self."[47]

The desire for "historical authenticity" has been uncovered as a paradigm of positivist scholarship and performance theory. On the other hand, "historical authenticity" has not been replaced by a new paradigm, being lost in a postmodern notion of subjectivity,[48] in a play with isolated elements, in the indeterminacy of the common. Leo Treitler's question, "Are we content to yield the decisions about what is interesting and beautiful and the formulation of our discourses about those things to the dynamics of commerce, technology, and politics?" is an important one to ask.[49] Yet whole cultures, unlike individuals, are generally reluctant to absorb normative forces. The paradigm of "historical authenticity," once recognised as such, will lose nothing of its savor but rather gain in momentum. And the criteria, which we cannot borrow from another epoch, and which are not necessarily coined by the dynamics of commerce, technology, and politics, will be regarded as temporary tools, to be overthrown by better tools.

The rediscovering of medieval music is as much a fascinating invention as a creative reconstruction. Both trends, namely the trend to completely avoid "music itself" (= the hermeneutic notion of music as text only) and the trend to completely avoid "historicity itself" (= the esoteric notion of music as feeling only) will be prevalent until some new, *post-postmodern paradigm* of scholarship and performance practice comes to the fore. In any case, it is important to uncover the premises on which images of medieval music – be they scholarly and written, artistic and written, scholarly and sounding or artistic and sounding – are built, in order to see the dependence of writing and thinking about medieval music on historic models, to start a rethinking of the tidal wave of medieval sounds in the late 20th and early 21st century, and to ask for their reasons. This should be the aim and we should continue the discourse on medieval music.[50] For nothing else is writing about medieval music. Less we cannot hope for and more we should not expect.

NOTES

1. The long history is: Annette Kreutziger-Herr, *Ein Traum vom Mittelalter: Die Wiederentdeckung mittelalterlicher Musik in der Neuzeit* [Dreaming the Middle Ages. The Rediscovery of Medieval Music in Modernity] (Cologne/Weimar: Böhlau Verlag, 2003). The endnotes of this article are relating only to primary sources or direct quotes. The study contains in an appendix an extensive lists documenting a complete overview of literature on medievalism in music, documenting the reception of the music by Guillaume de Machaut (from 1800–1899 and 1900–1957), a documentation of the early concert programmes presenting medieval music to the public since the 19th century until 1927, an index of names and subjects as well as fifty-one images, photographs and facsimiles.

2. Victor Hugo, *The Hunchback of Notre-Dame*, Third Book: A bird's eye view of Paris (London: 1996).

3. Compare Kathleen Biddick, *The Shock of Medievalism* (Durham/ London: Duke University Press, 1998) and Annette Kreutziger-Herr, "Postmodern Middle Ages: Medieval Music at the Dawn of the Twenty-First Century," in the Canadian Society of Medievalists, ed., *Florilegium* 15 (1998): 187–205.

4. Johann Wolfgang von Goethe, "Von deutscher Baukunst," in *Johann Wolfgang von Goethe: Werke* (= Hamburger Ausgabe in 14 Bänden, ed. by Erich Trunz), vol. 12: *Schriften zur Kunst* (Munich: Beck, 1998), pp. 7–15.

5. To name just a few: William Warburton: "An Epistle to Lord Burlington," in Alexander Pope, *Collected Works*, Vol. 3, William Warburton, ed. (London: 1751); James Hall, *Essays on the Origins, History and Principles of Gothic Architecture* (London: 1813); Friedrich Schlegel, "Grundzüge der gothischen Baukunst," in *Friedrich von Schlegel: Kritische Ausgabe sämtlicher Werke*, vol. 4, *Ansichten und Ideen von der christlichen Kunst*, Ernst Behler, ed. (Munich: 1958), p. 179 ff.

6. Charles du Fresne, Sieur Du Cange, *Glossarium ad scriptores mediae et infimae latinitatis . . .* (Paris ca. 1650 – the work was published many times). See also Tibor Kneif, 'Zur Entwicklung der musikalischen Mediävistik' (Göttingen 1963: unpublished Ph.D. thesis), 19–20.

7. Carpentier, *Glossarium novum ad scriptores mediae et infimae latinitatis* (Paris: 1766).

8. For collections of medieval treatises see for example the collections of Ursin Durand and Dom Edmond Martène, which included the 9th-century treatise *Musica disiplina* by Aurelianus Reomensis, now GS I, 27–63; for an early history of music see Pierre Bonnet-Bourdelot's *Histoire de la musique et de ses effets, depuis son orignie jusquà présent* (Paris: 1715); Martin Gerbert, *De cantu et musica sacra a prima ecclesiae aetate usque ad presens tempus* (St. Blasien im Schwarzwald: 1774).

9. Charles Burney, *A General History of Music from the Earliest Ages to the Present Period*, vol. 1 (London: 1776).

10. Charles Burney, *A General History of Music from the Earliest Ages to the Present Period*, vol. 2 (London: 1782), p. 67.

11. Burney, *General History* (1782), p. 41.

12. Burney, *General History* (1782), p. 173.

13. Kiesewetter and Fétis differ fundamentally on many points, though, including the worth of individual medieval genres such as the organum or the chansons for three voices by Adam de la Halle. Whereas for example Kiesewetter and Coussemaker describe these chansons as "clumsy and unbearable," Fétis finds them very important ("bien supérieures à l'état des connaissances indiqué dans les écrits de Francon"). See Fétis, *Histoire générale de la musique*, vol. 5 (Paris: 1876), 25–63; 265–82. How little of medieval music was widely known in the first half of the 19th century is evident in this: In 1822 Adam de la Halle's "Li gieus de Robin et Marion" was printed after the Paris sources for the Société des Bibliophiles de Paris in 25 copies, the only edition available at that time.

14. To name the romanticists Novalis, Ludwig Tieck and Wilhelm Heinrich Wackenroder and the later reception of their writings after the French/German war in 1870–71 and in the Weimarer Republic as well as the Nazi time.

15. See for example Johann Nicolaus Forkel, *Allgemeine Geschichte der Musik*, *Bd.II* (Leipzig: 1801); Drittes Kapitel: "Von Guido bis auf den Franchinus Gasor," *Erster Abschnitt*, §1–§39.

16. Katherine Bergeron, "A Lifetime of Chants," in Katherine Bergeron and Philip V. Bohlmann, ed., *Disciplining Music: Musicology and Its Canons* (Chicago/London: University of Chicago Press, 1995), 182–96, and Katherine Bergeron, *Decadent Enchantments: The Revival of Gregorian Chant at Solesmes* (Berkeley/Los Angeles/London: University of California Press, 1998).

17. Carl von Winterfeld, *Music of Gabrieli and his Time* (Ossining, NY: W. Salloch, 1960; Engl. translation of *Johannes Gabrieli und sein Zeitalter* (Breslau 1834), Introduction.

18. Karl Hampe, *Das Hochmittelalter: Geschichte des Abendlandes von 900–1250*, 4th edn. (Munster: Böhlau Verlag, 1953), 236.

19. Compare François-Joseph Fétis, *Esquisse de l'Histoire de l'Harmonie*, Engl. translation by Mary I. Arlin, Harmonologia Series No. 7 (New York: Stuyvesant, 1994), 4–5. For more information see John Stevens, "The Manuscript Presentation and Notation of Adam de la Halle's Courtly Chansons," in Ian Bent, ed., *Source materials and the interpretation of music. A memorial volume to Thurston Dart* (London: Stainer and Bell, 1981), 29–64.

20. Both at Staatsbibliothek zu Berlin – Preussischer Kulturbesitz.

21. See the appendix of Kreutziger-Herr, Traum.

22. Ib. The first Jugendmusikschule was founded in 1923 in Berlin.

23. See Heinrich Besseler, "Musik des Mittelalters in der Hamburger Musikhalle. 1.–8. April 1924," in *Zeitschrift für Musikwissenschaft* 7 (Oct. 1924–Sept., 1925), 42–54.

24. Peter J. Wagner, *Einführung in die gregorianischen Melodien: Ein Handbuch der Choralwissenschaft* (Freiburg, 1895), Engl. translation: Introduction to the Gregorian melodies, A Handbook of Plainsong (London: The Plainsong and Medieval Society, 1901).

25. Johannes Wolf, *Geschichte der Mensuralnotation von 1250 bis 1460* (Leipzig: 1904).

26. Friedrich Ludwig (1872–1930) made available all the important 13th-century sources of central polyphony, perhaps the most important achievement

made by one man in the study of medieval music. His catalogue of literally thousands of pieces is hard to appreciate in an age where the microfilm or the computer data-base have replaced the manuscript, but it laid the very foundation of the contemporary study of medieval sources.

27. For an overview see also Howard Mayer Brown, "Pedantry or Liberation? A sketch of the Historical Performance Movement," in Nicholas Kenyon, ed., *Authenticity and Early Music. A Symposium*, second edition (Oxford/New York: Oxford University Press, 1989), 27–56.

28. Rudolf von Ficker, "Die Musik des Mittelalters," in *Das Mittelalter in Einzeldarstellungen* (= Wissenschaft und Kultur, Bd.III) (Leipzig/Vienna, 1930), 113–14. The northern impulse, von Ficker talks about, reveals in addition to his amazement and wonder a more or less conscious nationalist trend. Von Ficker and Besseler speak often about "the northern impulse" and connect this term to "form" and "spirit," in contrast to "melody" and "the senses." See also Leo Treitler, "The Politics of Reception: Tailoring the Present as Fulfillment of a Desired Past," *Journal of the Royal Musical Association* 116, Part 2 (1991): 280–98.

29. Rudolf von Ficker, *Introduction to "Perotinus. Organum Quadruplum. Sederunt Principes"* (= *Musik der Gotik*), Klavierauszug mit Text und kritischer Übertragung (Vienna/Leipzig: Universal-Edition, 1930). Paul Hindemith, while working with the Collegium Musicum at Yale University presented also an interesting version of Sederunt Principes. See Andreas Traub, "Eine Perotin-Bearbeitung Hindemiths," *Hindemith-Jahrbuch 1994/XXIII* (Mainz/London/ Madrid: 1994), 30–60.

30. Robert Donington, *The Interpretation of Early Music: New Version* (London: Faber and Faber, 1977), 27–28. The earliest, and most important book on performance practice came out in 1916: Arnold Dolmetsch, *The Interpretation of the Music of the XVII and XVIII Centuries, revealed by Contemporary Evidence* (London: Novello and Company and Oxford University Press, 1916). Dolmetsch remarks, p. v: "For nine hundred years notation has progressed, and still it is far from perfect. We are not often conscious of this with regard to modern music, for most of what we wish to play is already known to us from previous hearing . . ." Thurston Dart in his famous study even notes: "The present-day performance of music written between 110 and 1500 presents the students of interpretation with immense problems, many of which will probably never be solved." Thurston Dart, *The Interpretation of Music* (New York/ Toronto/Melbourne: Hutchinson's University Library, 1954), 150.

31. Dart, *Interpretation*, 88.

32. Index-Card in "The Central Middle Ages: Ecole de Notre Dame," Pro Musica Antiqua, Safford Cape, rec. July 1956 (= Archive Production ARC 3051–14068 APM).

33. To be followed later after David Munrow's early death by The Medieval Ensemble of London.

34. Binkley died in the summer of 1995 and David Fallows honoured him in a memorial, noting that the Studio der Frühen Musik always performed from memory: "no music was ever allowed on the concert platform, and pieces rather evolved in the course of a tour, so that when it came to record them they existed in a

version that had little to do with anything on the page. This was of course in line with the nature of most medieval sources: the music varies from manuscript to manuscript." David Fallows, "Thomas Binkley, 1931–1995," in *Early Music* 22 (August 1995): 538.

35. Journals on Medieval Studies were founded much earlier, like for example *Speculum, A Journal of Medieval Studies*, published by the Medieval Academy of America since 1925.

36. J. M. Thomson, "Preface," in *Early Music*, vol. I, no. 1, Oxford, January 1973, 1.

37. Ian Fenlon, "Preface," in *Early Music History: Studies in Medieval and Early Modern Music*, vol. I (Cambridge: Cambridge University Press, 1981), vii. Interestingly enough, Fenlon would comment on the vivid discussions about early music itself and how they shaped musicology as a discipline: "Early Music History exists to stimulate further exploration of familiar phenomena through unfamiliar means, and to add to the growing appreciation of the value of interdisciplinary approaches and their potentialities. Another emphasis might be called the contextual. At present some music historians tend to concentrate on the internal analysis of a composition and its relation to a specific and usually narrowly defined historical frame. Indeed, much musicological writing presents by implication a formidable orthodoxy in which history is perceived as a succession of paradigms of musical language, style, and form. Some recent work has attempted explanation through exploration of a wider range of evidence, and Early Music History intends to strengthen this trend by encouraging studies that examine the economic, political and social ramifications of research. In that musicology itself can only benefit if its vision is extended and its methods refined and broadened, the board believes that Early Music History will mark a new departure in the development of the discipline while continuing to support its traditional tasks."

38. *Plainsong and Medieval Music*, vol. I, no. 1 (Cambridge: 1992). This publication succeeds the *Journal of the Members of the English Plainsong and Medieval Music Society*.

39. See Ethel Thurston, *The Works of Perotin. Music and Texts transcribed with explanatory preface and performance directions* (New York: Edwin F. Kalmus, 1970), 133.

40. Sederunt Principes may be found in the manuscript Wolfenbüttel 677 (= W 1); it may also be found in the manuscript Medicea-Laurenzia Plut. 29/1 (F), in the manuscript Wolfbüttel 1206 (W2) and in the manuscript Bibliotheca Nacional Madrid Hh 167 (M). The version in W2 is incomplete, as is that of M, but M also gives a troped version of the organum.

41. Perotin, *The Hilliard Ensemble* (= ECM New Series 1385 78118–21385–2), Munich 1988. Introduction "Perotin" by Paul Hillier.

42. Introduction to Perotin, *Hilliard Ensemble*.

43. John Levin, "Sax and Polyphony," in *RhythmMusic Magazine*, vol. 4, no. 2 (1995), 19.

44. Katherine Bergeron, "Finding God at Tower Records: The virtual sacred," *The New Republic*, February 27 (1995). See also Katherine Bergeron, "A Lifetime of Chants," in Katherine Bergeron and Philip V. Bohlman, ed., *Disciplining music*.

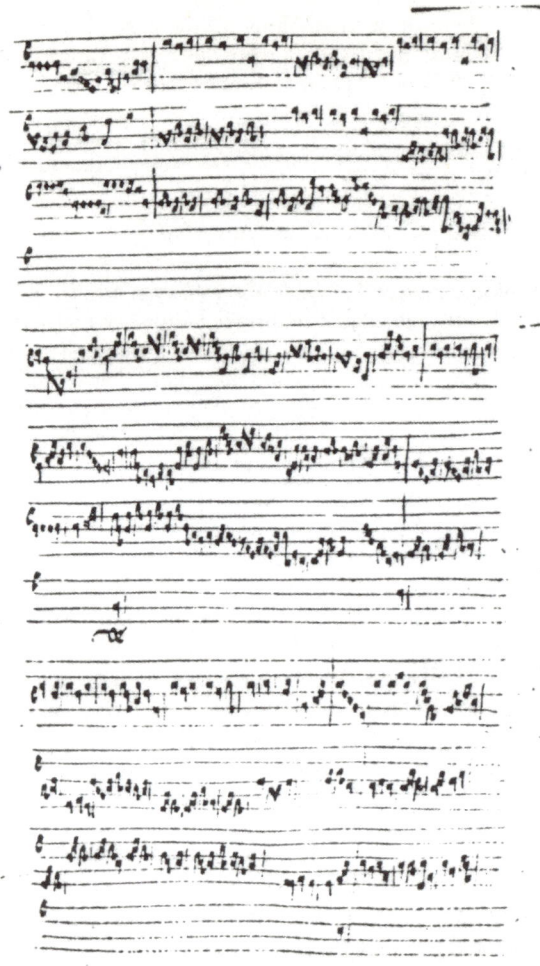

Excerpt from *Wolfenbüttel 617*, Sederunt Principes (Sample)

Musicology and its Canons (Chicago/London: University of Chicago Press, 1992), 182–96.

45. Jan Gabarek/The Hilliard Ensemble, *Officium* (= EM New Series 1525 78118–21525–2) (Munich, 1994).

46. Even if many critics of modernity would argue that probably the time for criteria has passed, pushing indeterminacy to its extremes, there are others, like Jürgen Habermas, pushing the Enlightenment further and arguing, that the defects of Enlightenment can only be made good by further enlightenment, not by the relinquishment of reason and judgement. "Modernity can and will no longer borrow the criteria by which it takes its orientation from the models supplied by another

epoch; it has to create its normativity out of itself," argues Habermas in his philosophical discourse "Modernity's Consciousness of time." See Jürgen Habermas, *The philosophical Discourse of Modernity: Twelve Lectures* (Cambridge MA: The MIT Press, 1987), 7; and Thomas McCarthy's introduction, xvii.

47. Treitler, "Politics," 290.

48. A different notion than Hegel's critique of "the higher criticism": "This higher criticism has been the pretext for introducing all the un-historical monstrosities a vain imagination could suggest. It too is a method of bringing the present into the past, namely by substituting subjective fancies for historical data – fancies which are considered the more excellent the bolder they are . . ." G. W. F. Hegel, *Lectures on the Philosophy of World History*, trans. H. B. Nisbet (Cambridge: Cambridge University Press, 1975), 23.

49. Leo Treitler, "Postmodern Signs in Musical Studies," *Journal of Musicology*, 13 (1) (1995): 3–17 (10).

50. I would like to thank Kerry Jago for editing my manuscript and Daniel Leech-Wilkinson for active academic exchange. His study *The Modern Invention of Medieval Music: Scholarship, Ideology, Performance* (Cambridge: Cambridge University Press, 2002) complements mine for the chapters focusing on the 20th century. I would also like to thank Dorette Kreutziger and Klaus-Hendrik Herr for unceasing interest and innumerable kindnesses.

The Medievalism of Carl Maria von Weber's *Euryanthe*[1]

Nils Holger Petersen

Introduction: Music and Romanticism

The German composer Carl Maria von Weber (1786–1826) is one of the most important figures associated with the beginnings of German musical romanticism, and the most famous of his operas, *Der Freischütz* (1821), is generally considered to constitute a new (and essentially romantic) departure in operatic history.[2] It is true that the concept of musical romanticism – and of romanticism in general – seems difficult to define and its usefulness is not entirely clear either. The notion, on the other hand, seems unavoidable because of its pervasive popular and scholarly use. A common approach in music history has been criticised as based on outdated literary scholarship by Edward Kravitt, who refers to generalised statements which describe romantic music through "separate, isolated, and often unrelated attributes, for example, interest in nature, medieval chivalry, mysticism, remoteness, and many others . . . ." Evoking the literary scholarship of M. H. Abrams, Kravitt proposes to understand musical romanticism rather through the idea of "the artist's estrangement from society and consequent reaction: to turn within."[3] Another music historian, Arnold Whittall, has wanted to avoid a definition of the notion. Taking his cue from Gustav Mahler's somewhat surprising endorsement of a dictum by Goethe, "What is Classical I call healthy, what is Romantic sick," Whittal intends "to describe and celebrate the diversity of Romantic music; not . . . to impose a convenient but artificial unity on it."[4] This point of view to a certain extent corresponds to what was characterised (by Kravitt) as the old definition of romanticism in highlighting various important characteristics of music pieces usually understood as "romantic" rather than understanding the concept in a broader way. Among the characteristics emphasised by Whittal are increasing chromaticism in spite of remaining tonality, irregularities of phrase structure, and a growing amount of extra-musical inspiration. He does, however, also point to the more general aspirations towards the "sublime" and the "infinite" as suggested by the writings of – among other literary figures – E. T. A. Hoffmann although he concludes his general discussion of the term romanticism in the following statement: "musical Romanticism is probably still best defined indirectly, through description and interpretation of particular compositions."[5] Carl Dahlhaus has also emphasised the difficulty in defining criteria for describing works as romantic or pre-romantic.[6] On the other hand, he has pointed to one major paradigmatic aspect of (especially) German musical romanticism: the development of the idea of absolute music.[7]

Around 1800, music attracted much attention from (so-called early romantic) writers and "critics." As Hans Lund, especially concerned with the relationship between "the arts," has pointed out, this does not mean that literature after 1770 oriented itself towards music in contrast to an earlier orientation towards the visual arts. According to Lund there was a clear continuity between the periods and the increased musical interest did not result in a decrease – but rather in a different understanding – of the significance of visual art in nineteenth-century literature.[8] Still, music was given a new status as the most "romantic" art in the early nineteenth century. The well-known statement by E. T. A. Hoffmann (1776–1822) that Beethoven was a purely romantic composer and consequently a truly musical composer may be taken as programmatic. Hoffmann distinguished between the truly musical [*das eigentlich Musikalische*] – anticipating the term "absolute music" (coined much later by Richard Wagner) – and the plastic or sculptural [*das Plastische*] in music (closer to program music) expressive of for instance particular (extra musical) feelings or even of a story.[9] The focal point for Hoffmann's (and other early romantic writers') idea of "the truly musical" was instrumental music – as for instance marked through his interest in Beethoven's symphonies. He found the "infinite longing" [*unendliche Sehnsucht*] constituting the "essence of romanticism" [*das Wesen der Romantik*] rather in Beethoven's instrumental music than in his vocal works.[10]

Both as a composer and performer, Weber's main interest was opera. The medieval setting of his opera *Euryanthe* (1823), composed to a libretto by Helmina von Chézy (1783–1856), and the use of the supernatural in the course of the action point to generally acknowledged "romantic" and medievalistic literary characteristics of this work. This opera is an early (though by no means the earliest) example of explicit medievalism in romantic opera. Weber's first succesful opera *Silvana* (1810) – to some (unknown) extent a mature recomposition of his early *Das Waldmädchen* (1800) – was set in the Middle Ages. A major early romantic opera is *Faust*

(1815) by Louis Spohr (1784–1859) which was conducted by Weber at its première in Prague. Also Franz Schubert's "Singspiel," *Des Teufels Lustschloss* (1815) and his opera *Alfons und Estrella* (1822), which antedates *Euryanthe* by only a year in being the first German romantic through-composed opera, are set in the Middle Ages. *Tancredi* (1813) and *Armida* (1817) by Gioachino Rossini (1792–1868) are set during the Crusades in the eleventh century (being, of course, very different from typical romantic operas). E. T. A. Hoffmann's opera *Undine* composed in 1816 to a libretto by Friedrich de la Motte Fouqué based on the latter's *Undine* (1811) does not have a very precise setting, but clearly suggests a medieval scenery around one of the protagonists, the knight Huldbrand. Weber reviewed the *Undine* very positively in the *Allgemeine Musikalische Zeitung* in 1817 after its première stating some of his own positions on operas.

The transition from the Enlightenment to early Romanticism was a gradual one, and the romantic fascination of the "age of chivalry" was anticipated in a number of operas from the end of the eighteenth century, among them *Richard coeur-de-lion* (1784) and *Guillaume Tell* (1791) by André-Ernest-Modeste Grétry (1741–1813), *Mélidore et Phrosine* (1794), *Ariodant* (1799), and *Ossian* (1804) by Jean Francois Le Sueur (1760–1837), *Uthal* (1806) by Étienne-Nicolas Méhul (1763–1817), and also – with the same interest in the Ossianic epic – the German *Colmal* (1809) by Peter Winter (1754–1825). Almost since the beginning of the history of the opera, themes and plots from medieval literature have been common (as can be seen in any handbook of opera history). At the end of the eighteenth and the beginning of the nineteenth centuries, medieval settings of operas stand out in new ways, in – for instance – the mentioned operas.[11] This period, of course, is a traditional main period for the study of medievalism, a concept which to some extent even has been identified with the notions of pre-romanticism and romanticism.[12]

The fascination with the Middle Ages in early nineteenth-century operas, however, has not generally received much attention in spite of the amount of such works even including, as mentioned, operas by Schubert whose last completed work in this genre, *Fierrabras* (1823) to a libretto by Josef Kupelwieser (1791–1862), was set in the time of Charlemagne and (among other sources) based on a *chanson de geste* from the twelfth century. Domenico Barbaja, the (Italian) director of the Kärntnertortheater (the court opera) since December 1821 had approached some German composers (among them Weber) in November of that year suggesting that they should write German operas for his theatre; a commission for *Euryanthe* was one result of this.[13] For Schubert a less formal contact resulted in *Fierrabras* which, however, in the end was rejected and not performed during Schubert's lifetime.[14] Schubert's operas,

Weber's *Euryanthe*, Schumann's *Genoveva* (1848) and other medievalist operas of the first half of the century have never been able to attract the amount of attention which the operas of Richard Wagner (and also Verdi's operas) from later in the century received.[15] The preoccupation with the Middle Ages in early operas of the century has also sometimes been dismissed as a question of a kind of local colour. This is the case, for instance, when Michael C. Tusa comments on the medievality of *Euryanthe*. He discusses to which degree the music of Weber seeks to portray the twelfth-century milieu of the opera and concludes that it only does so to a very small degree:

> *Euryanthe* makes few if any direct or obvious allusions to the music of the European Middle Ages, at least none that would be recognised as such by a twentieth-century listener with even a passing acquaintance with medieval music. Admittedly, practically nothing was known about medieval music during the early nineteenth century, and thus a composer like Weber would have had few sources to which to turn for "authentic" melodies. But neither does the opera strive at self-conscious archaisms to suggest the Middle Ages, as Grétry had done in *Richard cœur-de-lion*. The one musical feature in *Euryanthe* that perhaps betrays an obvious attempt at medieval colour is the conspicuous use of the zither as a stage prop in the first act . . .[16]

However, Tusa also comments on the fact that *Euryanthe* was received by contemporary critics as a medieval opera. In this connection he quotes a number of statements about the succes of Weber in his "faithful interpretation of the time and the place in which the event occurs," to cite only one.[17] This gives him the opportunity to characterise the poetic image of the Middle Ages of these writers as well as of Weber himself:

> However, these writers were probably responding less to concrete details of compositional technique and "authentic" medievalism than to their own poetic image of the Middle Ages, one rooted in the romantic literature of the day, that pictured the European Middle Ages as an "age of chivalry" replete with court pageant, solemn oath-taking, and trial-by-combat, in which duty and honour were more important than life itself, in which warriors were also sensitive poet-musicians and graceful dancers, in which conduct was guided by a refined code of etiquette and morality, in which women were placed upon a pedestal as objects of love and admiration and at the same time held to a severely strict code of fidelity and chastity, and in which the supernatural still

communicated with the living world. Presumably Weber shared this image as well, for he had, after all, selected the story and moulded a libretto that embodied all of these "romantic" clichés about the Middle Ages . . ."[18]

Tusa refrains from seeking for further traces of musical medievalism as Weber in this opera concentrated on the expression of human passion as "his ambition to conquer 'grand opera', the acme of operatic genres, brought with it notions about elevation and severity of style that not even a 'grand romantic opera' could violate."[19] Tusa refers in particular to a well-known statement of Weber in a letter to Franz Danzi (1 March, 1824) who was planning to perform *Euryanthe* in Karlsruhe:

> The care which you dedicate to my *Euryanthe* is a new proof for me of your friendship. Indeed, I need the true care of my friends for this opera since it has a precarious place in the world. The expectations of the masses were stirred up beyond reason through the miraculous success of the *Freischütz*; and now appears the simple, serious work, that seeks nothing but truth of expression, passion and characterisation, and dispenses with all of the manifold variety and stimulants of its predecessor. – Now, as God wishes![20]

Though it is not explicitly stated, in this statement (and other similar ones) Tusa seems to see a negation of the significance of the medievality of Weber's opera. If, however, one does not take the interest in the Middle Ages of the early romantics seriously, it becomes difficult to understand the continuity of medievalism, an important factor in European and American culture in enormously varied manifestations to this day.[21] In view of decades of studies of medievalism within all kinds of media, it seems evident that also the medievalism of *Euryanthe* must be taken seriously. I will argue that the means which Weber used in his music drama to represent the medieval setting also form a significant part of this. Since Weber never gave any clue as to the significance of the narrative to him,[22] except what can be deduced from the opera itself, the medievality of the opera must be approached as a "reading," i.e. as a modern interpretation. To be sure, Tusa is probably correct in believing that Weber (and Chézy) most likely had a rather vague poetic image of the "historical" Middle Ages. This, however, does not necessarily preclude the significance of the way the medieval narrative was represented in *Euryanthe*. In the following section the literary reception will be dealt with, after which I will discuss the musical representation of some main dramatic points.

The Literary Reception Behind Euryanthe

Weber composed *Euryanthe* between 1821 and 1823. In spite of its limited success *Euryanthe* has been recognised as a breakthrough for German opera and as an important step on the way to the music dramas of Richard Wagner.[23] *Euryanthe* seems to have been fairly well received at the première, enthusiasm was mixed with more critical voices, but *Euryanthe* never obtained a placement in the general operatic repertory like that of *Der Freischütz*. As an explanation for this, reference has normally been made to Chézy's libretto, which has been about as denounced as Weber's music in contrast has been praised for its innovative and artistic strengths, especially the features in which *Euryanthe* has been seen to anticipate the truly through-composed structure, the chromaticism and the Leitmotif technique of Wagner's music dramas. However, Weber himself seems to have been responsible for some of the much criticised features of the libretto.[24] For one critical statement (among many) concerning the libretto I quote John Warrack (who does modify his harsh criticism, however, in view of his comparisons with other problematic opera texts):

> More abuse has been heaped on this libretto than on any other in the history of opera, the more so since it has been generally accepted that this was the rock upon which a potential masterpiece became wrecked. Even in its painfully achieved final form, the weaknesses are glaring: the subject is artificial, the language stilted, the plot riddled with holes of which none is more gaping than the failure of Euryanthe to clear up the whole misunderstanding in Act 2 when she is first accused by Lysiart.[25]

One must wonder how far this "plot riddled with holes" is the creation of Chézy and Weber, and how much is owed to its medieval sources.

The medieval narrative about the beautiful and virtuous Euryant and her noble betrothed Gérard of Nevers which was used as the basis for the libretto of Euryanthe – with the name of the male protagonist Gérard changed to Adolar – is known in two versions:

(1) A verse romance *Le roman de la Violette* by Gerbert de Montreuil (first part of the thirteenth century) preserved in four medieval manuscripts, the earliest of these dating from the thirteenth century.[26]

(2) A prose version of the same romance by Gérard de Nevers, from the fifteenth century, preserved in two almost contemporary manuscripts.[27]

Helmina von Chézy translated the medieval story into German prose probably using (printed editions of) the prose version she had found in the

Bibliothèque Royale in Paris. Her version was published by Friedrich Schlegel in 1804. From the information given in Schlegel's preface it is not clear whether Chézy used the earlier verse romance or the later prose version (or both). Chézy (whose name was not mentioned in Schlegel's publication) published the same so-called translation separately (without mentioning Schlegel) in 1823. Here the subtitle of the publication specifies: "Aus dem Manuskript der königlichen Bibliothek zu Paris . . ." Today, the *Bibliothèque Nationale* contains manuscripts of both the verse and the prose version of the story. Later, in 1840, Chézy claimed not to have known the verse version and to have used an early printed edition of the prose version as the basis for her translation.[28] In the following I will comment on the relationship between the three versions mentioned of the story of Euryant and Gérard, from respectively the thirteenth, the fifteenth and the nineteenth centuries. The point is mainly to note the changes in the medieval literary traditions preserved or reflected in the version produced by Chézy.

Le roman de la Violette has been dated on inner criteria — above all the dedication to the Countess Marie de Ponthieu who was clearly alive when the dedication was made — by Douglas L. Buffum. Apparently it was written between 1227 and 1229.[29] Lawrence F. H. Lowe considers that the prose version by Gérard de Nevers was written between 1451 and 1464, his estimate also mainly based on a dedication, in this case to Count Charles I of Nevers.[30] The prose narrative contains an interpolated episode not found in any of the verse manuscripts. Chézy's version does not give this episode either. As a larger part around this interpolation is left out as well, there are, however, no weighty reasons to see the omission(s) as a sign of a dependency on the verse romance at this particular point.[31] Otherwise the prose version follows the action of the verse romance closely, but the new dedication and other details show that the prose story was meant as a new piece. Among other things a number of names of persons and places were changed.[32]

The Chézy "translation" did not preserve the dedications or the introductory remarks, neither as they are written in the prose nor in the verse version. From the start of the actual action, however, a number of differences between *V* (*Le roman de la Violette*) and *G* (*Gérard de Nevers*) make it possible to see how Chézy's "translation" differs from the verse version in much the same way as the prose version: In *V* the king is referred to plainly as Louis (Looÿs) whereas *G* uses the more precise designation Louis VI, "the fat" (Loÿs le Gros). He reigned 1108–35, but *G* at the same time places the action hundred years too early starting in 1010 in connection with a royal victory over rebellious vassals.[33] Louis VI did carry through such a victorious campaign, but in 1111–12.[34] Buffum has shown that the Looÿs referred to in *V* cannot be Louis VI, but rather Louis VIII (son of Philippe Auguste, reigning 1223–26), among other things because of the description of the

Royal Court at Pont de l'Arche, a Norman town that did not become French before 1204 (under Philippe Auguste).[35] *G* has preserved Pont de l'Arche as the place of the Royal celebration that opens the story.[36] Clearly then, the writer of the prose version in the fifteenth century had a somewhat distant idea about the history in which the story was set. Both in *G* and in *V* the historic frame is no more than a frame. *V* does not display any particular interest in the historic setting either, but clearly was written closer to the time of its setting than *G*. *V* does not refer to the campaign mentioned in *G*. The celebration which starts the action is described as a royal celebration connected with Easter and focuses primarily on the singing of *minnelieder* (and quoting from such songs) at the occasion. This naturally leads into the *minnelied*[37] sung by the young count Gerars[38] about his betrothed arousing envy and anger among some of the knights, among them count Lisïart.[39] In *G* the celebration has been moved to Pentecost instead of Easter. The love-songs are not quoted and the persons mentioned are only partly the same. *G* mentions more names than does V.[40]

On the whole Chézy's version remains very close to *G* though occasionally it appears drastically shortened.[41] The dating of the story and the designation of the king are as in *G* (even accepting the erroneous dating of Louis VI), similarly the connection to the just finished campaign, the time of Pentecost, the mentioning in passing also of a church celebration referred to in *G*, but not in *V*, as well as the lack of quotes from songs. In Chézy's version, however, the comments on the songs and their performers appear abbreviated in comparison with *G*. The wording of Chézy's description of Gérard also closely follows *G* though here, admittedly, *G* and *V* have much in common. However, *V* does not mention Euryant at this early point as do both *G* and Chézy.[42] In all three versions Gérard sings his *minnelied* about Euryant by request of *la chastellaine de Digon*.[43] *G* gives a prose account of this minnelied partly in direct speech. *V*, on the other hand, quotes lines of what appears to be more than one song, but also relates the contents of the song in direct speech outside the direct song quotes.[44] Both in *V* and in *G* one finds the metaphor of a ship without mast used about a person loving without being loved himself. Chézy composed for her "translation" a completely new poem using the mentioned metaphor for what is described as a hypocritical and restless longing for love, as opposed to love built on faithfulness and true feelings. In the following I give the original as well as English versions of the sections containing the metaphor of the mast from the mentioned accounts in *V* and *G* followed by Chézy's German re-writing of Gérard's song. I begin with *V*:

"Je ne sui mie en mer sans mast.
Chil est sans mast ki est amis,

> Quant en tel liu a son cuer mis,
> Ki ne set se on l'aimme point.
> Je di que cil est en tel point
> Con l'estrumans ki est en mer,
> Qui ne set cuidier ne esmer
> En quel liu puist venir a port,
> Quant il n'a mast ki son tref port,
> Ne gouvernail qui li ajut.
> Ensi sont li amant dechut,
> Qui aimment, s'il ne sont amé;
> Cil ont en gravele semé,
> Ou semenche ne puet reprendre;
> Mais or vous puis pour voir aprendre,
> Ne sui pas cil, j'os dire bien;
> Que plus m'aimme que nule rien
> Cele de cui me sui vantés,
> Qui tant a sens et loiautés. . . ."

> ["I am not at all at sea without a mast./ He is without a mast who is in love,/ When he has set his heart in some place,/ Who does not know at all if he is loved./ I say that he is in the same situation/ As the sailor who is at sea,/ Who cannot imagine or determine/ Where he may reach a port,/ When he has neither a mast carrying his sail/ Nor a helm to help him./ That is how betrayed lovers are,/ Who are in love, if they are not loved./ They have sown in gravel/ Where seeds cannot take root./ But now I can tell you truly:/ That I am not that man, I dare say/ For she of whom I have boasted/ Loves me more than anyone,/ She of whom I pride myself/ She who has so much wisdom and loyalty. . . ."][45]

This is the corresponding passage from G:

> Puis dist que en mer n'estoit mye sans mast, mais celluy estoit sans mast qui en tel lieu avoit son ceur mys ou il ne scet s'il est amé. "Et pour ce puis je bien dire et affermer que pas ne suis celluy quy aime sans partye, car d'elle suis amé plus que dire ne vous saroye . . ."

> [Then he said that he was not at sea without a mast, but that that man was without a mast who had set his heart in some place where he does not know if he is loved. "And for this reason I can well say and affirm that I am not one who loves unrequited, for I am loved by her more than I can tell you. . . ."][46]

Finally Chézy's version of Gérard's song as it appeared in her "translation":

1. "Wie heg ich im Herzen,
Aus Schmerzen so fröhlich entblühet,
Die Liebe, die Triebe, und Denken zur Süssen hin ziehet.
Ich sehne mich ferne
Zum Sterne, der freundlich mir funkelt,
Lust kenn ich nur, wenn ich sie nenne, die alles verdunkelt.
2. Wer heuchelndem Sinne
Der Minne vertraute, muss beben,
Wie rastlos sich mastlose Schiffe bald senken, bald heben;
Doch sicher vertrauet
Und bauet auf stürmende Fluten,
Wer freuen der Treuen sich mag und wahrhaftiger Gluten.
3. Drum sing ich, und freue
Der Treue mich, die uns verbunden,
Die mein, mit mir eins ist, in Liebe, so nie noch gefunden.
Drum preis ich im Sinne,
Der Minne der Schönsten ergeben,
Das Glück, ihr im Blicke zu schauen mein köstlichstes Leben."

[1. "How I cherish in my heart the love, the inclination and thoughts which draw me to my sweetheart and which joyfully have flourishes out of agony. I long for the distant star which sparkles kindly to me. I only know desire when I mention the one who obscures everything.
2. He who trusted love with a hypocritical mind must tremble, just as ships without masts move around restlessly. But he who may delight in faithfulness and true fervour may safely trust and build on the stormy waves.
3. Therefore I sing and rejoice in the faithfulness which ties us together, in her who is mine or is one with me in a love of which the like was never found. Therefore I praise in my mind that I have submitted to the love of the most beautiful, I praise the blessing that I shall be able to see her all through my priceless life."][47]

The style of Chézy's poem is far removed from the direct expressions of the thirteenth-century poem and the narrative prose of the fifteenth century. It is only possible to talk about an altogether new poem firmly rooted in a nineteenth-century poetic style although based on the narrative function of Gérard's *minnelied*. In spite of the stylistic distance, however, Chézy remained loyal to the basic ideas as well as the main metaphor of the medieval text(s). Both Chézy's text and *G* conclude this introductory section by referring to the enthusiasm of the king, queen and others for Gérard's *minnelied*[48] while *V* directly moves to the next point, the jealousy and the anger of some of the knights, mainly of Liziart.[49] In the libretto, Adolar's corresponding song is completely recast:

> "Unter blüh'nden Mandelbäumen,
> An der Loire grünem Strand,
> O wie selig ist's zu träumen,
> Wo ich meine Liebe fand.
> Sie, die Reine, Eine, Meine!
> Keusch wie Schnee, wie Rosen mild;
> Unter blüh'nden Mandelbäumen
> Schwebt um mich ihr süsses Bild.
>
> Bei dem goldnen Licht der Sterne,
> An der Loire Blüthenstrand,
> Gab der reinsten Liebe gerne
> Augenstern ein Himelspfand.
> Selig, minnig, hold und innig,
> Aug' in Auge, Mund an Mund,
> Bei dem Leuchten ew'ger Sterne
> Gab sich Herz dem Herzen kund!
>
> Heil'ger Treue schönste Rose,
> An der Loire Blumenrand,
> Ob auch Sturm und Welle tose,
> Blühest du, des Lenzes Pfand.
> Zarte, Reine, Süsse! Meine!
> Du mit mir ganz ein und mein,
> Heil'ger Treue schönste Rose
> Blüht in deiner Brust allein!"

> ["Under blossoming almond trees/ On the green banks of the Loire,/ How blissful it is to dream/ Of where I found my true love!/ She, my pure, my single love!/ Chaste as snow and soft as roses;/ Under blossoming almond trees/ Her sweet image hovers over me.//
> By the golden starlight/ On the blossoming banks of the Loire/ My true love freely gave/ With her loving glance a gage of sacred love./ Blissful tender, sublime, devoted,/ Eyes joined to eyes, lips to lips;/ By the light of the eternal stars/ Heart was promised to heart.//
> Sacred troth, fairest rose,/ On the flowering banks of the

Loire,/ Let storms rage and waves toss,/ You blossom as the pledge of spring./ Tender, pure, my sweet, my own!/ You, my one, my only love:/ The fair rose of our sacred troth/ Blossoms in your heart alone."]⁵⁰

The beginning and end of the medieval narrative formed the basis from which the action of *Euryanthe* was constructed. This frame, however, only takes up a relatively minor part of the medieval narrative: In *V*, in all 1931 verses out of a total of 6654 or less than a third, and a similar proportion in *G*. *V* seems to be dependent – particularly in the frame-story – on other medieval narratives, primarily the *Roman de la Rose ou Guillaume de Dole* (by Jehan Renart). Another medieval romance, *Le Comte de Poitiers*, containing very similar narrative material was until recently considered a possible source for *V*.⁵¹ The frame narrative in *V* takes its point of departure from the above mentioned jealousy of Count Liziart who – in the presence of the worried king – incites Gérard to accept a wager over their lands and titles concerning the infidelity of women. More precisely, Liziart claims to be able to have his way with Euryant within a week and to be able to show proofs of his success. When Liziart comes to Euryant in Nevers, she immediately proves him wrong; she is not in the least charmed by Liziart. In order to win the wager Liziart must fall back on trickery, helped by an evil old maid, Gondree, who makes sure that Liziart gets to hear about and see (through a hole in a door while Euryant is taking a bath) a birth mark in the shape of a violet (hence the title of the romance) on Euryant's right breast. Euryant has always preserved this birth mark as a secret, so that until this moment only Gérard knows of it. With his new knowledge as "proof" Liziart manages to convince the king and his court in Melun and even Gérard of the postulated infidelity of Euryant. Liziart has won the wager and Gérard leaves the court taking Euryant along with him into the forest intending to kill her. Euryant, however, saves Gérard by warning him against a dangerous dragon. After having killed the beast Gérard decides that he cannot be Euryant's judge anymore and leaves her alone in the forest.

Here two long and complicated lines of the narrative follow, one about the hardships of Euryant and one about Gérard. This part of the medieval story was not used in the opera (but of course included in Chézy's "translation" of the story), except for an episode following closely after the episode in the forest. Here Gérard goes to Nevers disguised as a *minnesinger* to explore the actions of Liziart (who has taken over Gérard's possessions). During this episode he realises the betrayal. This episode is brought to use in the operatic narrative, though in a very different way. The long and numerous adventures in Gérard's line of the medieval narrative are held together by his two strongly connected basic aims: To find Euryant and to make up for the wrong done against her. In the end Euryant and Gérard do meet again and Gérard is able to save his beloved from a most dangerous situation as she has been wrongly accused of a murder.

The story is concluded in essentially the same way in all three versions of the narrative.[52] The final confrontation between Gérard and Liziart where the former defeats the latter in a judiciary fight leads to Liziart's admission of his guilt, his conviction and execution. His accomplice in the initial trickery which led to the disastrous events for Euryant, Gondree (called Gundrieth by Chézy), is also executed, Gérard and Euryant are married and return to Nevers. A few narratively insignificant differences between the versions help clarify the relation of Chézy's version to *V* and *G*.

In *V* Gérard sends messengers to Nevers to arrest Gondree who is boiled to death. Gérard and Euryant are married in the presence of the king and the court. They then return to Nevers. The very end of the text is a kind of afterword where the author has included his own name: Gyrbers de Mosteruel. Also the patron of Gerbert, Marie de Ponthieu, is mentioned here again, before a concluding prayer and an announcement of the end of the story.[53] In *G* a messenger is sent to Nevers to arrest Gondree and bring her to the court. Here Gondree is burned and finally the wedding forms the festive ending of the course of events before the protagonists return to Nevers. The author refers to the happy life of Gérard and Euryant thereafter and to their two fair sons. As in *V*, also in *G* the narrative has a concluding short prayer. In *G* it is phrased so as to ask the Saviour to preserve the souls of the protagonists beside "les nostres" when departing from here, concluding, then, in the declaration of the end of the book.[54]

Chézy's text only briefly accounts for the execution of Gondree which seems to take place in Nevers (just as in *V*, but Gondree is burned here as in *G*). Most likely the rare difference from G is due to a somewhat shortened version of the narrative.[55] In *V* there is found a moralising remark in connection with Gondree: "Ensi va qui trahison mainne" [this is what happens to the one who commits treachery].[56] *G* has (objectively equivalent): "Ainsy fu la vielle payee de sa deserte" [in this way the old woman was paid as she deserved].[57] Chézy's text refers to the joy of the people at seeing their beloved master and mistress again but also to their being glad "die Gundrieth ihren Lohn empfangen zu sehen, welche auf einem Dornenfeuer verbrannt wurde, unter grossem Jubel des Volkes" [to see Gondree receive her payment: she was burned on a fire of thorns to the joy of the people].[58] Chézy again mainly seems to reflect *G*. The same is found also in the formulation of the concluding prayer and the declaration of the end of the book.

All through the narrative, deviations between Chézy's text and *G* seem rather to be explained by a relatively free treatment of the preserved material (maybe through several sources) than through recurrence to *V*. In any case, it must be underscored that Chézy's text – as well as G – loyally reflects the original narrative. Chézy managed to recreate a plain and lively atmosphere of chivalry in spite of liberties in relation to the medieval originals and in spite of occasional misrepresentations of the romance genre, as will be apparent from the discussion in the next section.

The Medievality of Euryanthe

In an early nineteenth-century edition of the medieval narrative,[59] the editor, Francisque Michel, discusses Weber's opera expressing a favourable opinion about Weber's music and what he considers its medievalistic approach.[60] Weber's opera had reached Paris in April 1831 at the Théâtre de l'Académie Royale de Musique in a French "translation" changing many aspects of the operatic treatment of the medieval romance. In June of the same year a German troupe performed the opera at the Italian theatre. Here are some of Michel's comments:

> This remarkable work – through its style and the versification, not by the disposition of the drama which has almost no connection to the romance except the names Euriant and Lysiart, the name of Gérard having been changed into Adolar – this work, I say, is even more remarkable for its music which is very beautiful, full of originality, of charm, of strength throughout, and which has a very pronounced medieval colour.[61]

In the (above mentioned) scene where Gérard takes Euryant to the forest to kill her because of her infidelity, a dragon (or serpent) – as mentioned above – suddenly appears.[62] Euryant saves the life of Gérard by warning him. In G (and similarly in Chézy's text and the libretto), she even offers to sacrifice herself with the intention that Gérard can escape, an offer which Gérard of course must refuse. Gérard fights the dragon and kills it. The dragon, or "le serpent," was rendered by Chézy by the word "Schlange" (snake), both in her "translation" and in the libretto. In the medieval narrative, the beast is described in dragon-like terms (basically correctly followed by Chézy): "une beste moult orrible et espoentable. Grosse avoit la teste et les yeulx plus ardant que feu, la coewe avoit moult grande et reserchelee" [a very horrible and fearful beast. It had a large head and eyes more burning than fire, also it had a very large, coiled tail].[63] In the Middle Ages, no clear distinction between dragons and snakes seems to have been drawn. Both were at the same time thought of as symbols for the Devil and as truly existing monsters/animals.[64] After Gérard has defeated the dragon an interesting difference between (both of) the medieval texts and Chézy's "translation" occurs. This concerns the different presentations of the considerations of

Gérard around his decision to leave behind Euryant in the forest. In *G* Gérard prays for help realising that he can no longer kill Euryant as she has saved him and shown a rare courage in wanting to save the one who was going to kill her. He then proceeds:

> "Certes a tousjours mais ara m'amour, mais nulz homs vivans ne le sara. Icy le lairay sans luy aultre mal faire. Dieux par sa grace le voelle pourveir et pardonner son mesfait." Il vint vers la damoiselle et luy dist: "Euryant, en la garde de Nostre Seigneur te laisse, auquel je prye humblement que de mal te voelle garder et a toy pardonner la faulte que vers moy as faitte."

> ["Certainly she shall have my love forevermore, but no man alive shall know it. Here I shall leave her without doing her any further harm. May God in his grace protect and pardon her for her misdeed." He went to the young lady and said to her: "Euryant, I leave you in the protection of Our Saviour, to whom I humbly pray that he will preserve you from ill and pardon you for the wrong you have committed against me."][65]

The emphasis is clearly on Gérard's concern for Euryant. In *V* the contents at this point – if not the wording – are closely related to *G* except for one important thing: there is no particular mention of a need for Euryant to be pardoned by God for her alleged misdeed. Gérard's reflection in *V* is solely based on his consideration for Euryant, except for what concerns the secrecy of his love for her:

> "Ceste a bien sa mort respitié,
> Et s'ai de li molt grant pitié,
> Quant seule le lais en cest bois.
> Fel soie jou se ja l'i bois;
> Mais tout adiés m'amour aura,
> Ne ja nus fors moi nel saura.
> Chi le lairai sans plus mesfaire.
> Diex, qui ensi le puet bien faire,
> Le consaut, qu'ele ara or mais
> Assés et painnes et esmais!"
> Lors li a dit: "Biele Eurïaut,
> Diex li peres, ki maint en haut,
> Vous doinst de ses biens! Je vous lais."

> ["She has indeed deferred her death,/ And I have great compassion for her,/ When I leave her alone in this forest./ I would be treacherous if I wrong her there now,/ She shall

have my love for evermore,/ But no-one but me will ever know it./ I will leave her here without doing any more harm./ May God, who can indeed do it,/ Preserve her, for she shall henceforth have/ plenty of suffering and troubles."/ Then he said to her: "Beautiful Euryant,/ May God the Father, who dwells on high,/ Give you his blessings! I leave you."]⁶⁶

In both *V* and *G* Gérard, in this scene, is no longer acting out of revenge or anger. It remains, however, a duty for him to punish Euryant. But his decision to leave her alone in the forest is basically seen as a pardon, an act of grace and love, a love, however, that must be secret at this point. In Chézy's "translation," by contrast, Gérard's love for Euryanthe is not mentioned. The only hint of the theme of grace is found in the formulation of Gérards quite conventional prayer for God's protection of Euryant which — not surprisingly — is congruent with the corresponding prayer in *G*:

> He raised his eyes towards Heaven and thanked the Lord that he had won over the monster; then he called out: "O God, may you help me, for how should it be possible for me to kill her who has just saved my life? Had she not been there, the monster would have strangled me! So I cannot do her any harm now, because when I had just drawn my sword to separate her head from her body she saw the terrible snake and shouted to me that I should save myself, which I would never have thought. For where can one find a woman who has the courage and will to save and protect against death someone who is ready to kill her? Thus I shall leave her alive, also since it is already a terrible misery to stay here alone, exposed to the wild animals. May God take her in his protection and forgive her misdeed against me." After Gerhart had decided this, he went to the lady and said to her: "Euryanthe, I will leave you in God's care and pray to him that he may forgive you the wrong you have done me."⁶⁷

In the opera libretto, a rubric points to the "inner struggle" in Adolar:

> Euryanthe: "Now let me die!" Adolar: "No, that cannot be. Honour demanded that I should kill you, but as you were willing to die for me I cannot be your executioner — stay here, alone, under God's protection." (He rushes away, a bitter inward struggle rending him, with a last backward look at Euryanthe.)⁶⁸

In a modern perspective, Gérard's (or Adolar's) act of leaving behind Euryant in the forest must appear as insensitive and inhuman. By contrast, in the medieval texts, as discussed above, Gérard's new intention clearly seems to be understood as an expression of his love for Euryant; the prayer for God's help should, correspondingly, be understood as operative so that Gérard's pardoning is more than empty words.

The symbolic meaning of the forest and – more generally – the wilderness in the Middle Ages throws light over the difference in mood between the dragon scene as it appears in Chézy's "translation" and in the two medieval narratives. As emphasised by Jacques Le Goff the forest was equated with the wilderness in the medieval mind. The wilderness appeared as a frightening place for ordinary people but at the same time also represented positive ideals, a place of repentance, an asylum from civilisation – at times endowed with an almost paradisiacal character.[69] The wilderness further carried with it a sense of holiness as seen in the urge of monks in the early Middle Ages to flee civilisation and go into the wilderness, tendencies that gained new importance in the quest for the primitive in certain new monastic movements in the eleventh and twelfth century and which was always present in attitudes of (and towards) hermits in the Middle Ages. In the Rule of Benedict the wilderness was seen (in the sixth century) as a solitary place for the fight of the individual believer against the Devil.[70] The new strengthening in the high Middle Ages of the urge to take up the challenge of the primitive is clearly expressed for instance in the life of the prolific theologian and writer Peter Damian (1007–72) and in the foundation of orders like the Carthusians, the Premonstratensians, and – most importantly – the Cistercians in the twelfth century.[71] Jacques Le Goff emphasises the important symbolic role of the forest in the courtly literature. The forest is used as a place of trial and adventure by the innovative twelfth-century romance writer Chrétien de Troyes (1135–83) and the wilderness preserved a similar important symbolic place all through the Middle Ages with a revival in the fourteenth and the fifteenth century.[72]

The dragon scene in *V* and *G* occurs at a turning point in the narrative. Both Gérard and Euryant are in a situation of chaos and despair. The dragon constitutes a challenge to their courage, but not only to their physical courage. Both of them win this first of many succeeding struggles through love and through courage to act out of love. The episode forms the beginning of a new course of action for Gérard. He goes to Nevers – out of an intuitive sense of necessity to see the place that no longer belongs to him. Disguised as a minnesinger he happens to overhear a conversation at Liziart's household between Gondree and Liziart which reveals the committed treachery. He realises that Euryant did not deceive him but that he was the naive victim of Liziart's wiles. Having recognised this he begins a journey through many adventures until he – in the end – finds Euryant. Gérard's journey mostly focuses on knightly adventures within the civilised world but also contains a few episodes in the wilderness. Similarly, the episode in the forest marks Euryant's transition to a state where she is only protected by God who has been invoked by Gérard for that very reason.

The dragon episode thus forms the beginning of a new direction in the overall structure of the narrative. In the wilderness – at a symbolically heavily charged place – both Euryant and Gérard are challenged to pursue the fight for their love and for the fulfilment of their lives. The dragon – symbolic of the Devil or evil – may be understood as representing the forces they have to fight against, everything that resists their originally innocent love and confidence. The attack of the evil forces started with the actions of Liziart. The dragon, on the other hand, turned up at the moment of the narrative where Gérard personally has succumbed to the evil and was about to kill Euryant. The dragon may be understood to provoke a deepening of Gérard's consciousness. In such a sense, the episode prepares Gérard for his journey and his fight. It is tempting to see this as a kind of "consecration" in the light of the liturgical exorcisms and renunciations of the Devil which during the Middle Ages formed an important part in the preparation of the catechumens for baptism.[73] During these rites evil forces were understood to be expelled from the catechumens through the power of prayer so that they could pursue the path of salvation, of love and virtue.[74]

There is no reason to believe that the dragon episode in any way should constitute a conscious representation of a liturgical ceremony. My point is rather that one can read parallels between plot structures and liturgical ceremonies – as for instance the exorcisms referred to here. The dragon episode which functions as the ultimate test of the innocence and purity of Euryant, forces Gérard not only to fight the beast but also to face the unselfish act of Euryant's (proposed) sacrifice. In the highly charged place of the forest, he is brought back to a consciousness of his love so that he can begin his journey to deserve his beloved. When the Devil was explicitly mentioned in prayers and exorcisms, the Roman-Frankish liturgy employed such unequivocal Biblical (and hence theologically safe) terms as *Satanas*, *Diabolus*, and *Spiritus inmundus*.[75] Representational liturgical ceremonies similarly seem mainly to have used the terms *Satanas* and *Diabolus* for the (quite limited) recorded evidence of direct participation of the Devil (for instance in ceremonies of the so-called *Descensus ad Inferos*, The Harrowing of Hell).[76] In the *Ordo Virtutum* (from the middle of the twelfth century) by Hildegard of Bingen (1098–1179), one finds the metaphorical use of *serpens* (five times) and of *draco* (once) for the Devil.[77] In other medieval poetic liturgical texts, the terms *serpens antiquus* and *draco* are also found: for instance in sequences and hymns by Peter Abaelard (1079–1142),[78] Peter the Venerable (abbot of Cluny, c. 1092–1156),[79] Adam of St. Victor (d.1192),[80] and the above mentioned Hildegard.[81] The more or less metaphorical and symbolic use in literature (and art) of serpent and dragon figures may thus be contextualised with liturgical expressions and theological reflection thereby widening the possible range of the dragon episode of the two medieval versions of the Euryant story.

Though essentially preserving the medieval plot, Chézy's nineteenth-century "translation" no longer contained the same connotations of a quasi-ritual and symbolic initiation of Gérard's journey. If it is possible to read the corresponding scene of the opera (Act 3, scene 1) in such a light, it is mainly due to the musical means which Weber used for his representation. As already indicated, the use of the snake in Chézy's rendering of the scene tends to remove or at least to minimise the symbolic and religious connotations which are readily found in the medieval narratives. It would seem likely that we should understand this simply as a consequence of a lack of knowledge of such connotations on the part of both Chézy and Weber.

Musically, I believe that Weber's representation can be understood to convey to the "dragon scene" a quasi-ritual sensation. Dramaturgically, in the opera, the scene has preserved its position as a dramatic turning point, even though Chézy's and Weber's alterations of the medieval narrative – especially the decision to create a completely different construction to use in stead of the birth mark secret for Count Lysiart's use as a "proof" of his seduction of Euryanthe, since the representation of a birth mark on stage seemed too daring to Weber – complicated the described frame narrative and pushed the dragon or snake scene back in the operatic plot. This scene still remains the fundamental crisis of the drama and brings with it the potential for the dénouement as Adolar in his despair goes to his (former) home place (Nevers) where he (although in a different way than in the medieval narratives) finds out about the fraud that Lysiart has committed against him.

Weber had chosen the narrative material for the opera from several suggestions from Chézy. It was Weber too who was mainly responsible for exactly those changes which have given rise to the most severe criticisms of the dramatic plot. He seems to have been the one who insisted on the supernatural "gothic" incorporation into the action of Adolar's sister Emma, who had committed suicide (before the operatic plot takes its beginning) in despair over the death of her beloved Udo, and her secret burial in a tomb placed in the garden of Adolar's castle. Because of her suicide Emma cannot find rest in her tomb until innocent tears are shed on the very ring from which she drank the poison that killed her.[82]

Helmina von Chézy, in her memoir, *Unvergessenes* (Leipzig 1858) related how she had wanted to keep as close as possible to the medieval narrative:

I wanted to treat the opera in an unassuming and troubadour-like way and not to lose track of the guiding principles of the old narrative. Weber had scruples about the birthmark on Euryanthe's breast, Ludwig Tieck strengthened these by his remarks. Weber, who later also in his *Oberon* proved how the domain of spirits was natural to him wanted a change of the action, in which that could become of use.[83]

In the operatic version, Euryanthe tells the secret about Emma, which she has promised Adolar never to reveal, to Eglantine, who (also) loves Adolar but has been rejected by him and is deeply jealous of Euryanthe's and Adolar's love. She has misled Euryanthe into thinking of her as a devoted friend. Lysiart and Eglantine become accomplices, Eglantine steals the ring from Emma's tomb and as Lysiart is able to disclose his thus obtained knowledge of the family secret and to hand over Emma's ring, this convinces Adolar as well as the court that Lysiart's claim to have seduced Euryanthe is true.

Whatever one thinks of this dramatic construction, it did provide the opera with a crisis which even incorporated some guilt in the figure of Euryanthe, since in this plot she did betray Adolar's confidence. This may explain to some degree why she does not come up with a more convincing defense at the court when accused. It may also explain her strange subdued mood at the beginning of the third act, the snake or dragon scene. This scene begins with a fairly long orchestral introduction (35 bars) during which Euryanthe and Adolar make their appearance on stage. The musical means used in this introduction are almost ascetic. Weber, who is famous for his orchestration and at other places (also in Euryanthe) uses orchestral colours in a virtuoso manner, here mainly used strings moving at a calm pace ("Adagio non lento") with no use of tremolos or other special "romantic" stylistic means. The atmosphere thus raised may be interpreted in connection with the interpretation given above as to the wilderness in medieval narratives. Only after the introduction and the gloomily understated expressions of Euryanthe ("Hier weilest du? hier darf ich ruhn?" [Here will you stay? Here may I rest?] and Adolar's equally gloomy, but more direct statement ("Dies ist der Ort, so schaurig öd' und still, wie meine That ihn will. Ich führte dich zum Tode fort" [This is the place, as grim, as bleak and silent as my deed might wish it. I have brought you to your death],[84] a more vivid dramatic representation begins to develop as Adolar reproaches Euryanthe for her infidelity and the ensuing argument – with no resolution – leads into the dramatic high point of the scene as the snake makes its entrance and leads to a temporary climax and triumph as Adolar, warned by Euryanthe, defeats the monster. Both the mentioned slow recitative-like instrumental introduction and the first lines of Euryanthe's and Adolar's recitatives appear quite bare, and are demonstratively unmelodic. Euryanthe's recitative is sung almost without orchestral accompaniment, and Adolar's death announcement may be heard as a hint of a liturgical recitation tone because of the emphasised repetition of its beginning tone (a "d").[85] After the defeat of the monster and Adolar's above mentioned decision to leave Euryanthe in the wildernes without killing her, the instrumental postlude (of 27 bars) ending the scene seems to represent a process of breakdown or crisis in a succession of fragmented musical figures and chords detached from the thematic or melodic materials used in the scene.[86] I do not claim that Weber's composition depends directly on the interpretation proposed above of the medieval narrative. Rather, I propose to read Weber's representation of the plot as an intuitive understanding which turned out to highlight a similar interpretation of the main dramatic point as in the medieval *aventure*. This intuitive medievalism, it seems to me, is deeply connected to the spiritual aspirations of both the romantic music ideology as outlined briefly in the introduction to this paper, and of Weber's own fascination, not only with the Middle Ages, but also with the supernatural.

In this respect it is important to look at the means used to represent the supernatural, not the least because these means are prevalently instrumental (cf. the introduction to the paper above). Weber had originally planned to have Emma's spirit represented on stage in the overture during a particular part of the music.[87] This music is a 15 bar long section of the overture which stands out markedly from everything else.[88] The same music reappears (in slight variations) at every point in the opera where Emma is mentioned.[89]

The "spirit of Emma" section of the overture is given in Weber's piano score reduction in the example on p. 129. The music can be read as a kind of chorale in an alienated and transformed form. The chromaticism and the ghostlike sound (the *divisi* and muted violins) distinguish it from such an ecclesiastical musical tradition. On the other hand, the steady progression of the music – basically in quarter notes – in a rhythmically and non-thematically very simple setting has obvious common points with a chorale. An immediate characterisation of the use of this element is that it curbs the musical flow (which after this section of the overture is regained through a large fugato section).[90] At all the occurrences of this element – though of course in the opera similar effects are achieved in other ways at other places – the narrative flow is brought to a halt in what may be understood as a supernatural, quasi-religious contemplation. A procedure which can be likened to what in a certain way can be seen to constitute a special genre of "liturgical drama" which gradually can be understood to have developed in the Middle Ages mainly during the eleventh to thirteenth centuries.[91] This is very much the case at the point in the opera where Eglantine breaks down, prompted by her fearful vision of Emma, and – seemingly insane, but in the opera

The 'spirit of Emma music' from the overture to *Euryanthe* (bars 129 to 143) in Weber's own piano reduction.

importantly viewed as the opposite – reveals the truth. The "spirit of Emma" music here occurs during the wedding procession which is highlighted by a flashy almost shrill instrumentation with brass and timpani, but notably by the use of piccolo flutes, to an extent which may almost be described as ironic.[92] After the wedding march the music breaks up the processional flow of the march in sharply detached musical figures and a dramatic outbreak of Eglantine, which leads into the mentioned auditively conveyed vision of Emma.[93] After this, the action resumes as Adolar and Lysiart enter into a struggle which is interrupted and ended by the arrival of the King and his entourage bringing with them Euryanthe whom they had found in the wildernes. From there the action moves straight to the final dénouement as briefly indicated above.

Weber's *Euryanthe* is a rich and complicated music drama. It has had the strange fate of being praised and rejected at the same time. I hope here to have shown that there are intricate connections between the medieval narrative upon which the opera was constructed and other contextually relevant materials on the one hand and the dramaturgical construction of the opera and the musical means which Weber chose to use.

NOTES

1. I am grateful for the support given, in the writing of this article, by the Danish National Research Foundation through its funding of the Centre for the Study of the Cultural Heritage of Medieval Rituals.

2. See for instance Wolfgang Michael Wagner, *Carl Maria von Weber und die deutsche Nationaloper*, Weber-studien II (Mainz: Schott, 1994), 78. Also John Warrack, *Carl Maria von Weber*, second edition (Cambridge: Cambridge University Press, 1976), 235. And cf. E. T. A. Hoffmann's review (written in 1821 as a report from its opening in Berlin) as reprinted in Martin Hürlimann, ed., *Carl Maria von Weber in seinen Schriften und in zeitgenössischen Dokumenten* (Zürich: Manesse Verlag, 1973), 161–81, esp. 166 where Hoffmann emphasises that something entirely new has appeared with this opera.

3. Edward Kravitt, "Romanticism Today," *The Musical Quarterly* 76 (1992): 93–109 (93 and 97–98). Kravitt refers to M. H. Abrams, *The Mirror and the Lamp: Romantic Theory and the Critical Tradition* (New York: Oxford University Press, 1953). On Kravitt's account, romantic composers, in contrast to their predecessors (who ultimately aimed for approval by their patrons), "rejected that final cause in favor of an introvert art generated by a consciousness of *self*". For Abrams, this new focus is the "one single real entity" of romanticism, the core from which its numerous attributes radiated (99).

4. Arnold Whittall, *Romantic Music. A concise history from Schubert to Sibelius* (London: Thames and Hudson, 1987), 7–9.

5. Whittall, 15.

6. Carl Dahlhaus, "Romantic Music," in Michael Raeburn and Alan Kendall, eds., *Heritage of Music, vol. II: The Romantic Era* (Oxford: Oxford University Press, 1990/1989), 111–25 (118 and 114–16).

7. Carl Dahlhaus, *Die Idee der absoluten Musik* (Kassel – München: Bärenreiter – Deutscher Taschenbuch-Verlag, 1978). English translation: Carl Dahlhaus, *The Idea of Absolute Music* (Chicago: Chicago University Press, 1989).

8. Hans Lund, *Texten som tavla*. Studier i litterär bildtransformation (Lund: Liber Förlag, 1982), 77–80 (English translation: Hans Lund, *Text as Picture*. Studies in the Literary Transformation of Pictures, Lewiston NY: Edwin Mellen Press, 1992).

9. Dahlhaus, *Die Idee*, 47–49. The cited text stems from Hoffmann's introduction to the review of Beethoven's fifth symphony (written in 1810). See also Steven Paul Scher, "Temporality and Mediation: W. H. Wackenroder and E. T. A. Hoffmann as Literary Historicists of Music," *Journal of English and Germanic Philology* LXXV (1976): 492–502 (500). Hoffmann's review was originally published in the *Allgemeine Musikalische Zeitung* (Leipzig). Together with another review (of Beethoven's piano trios op. 70) it was reworked into the essay *Beethovens Instrumental-Musik* and published 1813 in the *Zeitung für die elegante Welt* and again in 1814 as part of the *Kreisleriana* in Hoffmann's *Fantasiestücke in Callot's Manier*. See Hartmut Steinecke, ed., with Gerhard Allroggen and Wulf Segebrecht: E. T. A. Hoffmann: *Fantasiestücke in Callot's Manier*, Werke 1814, in Hartmut

Steinecke und Wulf Segebrecht, eds., *E. T. A. Hoffmann: Sämtliche Werke in sechs Bänden*. II, 1 (Frankfurt am Main: Deutscher Klassiker Verlag, 1993), 538–40, 627–28, and 663–65. Concerning the concept of absolute music and its history, see Dahlhaus, *Die Idee*, 24–46.

10. Steinecke und Segebrecht, eds., *Hoffmann: Sämtliche Werke*, II, 1, 54, see also Dahlhaus, *Die Idee*, 58–59 and 48–49. For a comparison between Hoffmann's idea (as a "topos of ineffability," see Dahlhaus, *Die Idee*, 66–68) and St Augustine's understanding of the *iubilus*, see Nils Holger Petersen, "Liturgy and Musical Composition," *Studia Theologica* 50 (1996), 125–43 (135), and Eyolf Østrem, "Music and the Ineffable," in Siglind Bruhn, ed., *Voicing the Ineffable. Musical Representations of Religious Experience*, Hillsdale (New York: Pendragon Press, 2002), 287–312 (293–99).

11. Concerning Weber and Spohr, see Warrack, 34–35, 78–86, and 172. For Schubert, see Elizabeth Norman McKay: *Franz Schubert's Music for the Theatre* (Tutzing: Hans Schneider, 1991), 93–105 and 209–29, and Till Gerrit Waidelich, *Franz Schubert: Alfonso und Estrella* (Tutzing: Hans Schneider, 1991), 93–119. See also Nils Holger Petersen, "Freedom, Oppression, and Celebration: Rossini's *Guillaume Tell*," in *Medievalism. The Year's Work for 2001*, ed. Gwendolyn Morgan (Bozeman, Montana, 2002), 21–36. Concerning *Undine*, see Friedrich de la Motte Fouqué, *Undine* (Stuttgart: Reclam, 1953), and the printed piano score: E. T. A. Hoffmann, *Undine, Zauberoper in drei Akten. Klavierauszug neu bearbeitet von Hans Pfitzner (1906)* (Leipzig: C. F. Peters Verlag, no date), no. 9296. Weber's review of *Undine* is reprinted in Hürlimann, ed., 3142.

12. See Ulrich Müller: "Das Nachleben der mittelalterlichen Stoffe," in Volker Mertens und Ulrich Müller, eds., *Epische Stoffe des Mittelalters* (Stuttgart: Alfred Kröner Verlag, 1984), 424–48 (427–28), and Leslie J. Workman, "Medievalism and Romanticism," *Poetica* 39–40 (1994), 1–40 (1–3 and 32–35).

13. Warrack, 273 and 280, Michael C. Tusa, *Euryanthe and Carl Maria von Weber's Dramaturgy of German Opera* (Oxford: Clarendon Press, 1991), 9–14.

14. McKay, 247–69, esp. 247 and 267–69.

15. David E. Barclay in his "Medievalism and Nationalism in Nineteenth-Century Germany," in Leslie Workman, ed., *Medievalism in Europe, Studies in Medievalism* 5 (1993): 5–22, esp. 15–16, claims that Wagner falls outside any categorisation and thus cannot be used as an example of nineteenth-century medievalism. But whether extreme or untypical, Wagner is an example of a marked interest in the Middle Ages.

16. Tusa, 75. The zither is used for Adolar's romance in act 1 – the operatic rendering of a *minnelied* where Euryanthe is praised at court. Compare also Annette Kreutziger-Herr's article in this volume concerning the knowledge of medieval music at the time.

17. Tusa, 75–76.

18. Tusa, 76.

19. Tusa, 77, and (discussing the genre of *Euryanthe*) 49–56. Tusa sums up, 55–56: "a number of German grand operas antedate *Euryanthe*, but no prior work of comparable stature had ever attempted to bring 'grand opera' into the nineteenth century with such a vengeance, by fusing its one salient compositional feature with

the stylistic, dramaturgic, and aesthetic principles of early romantic opera." Tusa points to the fact that 'grand opera' for Weber meant opera with a continuous orchestral accompaniment as different from both operas with spoken dialogue and operas with simple recitative. A grand opera was normally based on subjects from classical antiquity (or some times biblical subject matter). Tusa makes it clear that *Euryanthe* through its choice of a medieval narrative (as well as through its music dramatic form) developed a new genre by Weber denoted (rather precisely) *grosse romantische Oper*, a mixture of elevated "grand opera" with elements of German romanticism.

20. Translation quoted (and slightly extended) from Tusa, 57–58; original German text in Hans Christoph Worbs, ed., *Carl Maria von Weber Briefe* (Frankfurt am Main: Fischer Taschenbuch Verlag, 1982), 119: "Ein neuer Beweis Ihrer Freundschaft ist mir die Sorgfalt, die Sie meiner Euryanthe widmen, und allerdings muss ich auch die treue Sorge meiner Freunde dieser Oper sehr wünschen, da sie einen misslichen Platz in der Welt betritt. Die Erwartungen der Masse sind durch den wunderbaren Erfolg des Freischützen bis zum Unmöglichen in's Blaue hinauf gewirbelt; und nun kommt das einfach ernste Werk, das nichts als Wahrheit des Ausdrucks, der Leidenschaft und Charakterzeichnung sucht, und alle der mannigfachen Abwechslung und Anregungsmittel seines Vorgängers entbehrt. – Nun wie Gott will!"

21. See for general surveys for instance Tom Shippey and Richard Utz, eds., *Medievalism in the Modern World. Essays in Honour of Leslie Workman* (Turnhout: Brepols, 1998) and Annette Kreutziger-Herr und Dorothea Redepenning, eds., *Mittelalter-Sehnsucht?* (Kiel: Wissenschaftsverlag Vauk, 2000), and concerning the interest in the music of the Middle Ages, Annette Kreutziger-Herr, *Ein Traum von Mittelalter* (Vienna: Böhlau, 2003).

22. Tusa, 84.

23. Tusa, 2.

24. See the discussion of the long and complicated genesis of the libretto in Tusa, 81–140. Tusa concludes: "Weber's responsibility for the final shape of the libretto must be seen as greater than Chezy's. Whereas Chezy was responsible primarily for the versification, Weber dictated the outcome of the story, the disposition of the numbers, the sequence of situations, and in many cases the forms of the individual numbers." Tusa, 138.

25. Warrack, 287. Compare Tusa, 140: "That the final version of the libretto ultimately was not very succesful should therefore come as no surprise. Chezy was no librettist, and, for that matter, neither was Weber. From the standpoint of logical and consistent development of plot and character, Weber's revisions hardly improved the libretto, and in some cases they were even detrimental to the intelligibility and plausibility of the story."

26. Douglas Labaree Buffum, ed., *Le Roman de la Violette ou de Gerart de Nevers par Gerbert de Montreuil* (Paris: Librairie ancienne Honoré Champion, 1928), see especially introduction, VII–IX. Here the four sources are referred to as A, B, C and D; see also Michel Zink, *Belle. Essai sur les chansons de toile suivi d'une édition et d'une traduction*. Transcriptions musicales de Gérard Le Vot (Paris: Champion, 1978), (73):

A: Paris, Bibl. nat. fonds fr. 1533, from 1284 (referred to as *v* by Zink).
B: Paris, Bibl. nat. fonds fr. 1374, from around the middle of the thirteenth century. (Zink: *w*).
C: Leningrad, Bibl.publ. fr.F.r. XIV, no. 3 (no. 5 according to Zink, where the ms is referred to as *v1*) written between 1400 and 1420. The ms. was stolen during the French revolution and arrived in St.Petersburg at the latest in 1805 (Buffum, VIII).
D: New York, bibl. J.P. Morgan, Esq. (Pierpont-Morgan 36 according to Zink who refers to it as *w1*). Written in the middle of the fifteenth century.
B and C form one group as do A and D. In C and D there are rubrics (headlines for sections of the plot). Buffum, VIII–IX.

Concerning *Le roman de la Violette* see also the analysis in Rita Lejeune, "Jean Renart et le roman réaliste au XIIIe siècle," chapter C, II in: Jean Frappier et Reinhold R. Grimm, eds., *Le roman jusqu'a la fin du XIIIe siècle*. I (Partie historique), *Grundriss der romanischen Literaturen des Mittelalters*, IV (Heidelberg: Carl Winter Universitätsverlag, 1978), 400–53 (414–17), as well as the documentation in Reinhold Grimm, ed., *Le roman jusqu'a la fin du XIIIe siècle* II (Partie documentaire), *Grundriss der romanischen Literaturen des Mittelalters* IV (Heidelberg: Carl Winter Universitätsverlag, 1984), 127–29, where *Le Roman de la Violette* is discussed as no. 216.

Not much is known about Gerbert de Montreuil. Beside *Le roman de la Violette* he is the likely author of a continuation of the story of the Holy Grail, see Grimm, ed., 125–27, where it is proposed that he was a wandering clerk.

27. Lawrence F. H. Lowe, ed., *Gérard de Nevers*. Prose version of the *Roman de la Violette* (New York: Kraus Reprint Corporation, 1965), a reprint of the original edition: Princeton: Princeton University Press, 1928. See also Buffum, IX, n. 1. Here the manuscripts are referred to as B and P in the introduction, IX–XII:
B: Bibl. Royale de Bruxelles, no. 9631: Histoire de Gérard de Nevers. B is probably written around the middle of the fifteenth century, at least before 1467 where the manuscript for the first time can be found in the inventory for the library of the Duke of Burgundy which later turned into the Bibl. Royale in Bruxelles and which the manuscript in all likelyhood did not leave again.
P: Paris, Bibl. nat. No. 24378: Roman de la Violette ou de Gérard de Nevers, par Girbert de Montreuil. This manuscript is found in the mentioned inventory of the Duke of Burgundy in 1467 but it did not stay there. In 1784 it arrived at the Bibliothèque du Roi, (later the Biblioteque Nationale in Paris) where it then remained.

The text of Lowe's edition is based on B, the two manuscripts are closely related, however, and stem without any doubt from a common source (Lowe, X–XI). None of the four (known) sources for the verse romance can alone have been the source for the prose version(s), see Lowe, XII.

28. Chézy's reproduction was first published in Friedrich Schlegel, *Sammlung romantischer Dichtungen des Mittelalters*. Zweiter Teil, Leipzig 1804. The only information concerning the sources in this work is the general note: "Aus gedruckten und handschriftlichen Quellen" on the front pages of the volumes. See Liselotte Dieckmann, ed., *Friedrich Schlegel: Sammlung von Memoiren und romantischen Dichtungen des Mittelalters aus altfranzösischen und deutschen Quellen* Kritische

Friedrich-Schlegel-Ausgabe, 33 (Paderborn: Verlag Ferdinand Schöningh, 1980), Einleitung, X, XVIII–XIX and XXIII–XXV (cf. Warrack, 282). Chézy's text is printed in this volume, 315–75. According to Dieckmann no single known version corresponds completely to Chézy's translation. Concerning Chézy's statement in 1840, see Tusa, 84, n. 11. Here two sixteenth century printed editions of the prose version (from the *Bibliothèque Nationale*) are mentioned as possible sources for Chézy's version.

29. Buffum, ed., introduction, LV–LVII. Compare verse 49 ff, 58 and 6643 of the edition, 5 and 265.

30. Lowe, ed., X–XI, cf. the edition, 1.

31. See Lowe, ed., 100–105, and introduction, XIV–XVII. Compare Dieckmann, ed., 1980, 360 to Lowe, ed., 95 and 117. In Chézy's text the contents of the pages from 95 to 117 of the prose version is missing. Deviations from the fifteenth-century prose version may – at least partly – derive from Chézy's printed source(s). In any case, the point here is not to determine the exact way of transmission but rather to note what in the medieval (original) versions was preserved also in Chézy's text.

32. See Lowe, ed., XVII–XXIX, concluding: "A prose reworking of a poem inevitably contains certain alterations and expansions of its original, especially when a long period of years has elapsed between the original and the reworking. *Gérard de Nevers*, as we have seem, is no exception to the rule. A new episode is interpolated in the thread of the old narrative, new names of persons and places are introduced. But these changes are not due to mere chance invention by the author; rather are they retouchings inspired by the actual background of his epoch. The story told by the Violette has been renovated, as it were, and made realistic for the readers of the times." (XXIX).

33. Buffum, ed., 6 (v. 78). Henceforth the verse romance is referred to as *V* plus page (and, in most cases, verse) number. Lowe, ed., 3. Henceforth the prose version is referred to as *G* plus page number (sometimes also number of section).

34. Georges Duby, *France in the Middle Ages, 987–1460*. Translated by Juliet Vale 127–28 (Oxford: Blackwell, 1991 (orig. Paris, 1987)), 127–28.

35. Buffum, ed., introduction, LVI–LVII.

36. *G*, 3.

37. *V*, 9 (v. 154).

38. *V*, 10 (v. 180).

39. *V*, 13 (v. 247), envy in general is referred to p. 12 (v. 240).

40. Compare *V*, 5–9 (v. 65–154) to *G*, 3–4 (section 5–8).

41. Dieckmann, ed., 343–49, consisting of three sections with the following headings: "Wie Gerhart nach Köln kam, und von den grossen und wunderbaren Kämpfen, die er mit den Heiden hatte" (343–46). "Wie Gerhart am Hof empfangen wurde, und wie die schöne Eglantine und Florentine mit ihm sprachen" (346–47), and "Wie Gerhart von der Fräulein Eglantine geliebt wurde, und von einer Alten ein Liebesgift bekam" (347–49). The corresponding part of *G* contains the sections: "Comment Gerart vint a Coulougne, et des grans mervellez d'armez qu'il fist sur les Saines" (52–56), "Cy parle de la grant battaille quy fu devant Coulougne, ou Gerart fist mervelles" (56–58), "Comment le duc Mylon de

Coulougne gaigna la bataille sur les Saines par les grans proeces de Gerart de Nevers, et de la grant gloire quy ly fu faitte quant il rentra dedans Coulougne" (58–63), "Cy parle des damoyselle[s] quy commencherent de tenchier l'une a l'autre pour la grant amour qu'elles avoyent a Gerart" (63–67), "Comment Gerart de Nevers vint a court, ou il fu moult bien recheus, et comment la belle Aiglentine parla a luy, et de leurs devises" (67–70) and finally "Comment les deux damoisellez par jalousye tencherent l'une a l'autre, et de la vielle qui fist la poison" (70–73). As it appears, Chézy's version is highly abbreviated in comparison with *G*, certain parts of the narrative being given a lower priority.

    42. *G*, 5 (line 12): *Euryans*. Dieckmann, ed., 318: *Euryanthe*. Compare *V*, 6–15. Euryanthe is mentioned for the first time on p. 15, v. 312: *Orïaus*. The names vary – as is seen – between the three versions (as well as the spelling to a small degree inside the medieval versions). Generally *V* uses *Eurïaut* (and *Orïaut*), *G Euryant* and Chézy *Euryanthe*. Unless I refer specifically to a narrative context within one particular of the three versions I use Euryant throughout for the medieval narrative (also in Chézys version), but Euryanthe for the operatic narrative. For the male protagonist *V* uses *Gérart*, *G Gérard* and Chézy *Gerhart*, the medieval versions with slight inconsistencies of spelling. As above, I use the name from *G* in general references to the story. Similarly the villain of the story is called *Lisüart*, *Liziart* resp. *Lysiardus* in the three texts (again with minor spelling inconsistencies in *V* and *G*). I use Liziart in general.

    43. *V*, 10, v. 184 ff., *G*, 5, and Dieckmann, ed., 318.

    44. Cf. Buffum, ed., introduction, LXXXII–XCI.

    45. *V*, 11–12, verses 215–33. I thank Marta Weingartner from the French department of Indiana University, U.S.A. who (in 1995) provided me with a much needed help for an English version of these lines.

    46. *G*, 5 (section 11). Again I thank Marta Weingartner (see n. 45 above) for her help.

    47. Dieckmann, ed., 318.

    48. Dieckmann, ed., 319, resp. *G*, 5.

    49. *V*, 12, v. 240 ff.

    50. See the printed piano score: Carl Maria von Weber, *Euryanthe*. Vollständiger vom Componisten verfertigter Clavier-Auszug, No. 4519 (Vienna: Carl Haslinger, without date), Romanze, no. 2, 22(21)–24. (In the following I refer to this edition as *Euryanthe*). I also refer to the CD recording conducted by Marek Janowski, LC 6203, (Berlin: Berlin Classics, 1994), where the text and the English translation quoted here (by Bernd Zöllner) is found in the booklet, 24.

    51. Buffum, ed., introduction, p. xl. See Grimm, ed., 109 dating *Le Comte de Poitiers* to 1235–40, i.e. later than *V*. *Le Roman de la Rose ou Guillaume de Dole* is recently dated to 1208–10 and has generally been dated earlier than *V*, Grimm, ed., 127–28 and 156–57.

    52. *V*, 259–65, v. 6497–6654. *G*, 141–47. Dieckmann, ed., 372–75.

    53. Conclusion of the narrative, *V*, 262–64. The afterword, *V*, 264–65 (verses 6634–6654).

    54. *G*, 146–47.

    55. Dieckmann, ed., 374–75.

56. *V*, 262, v. 6571.
57. *G*, 146 (section 345).
58. Dieckmann, ed., 375.
59. *Roman de la Violette ou de Gérard de Nevers, en vers, du XIIIe siècle, par Gibert de Montreuil; publié, pour la première fois, d'après deux manuscrits de la Bibliothèque Royale, par Francisque Michel* (A Paris, chez Silvestre, Librairie, 1834). One copy is preserved under the pressmark Res. Ye. 4062 in the *Bibliothèque Nationale*, Paris, where I consulted it during a visit in the spring of 1996. It contains an introduction by the editor (Francisque Michel), i–xl, a description of the manuscripts, xl–lxiv, and an appendix comparing textual excerpts from various manuscripts. Michel also provides a list of early printed versions of the prose version belonging to the Bibliothèque Royale, xxvij ff., among them primarily two from 1520 and 1526, xxx and xxxij. He refers to an edition from 1586 which he has not been able to retrieve, to an edition from 1727, an edition by the comte de Tressan offering extracts of the *roman* from 1780, and another similar edition by an unknown editor dating from 1780.
60. Michel, ed., xxxv–xxxvij.
61. Michel, ed., xxxvi: "Cet ouvrage remarquable par le style et par la versification, et non par la disposition du drame, qui n'a presque d'autre rapport avec le roman que par les noms d'Euriant et de Lysiart, celui de Gérard ayant été changé en Adolar; cet ouvrage, dis-je, est encore bien plus remarquable par la musique, qui est fort belle, pleine d'originalité, de charme; de vigueur surtout, et qui a une couleur de moyen-âge très prononcé." In a note (same page) Michel gives the following reference: "Voyez un feuilleton signé xxx (Castil-Blaze), dans le Journal des Débats du 16 juin 1831." He quotes from this text: "Cet opéra, traduit ou plutôt refait par M. Castil-Blaze, a été représenté pour la première fois sur le théatre de l'Académie royale de Musique le 6 avril 1831. En conservant à peu près dans les deux premiers actes, dit l'auteur, la position des personnages et de la musique, j'ai donnés d'autres motifs à l'action en reproduisant l'aventure de la Violette, que la pièce allemande ne rapelle en aucune manière. Le fabliau de Gérard de Nevers, le Cymbeline de Shakespeare, m'ont fourni les principales situations de l'Euriante française." Another note here refers to the printed French libretto: *Euriante, opéra en trois actes* (Paris: imprimerie de Ch. Dezauche, 1831), 46.
62. *V*, 44–48 (verses 1008–1111); *G*, 22–27, and Dieckmann, ed., 327–30.
63. *G*, 25. Again here – as concerning all quotes in old French – I thank Marta Weingartner for her generous help in translating the passage. Cf. the description of Gérard's fight with the beast later on the same page. Compare also *V*, 45–46, where the beast is referred to as a "dyable" respectively "le grant serpent," and the fight is described. Chézy renders the quoted passage from *G* in the following form (Dieckmann, ed., 329): "sah das Fräulein, wie eine grosse erschreckliche Schlange herbei und auf sie zu kam, und sie rief Gerhart zu: Ach Herr, um Gotteswillen, rettet euch, seht ihr nicht dort das scheussliche entsetzliche Untier mit den Augen und Rachen, die wie Flammen glühen, und mit dem ungeheuern gewundenen Schwanze?" In the libretto, Euryanthe exclaims as she has seen "etwas Grässliches," *Euryanthe*, 161–62, and CD-booklet (as in n. 50), 54: "Entsetzen! rette dich! sieh! eine Schlange fürchterlich wälzt sich herbei durch das Gestein, hinweg! lass mich das

Opfer sein, für dich zu sterben . . ." In the English translation: "Horror! Save yourself! Look, a terrible serpent is slithering towards us through the rocks! Run, let me be its prey! To die for you . . ."

64. Jeffrey Burton Russell, *Lucifer: The Devil in the Middle Ages* (Ithaca: Cornell University Press, 1984), 67–68, 131, and 211 also presenting a very instructive photograph of the statue of Eve and the serpent from the Cathedral of Reims from the thirteenth century, 258. Cf. also *Lexikon des Mittelalters*, III, (München: Artemis Verlag, 1986), col. 1339 and col. 1344, and *Lexikon der Christlichen Ikonographie*, I and IV (Rom: Herder, 1968 and 1972), col. 516, respectively col. 75.

65. *G*, 26 (section 63).

66. *V*, 47, verses 1085–1097.

67. Dieckmann, ed., 330: "Er erhob nun die Augen gen Himmel und dankte dem Herrn, dass er über das grosse Ungeheuer den Sieg davon getragen; dann rief er aus: 'O Gott, du wollest mir helfen, denn wie sollt es mir möglich sein, die totzuschlagen, die mir das Leben gerettet? denn wenn sie nicht gewesen wäre, hätte mich das Untier gewürgt! So kann ich ihr denn kein Leid zufügen, denn da ich eben das Schwert gezückt hatte, um ihr Haupt vom Rumpf zu trennen, sah sie die grässliche Schlange, und schrie mir zu, ich sollte mich retten, welches ich nimmer geglaubt hätte, denn wo ist das Weib zu finden, welche den Mut und Willen hätte, den zu erretten und vor dem Tode zu bewahren, der bereit ist, sie zu erschlagen? So will ich ihr denn das Leben lassen, zumal da es schon ein grosser Jammer ist, hier allein zu bleiben, den wilden Tieren ausgesetzt. So wolle sie denn Gott in seinen Schutz nehmen, und ihre Untat an mir vergeben.' Nachdem Gerhart solches beschlossen, ging er zum Fräulein und sagte ihr: 'Euryanthe, ich lasse dich in Gottes Obhut, und bitte ihn, er wolle dir das Leid vergeben, das du mir zugefügt.' "

68. *Euryanthe*, 165–66 (the English translation from booklet, 56): "Euryanthe: 'Nun lass mich sterben!' Adolar: 'Nein! das sei mir fern. Dich tödten war der Ehre streng Geboth, du aber wolltest geh'n für mich in Tod, so kann ich nicht dein Richter sein, im Schutz des Höchsten bleibe hier allein!' (Adolar stürzt ab. nachdem er noch auf Euryanthen zurückblickend seinen innern schmerzlichen Kampf, sich loszureissen, zeigte.)"

69. Jacques Le Goff, *The Medieval Imagination* (Chicago: University of Chicago Press, 1988, an English translation of the original French edition, Paris 1985), 54–55. See especially the essay "The Wilderness in the Medieval West," 47–59.

70. See Timothy Fry, ed., *The Rule of St. Benedict. In Latin and English with Notes* (Collegeville: The Liturgical Press, 1981), 168–69, cf. C. H. Lawrence, *Medieval Monasticism*, 2nd edition (London: Longman, 1989), 26.

71. Le Goff, 50–54. Also Lawrence, 149–205.

72. Le Goff, 55–59.

73. The number of the so-called scrutinies in the Roman-Frankish liturgy grew from three to seven in the early Middle Ages. These are described and discussed in Henry Ansgar Kelly, *The Devil at Baptism* (Ithaca: Cornell University Press, 1985), 201–31, (201 and 210). See also the suggestive account in O. B. Hardison, *Christian Rite and Christian Drama in the Middle Ages* (Baltimore: The John Hopkins Press, 1965), 93–108 and 141–43. Concerning some non Roman-

Frankish liturgical 'dialects', see also Kelly, 71–72 (on the early Church), 145–46 (Cyril of Jerusalem), 167–69 and 171–72 (Byzantine liturgy), 191 and 199 (Armenian and Egyptian liturgy) and 241 (Gallican liturgy).

74. See, for instance, the following phrase from a prayer from the first scrutiny of the Romano-Germanic Pontifical, the influential liturgical order of the tenth century, whose baptismal liturgy was basically preserved unchanged until the post Tridentine liturgy of the sixteenth century – cf. Kelly, 254): "Omnipotens sempiterne Deus, pater domini nostri Iesu Christi, respicere dignare super hunc famulum tuum N. quem ad rudimenta fidei vocare dignatus es, omnem cecitatem cordis ab eo expelle, desrumpe omnes laqueos Satanae quibus fuerat colligatus, aperi ei, domine, pietatis tuae ianuam, ut signo sapientiae tuae imbutus, omnium cupiditatum fetoribus careat . . ." English translation: "Almighty and eternal God, Father of our Lord Jesus Christ, deign to look upon this your servant N. whom you had counted worthy to call to the beginnings of faith. Drive out all blindness of heart from him and break all the chains with which Satan has held him in bondage. Open to him, O Lord, the door of your mercy, so that having been signed with the mark of your wisdom, all desire for evil doing might lack in him . . ." Cyrille Vogel and Reinhard Elze, eds., *Le pontifical romano-germanique du dixième siècle* (Città del Vaticano: Biblioteca Apostolica Vaticana, 1963), vol. II, 25 (the same formula also found in the same book in the "Order for Baptizing Infants," 155). The translation given here is due to the late Professor C. Clifford Flanigan to whom I am much indebted for the understanding of medieval liturgy. Hardison, 97, stressed that the scrutinies were regarded as a "journey toward baptism." They started on the third Wednesday of Lent and ended Easter Saturday morning. The baptism then took place in the afternoon during the Easter vigil. Thematically the Lenten liturgy stressed personal combat with sin.

75. The order for baptising children which has incorporated much material from the scrutinies is found in Vogel and Elze, eds., vol. II, 155–64. Here the Devil is explicitly mentioned by the name *Satanas* six times, as *diabolus* three times and as *spiritus inmundus* (impure spirit) four times (not counting the five repetitions of the formula *Ergo maledicte diabole*, "Therefore, cursed Devil"). For the relationship between theological approaches to Evil and the folkloristic imagery penetrating into literature and art, see Russel, 208–9.

76. See Karl Young, *The Drama of the Medieval Church,* 2 vols (London: Clarendon Press, 1933), I, 149–51 and 425 (from an incorporation of a descensus scene in the Ludus Paschalis from Klosterneuburg of the thirteenth century, 421–29). The earliest mention of the participation of devils (here without any lines) seems to date from the eleventh century from the *Sponsus* using the term *Demones*, see Young, II, 364 and 366–67.

77. See the edition and translation of the verbal text of the *Ordo Virtutum* in Peter Dronke, ed., *Nine medieval Latin plays* (Cambridge: Cambridge University Press, 1994), 164–79. I quote two examples, first from the lines of *Humilitas* to *Diabolus* (164): "Ego cum meis sodalibus bene scio/ quod tu es ille antiquus dracho/ qui super summum volare voluisti – sed ipse deus in abyssum proiecit te." English translation (165): "My comrades and I know very well that you are the dragon of old, who craved to fly higher than the highest one: but God himself hurled you in

the abyss." Secondly the lines of Victoria, (Dronke, 170): "Ego Victoria velox et fortis pugnatrix sum –/ in lapide pugno, serpentem antiquum conculco." English translation (171): "I am Victory, the swift, brave champion: I fight with a stone, I tread the age-old serpent down."

78. See *Analecta Hymnica* (in the following *A.H.*), vol. XLVIII, edited by Guido Maria Dreves (Leipzig: O. R. Reisland, 1905), 183 and the introduction (141–42) concerning the hymn *Serpens erectus*. Also Josef Szövérffy, *Die Annalen der lateinischen Hymnendichtung* 2 vols. (Berlin: Erich Schmidt Verlag, 1964–65), II, 169. The "serpens erectus" would be the cobber snake that Moses was told to erect in the desert (Num. 21, 8–9) prefiguring Christ (cf. John. 3,14), whereas the "antiquus serpens" is the Devil. I quote the first two stanzas: "Serpens erectus/ Serpentum morsus/ Conspectu sanat,/ Antiqui virus/ Serpentis Christus/ Suspensus curat." English translation: "The erected serpent heals the bites of the serpents through sight, Christ hanging [on the cross] cures the poison of the Old Serpent."

79. See the hymn *Rhythmus in Laude Salvatoris*, *A.H.*, vol. XLVIII, 244–51, cf. the introduction, 233–34, and Szövérffy, II, 98. I quote the beginning of the fourth stanza: "Draco perimitur,/ Mundus redimitur/ Sanguinis pretio . . ." [The dragon is destroyed, the world redeemed through the ransom of blood . . .]

80. See an Easter hymn edited in the *A.H.*, vol. LIV, edited by Cl. Blume and H. M. Bannister (Leipzig: O. R. Reisland, 1915), 227–28, cf. introduction, V–XX. The ascribing of the hymn to Adam is not certain. Cf. Szövérffy, II, 110. In the stanzas 9 and 10 of the hymn one finds both the use of *draco*, *serpens*, and *anguis* (snake) as metaphors for the Devil.

81. See for instance the sequence "De Undecim Milibus Virginibus" (for saint Ursula) and the antiphon "in dedicatione ecclesiae," Hildegard von Bingen, *Lieder*. Nach den Handschriften herausgegeben von Pudentiana Barth, Immaculata Ritscher und Joseph Schmidt-Görg (Salzburg: Otto Müller Verlag, 1969), 270–75. Also edited with music, 118–22 and 127–28. I quote the last four lines of the sequence: "Hoc audiant omnes caeli/ et in summa symphonia laudent Agnum Dei,/ quia guttur serpentis antiqui in istis margaritis/ materiae Verbi Dei suffocatum est. (272) English translation: "Let all heavens hear/ and praise the Lamb of God all singing together:/ that the throat of the age-old serpent through these pearls/ made of the words of God was choked."

82. *Euryanthe*, 58–59.

83. Original text in the excerpt in Hürlimann, ed., 194–96: "Ich wünschte die Oper volkstümlich und zugleich troubadouresk zu behandeln, den Leitfaden des alten Fabliau nicht aus den Händen zu lassen. Weber hatte Bedenken wegen des Veilchens auf Euryanthens Brust, Ludwig Tieck vermehrte diese durch seine Bemerkungen. Weber, der auch später im *Oberon* bewiesen, wie sehr das Geisterelement sein eigenes war, wollte eine Umwandlung, bei welcher es angewendet würde." See also Constantin Floros, "Carl Maria von Weber, Grundsätzliches über sein Schaffen" in Constantin Floros et al., eds., *Carl Maria von Weber*. Musik-Konzepte 52 (München: Edition Text + Kritik, 1986), 5–21 (15).

84. *Euryanthe*, 154–55. Booklet, 52.

85. See – aside from the piano score referred to throughout this presentation – also the printed full score, Carl Maria von Weber, *Euryanthe: Grosse romantische*

Oper in drei Aufzügen. Dichtung von Helmine von Chezy, geb: Freyinn von Klencke. Partitur (Berlin: Verlag der Schlesinger'schen Buch u. Musikhandlung, no date). The score, however, has an introduction written by Ernst Rudorff, dated Cologne 1866. For the orchestral introduction to the third act and the mentioned recitatives, see 231–34 corresponding to *Euryanthe*, 153–55.

    86. *Euryanthe*, 166.

    87. Tusa, 30 and 249–52 and 259; also Warrack, 284, and Floros, 15.

    88. *Euryanthe*, 8, bars 129–43. See Tusa, 30 and 251.

    89. *Euryanthe*, 58–59 (cf. at n. 81 above); 197–98 (as Eglantine on her way to the planned wedding with Lysiard sees Emma, breaks down and confesses the crime); and 219 in a version in C major (whereas the earlier three versions are all in B minor) as the villains have been defeated, Adolar and Euryanthe reunited, and Adolar feels the redemption of Emma. (Compare with the famous modulation from B to C in *Der Freischütz* at the celebration of the denouement in the final scene.)

    90. Cf. Tusa, 251.

    91. Nils Holger Petersen, "*Danielis ludus* and the Latin Music Dramatic Traditions of the Middle Ages," in Laszlo Dobszay, ed., *The Past in the Present* (Budapest: Hungarian Academy of Sciences – Liszt Ferenc Academy of Music, 2003), 291–307 (298–307), with further references. The fundamental ideas rest mainly on the scholarship of O. B. Hardison and C. Clifford Flanigan.

    92. See the printed score of *Euryanthe* (cf. n. 84 above), 286–90, third act, beginning of no. 23.

    93. *Euryanthe*, 197–98.

"Those effigies which belonged to the English Nation": Antiquarianism, Nationalism and Charles Alfred Stothard's *Monumental Effigies of Great Britain*

Rachel Dressler

On May 27, 1821, having been commissioned by Daniel Lysons to produce drawings of the antiquities of Devon for his late brother Samuel's *Magna Britannia*, Charles Alfred Stothard F.S.A. secured permission from the Reverend Henry Hobart, vicar of Bere Ferrers Church, to make tracings of the eastern stained glass window devoted to the founder of the church and his wife. The next day, Stothard ascended a ladder placed in front of the window and proceeded to sketch. As he was working, the step on which he was standing gave way and he fell, striking his head on the slab of a knight's tomb placed in the chancel. He died shortly thereafter.[1] Stothard was 34 years old.

Stothard died as he had lived, devoted to the study of Britain's medieval remains. The manner of Stothard's death heightened its poignancy, for he had devoted himself to examining England's medieval and early modern effigies for much of his adult life. Stothard was an artist and antiquarian whose interests and work straddled the dividing line between recording, and thus preserving, monuments through drawings and etchings, and studying these same works for their historical import. At the time of his death, Stothard was completing Number 10 of his *Monumental Effigies of Great Britain*, a survey of English medieval and early modern tomb figures part of whose purpose can be gleaned from the subtitle: *Selected from our cathedrals and churches for the purpose of bringing together, and preserving correct representations of the best historical illustrations extant, from the Norman Conquest to the reign of Henry the Eighth*. His intended Preface, which was included in edited form in the final edition of his book and as the full text in his widow's *Memoirs of Charles A. Stothard* (1843), sheds further light on his intentions in presenting a study of these antiquities: "By these means, we live in other ages than our own, and become nearly as well acquainted with them. In some measure, we arrest the fleeting steps of Time, and again review those things his arm has past over and subdued, but not destroyed. The researches of the antiquary are worthless, if they do not impart to us this power, or give us other advantages; it is not to admire anything for its age or rust, that constitutes the interest of the object, but as conducive to our knowledge, the enlargement of human intellect and general improvement."[2]

Why would Stothard desire to revitalise the past through the preservation and presentation of obscure, often fragmentary, bits of funeral sculpture, and what general improvement would he look to in engaging his readers in this study? It is the contention of this essay that the political, social and cultural context in which he grew up and trained as an artist and antiquary prompted his exploration into England's medieval past. Stothard engaged in this work at precisely the period in which the English were fashioning an expanded national identity as British and struggling with the anxiety aroused by the threat of Catholic France and social uncertainties attendant upon the French and American Revolutions. The cultural turmoil occasioned by union with Scotland and Wales, on-going wars with France, and global empire building sparked a reconsideration of class privilege among the inhabitants of the British Isles. As part of this social sea-change, Stothard's greatest work, *The Monumental Effigies of Great Britain*, looked to the medieval past in its response to and participation in the British population's process of self-refashioning. Through his selection of effigies to represent, Stothard constructed a glorious history largely celebrating those forerunners of the privileged class of his own time: male aristocrats. The past constructed by artists and antiquarians like Stothard could be and was employed to consolidate class privilege at a time when it was under threat of upheaval from across the Channel and under scrutiny by critics within its own borders.

Anyone familiar with English cultural history from the Tudor period to the Victorian Age knows that Stothard's choice of subject matter was not unique in antiquarian circles. Medieval sepulchral monuments were objects of antiquarian inquiry going back as far as the sixteenth century. Prior to Stothard the two major works to survey England's funereal remains were John Weever's *Antient Funerall Monuments* (1631) and Richard Gough's *Sepulchral Monuments in Great Britain*, coming out in multiple parts between 1786 and 1796.[3] What sets *Monumental Effigies* apart from his predecessors' studies is Stothard's concern with artistic quality and stylistic consistency. In addition, his choice of subject located him squarely within the medieval revival, a cultural movement crucial to a new nationalism in the British Isles. Through his skill as an artist, as well as his antiquarian training, he claimed possession of a newly treasured medieval past for himself and made it his own.

Stothard may have inherited his artistic inclinations and nurtured them through training. Born in 1786, he was the second, and only surviving, son of Thomas Stothard R.A., a prominent artist of the medieval revival, the bulk of whose career was devoted to book illustration.[4] In 1802 Stothard accompanied his father, who had a commission to decorate a staircase, to Burleigh, seat of the Marquis of Exeter. While his father worked, Charles spent his time in the local parish churches making drawings of the various monuments they housed. Perhaps this experience encouraged his lifelong interest in antiquarian pursuits. Stothard entered the Royal Academy in 1807, where he studied painting by copying antique sculpture. In 1811 he created a sensation by exhibiting his painting of the death of Richard II at Pontefract Castle in which, according to his future brother-in-law, Alfred Kempe, Stothard was careful to render all the costumes with strict historical accuracy.[5] In this painting Stothard the artist merged with Stothard the antiquarian, a dual identity which was to characterise him from then on.

It was Stothard's antiquarian interests, as well as his artistic skill, that led to his involvement with the Society of Antiquaries. In 1815 Samuel Lysons, a prominent member of this antiquarian institution, commissioned the young artist to make drawings for his study of British antiquities entitled *Magna Britannia*. While Stothard was engaged in recording the monuments of northern England, Lysons had him appointed to the office of historical draughtsman to the Society.[6] It was in this capacity that Stothard journeyed to Normandy, where he was commissioned to make drawings of the famous *Bayeux Tapestry* in 1816, a project he completed two years later. Shortly thereafter, Stothard exhibited his drawings to members of the Society. He also included some remarks on the famous textile that attempted to demonstrate its late-eleventh-century date and deny any association with Matilda, William the Conqueror's consort, and alleged creator of the embroidery.[7] The overwhelmingly positive response to both the drawings and the explication led to Stothard's unanimous election as a Fellow of the Society of Antiquaries that same year. He drawings were published as part of the Society-sponsored *Vetusta Monumenta* in 1819.[8]

It was his trips to France, as well as his youthful sketching of monuments, that reinforced Stothard's antiquarian leanings, especially in regard to funeral sculpture. In 1816, while on a visit to the ruined abbey of Fontevraud in the Loire, Stothard discovered several effigies in more or less intact condition in a cellar.[9] These figures turned out to be the famous representations of the Plantagenet sovereigns Henry II, Eleanor of Acquitaine,

Richard I, and Isabel of Angouleme. It had been thought that these figures were destroyed during the course of the French Revolution. In view of their historical importance, Stothard formed the idea of appealing to the British government to have these sculptures brought to England and installed in Westminster Abbey in company with the other royal effigies. He failed to convince officials of this plan, but his discovery did alert the French government to the need to preserve these treasures. He also represented these sculptures in the *Monumental Effigies*.

Five years previous to his French excursions, Stothard began to publish what would be the major artistic and antiquarian enterprise of his career: *The Monumental Effigies of Great Britain*.[10] His widow, Eliza, later Mrs. Anna Eliza Bray, and his brother-in-law, Alfred John Kempe, issued the book posthumously as a complete volume in 1832. During his tragically short lifetime, Stothard had published nine of a projected twelve pamphlets of his etchings of English tomb sculpture.

As it exists today, *The Monumental Effigies of Great Britain* consists of some 142 etchings of tomb monuments, representing 98 individuals, dating from the late eleventh century through the early sixteenth. The earliest monument depicted is the coffin lid of Queen Matilda, wife of William the Conqueror, and the latest is the effigy of Sir John Peche, warrior and courtier in the reign of Henry VIII. The majority of the individuals represented by these tomb figures can be classified as elite: out of 98, 68 are of a knightly rank or higher nobility; 22 are royal, and 7 are ecclesiastical of the rank of bishop or archbishop. There is only one effigy, that of William Wantley, a fifteenth-century merchant, which is not aristocratic. Male figures dominate the selection, which consists of 72 males and 26 females.

To a certain degree, Stothard's selection was governed by the original medieval and early modern patronage, for many of the surviving three dimensional tombs of the period belonged to elite individuals.[11] Medieval European three-dimensional tomb sculpture dates back as far as the twelfth century, when the practice of carved commemorative monuments was well established among ecclesiastical and secular princes, aided by the financial and status benefits accruing to the church for burying the elite dead. In England, the earliest sculpted effigies were of high-ranking ecclesiastics, archbishops and bishops, and members of royal families. By c. 1240, however, those holding knightly rank also began commissioning tomb monuments. The thirteenth century witnessed an explosion of knightly patronage such that military effigies represent the largest surviving category of English medieval stone sculpture. The initial monuments were commissioned by titled families possessing large and multiple estates, and national importance, but by the late-thirteenth century, simple county knights with limited holdings and only local political influence were also being represented with great frequency.[12] In the later fifteenth century, when brasses had overtaken stone or alabaster sculpture as the most popular form of commemorative monument, members of the merchant and professional ranks were also commissioning tombs.[13]

Stothard's selection only partially reflects the demographics of tomb production in the later medieval and early modern periods. By the fifteenth century the number of figured tombs commemorating those from the ranks of county knights, civic officials, merchants and professionals outnumbered monuments to the highest levels of the aristocracy. By contrast, just over half of the figures included in the *Monumental Effigies* represent titled individuals – archbishops, bishops, monarchs, earls and dukes. Furthermore, Stothard includes very few brasses, a tomb type heavily patronised by the increasingly significant middle class, despite the fact that this less expensive alternative predominated by 1400. Stothard's decision to focus on three-dimensional stone and alabaster figures virtually ensured that the highest ranks of medieval society would receive greater representation in his survey.

The effigies are presented in chronological order from earliest to latest. Many of them are displayed in both frontal and profile views (Figures 1 and 2); furthermore, if the monument displayed double figures, husband and wife, Stothard often included a profile view of each individual figure (Figure 3). Most of the monuments are stone but a few brasses are also represented. In addition, Stothard, or one of his posthumous collaborators, frequently displayed a smaller, fully-coloured version of the effigy, or details of costume, on the same page with the major image.

It is unclear how Stothard arrived at the colours he employed for his illustrations. Most of the effigies included in his study have lost their original polychromy, but two hundred years ago they may have retained a bit more. His text makes no reference to his sources and his widow's memoir makes only scattered statements about this issue. For example, in the draft of his Preface, Stothard notes that the historical accuracy of the effigies' costumes can be confirmed by comparison with images in coeval illuminated manuscripts.[14] It is perhaps from the latter source that he also derived his colours. In addition, in a letter to a fellow antiquarian, Stothard boasts that his drawings of escutcheons, intended for the margins of his plates, would be faithful to the originals, unlike those created by the present-day Heralds' Colleges.[15] These remarks suggest that he may have consulted the arms rolls, another source for colour.

Medieval tomb effigies were frequently encased in architectural frames which could be as simple as plain arched wall niches or as elaborate as the multi-tiered, traceried structure surmounting the tomb of Edward II. In addition many of the figures lie on sizeable boxlike tombs, often with highly decorated sides. Stothard's illustrations eliminate most evidence of the effigies' original contexts and present them almost as free-standing figures against the empty, cream-coloured background of the paper used in the book. Not a single etching makes visual reference to any arched niche, although a number of the originals surely must have been located in such spaces. Nor is there any indication of elaborate tomb canopies, as his illustration of Edward II demonstrates.[16] All that survives of the tomb's decoration beyond the effigy are the angels supporting the monarch's head and the lion crouched at his feet. In most of his frontal views, Stothard also eliminates almost all signs of the rectangular chest on which many of these figures originally reposed. In his image of William Longespée the Elder, for example, it is impossible to tell that the Earl of Salisbury's gisant still resides on a table-type tomb in Salisbury Cathedral (Figure 4). There are occasional frontal examples in which the slab supporting the effigy is visible (Figures 5 and 6) and profile depictions sometimes include such indications as well.[17] Only the headplates for Queen Berengaria, Sir Robert de Shurland, William de Valence, Edward the Black Prince, Sir Guy Bryan, and Sir John Peche give any indications of tomb chests, canopies, or both (Figure 7). In a letter to William Stevenson, Stothard indicates that he originally intended separate plates, of equal dimensions to those representing the effigies, for tomb architecture but abandoned this idea in favour of half-page images of effigies with escutcheons occupying broad margins.[18] In the end, neither plan was carried out.

Excluding the figures and details rendered in colour, Stothard's images are delicately monochromatic. All of the figures except for the five brasses are a soft gray in tone, with slightly darker parallel and cross-hatched lines creating shadows and enhancing three-dimensionality. The chronological differences among the effigies are not manifested by any stylistic modifications, but there are variations in the etching line resulting from the use of multiple artists to complete the etchings left unfinished at Stothard's death. For example, a comparison between *Edward II*, drawn and etched by Stothard, and *A Lady and Child*, drawn by Stothard but etched by B. Hewlitt, reveals the former's use of a crisper, harder and darker line. It is difficult to judge how much the etchings depart from Stothard's original drawings since few of the latter works are known to be extant, and none of these pertain to the *Monumental Effigies*.[19] There are surviving drawings for an intended album of French effigies, which was never published.[20] They are very close in style to Stothard's etchings for his English volume.

In addition to the images, *Monumental Effigies* features an extensive text consisting of a twenty-three page Introduction and a biography, or "historical description" accompanying each tomb monument. The book as presently constituted also displays two different title pages, an advertisement from the printer, and two engravings: a portrait of Charles A. Stothard after a miniature by Alfred Chalon and an allegorical frontispiece by Thomas Stothard entitled *The Monumental Effigies rescued from Time*.

The finished volume of the *Monumental Effigies* results from the intervention of Anna Bray and Alfred Kempe. The 1832 publication contains a disclaimer from Stothard's widow in which she explains the necessity of issuing and charging for the Introduction and Historical Description, written by her brother (Kempe), separately from the etchings of the monuments themselves.[21] At his death, Stothard had completed all the drawings, but only some of the etchings, forcing his widow to hire artists at great expense to finish the work. In addition, the artist left behind fragmentary drawings of tomb elevations for the head-plates, but did not identify the monuments to which they belonged. According to an explanatory paragraph before the list of illustrations, Stothard only managed to complete eight of the historical descriptions: Queen Berengaria, Henry II, the Temple Church Military Effigies, William de Valence, Edward the Black Prince, Sir Guy Bryan, William Fitz-Alan, and Sir John Peche.[22] The rest of the descriptions were Kempe's creations.

Stothard's study follows immediately upon the beginning of that period characterised by cultural historians as the medieval revival. The medieval period had been scorned in England for almost the whole of the eighteenth century for its supposed superstition and barbarism, but by late in the century the Middle Ages had become not just acceptable but positively celebrated. As Mark Girouard puts it in *The Return to Camelot*: "By the second half of the eighteenth century there was a sizeable group of country gentlemen with antiquarian tastes, or antiquarians with friends among the gentry, all busy studying the Middle Ages, publishing the results of their researches and building Gothic buildings."[23] Horace Walpole's neo-Gothic home Strawberry Hill, built between 1749 and 1776, and James Wyatt's Fonthill Abbey, dated 1796–1812, are two famous examples of such medieval revival structures. Medieval nostalgia was also manifest in literature. Walpole's *Castle of Otranto*, which the author first published in 1764 as an alleged recovered medieval manuscript, was so popular that a second and third edition appeared within a year of the original.[24] This novel and Ann Radcliffe's *Mysteries of Udolpho* are considered among the founding works of literary medievalism.[25] Even George III, England's monarch, felt the pull of the past, for in 1787 he commissioned Benjamin West to decorate the walls of the Kings's Audience Chamber at Windsor Castle with a series devoted to his medieval predecessor Edward III.[26]

One of the Middle Ages' primary attractions for late-eighteenth-century Britons was its perceived social and religious stability. By contrast their own age was witness to great social upheaval attendant upon the merging of three nations into one. While the Act of Union of 1707, a

Parliamentary act joining Scotland to England and Wales, made Great Britain a political reality, the process of forging a unified national identity took much longer, almost 130 years according to historian Linda Colley.[27] Other scholars, such as Stephanie Barczewski, have questioned whether such an identity ever completely took hold and persisted.[28]

Aside from geographic proximity, the three nations of the new Great Britain had little in common. They had different, if related, histories; spoke different languages; ate different foods; and wore different clothes. For the English, the process of forming a national identity had been on-going since the early Tudor period of the sixteenth century, but now they had to incorporate their neighbors to the west and north into a new, expanded, British nation. Despite their cultural differences, the inhabitants of the British Isles succeeded in forging a single collective identity by the end of the eighteenth century. Colley argues that the struggles against France – Catholic, Revolutionary, and Napoleonic – provided an external adversary, and the opposition to this perceived threat the adhesive binding the disparate units together into Great Britain.[29]

England's conflict with France had roots in the Middle Ages, but the eighteenth-century manifestation of English Francophobia derived initially from France's role as the major continental Catholic power and later as the instigator of class warfare during the French Revolution. In general the English perceived their neighbors across the Channel as in all things the opposite of themselves: where the English were rational, virtuous and free, the French were superstitious, militaristic, decadent and enslaved to absolutism.[30]

In the nineteenth century Great Britain's hard-won unity began to break down again according to Barczewski. The incorporation of Ireland into the United Kingdom in 1800 brought Catholics in as at least partial citizens, while Catholic Emancipation in 1829 gave them greater rights. What had been constructed as an alien group, closely identified with France, was now part of the national framework. In addition, confrontation with the non-European peoples of the expanding empire, and the increasing clamour inside Britain for complete enfranchisement on the part of the lower classes, and even perhaps women, forced a re-evaluation of what it meant to be British. One response to a problematic identity was to emphasise pre-Act of Union allegiances, at least in England, which began to assert itself as the strongest component of the United Kingdom. By the end of the nineteenth century, English culture and history had begun to dominate British national identity. As Barczewski puts it: "A Briton could be made, but one had to be born English."[31]

Regardless of whether one accepts Colley's or Barczewski's analysis, one must recognise the centrality of the medieval revival in constructing or inventing the nation in the late eighteenth and early nineteenth century. The conflict with France, particularly on the heels of the French Revolution, may have given strong impetus to the nostalgia for the medieval past, especially among the elite of all parts of the British Isles. As they witnessed the violent overturning of French class hierarchies, and the execution of French monarchs, the British gentry, and the middle class, became increasingly conservative. For them, the Middle Ages came to represent a time of social stability when the monarchy was respected and a firm class structure held sway.[32] As such it offered a distinct and glorious historical precedent for a nation wrestling with a new identity and feeling under threat from across the Channel. In addition, Greek and Roman antiquity, which had functioned as the chief cultural exemplar since the Renaissance, was now closely linked to the ideology of the French Revolution, lessening its appeal to those in Great Britain fearful of violent reforms happening upon their own soil.[33] Even when France returned to centralised rule under Napoleon, the fact that his elite often advanced through effort rather than land or lineage offered no reassurance to Britain's landed class.[34]

British elites were right to fear social upheaval at home in that their privileged position in society came under attack from without and within. The spectre of the class warfare that sparked the French Revolution, in which their French counterparts were on the losing side, terrified British aristocrats. Furthermore, political, social, and economic factors had combined to make the governing class of Great Britain both very wealthy and very vulnerable to criticism. With increasing industrialisation and urbanisation, and imperial expansion abroad, Great Britain began to experience great economic growth and global power. With increased income from landed estates, the British elite benefited disproportionately from this new prosperity. As a result of intermarriage, wealth, and the power attendant upon it, became concentrated in the hands of a small, relatively homogeneous group, rendering them vulnerable to political attacks by Radicals. By the 1780s, on the heels of a defeat in the American Revolution, calling into question the governing class's competency to rule, open criticism of them as parasites had entered political discourse.[35] Criticism continued throughout the first two decades of the nineteenth century. In 1819 John Wade in the *Black Book: or corruption unmasked* wrote about patrician patronage:

> The aristocracy, usurping the power of the state, have the means under various pretexts of extorting for the junior branches of their families, a forced subsistence. They patronize a ponderous and sinecure church establishment; they wage long and unnecessary wars to create employments in the army and navy; they conquer and retain useless colonies; they set on foot expensive missions of

diplomacy and keep an ambassador or consul, and often both, at almost every petty state and pretty port in the world; they create offices without duties, grant unmerited pensions, keep up unnecessary places in the royal household, in the admiralty, the treasury, the customs, excise, courts of law, and every department of the public administration.[36]

One patrician response to such threats against their position was to invoke the medieval past as a golden age of social order and harmony where everyone knew his or her place. This nostalgia took several forms among which was an interest in medieval material culture – its architecture and costume. In 1802 George III commissioned James Wyatt, of Fonthill Abbey fame, to build a castle in Kew Gardens on the model of a curtain wall castle with corner towers, numerous turrets, and a battlemented gatehouse. Radicals nicknamed it the Bastille.[37] In 1806, Robert Smirke built a structure based on the Kew palace for the Tory magnate Lord Lonsdale, and in 1810 he designed a similar building for Lord Somers. The latter's politics can be discerned from the title of a pamphlet he published in 1817, *A defence of the constitution of Great Britain and Ireland, as by law established, against the innovating and levelling attempts of the friends to Annual Parliaments and Universal Suffrage*. In this publication he wrote: "It is Equality which jars with Liberty." He goes on to assert that gentlemen, nobility and clergy gave employment to the poor, dispensed justice to them, and protected them from oppression. Thus, the ruling class was entitled to its privileges and any criticism of it would result in harm to those below.[38] Among those privileges was the right to build a castle and symbolically claim its aristocratic chivalric associations.

As Gothic Revival "castles" went up all over England, their owners worked to fill them with appropriate accessories such as the ubiquitous suit of armour. Sir Walter Scott's *Abbotsford*, built in part to compensate the popular Gothic novelist for the loss of his family's ancestral holdings at Dryburgh Abbey, had a hall full of dark wood, plate armour and antlers, making it a prime example of the use of "Gothic" to suggest an elevated pedigree.[39] By the first decades of the nineteenth century medieval body defenses were being displayed in newly Gothicised halls and in more accessible venues. In 1817 there were two collections on display in London: Thomas Gwennap's in Lower Brook Street and William Bullock's in the Egyptian Hall in Piccadilly. Such open displays allowed the general public to come and admire these relics of the chivalric past.[40]

In addition to recreating or collecting tangible remains of medieval civilisation, patricians, men in particular, appealed to the ancient practice of chivalry in order to fend off criticism by constructing themselves as a military service elite in the tradition of knighthood.[41] Military glory was very much in vogue during the years of warfare with France, and the aristocracy, who provided a large percentage of the officers in the British army and navy, benefited from an emerging cult of heroism. By associating themselves with military heroes, especially those paying the ultimate patriotic price, patricians made claims to being a service elite.[42] Paintings such as *The Death of General Wolfe* (1770), by Benjamin West, and *The Death of General Pierson* (1783), by John Singleton Copley, intensified the link between elite social status and patriotism by visually transforming these ranking military heroes into martyrs for their country. That these paintings, and others like them, were reproduced on a mass scale in prints, on fabrics and ceramics, testifies to the powerful hold patrician wartime sacrifice had on the artistic and public imagination.[43] So does the decision by Parliament in the early 1790s to allocate money in order to erect statues to army and naval heroes in St. Paul's Cathedral. The patrician obsession with the military came to govern the mission of elite public schools such as Eton, Harrow, Winchester, and Westminster, where it took the form of celebrations of British military victories and a stress on studying those classical authors most concerned with stories of war, empire, and sacrifice for the state. The sport of fox-hunting with its dependence on speed, horsemanship, and physical courage could be readily analogised to battle experience; it became increasingly popular among the elite class in the early nineteenth century. Happily, since foxes were considered vermin, elites could claim to perform a valuable service to the country while enjoying the sport immensely.[44] Of course, all this "real men" activity also placed British elite males in opposition to French men, who were generally regarded as effete.

Nothing was more compatible with the contemporary cult of military glory, and the construction of masculinity as aristocratic, physically gifted, courageous, and patriotic than medieval chivalry and the cult of knighthood. Cultural interest in chivalric material confirms Britain's obsession with this part of its medieval history. The first three decades of the nineteenth century saw the publication of numerous translations of medieval knightly romances or ballads as well as the chronicles of Froissart and de Joinville. New editions of Malory's *Morte d'Arthur* came out in 1816 and 1817; Charles Mills published his *History of the Crusades* in 1820 and his *History of Chivalry* in 1825.[45] In the construction of a nationalist history, which stressed the stability of social order with a deserving aristocracy at its head, in contrast to the violent overthrows characterising the hated French, the Middle Ages played a crucial role.

It is difficult to determine precisely Charles Stothard's attitude towards the rage for all things medieval that marked pre-Victorian Great Britain. According to his widow, Stothard's interest in the Middle Ages emerged when he was quite young. As a child he was the favourite of his aunt, who required him to sit with her while she engaged in needlework. According to Bray:

> Seated on a low stool in the chimney-corner, whilst the good lady was employed with her needle, little Charles would read Shakspear (sic), or the histories of our Gothic times, till his heart was agitated with a quicker pulsation; and his imagination pictured to him in such glowing colours, "the pride, pomp, and 'circumstance' of knights and tournaments," that scarcely knowing how to restrain his feelings, and wishing to give them vent, he would leave the house, and rambling into the pine forest in the neighborhood, there indulge his reveries on past times, till he reluctantly returned, deeply lamenting there were now neither knights, nor tournaments, nor glittering arms.[46]

We are also reminded that he was son to one of the day's most highly regarded painters and illustrators of medieval themes, and that Charles's presentation piece to the Royal Academy also had a medieval theme. Yet, his published letters contain only one direct reference to any part of the medieval revival, which seems to contradict his earlier stance. This is his opinion of the newly "Gothicised" Arundel Castle found in a letter to his father, Thomas, dated Oct. 1, 1814:

> I have been highly favored by the kindness, the attentions, and politeness of Mr. Lane, who is ever ready to show me any thing. Yesterday morning I went over to Arundel castle with him; which, for all the expense bestowed upon it, is not worth seeing: excepting three or four whole length portraits, of the time of Henry the Eighth and Queen Elizabeth, there are no pictures but the vilest trash. In the castle, all is modern Gothic; so tasteless and overloaded with ornament, that you feel quite surfeited. You here find Grecian figures (if they deserve the name) intermixed. To give the most complete idea of the taste which pervades the castle, I need only speak of the library. It is of course in the *Gothic* (sic) style; the whole of mahogany and cedar, polished and varnished to excess.[47]

This passage suggests his contempt for at least one example of medievalist madness, and seems in contradiction to his wife's description of his boyhood fantasies.

A comparison between Stothard's historical descriptions in the *Monumental Effigies* and his brother-in-law Kempe's contributions seems to bear this contradiction out. Stothard does note the subject's military experience but seems more concerned with the description of the effigy. Kempe, on the other hand, is enthralled with the romance of the Middle Ages and is more likely to dwell on the subject's deeds of chivalry or miraculous experiences, often in rather florid prose. In his entry on Sir Guy Bryan, for example, Stothard devotes the first paragraph to the knight's military service: "During the reigns of Edward III and Richard II no one appears to have been more actively or variously engaged than Sir Guy Bryan. He first presents himself to notice, 23rd Edward III. at the Battle of Calais, in which he bore the king's standard, when for his gallant carriage with that trust he granted him two hundred marks per annum."[48] That is about as enthusiastic as Stothard gets. He goes on more or less to list Sir Guy's other service before turning to the effigy itself. This paragraph is much longer and more detailed as to the condition of the effigy, costume attributes and blazoning of the arms. By contrast, Kempe's account of the life of William Longespée, Earl of Salisbury, is much more fulsome concerning the earl's chivalric worth. He begins by citing William's parentage before turning to his military career. After mentioning the earl's support of King John against the barons and his subsequent switch to the barons' side, Kempe tells this anecdote:

> In 1224 he went over into Gascony with Richard Earl of Cornwall, to subdue certain towns and castles to obedience to King Henry their lord. Returning in the following year they were overtaken at sea by a violent tempest; after beating about for many nights and days they were carried far out of their course; and giving themselves up for lost, committed all their treasure and rich garments to the deep. While they remained in darkness and despair, on a sudden the whole vessel was illuminated by the brilliant flame of a huge wax taper, which appeared on the prow, and by it a damsel of exceeding beauty, who protected the light with her garment from force of the wind and rain. While the crew were lost in wonder at this miraculous nocturnal vision, the Earl of Salisbury proclaimed that their thanks were due to the Blessed Virgin for this merciful interposition, at whose shrine, on the day of his knighthood, he had offered a taper to be kept constantly burning on the daily celebration of the offices to her honour.[49]

What more stirring and romantic vision of this virtuous knight could one ask for?

Stothard's boyhood romance with the Middle Ages can be reconciled with his later attitude if we recognise that what we see in him is not so much a complete rejection of his contemporaries' idealised Middle Ages as an overriding concern with authenticity, which was a legacy of his antiquarian training. We have already noted that one of Stothard's goals for *Monumental*

Effigies was to provide history painters with accurate examples of medieval costumes to copy.[50] The desire for accuracy can be attached to even the earliest antiquarian productions. Beginning with John Leland's *Itinerary* (1533) antiquaries made a point of on-site observation and recording of monuments and inscriptions in English churches.[51] In the seventeenth century, William Dugdale conducted a similar tour with the arms painter William Sedgwick in service of his *Monasticon Anglicanum*.[52] His publication also contains illustrations by Wenceslaus Hollar and Daniel King. Both John Weever and Richard Gough followed the same practice in their studies of England's medieval funerary remains: they recorded written inscriptions and published illustrations produced by other hands. By contrast Stothard strove to record monuments in his own hand and, as we have seen, intended to produce all of the finished etchings himself.

During his travels, Stothard encountered numerous examples of tomb monuments damaged through misguided restoration. Over and over again, his published letters express dismay over the nineteenth-century love of restoration and subsequent damage to the historical accuracy of medieval remains. For example, in September, 1815 he writes to his brother-in-law of the proposed restoration of the Arundel Chapel chancel: "One of the causes for my giving up the Canterbury scheme was, having heard from very good authority that it is now in agitation to restore the Arundel chancel, and the monuments, according to the ideas of what they originally were. How far such improvements are to be feared you will judge, when you see for yourself what is already done in the architectural way here."[53]

Stothard's insistence on historical integrity makes itself evident in the *Monumental Effigies* in his titles for the plates. In the matter of attribution, Stothard often opts for caution. For example, his etching of a thirteenth-century knight's effigy located in Salisbury Cathedral is entitled *Monumental Effigy of a Knight Templar in Salisbury Cathedral*. Kempe, on the other hand, is much more willing to speculate as to attribution. His historical description of this same figure is entitled *William Longespee the Younger*.

Stothard was sometimes willing to take extreme measures in order to present the most complete and accurate image possible of his chosen monuments (Figures 8 and 9). An extract of his account of recording the monument to Richard Beauchamp found in a letter to his father dated August 31, 1813 demonstrates his zeal for thoroughness:

> On Saturday last I made a discovery that the figure was loose; and, with considerable difficulty, having raised it an inch or two, found, to my great surprise, that the back was nearly as highly finished as the front. To get leave to turn the figure was a matter of great difficulty; my request having been put by, with its being hazardous,

Charles Stothard's *Effigies*

and requiring the assistance of three or four men. This morning, on re-examination, I conceived a mode of executing my purpose. Having locked the doors for fear of interruptions, with the asistance of a mason, who by good luck was working in the church, I succeeded , in the course of ten minutes, in turning this massy figure completely over, laying him face downwards. The drawing I have begun of this view, though unsightly, will unriddle many things which till to-day I did not understand.[54]

It was Stothard's training as an artist, as well as his antiquarian studies, that allowed him to exert almost complete control over the *Monumental Effigies*. As a result, there is a dramatic difference between the overall impact of his book and the impression one receives from viewing either Weever's or Gough's publication. Weever's *Antient Funerall Monuments* contains illustrations of diverse mortuary-related objects in a multiplicity of styles. Woodcut images of tomb slabs, stained glass donor portraits and three-dimensional monuments all appear within the pages of his work. While he makes no direct reference to how he obtained his illustrations, it is clear from their appearance that whoever produced these woodcuts made an effort to reproduce the style of the period to which the object belonged. Thus, Weever's illustration of Lady Katherine Howard's fifteenth-century effigy looks like a woodcut of that period while the image of the sixteenth-century representation of Lord John Howard mimics Tudor style. This sensitivity to period style emphasises the temporal context of the object's production. Gough's illustrations are not so chronologically attuned, but, because they were produced by many different people, a fact which Gough openly acknowledges, they take on a bewildering, if entertaining diversity.[55] For example, the effigy of Eleanor of Castille from Westminster Abbey is shown as both a full-length figure and a detail. The bust-length detail makes the medieval gisant look like an eighteenth-century portrait miniature. The visual chaos is heightened by the lack of uniform dimensions for these images.

The second-hand approach to illustrating sepulchral material was unacceptable to Stothard; in fact, he was highly critical of Gough's study precisely on these grounds. He says in his preface:

> It is true indeed, that a very voluminous work of this kind has been published by the late Mr. Gough, which was undertaken with the best intentions: but whatever information we may receive from his writings, the delineating part is so extremely incorrect and full of errors, that at a future period, when the originals no longer exist, it will be impossible to form any correct idea of what they really were. Had Mr. Gough been draughtsman sufficient to have executed his own drawings, he might have avoided these

innumerable mistakes, which, from circumstances and the nature of the subject, must unavoidably have arisen.[56]

One example of Gough's errors is to be found in the image of a De Ros from the Temple Church, in which Gough's artist has depicted the figure as balding, but Stothard's etching displays the small tufts of hair on the forehead which are also clearly visible on the actual figure.

When we examine Stothard's book, we find a remarkable stylistic consistency regardless of the period to which the effigy belongs. He does differentiate brasses from three dimensional figures by colour, but he presents most figures as discrete objects rather than as parts of larger sculptural ensembles. By contrast, Weever reproduces woodcuts of ecclesiastical embellishments such as stained glass donor portraits and even whole tombs with accompanying mourners. Similarly, Gough's illustrations occasionally offer views of entire tombs situated within chapels or sanctuaries. In both publications, the display of church furnishings and ecclesiastical interiors acts as forceful reminders that medieval funeral monuments were inseparable from medieval religious spaces.

Why does Stothard choose to extract his effigies from their original sacred contexts and present them as isolated statues? In large part, this is the result of the standard artistic training of his day in which students drew from plaster casts of antique sculpture.[57] Stothard's illustrations treat medieval effigies as if they were ancient statuary, pristinely monochrome and removed from any specific setting. Furthermore, their lack of an overt medievalness signaled by the surrounding panoply of Gothic ecclesiastical furnishings has the effect of extricating these figures from their own time and locating them in a zone transcending fixed chronological and spatial boundaries. By removing them from their own historical context, Stothard claims ownership over these relics of the medieval past and renders them freely available to act as desirable icons for his own time and place.

It is possible that Stothard's elimination of overt medievalising characteristics in his illustrations was in its own way an attempt at restoring and improving these figures, similar to the whitewashing that he complained about so strenuously in his letters. By reducing his representations to figures isolated from their tomb base and Gothic architectural framing, Stothard may have also wished to remove any associations between his learned, antiquarian enterprise and the excesses of Gothic Revival flourishing all around him. His opinion of modern Gothic is quite clear – it is overly ornamented, tasteless and, worst of all, inaccurate. His austere, monochromatic and isolated rendering of these effigies could be a way of avoiding the outrages which, in his mind, plagued other medievalist works.

Stothard's Spartan style may have also served to negotiate a difficult dilemma for him and all those interested in the material evidence of the medieval past: the undeniable association between medieval artifacts and that period's Catholicism. English medievalism was fraught with ambivalence about the medieval Catholic Church and its present-day descendant. While patricians, writers and artists might admire and imitate medieval buildings, most were not similarly enamored of medieval religion, which they considered replete with religious tyranny and barbarism. Furthermore, Roman Catholicism was the dominant faith of the hated French, reinforcing English antipathy to its observance. Indeed, English Protestant religious and ethnic bigotry was long-standing, having been a social and political factor since the Reformation.[58] Gothic novels featuring supernatural horrors such as *The Castle of Otranto* and *The Mysteries of Udolpho* were frequently set in southern Europe because it was an area considered rife with exoticism and superstition due to its Roman Catholicism.[59]

For antiquarians medieval religion was an especially pressing problem, for they saw as their mission the preservation of artifacts with undeniable Catholic associations, a stance which left them vulnerable to attack from anti-Catholics. Even such a respected work as Dugdale's *Monasticon Anglicanum* was criticised by the Puritans for its alleged pro-Catholic sentiments.[60] One antiquarian response to this quandary was to distance English Christianity from Continental religion; another response was to suggest that medieval piety, while certainly credulous, did had some positive value. Weever, for example, wrote eloquently of monastic foundations' devotion to God as evidenced by their building of churches, oratories and other sacred buildings.[61] Stothard may well have felt the same ambivalence towards medieval religion as his predecessors and resolved his discomfort by editing out the most obvious indicators of cult practices: ecclesiastical spaces and furnishings. Without visual evidence of their original religious context these effigies become almost completely secular, leaving room for their more nationalistic associations to emerge. In short, through Stothard's laconic presentation, the monumental effigies become less Catholic and, therefore, more English.

Through his style, Stothard removes undesirable associations from these figures; through his selection, he participates in the nineteenth-century patrician self-justifying agenda. In his preface, Stothard explains that he was able to include only a twentieth part of surviving monumental effigies; it is to be presumed that he shows those he feels to be most significant.[62] It is no coincidence that he favours effigies of armoured knights and crowned sovereigns, exactly those medieval elites offered as exemplars of deserving privilege and power used to justify the position of their pre-Victorian successors. The relentless repetition of armoured or crowned figures functions as visual proof of the rightful dominance of the military and royal elite then, and now. He also chooses to illustrate exclusively English effigies, suggesting that Barzcewski's analysis of the breakdown of a unified identity beginning in the nineteenth century is correct.

I would like to conclude by considering Stothard's motives in undertaking this study. Was he compelled to publish his celebratory sepulchral account of a glorious English history out of the same anxious patriotism evidenced by his fellow Englishmen on the heels of the French wars? Certainly, his letters suggest a degree of anti-French feeling characteristic of many English people of his day. In his journal record of a trip to France he made in 1817 he says of the French people, "The French can talk of Semiramis and Jules Caesar, and of things of which they are most likely to know the least; yet do not know anything of their own country. The common people, I believe, have but their five senses; and these they do not often use."[63] He mocks a religious festival which he witnessed at Chartres Cathedral, labeling it a farce, and is frequently critical of the French cuisine he encountered while traveling there.[64] His wife says of him in her *Memoirs*, "Charles was by no means a general admirer of the French. He detested the instances that he so often met with, of their egotism and impertinence; nor did he ever suffer the latter to pass without a check . . . One of these insulting politicians remarked to him, that the English were slaves, that they merely thought themselves free, whilst in reality their only distinction was of having gilded their chains. 'No sir,' said Charles, 'you are mistaken, we have only gilt the chain we placed on France.' "[65] At the same time, Stothard's Francophobia is not unique to him, but, as we have seen, standard for the English of his day.

It is his response to discovering the Plantagenet effigies intact that suggests part of his agenda for the *Monumental Effigies*: a desire to preserve and celebrate a glorious and English past. His journal of his French journey of 1817, published in Bray's *Memoirs*, clearly reveals his understanding of the dynasty's French associations. When he views the enameled tomb plaque of Geoffrey le Bel in the Museum of the Prefecture at Le Mans, for example, he correctly identifies the figure as "Geoffrey le Bel, (surnamed Plantagenet,) Comte de Mans, and father of Henry II."[66] But even though the Plantagenets could be considered as much "French" as "English," Stothard is determined to claim them for his native country. In a letter to the Reverend Thomas Kerrick he states:

> You have heard, I believe, of my expedition to France, for the purpose of making drawings from that barbarous, but very interesting work, the Bayeux Tapestry. You have also heard, I believe, from Mr. Douce, that I have made this in some degree subservient to my purpose of procuring drawings for my own work, from the

effigies of *our* kings and queens at Fontevraud. I do not know if you will allow it to be a fair mode of carrying my series up towards the conquest. However, King John does not now appear so formidable, *provided you do not receive my two kings in No. 8 as Frenchmen* (italics mine).[67]

The only monarchs included in No. 8 of the *Monumental Effigies* were Henry II and Richard I. Finally, his desire to remove the Plantagenet figures from their hiding place at Fontevraud and relocate them in Westminster Abbey, along side the other English royal tombs, reveals Stothard's wish that they be considered exclusively English. In the end, perhaps, his efforts toward securing the Plantagenet effigies for the Crown speak clearly to us of his overall concerns as he worked unceasingly to discover "what had been the fate of those effigies which belonged to the English nation."[68]

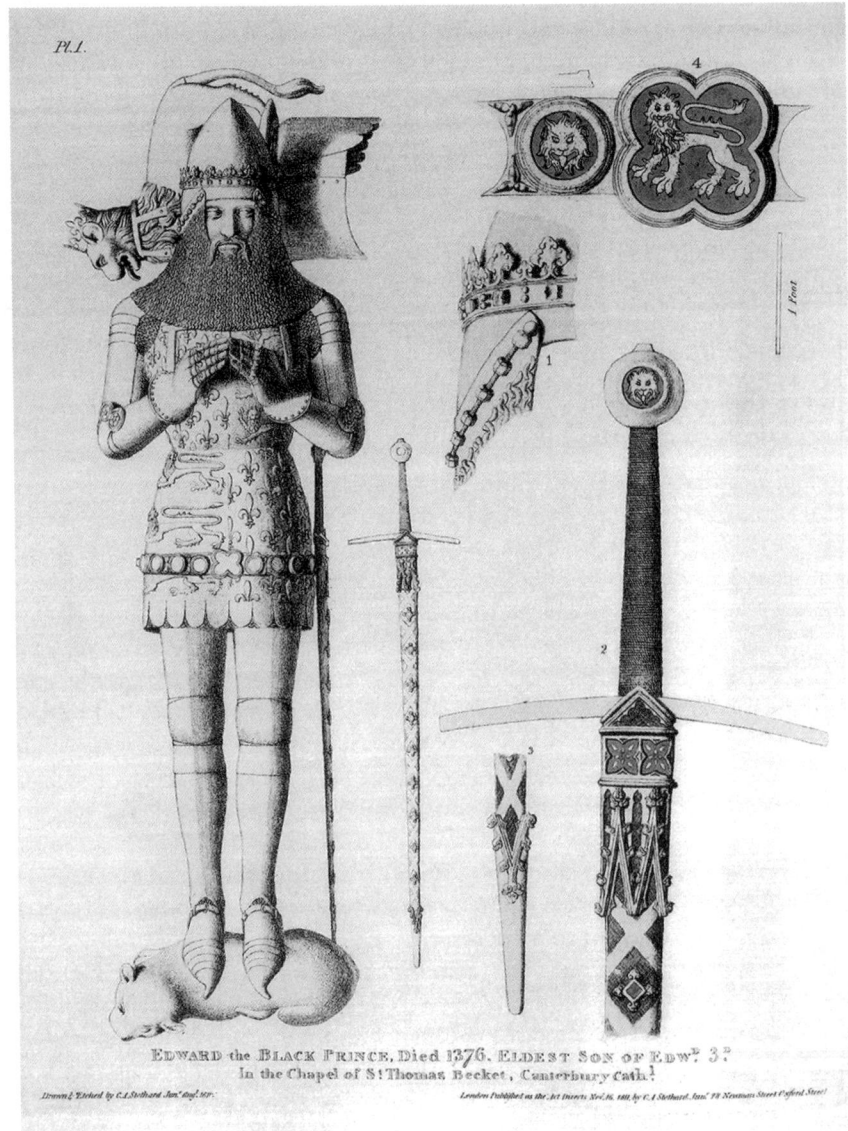

Figure 1. Charles A. Stothard, *Edward the Black Prince, Died 1376. Eldest Son of Edward 3d. In the Chapel of St. Thomas Becket, Canterbury Cathedral*, from *The Monumental Effigies of Great Britain*, 1817–32, etching. Photo by author.

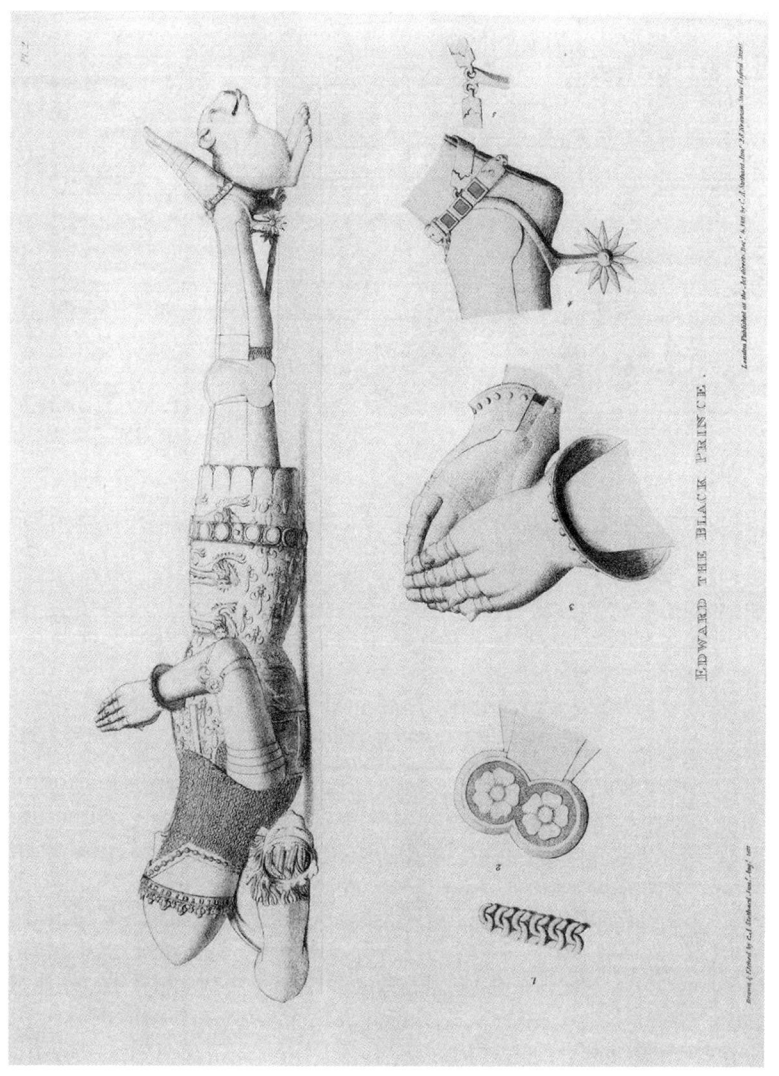

Figure 2. Charles A. Stothard, *Edward the Black Prince*, from *The Monumental Effigies of Great Britain*, 1817–32, etching. Photo by author.

Figure 3. C. J. Smith after Charles A. Stothard, *Ralph Neville Earl of Westmoreland and his Wives, Staindrop Church, Durham*, from *The Monumental Effigies of Great Britain*, 1817–32, etching. Photo by author.

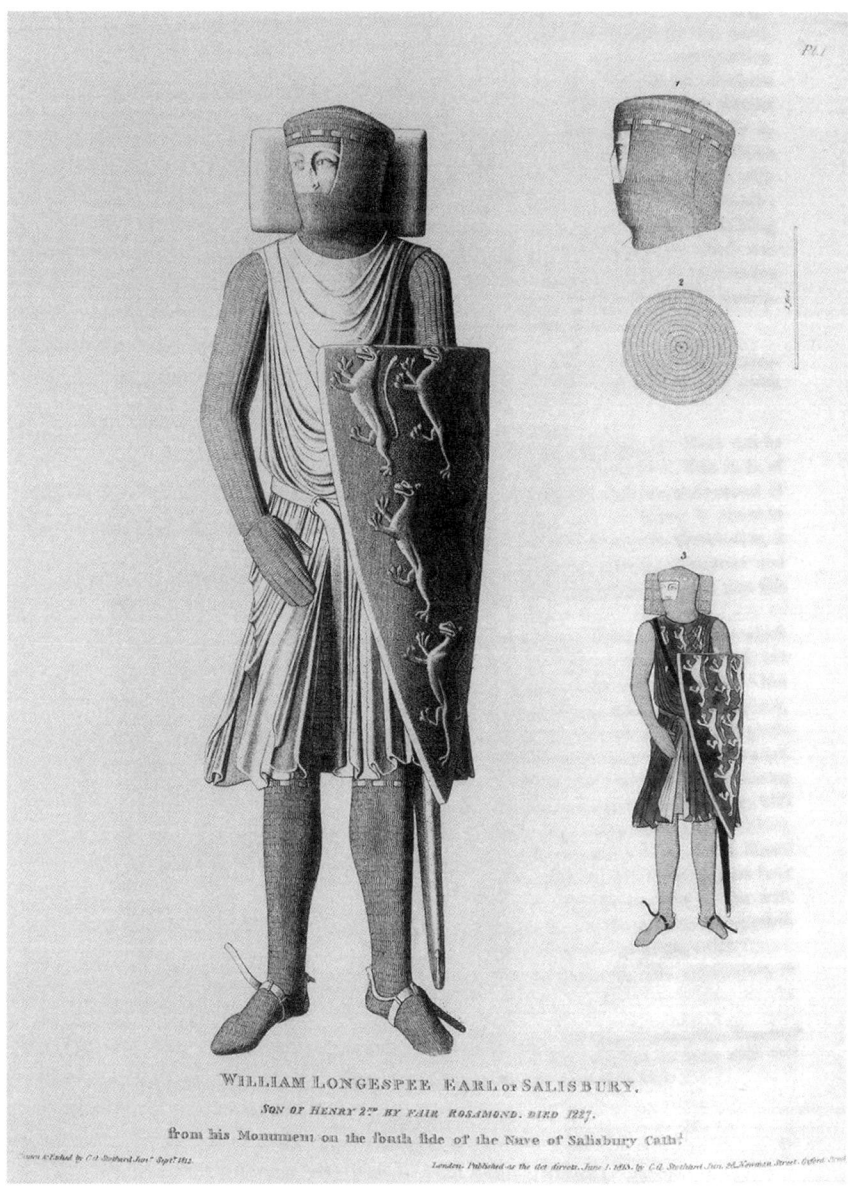

Figure 4. Charles A. Stothard, *William Longespee Earl of Salisbury. Son of Henry 2nd. by Fair Rosamund. Died 1227. From his Monument on the South Side of the Nave of Salisbury Cath.* from *The Monumental Effigies of Great Britain*, 1817–32, etching. Photo by author.

Figure 5. Charles A. Stothard, *King John, died 1216, from his Effigy in the choir of Worcester Cathedral*, from *The Monumental Effigies of Great Britain*, 1817–32, etching. Photo by author.

Figure 6. Charles A. Stothard, *Henry the Second,* from *The Monumental Effigies of Great Britain*, 1817–32, etching. Photo by author.

Figure 7. After Charles A. Stothard, *Head-Plate for Sir Guy Bryan*, from *The Monumental Effigies of Great Britain*, 1817–32, etching. Photo by author.

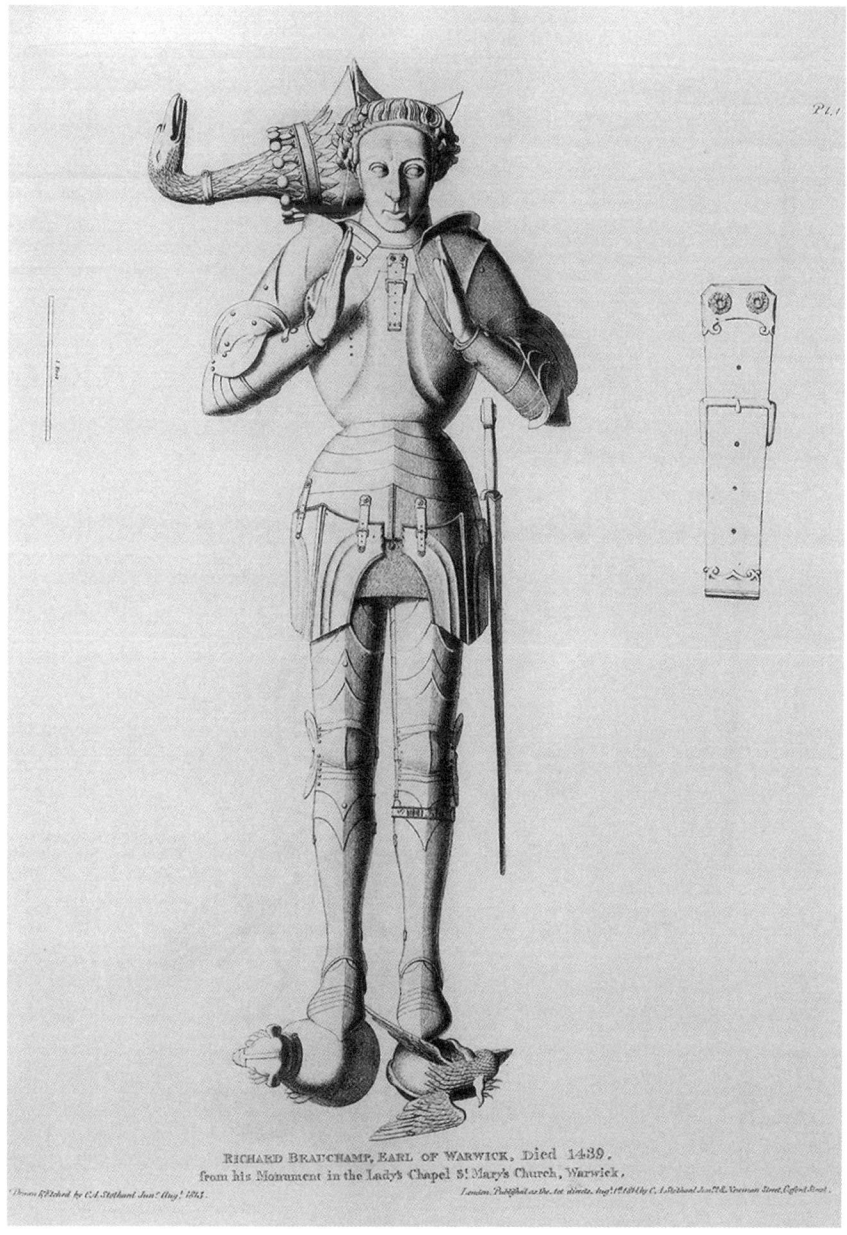

Figure 8. Charles A. Stothard, *Richard Beauchamp, Earl of Warwick, Died 1439. from his Monument in the Lady's Chapel St. Mary's Church, Warwick*, from *The Monumental Effigies of Great Britain*, 1817–32, etching. Photo by author.

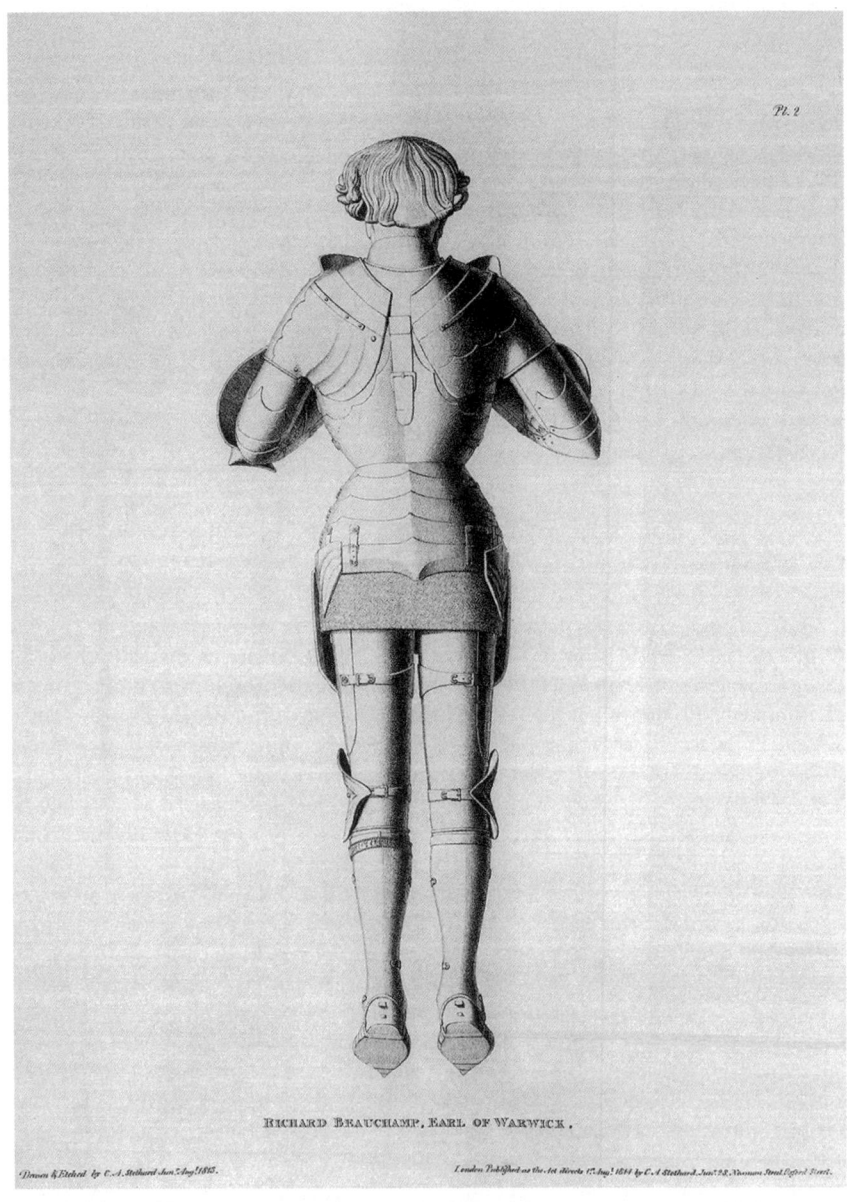

Figure 9. Charles A. Stothard, *Richard Beauchamp, Earl of Warwick*, from *The Monumental Effigies of Great Britain*, 1817–32, etching. Photo by author.

NOTES

1. Alfred Kempe, "Introduction" to Stothard, *Monumental Effigies of Great Britain* (London, 1832), 1–23, here 22.
2. Kempe, "Introduction" to *Monumental Effigies of Great Britain*, p. 2; Mrs. Charles Stothard (Anna Eliza Bray), *Memoirs, including Original Journals, Letters, Papers, and Antiquarian Tracts, of the Late Charles Alfred Stothard, F. S. A. author of The Monumental Effigies of Great Britain. With Connective notices of His Life, and some account of a Journey in the Netherlands* (London, 1823), 22–23.
3. John Weever, *Ancient funerall monuments within the united monarchie of Great Britain, Ireland, and the islands adjacent, with the dissolved monasteries therein contained: their founders, and what eminent persons have beene in the same interred. As also the death and buriall of certaine of the bloud royall; the nobilities and gentrie of these kingdomes entombed in forraine nations* (London, printed by T. Harper, 1631); Richard Gough, *Sepulchral monuments in Great Britain: applied to illustrate the history of families, manners, habits and arts, at the different periods from the Norman Conquest to the seventeenth century: with introductory observations* (London, printed by J. Nichols, for the author, 1786–96).
4. From *Dictionary of National Biography* and Kempe, "Introduction" to *Monumental Effigies*, p. 17. For Thomas Stothard's dispute with William Blake over their respective representations of *Pilgrims to Canterbury* see Betsy Bowden, "Transportation to Canterbury: the Rival Envisionings by Stothard and Blake," *Studies in Medievalism* 11 (2001): 73–111.
5. Kempe, "Introduction" to *Monumental Effigies*, p. 17.
6. Kempe, "Introduction" to *Monumental Effigies*, p. 19.
7. Bray, *Memoirs*, 289–90; text of his conclusions pp. 291–303, also *Archaeologia*, 19.
8. Richard Knowles, "French Excursions: Charles Alfred Stothard and the Monumental Effigies of France," *Church Monuments* 13 (1998): 45–69, here 51.
9. Bray, *Memoirs*, 273–74.
10. According to Richard Knowles, Stothard intended a follow-up volume to be called *The Monumental Effigies of France*. He made several trips to France to sketch monuments but died before any real work could be done on the next book. See Knowles, "French Excursions," 48 and "A Further Album of Stothard Drawings," *Church Monuments* 14 (1999): 38–40. Accounts of his trips can be found in letters published by his widow in her *Memoirs* and in her *Letters Written during a Tour through Normandy, Brittany and other parts of France in 1818: including local and historical descriptions; with remarks on the manners and characters of the people* (London, 1820).
11. For an overview of English thirteenth- and fourteenth-century effigies see Rachel Dressler, *Of Armor and Men in Medieval England: Three English Knights' Effigies and the Rhetoric of Chivalry* (Hammersmith and Burlington, VT.: Ashgate, 2004), chs. 1 and 3. See also Harry A. Tummers, *Early Secular Effigies in England* (Leiden: E. J. Brill, 1980) and Judith Hurtig, *The Armored Gisant Before 1400* (New York: Garland Press, 1979).

12. Peter Coss, *The Knight in Medieval England 1000–1400* (Phoenix Mill: Alan Sutton, 1993; reprint 1996), 72–73.

13. Muriel Clayton, *Catalogue of Rubbings of Brasses and Incised Slabs* (London, Victorian and Albert Museum, 1979). The selection of brasses represented indicates the changing class patronage from the fourteenth through the sixteenth centuries. See also Nigel Saul, " 'Forget-Me-Nots': Patronage in Gothic England," in Nigel Saul, ed., *Age of Chivalry: Art and Society in Late Medieval England* (New York: St. Martin's Press, 1992), 45–46.

14. Bray, *Memoirs*, 24.

15. Bray, *Memoirs*, 172. His widow describes the death of Henry Oldner, whom she identifies as the colourist for *Monumental Effigies*. See p. 343. His plans for these escutcheons went unexecuted for the most part.

16. Stothard also edits out the superstructure of Edmund Crouchback's tomb in Westminster Abbey.

17. Stothard is careful to depict the extraordinary pebbled looking surfaces of the tombs slabs of Sir Roger de Kerdeston and Sir Oliver Ingham. These are the only two known instances of this type of slab, which is no doubt why Stothard included them.

18. Bray, *Memoirs*, 171–2.

19. Knowles, "French Excursions," 45–46.

20. Knowles, "French Excursions," 45–46.

21. *Monumental Effigies*, Advertisement.

22. Stothard, *Monumental Effigies*, 107.

23. Mark Girouard, *The Return to Camelot: Chivalry and the English Gentleman* (New Haven and London: Yale University Press, 1981), 21. Girouard refers to Stothard and *The Monumental Effigies* on p. 43. Stephen Bann offers a more extensive historiographic analysis of *The Monumental Effigies* in *The Clothing of Clio: A Study of the Representation of History in Nineteenth-Century Britain and France* (Cambridge: Cambridge University Press, 1984), 64–66. See also *The Inventions of History: Essays on the Representation of the Past* (Manchester and New York: Manchester University Press, 1990), 130–31.

24. Valdine Clemens, *The Return of the Repressed: Gothic Horror from The Castle of Otranto to Alien* (Albany, NY: State University of New York Press, 1999), 29–30.

25. Fred Botting, *Gothic* (London and New York: Routledge, 1996), 21.

26. Girouard, *Return to Camelot*, 19–20.

27. Linda Colley, *Britons: Forging the Nation* (New Haven and London: Yale University Press, 1992), 1.

28. Stephanie L. Barczewski, *Myth and National Identity in Nineteenth-Century Britain: The Legends of King Arthur and Robin Hood* (Oxford: Oxford University Press, 2000), 5–6.

29. Colley, *Britons*, 5 and 13–14.

30. Kathleen Wilson, "The Good, the Bad, and the Impotent: Imperialism and the Politics of Identity in Georgian England," in Ann Bermingham and John Brewer, eds., *The Consumption of Culture 1600–1800: Image, Object, Text* (London and New York: Routledge, 1995), 242–43.

31. Barczewski, *Myth and National Identity*, 6. Colley does note that the political movement inspired by John Wilkes grew out of the fears of a certain portion of the English population that they would lose their English identity in Britishness. See *Britons*, 105–06 and 111–12.

32. Girouard, *Return to Camelot*, 23.
33. Barczewski, *Myth and National Identity*, 27 and 33.
34. Colley, *Britons*, 140.
35. Colley, *Britons*, 152–5.
36. Cited in Colley, *Britons*, 152–3.
37. Girouard, *Return to Camelot*, 24–25.
38. Girouard, *Return to Camelot*, 49–50.
39. Bann, *Clio*, 104–05.
40. Bann, *Clio*, 50–51.
41. Bann, *Clio*, 41.
42. Colley, *Britons*, 145, 177ff.
43. Colley, *Britons*, 181–2.
44. Colley, *Britons*, 172, 193.
45. Girouard, *Return to Camelot*, 42.
46. Bray, *Memoirs*, 4.
47. Bray, *Memoirs*, 168–69.
48. Stothard, *Monumental Effigies*, 73.
49. Stothard, *Monumental Effigies*, 21.
50. Stothard, *Monumental Effigies*, 22.
51. John Chandler, ed., *John Leland's Itinerary: Travels in Tudor England* (Stroud, Gloucestershire: Sutton Publishers, 1998).
52. William Dugdale, *Monasticon Anglicanum, or, the history of the ancient abbies, and other monasteries, hospitals, cathedral and collegiate churches, in England and Wales: with divers French, Irish, and Scotch monasteries formerly relating to England* (London: Printed for Sam Keble, 1693).
53. Bray, *Memoirs*, 156.
54. Bray, *Memoirs*, 103–04.
55. Gough, *Sepulchral Monuments*, Vol. 1, 9.
56. Stothard, *Monumental Effigies*, 4–5.
57. Bray, *Memoirs*, 6–7.
58. Colley, *Britons*, ch. 1, "Protestants," 11–54.
59. Botting, *Gothic*, 48. For an extensive tratment of the medieval religious revival in all genres of Victorian literature see Kevin L. Morris, *The Image of the Middle Ages in Romantic and Victorian Literature* (London, Sydney, Dover, NH: Croom Helm, Ltd., 1984).
60. Graham Parry, *The Trophies of Time: English Antiquarians of the Seventeenth Century* (New York and London: Oxford University Press, 1995), 228.
61. Weever, *Ancient Funerall Monuments*, "Epistle to the Reader."
62. Bray, *Memoirs*, 26.
63. Bray, *Memoirs*, 232.
64. Bray, *Memoirs*, 240 and 254.
65. Bray, *Memoirs*, 278–79.

66. Bray, *Memoirs*, 243. He repeats this identification in a letter to his father. See Bray, *Memoirs*, 256.
67. Bray, *Memoirs*, 262.
68. Bray, *Memoirs*, 273.

Commedia Images in the Neo-Gothic Age(s)[1]

Karl Fugelso

In the mid-eighteenth century, at the start of the so-called "Neo-Gothic Age," critics redefined the sublime and gave it a new prominence in art.[2] Longinus and other ancient writers had treated the sublime as essentially an overwhelming form of beauty and, in the spirit of Neo-Platonism, had suggested that it could bring viewers closer to the Divine.[3] But after Nicolas Boileau re-introduced the concept in the late seventeenth century, critics increasingly defined the sublime as precisely the opposite of beauty and treated its impact as less metaphysical than psychological.[4] For example, in *Philosophical Enquiry into the Origins of our Ideas of the Sublime and the Beautiful*, which was published in 1757, Edmund Burke describes the sublime as that which repels, as "whatever is fitted in any sort to excite the ideas of pain and danger, that is to say, whatever is in any sort terrible."[5] He does not discuss the sublime in relationship to particular works of art, but he does note that "dark, confused, uncertain images have a greater power on the fancy to form the grander passions than those which are more clear and determinate."[6] And his contemporaries often associate the sublime with not only darkness and ambiguity but also extreme distortion, particularly great exaggeration of scale.[7] Thus, in relatively short order, the sublime acquired a radically new artistic identity, a distinctive character that has often been treated as a reflection of the age from which it emerged.

And, of course, not without reason, for the Neo-Gothic definition of the sublime is prominent in many works of the period, such as Henry Fuseli's *Commedia* illustrations from the late eighteenth and early nineteenth centuries.[8] In executing these six pen-and-ink drawings of Dante's text, Fuseli suffused them with stereotypical Neo-Gothic qualities.[9] For example, they are often so dark as to be extremely ominous and to allow that they hide even worse horrors than the considerable ones on which Fuseli dwells; their figures often strike poses that are so dramatic as to suggest almost unimaginable shock or suffering; and their settings are often so vast as to imply the potential infinity of God's retribution. Moreover, these qualities frequently articulate the most sublime of subjects, for, in choosing which moments to depict, Fuseli usually privileges the most dramatic of scenes, as when the Pilgrim kicks Bocca degli Abati during *Inferno* XXXII, or when the Pilgrim descends to lower hell via Geryon in *Inferno* XVII.

Indeed, even when Fuseli depicts a moment that seems relatively tranquil in the text, he suggests that it is in fact highly emotional. For instance, in his illustration of *Inferno* X, he rather dramatically departs from the text in having the Pilgrim flee from the arch-heretics to the strangely casual figure of Virgil (Figure 1). Dante as author notes that the Pilgrim is somewhat shocked at first hearing a voice emerge from the burning sarcophagi of the arch-heretics and that the Pilgrim therefore draws a little closer to Virgil (*Inf.* 10.28–30).[10] But after Farinata degli Uberti and Cavalcante dei Cavalcanti rise from their tomb, as they have in the illustration, Dante's protagonist does not express any emotion beyond mild irritation at Farinata's pride and quarrelsomeness.[11] And at no time during the canto does the Pilgrim exhibit the tremendous terror embodied in Fuseli's figure of him. As Virgil leans in a gentle "S" pose against the jamb at left, Dante throws his arms out, cranes his head backwards, and, to a degree almost contrary to the laws of biomechanics, lunges hip first at his guide. Moreover, while Virgil's hair modestly wraps around his head and his drapery calmly clings to his body, Dante's hair blows almost straight to the left and his cloak billows out in a dramatic arc to the right. Thus, almost every aspect of the figures, from their clothing to their pose, underscores their emotional polarity and highlights the Pilgrim's somewhat histrionic response to Farinata and Cavalcante.

In fact, even the setting appears to reflect that polarity, for in contrast to the stable vertical and horizontal vectors of the architecture, flames or fumes dance across the image from lower right to upper left. While Virgil's melancholic resignation echoes throughout the low, heavy lintel of the arch, throughout the rectilinear contours of the blocks in that arch, and throughout the grid of the backdrop, the Pilgrim's dynamic anxiety is embodied in the wavering contours, overt pen strokes, and diagonality of the flames or fumes, particularly as they parallel his hair. Thus, the flames or fumes seem to join the Pilgrim in sublimely destabilising the scene and in conveying his horror at meeting Farinata and Cavalcante. That is to say, the setting seems to join the figures in establishing an emotional polarity that underscores the drama of the Pilgrim's response to his environment.

Of course, the flames or fumes are also sublime in the scale of the perils they represent and in their obliqueness doing so, for they seem to be just the very tip of a great fire beyond the archway and to the lower right. In the depiction of those flames or fumes as a nearly solid sheet extending from the lower right to upper left corner of the illustration, they seem to represent a conflagration of enormous size, an unforgiving and perhaps unavoidable danger that is far greater than any other hurdle the pilgrim has yet faced. But it is difficult to be sure of the precise degree or scale of that hazard, for the main body of the fire appears to lie just beyond the foreground architecture and outside of the illustration. That is to say, Fuseli has sublimely left important details of the protagonist's immediate future to the viewer's imagination.

Yet, as sublime as this and Fuseli's other *Commedia* images may be, they often seem farther from eighteenth-century principles for the sublime, and, indeed, from the spirit of Neo-Gothicism as a whole, than do many later illustrations of Dante's text. In the late nineteenth and twentieth centuries, as we shall see, Gustave Doré, Rico Lebrun, Renato Guttuso, Robert Rauschenberg, and Leonard Baskin also illustrated the *Commedia* with dark tones, distorted forms, and exaggerated proportions.[12] But these five artists adapted, expanded, and sometimes augmented those means in such a manner and to such a degree as to promote the sublime even more thoroughly and forcefully than does Fuseli. Moreover, Lebrun, Guttuso, Rauschenberg, and Baskin sometimes apply those means to iconography that is so clearly damning in its overtness, yet so idiosyncratic in its details, that it epitomises the expressive ambiguity ascribed by Burke and other critics to the sublime. Thus, Lebrun and his three contemporaries, as well as Doré, undermine any association of the sublime exclusively with the Neo-Gothic period, and, given the penchant of art historians to orient definitions of that period around the sublime, concomitantly call into question the very identity of that period. Indeed, in the light of tendencies to characterise the past according to style, Lebrun and company call into question the foundations of many historiographical models. That is to say, they suggest that at least some taxonomies for the past, particularly those based on definitions of artistic style, may not be as clearcut or as accurate as is often suggested, that many models for art history, and perhaps for other branches of history, should be reconsidered.

Among the many artists who illustrated the *Commedia* after Fuseli, perhaps the most faithful adherent to the Neo-Gothic tradition was Gustave Doré.[13] Commissioned by subscription in the 1860s to depict at least one scene from every canto, he treated the project as an opportunity to demonstrate the power of engraving, a medium that the French had previously held in low regard. Indeed, for perhaps the first time in his career, he oversaw every phase of a project from design to printing.[14] Moreover, he inundated his *Commedia* illustrations with an unprecedented range and degree of dramatic effects.[15] That is to say, he employed sublime quantities of sublime qualities in the service of subjects that are themselves rather sublime.

Given a choice of topics, he seems to have almost always joined Fuseli in privileging the most emotional moment(s) in a canto, as when the Pilgrim suddenly realises he is in peril while passing through the "savage" woods of *Inferno* I.[16] And even when relatively innocuous cantos gave Doré few such opportunities to depict inherently dramatic scenes, he portrayed his subjects in a highly dramatic fashion. For instance, though his illustration of *Inferno* X is far closer to Dante's sedate account than is Fuseli's, for Doré has the Pilgrim turn only slightly towards Virgil and merely lay a hand on his guide, Doré energises the image by deploying extreme differences in tone (Figure 2). In contrast to the inky darkness that veils much of the scene, a brilliant white light radiates from Farinata's tomb. As that glow refracts through the clouds of smoke at right, reflects off the body of Farinata at left, and highlights details elsewhere in the illustration, it seems not only to depart from the black background but to interrupt it, to disrupt scansion of the image and to concomitantly add dynamism to the scene.

The sharpness of those juxtapositions, moreover, strongly underscores the purity of their tones and the dramatic properties associated with black and/or white. That is to say, the white is so bright as to heavily invoke the conventional association of light with a divine presence, with, in this case, the wrath of He who made the flames that will eternally torment the arch-heretics, and the background is so dark as to overtly invoke the dangers associated with night and its power to overcome sight. Indeed, the impenetrability of that murk, like the impenetrability of the white background in Doré's *Paradiso* illustrations, allows that the setting may be sublimely infinite in and of itself and, in the case of the *Inferno*, allows that the setting may shelter dangers that are sublime in both their number and their individual or collective power. Thus, the viewer may be overwhelmed by not only the scale of the protagonist's surroundings but also the potential peril that the Pilgrim's setting may harbor.

In fact, the viewer may be overwhelmed not only twice over but thrice over, for Doré also confronts him or her with a sublime minuteness of detail and craftsmanship. Though Doré did not engrave these images himself, he did, as mentioned earlier, closely oversee their production and evidently made sure they were among the most meticulously articulated prints of their time. For example, almost every one of Farinata's veins and sinews seems to be highly defined, and the differences in texture between, say, the inside and outside of Farinata's sarcophagus or between his skin and his drapery are extremely overt. That is to say, the viewer's eye is encouraged to glide over the sinner's smooth stomach with a speed and ease that would be more difficult across his woven garment, much less across the fine grooves of his sarcophagus interior or the crude bumps of its exterior. Thus, the world outside the frame, at least as that world was evidently envisioned by Doré, is represented with so much apparent verisimilitude as to potentially overwhelm the viewer with visual and perhaps tactile information.

Yet, of course, this very attempt to represent the world as it exists outside of the illustration paradoxically underscores the artifice of the image.[17] As long as the viewer recalls on some level that he or she is looking at an illustration, as long as he or she cannot fully suspend disbelief, efforts at representing the world outside of the image are revealed as precisely that mere efforts. Indeed, the closer an artist comes to accurately representing something without fully duplicating it, the more he or she may highlight the manufacturing of that representation and concomitantly advertise his or her own participation in its production. That is to say, the very attempt at verisimilitude in Doré's engravings may underscore its crafting and, in the meticulousness of that attempt, may overwhelm the viewer with both the artifice of the image and the degree to which Doré highlights his own contributions to it. Thus, through not only shading but also line and detail, Doré may invoke the sublime to an even greater degree than do Fuseli and other *Commedia* illustrators who are chronologically closer to the traditional apogee of Neo-Gothicism.

However, Doré may in turn be outdone by Rico Lebrun.[18] The latter's 36 *Commedia* drawings, which were executed between 1959 and 1961, also deploy line for an expressiveness that invokes eighteenth- and nineteenth-century definitions of the sublime, but they do so not as much through the descriptive properties of contour and detail as through the opposite of those properties, through expressive departures from descriptive realism. Like Fuseli, Lebrun enjoyed exceptional freedom in composing his images of Dante's text. Having immigrated from Italy to New York in 1924, he began working as a commercial artist shortly after his arrival and had established financial independence by the time he retired from that profession in 1935. He then concentrated on a solo career in the fine arts and, before assuming leadership of a California artistic community in 1937, established his creative independence. Thus, by the time he illustrated the *Commedia* in the late 1950s and early 1960s, he was no longer beholden to a single mentor or to a particular patron. That is to say, though he may in fact have constructed his images around expectations of viewer response, and though his illustrations were published shortly before his death in 1964, he was evidently free to respond as he wished to Dante's text.

And, indeed, he treated his *Commedia* illustrations as highly intimate interpretations of Dante's work. In introducing some of the drawings for a 1961 exhibition at the University of Southern California, he claimed that "to try to illustrate Dante without a contributing share of personal 'hell' seems impossible," for, according to Lebrun, Dante's images call for the draughtsman to bring with him "the lock, stock and barrel of his miserable gauge and limited range, of his daily gaspings, cut-rate pretenses, struggles to keep his life intact, and pathetic strategies for self reassurance."[19] In particular, these illustrations were, he suggests, a direct outgrowth of the personal issues and concerns that motivated other works he had recently completed, most notably his celebrated Concentration Camp series of the mid-1950s. Like the painting "Buchenwald Pit", for example, Lebrun's *Commedia* images portray a hell filled with distorted and often overlapping victims who are sometimes sharply defined by heavy contours and a dark, almost monochromatic palette, but who are at other times somewhat obscured by those very same means. That is to say, Lebrun's interpretations of Dante's text are, like the concentration camp series, an example of sublime means applied in a sublime fashion to sublime subjects seen through a sublimely personal and expressive vision.

Much of that expressiveness stems from the overtly sublime character and deployment of Lebrun's tones, particularly with regard to his settings, for many of his backdrops are even darker than those of Doré. For example, in Lebrun's first of four illustrations of a transmogrifying thief in *Inferno* XXV (Figure 3), the figure is heavily shadowed and surrounded by little more than a deep, dark murk. Moreover, that darkness is not alleviated by the small white dots and dashes that usually appear amid Doré's nocturnal tones. Thus, Lebrun's images seem to resist the viewer's sight even more thoroughly than do Doré's illustrations, which, as noted earlier, are still dark enough to represent an infinite expanse of space and to hide an infinite number of perils. And in that greater veiling, in suggesting to an even greater degree that the setting may be endless and may harbor hazards of infinite number and/or power, many of Lebrun's images are perhaps more sublime in style than are those of Doré, much less those of Fuseli and of other late eighteenth- or early nineteenth-century illustrators of the *Commedia*.

Indeed, even those of Lebrun's *Inferno* settings that are not black may enhance the sublimity of their images, for those backdrops are often pure white. Though these settings do not of course invoke the ominous associations of darkness, they do, like the black backgrounds elsewhere in the cycle, convey a sense of limitlessness, of an infinite space that may harbor infinite peril. Moreover, in the sterility of their whiteness, they may invoke the cold, heartless setting of a hospital or other medical establishment. That is to say, rather than welcome the viewer to a familiar outdoor setting or to an interior that advertises the subjectivity of its designers, they may repel the viewer by invoking an environment that assumes a pretense of objectivity and of cleanliness to the point of lifelessness.

In fact, those and all other associations with white may be underscored by the very purity with which Lebrun represents that tone and by his frequent juxtapositions of it with black backgrounds. Lebrun often alternates his tones from one folio to the next, as in his other three illustrations for *Inferno* XXV. And he sometimes transposes one tone upon the other within the same folio. For example, in his first illustration of the transmogrifying thief, the scene comprises a black circle set against the white rectangle of the folio itself. Thus, the extraordinary whiteness of the paper is accentuated at the same time that it underscores the darkness of the black circle it frames. That is to say, the two tonal extremes form a symbiotic relationship on one level that promotes their joint and individual properties, that underscores the infinite space and danger they both may harbor and the ominousness or chilliness they respectively represent.

Of course, the whiteness of the folio also forms a sharp contrast to the thick, black contours of Lebrun's figures and accentuates the extraordinary linearity of his illustrations. Although Lebrun sometimes introduces gradations of tone and suggests shadows through the use of washes, most of his images are largely defined by penstrokes. These lines are usually highly descriptive in that they allow identification of the subject. Moreover, they sometimes also suggest that the subject transcends its two-dimensional format, that it protrudes or recedes from the surface of the folios on which the images appear. But to some degree in all of Lebrun's *Commedia* illustrations, and to a considerable degree in a few of them, his lines depart from optical realism. As in his first image of the transmogrifying thief, they stray across fields of pure white without contributing to the descriptive function of that field. Indeed, they may undermine the optical realism of a composition. For example, the wavy lines that cross open fields of white on the legs of the thief are too asymmetrical and curvaceous within each leg to represent the scales that seem to appearing elsewhere on the figure, and those lines are too dissimilar from one leg to the next to represent the articulation of muscles, bones, or other subcutaneous structures. Thus, like the meticulousness of Doré's engravings, the overt linearity of Lebrun's drawings advertises the artificiality of the images in which it appears. It declares them to be the product of an artist and thereby literally and figuratively foregrounds the latter's participation in the work.

Indeed, Lebrun's lines underscore his presence as not only a generic generator of these images but also a particular personality that shaped the character and appearance of the illustrations. In other words, though his lines may be misleading in their representation of the artist, they at least pretend to embody how he actually felt about Dante's text. For example, a merging of response and theme is articulated by the shaky lines that occasionally stray across the serpentine body in his first illustration of the transmogrifying thief and suggest Lebrun was deeply affected by this sinner's agonisingly volatile fate. And that response is subdued in relationship to the one implied by Lebrun's depiction of Count Ugolino draped over Archbishop Ruggieri and gnawing on his head in the drawing of *Inferno* XXXIII (Figure 4), for in this illustration of a traitor exacting revenge on the man who may in fact have betrayed him, the artist has strayed so often and so far from describing the figures or the frozen river in which they are largely immersed that the image seems to be more a study than a finished work of art. As is suggested by the light sketch of a fully frontal figure on the left side of the folio, it seems to be a raw image of personal responses quickly recorded. That is to say, the contours of Ugolino and Ruggieri are often blurred by multiple overlapping strokes, particularly in relationship to their legs and arms. Moreover, even where lines do form relatively crisp edges, they do not always seem to describe an optically realistic figure. Indeed, as in articulating Ugolino's head, they sometimes suggest distortion bordering on caricature, a grotesqueness that, in this case, both suits the cannibalistic overtones of the episode depicted and suggests the strong response that such an extreme transgression may provoke. That is to say, as line once again stylistically echoes the volatility of merging figures, it suggests that Lebrun found this episode to be particularly abhorrent and that, in accord with late eighteenth- and early nineteenth-century principles of the sublime, he could not help but express his feelings on a subject in terms that are in and of themselves sublime.

Yet as evocative as is Lebrun's line, it seems controlled and descriptive relative to that of his countryman and contemporary, Renato Guttuso.[20] The latter published his 56 pen, ink, and watercolour illustrations of the *Commedia* in 1961, during a period of his greatest social activism. As a diehard, lifelong Marxist, he was spending much of his time publishing critiques of realism and other issues that ultimately reflect disapproval of the right-wing political establishment in Italy. And perhaps as part of his campaign to reform Italy, he transformed Dante's fourteenth-century diatribe against various forms of corruption into a highly personal commentary on the recent history of Italian – and, to a lesser extent, global – politics.

In fact, his *Commedia* images are so overtly expressive in their political allusions yet so idiosyncratic in their precise agenda that they exceed even Fuseli's and Lebrun's illustrations in fulfilling late eighteenth- and early nineteenth-century definitions of the sublime as expressive ambiguity. By the late 1950s, Guttuso was not beholden to a particular patron or model in depicting Dante's text. And, in choosing his topics, he evidently took great advantage of this freedom, for his subjects often depart from the canon that had dominated *Commedia* illustration since the mid-fourteenth century.[21] To begin with, they are exceptionally asymmetrical in representing the cantiche, with 31 based on the *Inferno*, 19 on *Purgatorio*, and 6 on *Paradiso*. Moreover, they do not overtly pursue any of the themes that have been discussed above in relationship to his predecessors' series. For every violent or emotional climax, such as that of the wrathful in *Purgatorio* XVI (Figure 5), there is at least one peaceful scene, such as that of the sea in *Purgatorio* I (Figure 6).

Yet there are, in fact, consistencies among Guttuso's illustrations, most notably a confluence of subject and style in terms of linear expressiveness. In calm images, such as that of *Purgatorio* I, the contours are largely descriptive and evidently controlled, for they invoke optical realism to an extraordinary degree and suggest the scene is thoroughly congruent with the world outside of its borders. In more emotional scenes, however, Guttuso's lines stray even farther from descriptive realism than do those of Lebrun. For example, in the image of *Purgatorio* XVI, several thin, highly quivery lines depart from the borders of the white frontal figure at left and rather abstractly cross his thighs. Moreover, on the legs of the figure bending over at right in the foreground, many thicker and more assertive lines cross fields of tone or colour in a manner that is inconsistent with the typical properties of pants or human anatomy. Indeed, at least some of those lines so thoroughly depart from optical realism as to overtly resist the descriptive properties of the lines that do in fact contribute to accurately representing the figure and his clothing. That is to say, the seemingly stray lines introduce expressiveness to an extraordinary degree, for they suggest that this episode triggered emotions in the artist that were so strong as to overcome his evident preoccupation elsewhere with optically realistic and largely literal descriptions of Dante's text. To a degree even greater than that of Lebrun's less numerous and abstract lines, they announce the presence of the artist and, particularly in juxtaposition with the far more descriptive lines in this and neighboring images, sublimely introduce his particular personality as a determining factor in the appearance of these illustrations.

In that expressiveness, Guttuso's line is to some degree reinforced by his colour. In his illustration of *Purgatorio* I, for example, colour joins line in contributing to the optical realism of the image, in suggesting a calm, somewhat objective perception of the subject: the sky is an appropriate shade of cerulean blue; the shore comprises rocks and ridges of realistically modulated reds and browns; and the sea fades from a subtle blend of red and blue, of earth and sky, to a white that naturally merges with the clouds on the horizon.[22] And in other, more dramatic illustrations, Guttuso's colours appropriately depart from optical realism to a greater degree than they do in the illustration of *Purgatorio* I. Indeed, they seem to depart from optical realism in proportion to the emotional content of the subject at hand. In the illustration of *Purgatorio* XVI, for instance, many of the figures are blank.[23] And those that do have colour rarely have it in more than one region of their body, as in the woman wearing a yellow dress in the upper centre of the image, or the corpulent man with the oval, flesh-coloured head at right.

Moreover, the subtle modulations of hue and tone in the image of *Purgatorio* I give way in the illustration of canto sixteen to blocks of pure colour that do not articulate the way fabrics and other surfaces would actually respond to light. That is to say, though Guttuso's penwork occasionally adds tonal contrasts suggesting depth and relief for a fold, for a body, or for another spatial projection, the colouring in each field generally has a rather abstract solidity that joins Guttuso's stray lines in evoking the presence of the artist.

Indeed, Guttuso's selective colouring often invokes a political agenda that is closely in tune with his commitment to Marxism, for he often seems to deploy colours in hues and locations that condemn right-wing politics and its proponents. For example, the bright yellow and crimson of the burning cross behind the wrathful in his illustration of *Purgatorio* XVI underscore the association of that Ku Klux Klan symbol with anger and intolerance. Moreover, the vehemence and presumably the concomitant detestability of the wrathful are accentuated by the fact that their colouring is often reserved for the most violent among them, such as the kicking figure in the left foreground and the bludgeoning figure in the right foreground. Indeed, perhaps lest the viewer miss that message or otherwise lack empathy for the victims of intolerance, the figure being pummeled in the central foreground is dabbled with a crimson that not only suggests blood but also echoes the burning cross.

Of course, the political implications of Guttuso's colouring are generally reinforced by his abstract lines, as the latter suggest the extreme emotion of the figures and perhaps of Guttuso's response to the subject. But his agenda may be even more thoroughly embodied in his descriptive lines, for many of them define well-known right-wing figures in compromised positions. For example, the wrathful in *Purgatorio* XVI include portraits of several minor fascist politicians and writers. And the tyrants in *Inferno* XII include famous right-wing figures such as Mussolini and Stalin, as well as such symbols of conservative intolerance as a hooded Ku Klux Klan or confraternity figure. Thus, Guttuso employs the *Commedia* as a vehicle through which to refract criticism of twentieth-century politics by casting modern subjects in roles that Dante has clearly condemned. That is to say, in accord with late eighteenth- and early nineteenth-century definitions of the sublime, Guttuso has overtly expressed an agenda that is clear in its general orientation, yet remains highly personal and idiosyncratic in its specific articulation.

Nevertheless, Guttuso's commentary may be both far less expressive and far more revealing than that in Robert Rauschenberg's *Commedia* images, for the latter feature far more polyvalent and overtly anachronistic allusions juxtaposed via one of the most blatantly modern of techniques.[24] All 34 of

Rauschenberg's illustrations address the *Inferno* and were executed in 1959 and 1960 by transferring excerpts from newspapers onto large sheets of heavy paper, which were then selectively coated with coloured pencils, crayons, gouache, watercolours, and washes.[25] Though this particular approach is rare among the works of Rauschenberg and his contemporaries, it is closely in tune with many artistic trends of the late 1950s and early 1960s. Indeed, in deriving imagery from newspapers, it epitomises the Pop strategy of commenting on modern culture via the very language of that culture. Moreover, as in many Pop works, the acerbity of Rauschenberg's critique is magnified by refracting that attack through a highly traditional context – in this case, of course, the *Commedia*. Thus, Rauschenberg constructs a commentary that, while personal and idiosyncratic in its details, is highly overt in its condemnation of the middle-class world around him, in its expression of his response to some socio-political circumstances in late 1950s and early 1960s America.

Though Rauschenberg critiques his era on many levels, he does so most directly, perhaps, through the subjects depicted in his transferred images and by their location in relationship to the plot of the *Commedia*. On some occasions those modern references are sprinkled amid literal translations of Dante's text, as in the mixture of trees and loading cranes that appear at the upper left corner of folio one and represent the savage woods in which the Pilgrim begins his journey (Figure 7). On other occasions, Rauschenberg's modern references may physically resemble their textual counterparts yet largely displace them, as in his canto eight substitution of a factory or power plant for Dis, the inner city of Hell. And, on a few occasions, Rauschenberg augments the *Inferno* with references that, while perhaps appropriate to the spirit of Dante's text, fully depart from the letter of its description, as in the flying bird found at the top of the second folio and presumably representing the Pilgrim's fear of the world he is about to face. Thus, Rauschenberg iconographically condemns the commercial culture of modern America by refracting images of that culture, as well as the dread it inspires, through the *Commedia*.[26]

Indeed, to some degree, Rauschenberg projects his agenda through Dante's own condemnation of corporate culture. As Joan Ferrante has noted, Dante draws close analogies between Hell and the Florence of his time.[27] He constructs the underworld, particularly Dis, from the monuments for which his former hometown was famous, such as walls, towers, and ruins; he fills that setting with more Florentines than identifiable Italians from all other cities combined; and he even has the narrator explicitly invoke Florence by declaring at the beginning of canto twenty six that the city should be proud indeed "since (it is) so great that over sea and land (it beats its) wings, and (its) name is spread through Hell!" (*Inf.* 26.1–3). Consequently, as

Rauschenberg identifies Dante's hell with modern commercialism, he ultimately anchors that condemnation in Dante's own extensive damnation of corporate culture.

In fact, Rauschenberg joins Dante in couching their attacks in the language of their apparent targets, for the humble source from which Rauschenberg gleaned his images, newspaper, could be compared to the vernacular tongue in which the *Commedia* is articulated and in which much business was conducted in Dante's time. Both sources have been treated as less intellectual than other comparable media of their time and have often been associated with the lower classes. Indeed, both have frequently been defined as crude outlets unsuited to any expression more refined than the mere transmission of information and gossip. Thus, their use by Dante and Rauschenberg in works that evidently aspire to sophisticated contexts, to epic poetry or gallery exhibitions, suggests attempts both to elevate the languages in which these works are couched and to undermine the use of these languages in the exploitation of the audiences with which those languages are customarily associated.

In the spirit of Pop art, however, Rauschenberg expands on that parallel to Dante by heavily invoking and ultimately subverting the specific contexts from which he elicited his images. For example, Rauschenberg's most common illustration of the Pilgrim derives from a golf-club advertisement that features four men and a woman, all of whom stand in a row against a sterile white background, wear nothing more than small towels, and evidently represent the wide range of human bodies to which the golf-club manufacturers could adapt their product. In other words, the naive protagonist is represented in these instances by a generic participant in an activity that is the virtual epitome of white middle-class culture in the 1950s, that, as the pursuit of a small white ball around a highly artificial substitute for natural settings, may be the consummate embodiment of the degree to which golf-club companies and other corporations could condition consumers.

Yet, as overt as Rauschenberg's satire could sometimes be, it is ultimately part of a highly idiosyncratic body of references to his personal experiences and influences. Though some of the sources for his images, such as the golf-club advertisement, are relatively well-known, many others have been lost over time, particularly in the wake of Rauschenberg's abbreviation and/or obfuscation of the images. Moreover, the precise meanings of his sources, much less the full implications of his images, are impossible to fully confirm, of course, for they may not even have been clear to Rauschenberg himself. Indeed, the images often participate in juxtapositions that seem overtly cryptic with regard to the relationships among not only themselves but also their sources. For example, the gate of hell in his illustration of

Inferno III features a reversed reproduction of the inscription over the portal in Dante's text next to transferred banners in English welcoming readers to a prom or similar event. Thus, even as the images assert that they are idiosyncratic expressions of a particular individual, they resist revealing the precise nature of that expression and the character of that individual. That is to say, they join the images by Guttuso in iconographically fulfilling late eighteenth- and early nineteenth-century definitions of the sublime as expressive ambiguity.

Of course, as suggested above, that veil is constructed by not only Rauschenberg's subject matter but also his style, for, in resisting interpretation, his iconographic ambiguity is joined by the visual obfuscation of his images. Though Rauschenberg could have preserved the clarity of his sources as he transferred his images, he often allowed the latter to blur and/or fade. Moreover, in many instances, he then veiled the images behind layers of pencil, crayon, gouache, wash, or watercolour. In some cases, particularly at the more cheerful junctures of the narrative, these coatings comprise pale yellow and orange or other light, largely transparent colours. But in many cases the overlapping layers are formed from dark hues, such as deep purple or muddy brown. And they are usually applied in overt strokes whose patterns distract from, and at times outright screen, the contours of the figures beneath them. Thus, the images embody expressive ambiguity in not only their subject matter but also their presentation. That is to say, they deploy sublime means, particularly obfuscation through darkness, to construct subjects that are as extraordinarily sublime in the veiling of their precise meaning as in the blatancy of their expressiveness.

Yet, as oblique as are many of Rauschenberg's illustrations, they rarely approach the ambiguity of Leonard Baskin's 115 *Commedia* images.[28] Not long after publishing Lebrun's illustrations in 1963, Baskin began his own series of responses to Dante's text.[29] And, like Lebrun's images, Baskin's are executed in black, white, and shades of gray, for he, too, worked with pen, ink, and wash. Moreover, like Lebrun, Baskin usually set his figures against monochromatic backgrounds, largely articulated his subjects by means of delicate lines inside crude contours, and departed from optical realism by distorting proportions and allowing lines to stray towards abstraction. But Baskin's penchant for stylistic abstraction is matched by an iconographic abstraction that departs from Lebrun's work, as well as that of Guttuso, Doré, and to a lesser degree, Rauschenberg. While Lebrun and the other three post-Fuselian artists we have examined can all in some senses be seen as illustrating the *Commedia*, as interpreting Dante's plot and themes literally, Baskin sometimes seems to completely depart from the text. For example, rather than show any particular group of the sinners described in *Inferno* XII through XVII, such as the violent against their neighbors, Baskin replaces them with a spiritually composite figure entitled "The Violent Against Nature," with a small, bat-like head emerging from a fissure in the forehead of a more anthropomorphic head that is perched on short, taloned limbs (Figure 8). That is to say, he invents an embodiment of visual themes generally associated with violence, such as bestiality and viciousness; he exceeds even Rauschenberg in advertising his own presence as an interpreter while simultaneously veiling the precise meaning and character of his vision.

Of course, that is not to deny that Baskin's images are explicitly and substantially ominous. Indeed, as suggested above, the sublime expressiveness and idiosyncrasy of the Violent Against Nature are largely conveyed by stereotypically sublime means. For example, as in many of Baskin's other *Commedia* images, the setting is almost completely black. Like the numerous opaque backdrops in the illustrations by Doré, Lebrun, and Rauschenberg, it invokes the many negative values commonly associated in the West with darkness and threatens to overwhelm the viewer with infinite space and/or infinite hazards. Moreover, in eliminating all indices of the beast's scale or proximity other than the frame, it helps the latter project that monster towards the viewer. That is to say it suppresses opposition to the appearance that, in nearly filling the frame, the figure of the Violent is large and close to the viewer. Thus, the viewer is confronted by a vicious-looking figure that reaches out with taloned claws, sharp teeth, and a vacant stare from a potentially limitless space, from a setting that is as sublime in its potential infinity as in the possibility that it harbors hazards even greater than those depicted.

In thereby articulating the *Commedia* through a pictorial language that closely adheres to Neo-Gothic definitions of the sublime, Baskin joins Doré, Lebrun, Guttuso, and Rauschenberg in undermining the tradition of tying those definitions exclusively to late eighteenth- and early nineteenth-century culture. In fact, by perhaps exceeding the sublimity of late eighteenth- and early nineteenth-century *Commedia* illustrations, Baskin and his colleagues suggest that the values associated with the sublime may have been even stronger in the late nineteenth and twentieth centuries than during the period from which those associations emerged. In other words, the traditional characterisation of Neo-Gothic art may apply more to a fluid and recurring mindset or response than to a set of objects chronologically delimited by acknowledged efforts at embodying the sublime, much less to the period itself. And in thus calling into question the assignation of Neo-Gothicism to a specific period or to the culture of that period, Baskin and his colleagues invite a re-examination of all chronological taxonomies grounded in style. That is to say, they encourage cultural critics to reconsider the premises and models on which their entire disciplines are often founded, and to re-evaluate the format and assumptions on which many of their historical surveys are still based.

Figure 1. Henry Fuseli, Virgil and Dante with Farinata and Cavalcante, *Inferno* X, 1774, Zurich, Kunsthaus.

Figure 2. Gustave Doré, Virgil and Dante with Farinata, *Inferno* X, 1868, from *L'Enfer de Dante Alighieri, avec les dessins de Gustave Doré* (Paris, 1868), vol. 1.

Commedia Images

Figure 3. Rico Lebrun, A Transmogrifying Thief, *Inferno* XXV, 1959–61, from *Lebrun's Drawings for Dante's "Inferno"* (Kanthos Press, 1963).

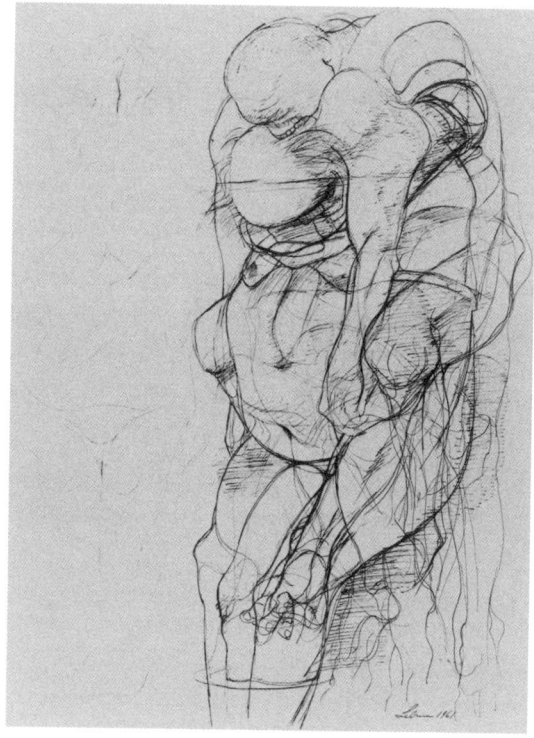

Figure 4. Rico Lebrun, Count Ugolino and Archbishop Ruggieri, *Inferno* XXXIII, 1959–61, from *Lebrun's Drawings for Dante's "Inferno"* (Kanthos Press, 1963).

Figure 5. Renato Guttuso, The Wrathful, *Purgatorio* XVI, 1961, from *Il Dante di Guttuso: Cinquantasei tavole dantesche disegnate da Renato Guttuso* (Milan, 1970).

Figure 6. Renato Guttuso, The Shore of Purgatory, *Purgatorio* I, 1961, from *Il Dante di Guttuso: Cinquantasei tavole dantesche disegnate da Renato Guttuso* (Milan, 1970).

Figure 7. Robert Rauschenberg, *Inferno* I, 1959–60, New York, Museum of Modern Art.

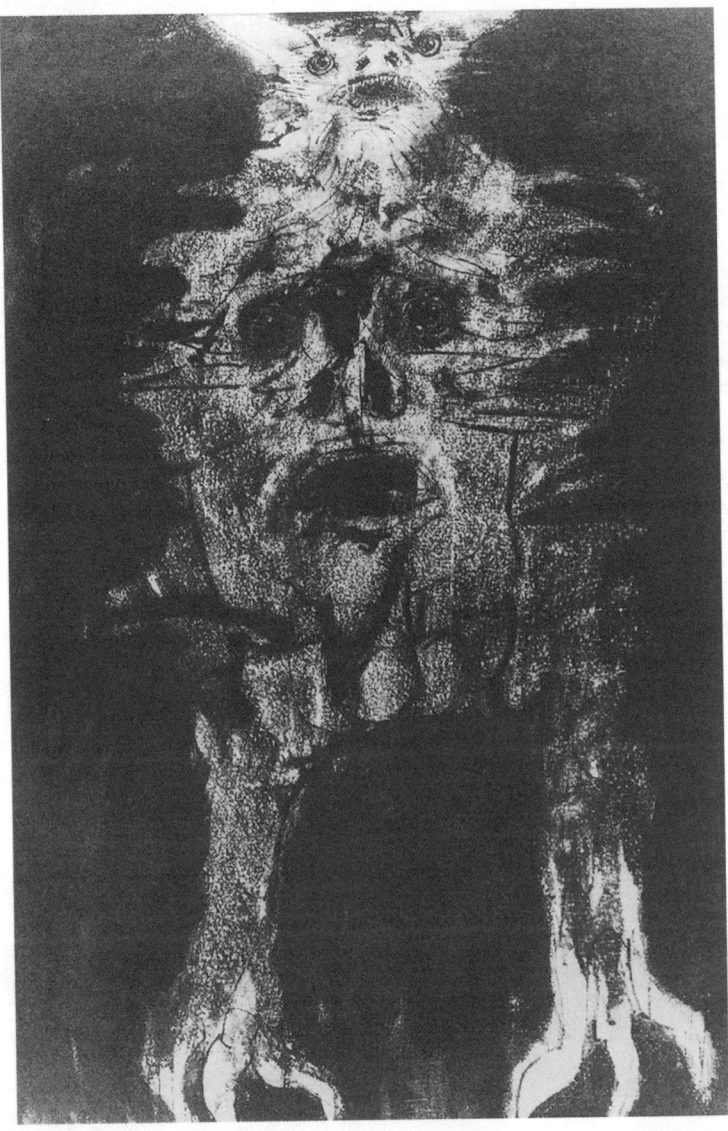

Figure 8. Leonard Baskin, The Violent Against Nature, *Inferno* XII–XVII, 1960s, from *Illustrations to the "Divine Comedy" of Dante*, Graphic Arts Exhibition catalog, Introduction Dale Roylance (New Haven, 1970). Amherst, Mass. R. Michelson Galleries.

NOTES

1. An early version of this paper was delivered at The Eighteenth International Conference on Medievalism, October 18, 2003 at Saint Louis University. For their questions and comments at that time, I would like to thank the audience, particularly Gwen Morgan and Kathleen Verduin.

2. The sublime and its cousin, the picturesque, have received a great deal of attention as of late. For a couple of the best succinct introductions to it, see William Vaughan, *Romantic Art* (New York and London: Thames and Hudson, 1978), esp. 32–36; and Joshua C. Taylor's introduction to William Gilpin's "Essay on Picturesque Beauty," in *Nineteenth-Century Theories of Art* (Berkeley, Los Angeles, and London: University of California Press, 1987), esp. 47. For more extended treatments, see James B. Twitchell, *Romantic Horizons: Aspects of the Sublime in English Poetry and Painting, 1770–1850* (Columbia: University of Missouri Press, 1983); Paul Crowther, *The Kantian Sublime: From Morality to Art* (New York and Oxford: Oxford University Press, 1989); Andrew Ashfield and Peter De Bolla, ed., *The Sublime: A Reader in British Eighteenth-Century Aesthetic Theory* (New York and Cambridge: Cambridge University Press, 1996); and the various essays in *Postérité du sublime: avatars d'un mode dans la littérature anglo-saxonne du XVIIIème au XXème siècles: The Sublime and after: colloque de l'Université de Provence, 13 et 14 novembre 1998* (Paris: Mallard Editions, 2000).

3. As noted by Vaughan (32–33).

4. As noted by Taylor (47). For more on the seventeenth- and eighteenth-century reintroduction of the sublime, see Théodore A. Litman, *Le sublime en France (1660–1714)* (Paris: A. G. Nizet, 1971); Sophie Hache, *La langue du ciel: le sublime en France au XVIIe siècle* (Paris: H. Champion, 2000); and Lawrence Carl Kerslake, *Essays on the Sublime: Analyses of French Writings on the Sublime from Boileau to La Harpe* (Bern and New York: Peter Lang, 2000).

5. *Philosophical Enquiry into the Origins of our Ideas of the Sublime and the Beautiful*, ed. Adam Phillips (1757; repr. New York and Oxford: Oxford University Press, 1990), 36.

6. Burke, *Philosophical Enquiry . . .*, 58.

7. See, for example, William Gilpin's *Three essays on picturesque beauty; on picturesque travel; and on sketching landscape, to which is added a poem, On Landscape Painting* (London: R. Blamire, 1794); and Uvedale Price, *An Essay on the Picturesque as Compared with the Sublime and the Beautiful; and on the Use of Studying Pictures for the Purpose of Improving Real Landscape* (London: J. Robson, 1794).

8. For more on Fuseli's *Commedia* illustrations, see Anita Joyce Coles, "The Divine Comedy in English Art, 1772–1827: Flaxman, Blake, and Fuseli," honors thesis, College of William and Mary (1972); Corrado Gizzi, *Füssli e Dante* (Milan: Mazzotta, 1985); and Luke Herrmann, *Nineteenth Century British Painting* (London: Giles de la Mare, 2000). For relatively recent sources on Fuseli's life and career in general, see Paul Ganz, *The Drawings of Henry Fuseli* (New York: Chanticleer Press, 1949); P. A. Tomory, *The Life and Art of Henry Fuseli* (London: Thames and Hudson, 1972); Frederick Antal, *Füssli Studien* (Dresden: Verlag der Kunst,

1973); Gert Shiff, *Johann Heinrich Fussli* (Zurich and Munich: Verlag Berichthaus, 1973); Carolyn Keay, *Henry Fuseli* (New York: St. Martin's Press, 1974); Gert Shiff and Werner Hofmann, *Henry Fuseli* (London: Tate Gallery, 1975); Paola Viotto, *L'opera completa di Fussli* (Milan: Rizzoli, 1977); John Knowles, *The Life and Writings of Henry Fuseli* (Millwood, NY: Kraus, 1982); David H. Weinglass, *Henry Fuseli and the Engraver's Art* (Boston: World Wide Books, 1982); Christian Klemm, ed., *Johann Heinrich Füssli: Zeichnungen* (Zürich: Kunsthaus Zürich, 1986); David H. Weinglass, *Prints and Engraved Illustrations by and after Henry Fuseli* (Brookfield, VT: Ashgate, 1994); and Martin Myrone, *Henry Fuseli* (Princeton: Princeton University Press, 2001).

9. Note that Fuseli later did several oil paintings based on the *Commedia*, including a highly controversial version of Count Ugolino in *Inferno* XXXIII (1806).

10. All references to the *Commedia* are based on Giorgio Petrocchi's four-volume edition *La "Commedia" secondo l'antica vulgata* (Milan: Mondadori, 1966–68).

11. The precise emotions in the exchange between Farinata and the Pilgrim are not clear and have been the subject of much debate among Dante scholars. However, there does seem to be something of a spiteful tone in Dante's reply to Farinata's claim to have driven Dante's ancestors out of Florence: " 'S'ei fur cacciati, ei tornar d'ogne parte,' rispuos' io lui, 'l'una e l'antra fiata; ma I vostri non appreser ben quell'arte.' " (*Inf.* 10.49–51).

12. For general introductions to *Commedia* illustrations from the eighteenth century and later, see Alfred Bassermann, *Dantes Spuren in Italien* (Munich: Oldenbourg, 1898); Ludwig Volkmann, *Iconografia dantesca* (London: Grevel, 1899); Jean-Pierre Barricelli, *Dante's Vision and the Artist* (New York: Peter Lang, 1992); Eugene Paul Nassar, *Illustrations to Dante's "Inferno"* (Rutherford, NJ: Fairleigh Dickinson University Press, 1994); Ralph Pite, "Illustrating Dante," in *The Circle of Our Vision: Dante's Presence in English Romantic Poetry* (Oxford, Clarendon Press, 1994), 39–67; and Charles H. Taylor and Patricia Finley, *Images of the Journey in Dante's "Divine Comedy"* (New Haven and London: Yale University Press, 1997). For more monographic yet general sources on Doré, Lebrun, Guttuso, Rauschenberg, and Baskin, as well as for specific sources on their *Commedia* images, see the bibliographies in the notes below.

13. Doré's work has received a tremendous amount of attention relative to that of other *Commedia* illustrators. For a good introduction and fairly recent bibliography on his *Commedia* images, see Peer Zietz, "Der 5. Hollengesang: die Illustrationen von Gustave Doré zur Göttlichen Komödie," in *Gustave Doré* (Dortmund: G. Langen, 1982), 119–30; and William Cole, "Literal Art? A New Look at Doré's Illustrations for Dante's Inferno," *Word & Image* 10 (April–June, 1994), 95–106. For more on Doré's life and art in general, see the discussion and thorough bibliography in Dan Malan, *Gustave Doré: Adrift on Dreams of Splendor: A Comprehensive Biography & Bibliography* (St. Louis, MO: Malan Classical Enterprises, 1995). For reproductions of the images mentioned above, see Taylor and Finley. For all of Doré's *Commedia* illustrations, see his original edition of the *Commedia* (Paris: Librairie de L. Hachette et cie, 1868); or one of the many more

recent reprintings of those illustrations, such as *The Doré Illustrations for Dante's "Divine Comedy"* (New York: Dover Publications, 1976).

14. As noted by Nassar (21–22).

15. Nassar notes (21–22) that Doré invented a new technique that allowed a far greater range of tones than had previously been possible.

16. All translations of the *Commedia* are from Charles Singleton's three-volume edition (Princeton: Princeton University Press, 1970–75).

17. Mimesis has, of course, received a great deal of attention in art history and other areas of cultural studies. For a fundamental introduction to it as a topic of the humanities, see Erich Auerbach, *Mimesis: The Representation of Reality in Western Literature* (Princeton: Princeton University Press, 1953; repr. 2003). For a fairly extensive, recent bibliography on the topic in general, see Thomas Metscher, *Mimesis* (Bielefeld: Aisthesis, 2001). For recent broad introductions to the relevance of mimesis (and its historiography) for art history, see Gunter Gebauer and Christoph Wulf, *Mimesis: Culture, Art, Society* (Berkeley: University of California Press, 1995); Karol Berger, *A Theory of Art* (New York: Oxford University Press, 2000); Robert S. Nelson, ed., *Visuality before and beyond the Renaissance: Seeing as Others Saw* (New York and Cambridge: Cambridge University Press, 2000); Stephen Halliwell, *The Aesthetics of Mimesis: Ancient Texts and Modern Problems* (Princeton: Princeton University Press, 2002). And for a fundamental discussion of its duality in art history and elsewhere, see Llowry Nelson, Jr., "The Fictive Reader and Literary Self-Reflexiveness," in *The Disciplines of Criticism: Essays in Literary Theory, Interpretation and History*, ed. Peter Demetz, Thomas Greene, and Lowry Nelson, Jr. (New Haven and London: Yale University Press, 1968), 173–91; and, more recently, Andrew E. Benjamin, *Art, Mimesis, and the Avant-Garde: Aspects of a Philosophy of Difference* (New York and London: Routledge, 1991); and Pierre Glaudes, *La représentation dans la littérature et les arts: anthologie* (Toulouse: Presses universitaires du Mirail, 2000).

18. For more on Lebrun's life and work in general, see John Ciardi, *In Memoriam: Rico Lebrun* (n.p.: N. Young, 1964); Leonard Baskin and the American Academy of Arts and Letters, *Rico Lebrun, Memorial Exhibition: Paintings and Drawings* (New York: The American Academy of Arts and Letters, 1966); Henry J. Seldis's introduction to *Rico Lebrun (1900–1964); An Exhibition of Drawings, Paintings* (Los Angeles: n.d., 1967); Richard McNaught Blank, "A Study of Rico Lebrun," M.A. thesis, Arizona State University, 1966; Rico Lebrun, *Rico Lebrun Drawings* (Berkeley: University of California Press; repr. 1968); George Ellis Merrill, "Rico Lebrun: Draftsman," M.A. thesis, University of Wyoming, 1968; and the anonymous introduction to *Rico Lebrun, 1900–1964: Works on Paper* (Los Angeles: Mekler Gallery, 1979). For examples and specific discussions of his *Commedia* illustrations, see Daniel Catton Rich, ed., *Illustrations for Dante's "Inferno,"* exh. cat. Worcester Art Museum, March 22–May 6, 1962 (Worcester, MA: Worcester Art Museum, 1962); *Drawings for Dante's "Inferno"* (n.p.: Kanthos Press, 1963); and Saundra Louise Goldman, "Interpretations of Dante in the Twentieth Century: *Inferno* Drawings by Rico Lebrun and Robert Rauschenberg," M.A. thesis, University of California, Berkeley, May 1985.

19. See *Rico Lebrun: Paintings & Drawings 1946–1961*, exh. cat. University of

Southern California, Los Angeles, April 1961 (Los Angeles: University of Southern California, 1961), 14.

20. For recent broad introductions to Guttuso's life and career, see Cesare Brandi, et al., *Guttuso: opere dal 1931 al 1981* (Florence: Sansoni, 1982); Cesare Brandi and Vittore Rubiu, *Guttuso* (Milan: Gruppo Editoriale Fabbri, 1983); Vittore Rubiu, *Guttuso: grandi opere* (Milan: Mazzotta, 1984); Vittore Rubiu, *Guttuso: opere dal 1938 al 1985* (Milan: Mazzotta, 1986); Giorgio Cortenova and Enrico Mascelloni, *Guttuso: 50 anni di pittura* (Milan: Mazzotta, 1987); Marco Carapezza, *Guttuso* (Palermo: Novecento and London: Thames and Hudson, 1996); Giorgio Chierici and Enrico Crispolti, *Renato Guttuso: disegni: opera dal 1935 al 1985* (Aan Polo di Reggio Emilia: La scaletta, 1997); Fabio Carapezza Guttuso, *Guttuso* (Milan: Rizzoli, 1999); and Giorgio Barberis and Marzio Dall'Acqua, *Renato Guttuso (1911–1987)* (Cherasco: Edizioni Città di Cherasco, 2001). For more on his *Commedia* illustrations, see *Il Dante di Guttuso: Cinquantasei tavole dantesche disegnate da Renato Guttuso* (Milan: Mondadori, 1970); Giuseppe Ungaretti, *Renato Guttuso: Zeichnungen 1930–1970* (Berlin and Vienna: Propyläen-Verl., 1970); *Guttuso e Dante: mostra patrocinata dalla Regione Abruzzo: Casa di Dante in Abruzzo Castello Gizzi, Torre de'Passeri (Pescara), settembre-ottobre, 1982* (Milan: I.D.E.A. Studio, 1982); and *Renato Guttuso: desegni danteschi* (Rome: Galleria d'arte il gabbiano via della frezza, n.d.).

21. On the dating of the canon and its original form, see Peter Brieger, "Pictorial Commentaries to the *Commedia*," in *Illuminated Manuscripts of the "Divine Comedy*," ed. Peter Brieger, Millard Meiss, and Charles Singleton, 2 vols. (Princeton: Princeton University Press, 1969), I, 84–85.

22. For a colour reproduction of this image, see Taylor and Finley, Figure 113.

23. For a colour reproduction of this image, see Taylor and Finley, Figure 151.

24. Rauschenberg's *Commedia* illustrations have been discussed at least tangentially in many of the numerous sources on his life and career. For some of the most focused discussions of those images, see Dore Ashton's introduction to *Rauschenberg: XXXIV Drawings for Dante's "Inferno"* (New York: H. N. Abrams, 1964); William Slattery Lieberman's introduction to *Robert Rauschenberg: illustrations pour "l'Enfer" du Dante, 30 septembre–27 octobre 1965, Palais des Beaux-Arts de Bruxelles* (Brussels: Palais des Beaux-Arts, 1965), esp. 118–19; Barricelli, esp. 65–79; Janet R. Mikolajczyk, "The Dante Drawings of Sandro Botticelli and Robert Rauschenberg," M.A. thesis, Kent State, 1993; and David L. Pike's introduction to *Passage through Hell: Modernist Descents, Medieval Underworlds* (Ithaca and London: Cornell University Press, 1997), esp. vii–xi. For recent, widely accessible introductions to his work in general, see Walter Hopps, et al., *Robert Rauschenberg: A Retrospective*, exh. cat. Solomon R. Guggenheim Museum, New York, September 19, 1997–January 7, 1998 (New York: Guggenheim Museum, 1999); Sam Hunter, *Robert Rauschenberg* (New York: Rizzoli, 1999); Branden Wayne Joseph, *Robert Rauschenberg* (Cambridge, MA, MIT Press, 2002); Robert Saltonstall Mattison, *Robert Rauschenberg: Breaking Boundaries* (New Haven: Yale University Press, 2003). For reproductions of all 34 of Rauschenberg's images, see *Rauschenberg: XXXIV Drawings for Dante's "Inferno*."

25. Though Rauschenberg's illustrations of the early cantos indisputably

comprise clippings that have been cut and pasted from newspapers, there is some ambiguity in the reports of how his other images were transferred. The title page of *Rauschenberg: XXXIV Drawings for Dante's "Inferno"* describes the process generically as a "transfer"; Lieberman suggests (118) that the medium was turpentine or lighter fluid; and Barricelli insists (65) the medium was ligher fluid.

26. For more on Rauschenberg's condemnation of commercial culture, particularly via his *Commedia* illustrations, see Alberto Boatto, *Pop Art in U.S.A.: Dichiarazioni di Dine, Johns, Lichtenstein, Oldenburg, Rauschenberg, Rosenquist, Segal, Warhol* (Milan: Lerici, 1967); Jonathan David Fineberg, *Art since 1940: Strategies of Being* (New York: H. N. Abrams, 1995); Pike, esp. vii–x; David Hopkins, *After Modern Art: 1945–2000* (New York and Oxford: Oxford University Press, 2000); and Donald Kennison and Jesse Washburne-Harris, *Pop Art: The John and Kimiko Powers Collection* (New York: Gagosian Gallery, 2001).

27. Ferrante, *The Political Vision of the "Divine Comedy"* (Princeton: Princeton University Press, 1984), esp. 62–73. For further discussion of the degree to which the *Commedia* is structured around Dante's political program, see Stewart Farnell, *The Political Ideas of the "Divine Comedy"* (Lanham, MD: University Press of America, 1985); E. L. Fortin, *Dissidence et philosophie au moyen âge: Dante et ses antécédents* (Montreal and Paris: Bellarmin and Vrin, 1981); and Karl Maurer, "Dante als politischer Dicter," *Poetica* 7 (1975), 158–88. For a recent summary of Dante's politics and a good, updated bibliography on the issue, see Ferrante, "Dante and Politics," in *Dante: Contemporary Perspectives*, ed. Amilcare A. Iannucci (Toronto, Buffalo, and London: University of Toronto Press, 1997), 181–94.

28. For a general introduction to Baskin's life and career, see Irma B. Jaffe, *The Sculpture of Leonard Baskin* (New York: Viking Press, 1980); and Alan Maxwell Fern, *The Complete Prints of Leonard Baskin: A Catalogue Raisonné 1948–1983* (Boston: Little, Brown, 1984). For more on his *Commedia* illustrations and some examples, see *Illustrations to the "Divine Comedy" of Dante, Graphic Arts*, exh. cat., intro. Dale Roylance, New Haven, 1970 (New York: Grossman, 1969); and Fern.

29. The precise date at which Baskin began his *Commedia* images is not clear, though it was after his Kanthos Press published Lebrun's images and apparently much earlier than 1970, when Baskin's images were published.

Harriet Monroe as Queen-Critic of Chaucer and Langland (*viz.* Ezra Pound)

William A. Quinn

The name of Harriet Monroe, founding editor of *Poetry, A Magazine of Verse*, is in comparison to many of the modern poets she fostered, including T. S. Eliot, Wallace Stevens, and, most contentious of all, Ezra Pound. Yet, Monroe's imprint on the success of the free verse movement cannot be overestimated. By 1912, Harriet Monroe had already achieved a modicum of fame for herself in Chicago. She was a persistent poet and a largely unsuccessful playwright. Her own most celebrated poem to date had been a prize-winning dedicatory ode for the Columbian Exposition of 1892.[1] Subsequently, Monroe remained fairly well-known in Chicago's society primarily as an art and architecture critic for the *Tribune*. But in October of 1912, at the age of fifty-one, Harriet Monroe also published the first issue of *Poetry*. By nurturing the magazine for the next twenty-four years, Monroe acquired most of her own, still enduring international renown.

Monroe's personal success, her magazine's financial security, and the prestige of the free verse movement in America are inseparable considerations. As Ellen Williams has remarked, it was Monroe's "hope and her faith that *Poetry* had ushered in a great era of poetry, and that faith was justified."[2] Furthermore, Monroe would help define "the era when," according to Ann Massa, "Chicago was its women."[3] But, given the subsequent success of both the magazine and the poetic movement it fostered, it is easy to forget the extraordinary struggles (both fiscal and formal) that Monroe originally faced. As Frederick Hoffman recalls: "Indubitably there were few persons in America of 1912 better qualified to lead the fight for a new poetry. And it was a fight – nerve-wracking, often bitterly discouraging."[4] Upon Monroe's death in 1936, Ezra Pound wrote, "No one in our time or in any time has ever served the cause of an art with greater devotion, patience, and unflagging kindness."⁵ Harriet Monroe is herself, therefore, owed homage as a midwife if not the mother of modern poetry in America.

Within her very own magazine, Harriet Monroe encouraged – or at least tolerated – a long and complicated debate about what *modern* English poetry should or should not be. In the context of this critical controversy about modernity itself, Monroe allowed herself a time-out, as it were, to reconsider a precedent decision about what *medieval* English poetry should or should not have been. In the September 1915 issue of *Poetry*, Monroe published an essay in which she reassessed the relative merits of "Chaucer and Langland" as poets.⁶ The significance of her intriguing analysis of the basic contrast between England's rhyming and alliterative traditions and of their respective relevance for modern poetry has been somewhat overshadowed in the magazine's illustrious history by the appearance of "The Love Song of J. Alfred Prufrock" earlier that same year. Monroe herself originally did not like the peculiarly *modern* melancholy of T. S. Eliot's "Love Song" at all; it was printed in *Poetry* largely because of the editorial influence of Ezra Pound.⁷ The impact of Eliot's poem on subsequent poetry has, of course, proven inestimable. The influence of Monroe's opinions regarding Chaucer and Langland themselves is rather negligible. To professional medievalists and prosodists, Monroe's remarks about fourteenth-century English verse now seem merely quaint. For modernists, her analysis of a putative contest between alternative medieval prosodies offers, at most, a tangential insight. But Monroe's devaluation of the dominant (i.e., Chaucerian) heritage of English verse once offered a highly influential challenge to those who presumed to define the future of modern poetry – especially Ezra Pound.

Although the circulation of *Poetry* when "Chaucer and Langland" first appeared consisted of fewer than 2000 subscribers,⁸ "[t]he list of poets who published in *Poetry* includes almost everyone who has since become important in American and British letters."⁹ Harriet Monroe questioned the fundamental importance of Chaucer to her own readership. As a woman reader empowered by her editorship both to evaluate the new poetry and to review the old, Monroe's provocative (and perhaps not entirely sincere) contention was that William Langland should henceforth be considered a more significant role model for modern poets than Geoffrey Chaucer, who had initiated a false, because both foreign and esthete, literary tradition – as Pound apparently intended to do again.¹⁰

Monroe's preference of Langland as the more proto-American because home-grown and democratic poet – instead of Frenchified Chaucer – would have seemed no less bizarre in her own time than it does today.¹¹ Prior to the rise of an academic "Chaucer Industry" starting in the early 1930s, Chaucer was perhaps not so idolized as he is now, but his preeminence as *the* Middle English poet was secure early in the twentieth century.

In retrospect, what might astonish many still "congenial"[12] Chaucerians is Ms. Monroe's uppity lack of taste. But there is a clear (if not entirely legitimate) rationale for Harriet Monroe's deliberately contentious invitation to rethink Chaucer's status as the Father of English Poetry. Monroe recommends that the readers of *Poetry* prefer Langland because he could serve as both a more formally vital and politically significant exemplar of the modern poet than Chaucer.

Harriet Monroe did not intend simply to aggrandize her own prestige as arbiter of the literary tradition by dismissing Chaucer from the canon – that would be reading "like a man," a stereotype of assertive taste that much more readily labels Ezra Pound's criticism.[13] Ezra Pound considered himself – rightly, as most would now concede – not only the better poet but a better medievalist than Harriet Monroe. Monroe's critique of Chaucer functioned primarily, I believe, as a self-conscious rebuttal of Pound's recent recommendations regarding the future of *Poetry* in particular and of modern poetry in general. Her "Chaucer and Langland" should be read, therefore, as a graciously regal admonition rather than an amateur's quaintly absurd opinion. On the one hand, Monroe intended to offer a prosodically informed reconsideration of the history of English poetry, rather than a mere display of her editorial privilege. On the other hand, Monroe's essay also presents a public exercise of her status as editor, an empowered woman reader's response to the Father of English Poetry largely unheard since the fourteenth century – that of a critical queen.

Harriet Monroe maintained a flexible but final control over the publication of *Poetry*.[14] Her initial managerial success as editor had been to achieve financial support for the magazine; her power of the purse then authorized her own critical choices. She decided each issue's table of contents, and she held copyright to all the contents of *Poetry* in her own name. She was quite entitled, therefore, to imagine herself a "Quene of comfort and of gode companye" (Chaucer's "Complaint to His Purse," l. 13)[15] ruling over a rather tumultuous court of more accomplished and often only grudgingly *submissive* poets (in the sense that they had to court her acceptance of their submissions). Precisely because the predominantly male contributors to *Poetry* achieved so much more fame than its editor, it is easy to ignore Monroe's creatively critical presence behind their printed pages.[16]

Monroe's overtly formal and thematic criticism of "Chaucer and Langland" resonates with the gender tensions that were threatening her very status as editor of *Poetry*. For the first six years of the magazine's existence, Ezra Pound – the "instinctive rebel,"[17] whom Monroe had personally recruited as the magazine's first "foreign correspondent" in August of 1912 (when he was only twenty-seven years old) – most aggressively attempted to influence her editorial decisions.[18] Whereas Monroe consistently wished to allow diversity, Pound repeatedly wanted to launch the next new thing.[19] "Harriet Monroe, in many quarters, came gradually to be looked upon not as a rebel, but as a conservative."[20]

Harriet Monroe's ruling taste as editor of *Poetry* magazine has been both applauded and derided as "open door" or "catholic" or "eclectic"or "elastic."[21] On the one hand, *Poetry* had a strong international cachet – primarily because of Ezra Pound. On the other hand, Monroe herself fostered a regional renaissance.[22] On the one hand, she would champion radical experimentation; on the other hand, she could accept utterly conventional verse. Monroe was considered a cordial and cooperative editor by most of her contributors, but she held the blue-pencil as her critical sceptre and was sometimes accused of hauteur.[23] Now, most literary historians agree with E. Jayne Marek's approval of Monroe's open-mindedness:

> *Poetry* provided a democratic space that encouraged inclusiveness and extensive scope in modernism at a crucial time. Far from being timid, frail, and provincial, Monroe showed a courage and equanimity that continually tried to preserve idealism and cooperation.[24]

Ezra Pound, however, found many of the poets that Monroe forced him to keep company with in the pages of *Poetry* "even less satisfactory than those in the *Egoist*."[25] In the end, however, even Pound had to accept that Harriet Monroe's good favour was absolutely necessary for a submitted poem to be admitted into the realm of American *Poetry*.

After four years of publishing the magazine, Monroe felt "like that goblin in the quaint old myth who, blowing the fog out of his face, started a tornado which went careering around the world. A great wind was blowing Cinderella's ashes away, and on the horizon were rolling clouds of words."[26] In "Chaucer and Langland," Monroe contrived an occasion to reconsider what she thought to have been an analogous crisis in the history of English poetry, a moment when a clear (though ultimately erroneous) choice was made between two competing poetic styles. Indeed, as Derek Brewer has perceived, Monroe's "Chaucer and Langland are made to appear rather as two different sides of Ezra Pound."[27] For Monroe, Langland personified a poetic road not taken . . . a right road that modern writers were increasingly in danger of not taking again.

Monroe imagines a near collision between the two medieval English poets on the streets of London as a sort of pedestrian tilt for vatic superiority:

> Not that the two champions consciously faced each other in their intellectual lists. Neither may have known of the other's existence; or, if they ever met in those narrow mudways, no doubt the

courtly Chaucer smiled when surly "Long Will" refused to make way for him, or take off his ragged cap to this retainer of kings. Neither suspected, probably, that the future of England, or at least of English, lay between them, that one or the other of them was molding a world-encircling language and cutting the patterns of an immortal art.[28]

Monroe almost regrets, however, that Geoffrey Chaucer, the proto-regularizer of England's future verse, won.

Monroe's critique of Chaucer avoids several expected stereotypes. As an American, Harriet Monroe might have reverenced Chaucer as a sort of down-home poet – as did Henry David Thoreau.[29] But she thinks Chaucer an aristocrat. Raised in a Victorian milieu, Monroe might have also been embarrassed by Chaucer's intermittent indecency – as she would be offended by D. H. Lawrence's chronic obscenity. But Monroe considers Chaucer to have been a thorough gentleman.[30] Most surprisingly, Monroe seems utterly indifferent to the question of whether Chaucer was, as Gavin Douglas claimed in the early Fifteenth Century, "evir (God wait) all womanis frend" (*Eneados* Prologue to Book I, ll. 445–9), or merely another medieval misogynist.[31] Monroe celebrates rather Chaucer's sophisticated congeniality: "then as now" Chaucer "was irresistible. Well born, well reared, learned in three or four languages, a cosmopolite . . . it was no wonder that Chaucer had it all his own way. English poets have done his will for centuries."[32]

It is precisely this all but universally acknowledged prestige of Geoffrey Chaucer as the formal Father of English Poetry that posed a target of opportunity for Harriet Monroe as parent-editor of *Poetry*. Monroe felt obliged to concede that English "which the Germans call 'the bastard tongue' 'the insignificant pirate dialect' " began to triumph as a (colonising) literary language – "that powerful, flexible, and richly tuned organ which was to be heard around the world"[33] – largely because of Chaucer's achievements:

> Indeed, it was proof of Chaucer's broad sympathy, of his strong mind and big heart, that he did not abandon English altogether, that he, like Dante, loved his "dames tongue," and insisted on writing his poems in it instead of in courtly French or learned Latin.[34]

Monroe especially approves Chaucer's faithfulness to the vernacular:

> It was a fortunate day for us all when Chaucer said: "Let clerks enditen in Latin, for they have the property of science and the knowinge in that faculty; and let Frenchmen in their French also endite their quaint terms, for it is kindly to their mouths; and let

us show our fantasies in such words as we learneden of our dames tongue."³⁵

Regrettably for her argument, this particular citation – the only excerpt from Chaucer that Monroe actually quotes – was not written by Geoffrey Chaucer.³⁶ Nevertheless, Monroe's approval of Chaucer as England's Dante is certainly in harmony with the prevailing scholarly authority of her time.³⁷ More to the point, Monroe's excursus into philology is merely a critical prelude to a subversive prosodic compliment.

Monroe acknowledges that Chaucer did open "the way for some of the greatest rhythmists who ever lived – Shakespeare, Spenser, Milton, Coleridge, Shelley, Swinburne and others"³⁸ – but only by taking English poetry down a formally foreign road. Monroe then addresses at length the shortcomings of Chaucer's rhyming verse line relative to Long Will's alliteration. Monroe admits that Chaucer achieved admirable if imperfect success in his efforts to domesticate quantitative meter in English. If only because of his French upbringing, "he naturally preferred rhyme" as well. As the victorious formal Father, Chaucer spawned the bastard child of so much later English poetry – the iambic pentameter couplet. "Thus Langland was left far behind, *Piers Plowman* was forgotten except by scholars."³⁹ Chaucer's artificial heritage was imported to America where, as William Calin observes, "Longfellow felt that he also could be a poet of the dawn, that he could do for America what Chaucer had done for England by bringing in European culture . . . like Chaucer, Longfellow turned to the Continent, not the Anglo-Saxon mother land."⁴⁰

To validate her own preference for an allegedly native and so more natural though now dispossessed versecraft, Monroe displays her technical expertise as a prosodist and literary historian – in other words, her editorial right to reject contrary opinions:

> Four-time measures were almost abandoned, being found only in a few Elizabethan songs, in parts of Dryden's two music-praising odes, and in a few other experiments. The iambus "reigned supreme," usually in the five-footed line which Chaucer's fine instinct had preferred to the French hexameter as better suited to the genius of the new language. And even when Coleridge – in the *Ancient Mariner* and a few other poems, Shelley – in *The Cloud*, *The Skylark*, and others, and Byron – in *There be none of beauty's daughters*, and one or two other songs, began to vary the music of English verse with four-time measures, their experiments bore little relation to Langland, or to the earlier Saxon bards. And while Swinburne's varied rhythms wove with infinite delicacy new renaissance patterns, they never went back to the stern Gothic motive.⁴¹

However out of date – or simply wrong – this diachronic overview of English prosody may now seem, it sounds majestic and was meant primarily to serve, I believe, as a rhetorical gesture that legitimized Monroe's rulings on modern poetry. Furthermore, Monroe's skepticism regarding "the utter inadequacy of the grammarians' still-medieval system" of scansion was not utterly unwarranted.[42]

Monroe proposes that Walt Whitman, as the "first great modern poet, no doubt, to put aside" regular verse forms derived from "the renaissance patterns" initiated by Chaucer, may have not consciously seeking "the music of the sagas – the Gothic motive, as it may be called . . . yet his free verse is more allied to Langland than to Chaucer."[43] Harriet Monroe thus reads *Piers Plowman* as a precursor of free verse – to her it seemed an authentic, unconventional, and experimental poem (if only because the almost complete extinction of the Alliterative Revival by 1425 had made its fossils seem novel again in early Twentieth Century): "perhaps Langland is like to bridge the centuries and clasp hands with poets of the future, the prophets of the new era."[44]

As patroness of the free verse movement, Monroe herewith decrees that *modern* poetry should mean the end of an exclusive formal definition of the regular verse line initiated by Chaucer. Monroe's promotion of Langland instead is not merely a stylistic preference, however. Monroe invites the readers of *Poetry* to read Langland not just as a school assignment but for the "immediate beauty and fecundity" of his message.[45] Monroe also prefers Langland's allegorical seriousness to Chaucer's ironic realism. Although she banished propagandistic poetry from her magazine, Monroe approves of Langland as the far more revolutionary and, hence, more inspiring precursor of modern poetry:

> And thus Langland, after more than five centuries, may have come into his own at last. The world may rediscover that modern socialist, anarchist, anti-militarist, who in the king-ruled, monk-ridden, war-lorded fourteenth century, lifted up his prophet's voice for the brotherhood of man, and was called crazy for his pains.[46]

In contrast, Monroe comes closest to condemning Chaucer outright when she criticizes his privileged insouciance as opposed to Langland's reformist intensity:

> The urbane Chaucer for five centuries has led the poets his successors: in motive as well as technique they have been mostly of his mind, accepting his aristocratic point of view, his delight in upper-class pageant, and almost ignoring the burden-bearing poor.[47]

Monroe argues that modern poetry should turn away from any such future conception of poetry as an elitist avocation. She prefers a progressive, Christian, socialist champion-poet of modernity such as William Morris and Florence Converse had invited turn-of-the-century readers to imagine William Langland to be.[48]

Monroe's specific criticisms of Chaucer seem *prima facie* rather conventional for her time. In fact, her perceptions of his failings as a poet largely concur with the long-standing and then authoritative opinions of John Dryden and Matthew Arnold. Dryden, whom Joseph A. Dane acknowledges as the *"fons et origo* for American Chaucer criticism,"[49] greatly admired Chaucer as "a rough Diamond." Dryden's disappointment with Chaucer's metricality is, of course, based primarily on a misapprehension of Middle English pronunciation. Matthew Arnold, however, questioned Chaucer's very substance as a poet. Arnold – who in fact greatly admired Chaucer and conceded his ability to teach a benign truth – had most famously lamented Chaucer's lack of "σπουδαιότης, the high and excellent seriousness, which Aristotle assigns as one of the grand virtues of poetry."[50] T. S. Eliot, who had "not a scrap of sympathy with or interest in Chaucer,"[51] thought much the same of Chaucer's shortcomings as did Arnold and Dryden and Harriet Monroe. But Ezra Pound adored Geoffrey Chaucer.

A year before Monroe's essay on "Chaucer and Langland" appeared in *Poetry*, Pound had declared his genuine enthusiasm for Geoffrey Chaucer: "Chaucer should be on every man's shelf. Milton is the worst sort of poison."[52] In the *Egoist*, Pound had also recently and publically challenged Monroe "to modernize herself considerably more, and stay modernized."[53] By contesting Pound's extravagant admiration for Chaucer,[54] Monroe displays both her own privilege as editor of *Poetry* and her *gentilesse* as a reader of the poetic tradition. It is this rather in-house context that imbues Monroe's otherwise purely academic and apparently objective reconsideration of medieval poetry with a fondly patronizing voice.

Though Monroe would shrink Chaucer's prestige, she never attempts simply to castrate the Father of English Poetry – as Camille Paglia has rather recently attempted to do.[55] More ladylike, Monroe celebrates Chaucer's achievements as an individual poet even as she laments his influence. Similarly, Monroe pillows her implicit admonition of Ezra Pound with an explicit compliment in "Chaucer and Langland." She invites all readers of *Poetry* to enjoy Ezra Pound's "truly wonderful paraphrase, *The Sea-farer*" as an example of "modern presentations of mediaeval music."[56]

Not unlike most of her contemporaries, Monroe's delight in England's "mediaeval music" seems to have heard the consonances of both Old and Middle English alliterative poems as one irregular (and so "free") prosody. She was not alone; "Mid-19th-century England abounded in amiable enthusiasts for Saxon roots . . . The time's enthusiasm for Anglo-Saxon studies was transmitted to Pound by Professor Ibbotson at Hamilton."[57] According to Fred C. Robinson, a magisterial advocate, Pound's translation of "The Seafarer" itself displayed what for the time was a rather remarkable expertise with Old English poetic conventions.[58] And Pound's "Seafarer" probably provided Harriet Monroe with her single most significant exemplar of the "Gothick" style of Old/Middle English alliterative verse.

Although herself no slouch as a connoisseur of pre-modern poetry, and although herself a rather sophisticated prosodist who greatly admired the revolutionary theories of Sidney Lanier – whose *The Science of English Verse* (1880) also inspired John C. Pope's *The Rhythm of Beowulf* (1942) – Harriet Monroe seems to have remained happily unconcerned as a critic by the systematic rigor of Eduard Sievers's *Altgermanische Metrik* (1893). Fully confident in her natural ability to appreciate the affective qualities of such verse, Monroe approves the lost liberty of Langland's Anglo-Saxonish alliterations:

> The run-away Anglo-Saxon sone and heir, far off in his isolated island, had at first shown a rebellious disregard of family rules and precepts; but a great poet named Chaucer had taken him in hand at just the right formative moment, and impressed upon him the superiority of the iambic Gallic paces over the heavy lumbering hoof-beats of song which his saga-singing mother had been crooning to him from her northern memories.[59]

Monroe would have Pound merely continue to be true to the native rhythms of this "dame's tongue"; Monroe thus admires Pound's genius as a scholar-poet even as she feels compelled to rebuke his increasingly foreign-minded definitions of modernity.

In her "Introduction" to the 1917 edition of *The New Poetry*, Monroe reiterated much the same convictions that Chaucer was almost individually responsible for derailing a free verse movement in English. Again, Monroe concedes the enduring appeal of Chaucer's "great genius." She softens her criticism of his poetry as an opiate of the upper classes – a bit: "he was, an aristocrat by birth and breeding, and a democrat by feeling and sympathy." But Chaucer-the-rhymer chose a non-native prosody:

> Chaucer may have had it in his power to turn the whole stream of English poetry into either the French or the Anglo-Saxon channel. Knowing and loving the old French epics better than the Norse sagas, he naturally chose the French channel, and he was so great and so beloved that his world followed him.

The subsequent rise of regular end-rhyme in English verse was inevitable though unnatural: "Thus there was no longer any question – the iambic measure and rhyme, both dear to the French-trained ears of England's Norman masters, became fixed as the standard type of poetic form."

For a time – the most crucial moment in English prosody, perhaps, prior to the early twentieth century – "it was possibly a toss-up." Like Monroe's perception of the present state of modern poetry:

> the scale hung almost even in that formative fourteenth century. If Chaucer's contemporary Langland – the great democrat, revolutionist, mystic – had had Chaucer's authority and universal sympathy, English poetry might have followed his example instead of Chaucer's.

Her challenge for new poets reading *The New Poetry* is to rediscover the integrity of this old option: "If our criticism is to have any value, it must insist upon the obvious truth that poetry existed before the English language began to form itself out of the débris of other tongues, and that it now exists in forms of great beauty among many far-away peoples who never heard of our special rules."[60] Almost every philological, prosodic, and interpretive assertion that Monroe makes here about the relative merits of Langland's "rum, ram, ruf" *vs*. Chaucer's "gesting" may now seem vague and debatable. But her fundamental challenge that "the Pound era" should promote a largely forgotten, rough, tough medieval conception of popular poetry was at the time deliberately targeted and clearly provocative.

Monroe's implicit invitation to heed her editorial advice was largely ignored by Ezra Pound. By 1917, Monroe felt compelled to achieve "a new understanding" with him.[61] Pound distanced himself from *Poetry*, informally resigning as its foreign correspondent; he continued, however, to submit poems which Monroe graciously printed.[62] By the mid-1920s, when *Poetry* is generally thought to have declined into being a mere "trade-journal,"[63] Monroe conversely thought that Pound and Eliot had fallen into supersophisticated elitism – Chaucer's urbanity gone bad.[64] It was primarily in an effort to forestall this trend in modern poetry that Harriet Monroe had attempted to resurrect an optional appreciation of medieval English poetry's original form and function in "Chaucer and Langland."

As the editor of *Poetry* and as a connoisseur of all poetry – and only ambivalently empowered in both contexts as a modern woman – Harriet Monroe assumed a critical posture probably not witnessed since the 1380s – the status of a patron queen as portrayed in Chaucer's Prologue to *The Legend of Good Women*. Chaucer appeals to his patronness "the quene Alceste" (F 511) to defend him against a pending charge: that he had misdirected English poetry (i.e., by slandering womankind and love). Alceste apologizes for – and so advertises – Chaucer's shortcomings as a poet:

> And eke, peraunter, for this man ys nyce,
> He myght doon yt, gessyng no malice,
> But for he useth thynges for to make;
> Hym rekketh noght what matere he take. (F 362–5)

Alceste (which is to say Chaucer himself) here initiates what has conventionally come to be identified as Matthew Arnold's critique of the poet's *niceness*, or lack of high seriousness. If not on account of his servile incompetence, Chaucer's artlessness should be excused by virtue his sincere regret:

> Or hym was boden maken thilke tweye
> Of som persone, and durste yt nat withseye;
> Or hym repenteth outrely of this. (F 366–7)[65]

Alceste also predicts what is now normally designated John Dryden's critique of Chaucer's rude verse: "Al be hit that he kan nat wel endite,/ Yet hath he maked lewed folk delyte" (F 414–15).[66]

Five hundred years later, Harriet Monroe essentially proposed that Alceste's taste comprises an equally *modern* perception of both the formal and thematic worth of Chaucer's poetry. Monroe's graciously negative tone – when criticizing Ezra Pound as well as Chaucer, that is – sounds highly recollective of the Queen's pseudo-apologetic (and probably ironic) voice. Chaucer himself anticipated this condescending, hostile affection from "every lady bright of hewe,/ And every gentil womman, what she be" (*Troilus and Criseyde* 5 1772–3). The curious correspondence between the rhetorical poses of Harriet Monroe and Queen Alceste (herself probably an image of the real Queen Anne) seems more situational than chromosomal, however; it is Alceste's regal status as the appointed judge of Chaucer in Cupid's court rather than merely her gender as a lady-in-waiting that Monroe echoes.

In one of her own poems, Harriet Monroe seems to have likewise anticipated that critical sparks would be generated by her own enthronement as a female arbiter of modernity. In 1910, Monroe personified "The Turbine," one of "the prodigious works of modern man,"[67] as a generous but powerful and so dangerous benefactress:

> Look at her – there she sits upon her throne
> As ladylike and quiet as a nun!
> But if you cross her – whew! Her thunderbolts
> Will shake the earth! She's proud as any queen.

This electric Luna rules "When her gay lord, the sun, gives up his job."

Monroe's portrayal of the lyric's "I" is most illuminating as a foreshadowing of Ezra Pound's perception of a female boss. The poem assumes the point of view of male attendant who serves the electric queen as "her slave . . . I do her will/ And dare not disobey." Monroe imagines his acknowledgment of her superiority: "Sometimes I wonder why she stoops/ To be my friend . . . Though I am trivial and she sublime." She also has him imagine (and so confesses) her feminine fatigue from fighting the male ego: "But there are moments – hush! –/ When my turn comes; her slave can be her master, Conquering her he serves. For she's a woman,/ Gets bored there on her throne, tired of herself."[68] But, when not concessive or exhausted or open-minded or indifferent, Harriet Monroe ruled her own domain of *Poetry, A Magazine of Verse* as its Queen-Critic, *pace* Pound.

NOTES

1. Harriet Monroe won a $1000.00 prize. The *New York World* published her "Columbian Ode" without permission prior to its scheduled recitation at the Exposition's opening ceremonies. Monroe's father successfully sued the newspaper for $5000.00. Daniel J. Cahill explains that "The *Monroe* case" was so important "because it was without legal precedent" and it "established the rights of authors to control their own unpublished works," in *Harriet Monroe* (New York: Twayne Publishers, 1973), 25.

2. Ellen Williams, *Harriet Monroe and the Poetry Renaissance: The First Ten Years of "Poetry," 1912–1922* (Urbana: University of Illinois Press, 1977), 294.

3. Ann Massa, "Form Follows Function: The Construction of Harriet Monroe and *Poetry, A Magazine of Verse*," in Susan Albertine, ed., *A Living in Words: American Women in Print Culture* (Knoxville: University of Tennessee Press, 1995), 115–31 (125).

4. Frederick J. Hoffman, Charles Allen and Carolyn F. Ulrich, eds., *The Little Magazine: A History and Bibliography* (Princeton: Princeton University Press, 1946), 39.

5. Rpt. in "Epilogue" to Harriet Monroe, *A Poet's Life* (New York: Macmillan, 1938), 469.

6. Harriet Monroe, ed. *Poetry, A Magazine of Verse* (Chicago: Seymour, Daughaday & Co., 1915), vol. VI, no. VI, 297–301. Rpt. in Harriet Monroe, *Poets & Their Art* (New York: Macmillan, 1926), 141–5.

7. Monroe, *Poetry*, vol. VI, no. III, 130–35.

8. In her "Appendix: Figures on Poetry's Income, Expenditures, and Circulation," Ellen Williams calculates the maximum possible circulation for 1914–15 to be 1,549 and for 1915–16 to be 1,938 in *Poetry Renaissance*, 296. Monroe's influence as *arbiter gustibus* was more firmly established by the anthology *The New Poetry* (1917, 1923, 1932). In "Publishing the New Poetry: Harriet Monroe's Anthology," *Journal of Modern Literature* 11 (1984): 89–108, Craig S. Abbott explains that "the anthology, more successfully than *Poetry*, reached Monroe's great

audience. Moreover, as it progressed through its several editions, it served as a review of *Poetry* and of the new poetry movement in general. It packaged the poetic renaissance for public consumption, especially in the schools" (90). Like her magazine, Monroe's anthology was widely criticized for its inclusiveness (95–96).

9. Hoffman, *Little Magazine*, 242.

10. Monroe's preference of Langland to Chaucer is as vulnerable to ridicule as several of her other editorial choices. Most notoriously, Monroe thought Lew Sarett's *The Box of God* superior to *The Waste Land*, an opinion that led Ian Hamilton to characterize her as a simple-minded pioneer *in The Little Magazines: A Study of Six Editors* (London: Weidenfield and Nicolson, 1976), 64–65. Craig Abbott offers a guarded apology for Monroe's taste; her "predilections may have been simple-minded, but she knew what they were and was not greatly limited by them," "Publishing," 108.

11. In the 11th Edition of the *Encyclopedia Britannica*, vol. VI (1910), A. W. Pollard celebrated "Chaucer's gifts of vivid colouring" and his "wonderful character sketches . . . For fully three centuries" appreciation of Chaucer's artistic achievement "was sustained solely by his narrative power, his warmest panegyrists betraying no consciousness that they were praising one of the greatest technical masters of poetry. Even when thus maimed, however, his works found readers and lovers in every generation, and every improvement in his text has set his fame on a surer basis," 15b–17a. Pollard was also editor of the highly influential "Globe Edition" of *Chaucer*, with H. Frank Heath, Mark H. Liddell, and W. S. McCormick, eds., *The Works of Geoffrey Chaucer* (London: Macmillan and Co., Ltd, 1898).

The unsigned article on "Langland, William," in the 11th *Britannica*, vol. XVI acknowledges the importance if not the immediate appeal of *Piers Plowman*: "The theological disquisitions which are occasionally introduced are somewhat dull and tedious, but the earnestness of the author's purpose and his energy of language tend to relieve them . . . The poem is essentially one of those which improve on a second reading" though its alliterative meter is "not very regular," 175a.

12. Stephanie Trigg, *Congenial Souls: Reading Chaucer from Medieval to Postmodern* (Minneapolis: University of Minnesota Press, 2002).

13. Carolyn Dinshaw defines "reading like a man" essentially as the imperative to take possession of the *corpus* of the text, whereas "reading like a woman" is essentially . . . something else. Women can read like men "and – perhaps more importantly – men don't have to read like men" in *Chaucer's Sexual Poetics* (Madison: University of Wisconsin Press, 1989), 12. Jill Mann contends that a fully " 'feminist reading' of Chaucer is not (as it might well be with other writers) essentially different from a reading *tout court*" in *Geoffrey Chaucer* (Atlantic Highlands, NJ: Humanities Press International, 1991), 2.

A curious example of the notion that Monroe prided herself on writing *like a man* may be found in her citation of Robert Louis Stevenson's May 25, 1886, reply to her first letter: "It may interest you to know that I read to the signature without suspecting my correspondent was a woman; though in one point (a reference to the Countesss) I might have found a hint of the truth" in Monroe, *Life*, 65.

14. Ann Massa sees an analogy between Monroe's ability to sell the quasi-operatic presentation of her "Columbian Ode" in 1892 and her launching of

the magazine *Poetry* in 1912: "she was able to sell her sponsors two products: poetry and herself" in "The Columbian Ode and *Poetry, A Magazine of Verse*: Harriet Monroe's Entrepreneurial Triumphs," *Journal of American Studies* 20 (1986): 52–69 (69). Monroe became convinced that, in order to earn more respect for poetry in America, modern poets needed to be awarded more money. She acquired funding for her editorial *largesse* by cultivating both sponsors and a marketplace for *Poetry*.

15. Unless otherwise noted, all citations of Chaucer are from Larry Benson, gen. ed., *The Riverside Chaucer*, 3rd edn. (Boston: Houghton Mifflin, 1987).

16. Lawrence Rainey does not focus extensively on Harriet Monroe in particular but considers how "Strategies of authorial construction changed as authors sought to address different publics, ranging from patron-*salonniers* to mass audiences, or from patron-investors, dealers, and speculators to a broader (if numerically restricted) corpus of critics and educated readers" in *Institutions of Modernism: Literary Elites and Public Culture* (New Haven: Yale University Press, 1998), 4. Medievalists are no less inclined to emphasize the impact of an anticipated audience on specific poetic projects; Paul Strohm, for example, explores "the assumption that Chaucer addressed much of his poetry to a circle of social equals and near equals" in *Social Chaucer* (Cambridge, MA: Harvard University Press, 1989), 50.

17. Monroe, *Poet's Life*, 404.

18. E. Jayne Marek remarks that "From the earliest months of his relationship with *Poetry*, Pound set out to stir things up. Interestingly, although literary history has usually ignored the collaborative nature of *Poetry*'s editorship, Pound saw Monroe and [Alice Corbin] Henderson's interaction as a means by which he might wield influence" in *Women Editing Modernism: "Little" Magazines and Literary History* (Lexington: Univ. of Kentucky Press, 1995), 180.

19. In his memorial to Monroe (*Poetry*, December 1936), Ezra Pound conceded the pragmatic rightness of her "inclusive policy (however much the inclusiveness may have rankled one and all factions)" rpt. in "Epilogue" to Monroe, *Poet's Life*, 470.

20. Hoffman, *Little Magazine*, 42.

21. As Marek observes, "Monroe's standards provided grounds for criticism no matter from which direction the critical winds blew," *Women Editing*, ix. Critics and biographers often attribute Monroe's sometimes self-contradictory policies as editor to some basic paradox in her psyche. E. Williams considers her ambivalent status as a populist who socialized with the upperclass but was not wealthy, *Poetry Renaissance*, 8. Massa suggests that Monroe's "complex attitudes determined that the kind of men for whom she formed deep emotional attachments were inaccessible and unattainable," "Construction," 121.

22. In his reply to Monroe's initial invitation to contribute, Ezra Pound asked "Are you for American poetry or for poetry? The latter is more important, but it is important that America should boost the former, provided it don't mean a blindness to the art" as reported in Monroe, *Poet's Life*, 259.

23. E. Williams argues that "Although Harriet Monroe's tendency to rewrite, revise, and correct submissions came to seem magisterial to a later generation of writers, or simply philistine to a writer like [William Carlos] Williams . . . it originated innocently," *Poetry Renaissance*, 65. In her autobiography, Monroe cites the

example of a long letter written in 1913 by William Carlos Williams regarding her request for revision of a submission: "I am startled to see that you are fast gravitating to the usual editorial position . . . that as soon as one says, 'I am an editor!' he having been in the march of the poets faces about upon them . . . Anyhow, I'm a great poet, and you don't think so, and there we are. And so allow me to send you a revised 'Postlude' (when it is done) hoping to gain your good favor in that way – for I must succeed, you know" as recorded in Monroe, *Poet's Life*, 270–1.

24. Marek, *Women Editing*, 58.

25. Timothy Materer, "Make It Sell! Ezra Pound Advertises Modernism," in Kevin J. H. Dettmar and Stephen Watt, eds., *Marketing Modernisms: Self-Promotion, Canonization, Rereading* (Ann Arbor: University of Michigan Press, 1996), 17–36 (21).

26. Monroe, *Poet's Life*, 404.

27. Derek Brewer, ed., *Chaucer: The Critical Heritage* (London: Routledge and Kegan Paul, 1978), vols. I (1385–1837) & II (1837–1933), II 334.

28. Monroe, *Poetry*, VI 298.

29. Brewer, *Heritage*, II 50–57.

30. See examples listed in the Index to Caroline Spurgeon, *Five Hundred Years of Chaucer's Criticism and Allusion 1357–1900*, 3 vols. (Cambridge: Cambridge University Press, 1925) under the heading "Indecency: frivolity," vol. 3, 18–19.

31. When it comes to such gender issues, Francis Lee Utley explains "Boccaccio and Chaucer piled satire and defense on one another in inextricable confusion" in *The Crooked Rib: An Analytical Index to the Argument about Women in English and Scots Literature to the End of the Year 1568* (Columbus: The Ohio State University Press, 1944; rpt. New York: Octagon Books, 1970), 36. Alcuin Blamires likewise considers the Wife of Bath's Prologue "a kind of interface between readings from anti-feminism and responses to anti-feminism" in Alcuin Blamires, ed., with Karen Pratt and C. W. Marx, *Woman Defamed and Woman Defended* (Oxford: Clarendon Press, 1992), 198.

32. Monroe, *Poetry*, VI 298.

33. Monroe, *Poetry*, VI 297.

34. Monroe, *Poetry*, VI 299.

35. Monroe, *Poetry*, VI 299.

36. The passage quoted is from the Prologue to *The Testament of Love* (ca. 1387) by Thomas Usk. W. W. Skeat's 1897 edition of the excerpt (correctly attributed to Thomas Usk) reads: "Let than clerkes endyten in Latin, for they have the propertee of science, and the knowing in that facultee; and let Frenchmen in their Frenche also endyten their queynt termes, for it is kyndely to their mouthes; and let us shewe our fantasyes in suche wordes as we lerneden of our dames tonge" in *The Complete Works of Geoffrey Chaucer*, vol. VII, "Chaucerian and Other Pieces" (London: Oxford University Press, 1897), 2. *The Testament* had been attributed to Chaucer in William Thynne's 1532 edition. Rossell Hope Robbins notes that it is "perhaps the most firmly linked to Chaucer of any of these apocryphal pieces," in "The Chaucerian Apocrypha" in Albert E. Hartung, gen. ed., *A Manual of Writings in Middle English 1050–1500*, vol. 4 (New Haven: The Connecticut Academy of Arts and Sciences, 1973), 1062.

37. In the *Encyclopedia Britannica* 11th Edition, vol. 6, A. W. Pollard affirmed that "Chaucer's service to the English language lies in his decisive success having made it impossible for any later English poet to attain fame, as Gower had done, by writing alternatively in Latin and French," 16b.

38. Monroe, *Poetry*, VI 299.

39. Monroe, *Poetry*, VI 298–9.

40. William Calin, "What *Tales of a Wayside Inn* Tells Us about Longfellow and about Chaucer," *Studies in Medievalism* 12 (2002): 197–213 (202).

41. Monroe, *Poetry*, VI 299–300.

42. Monroe, *Poet's Life*, 364.

43. Monroe, *Poetry*, VI 300.

44. Monroe, *Poetry*, VI 301.

45. Monroe, *Poetry*, VI 301.

46. Monroe, *Poetry*, VI 301.

47. Monroe, *Poetry*, VI 301.

48. Paul Hardwick, " 'Biddeth Peres Ploughman go to his werk': Appropriations of *Piers Plowman* in the Nineteenth and Twentieth Centuries," *Studies in Medievalism* 12 (2002): 171–95.

49. Joseph A. Dane, *Who is Buried in Chaucer's Tomb?* (East Lansing: Michigan State University Press, 1998), 161.

50. Brewer, *Heritage*, II 219.

51. Brewer, *Heritage*, II 489.

52. *The Renaissance*, "Poetry" [1914]; "Literary Essays" 216; Brewer II 329.

53. June 1, 1914, p. 215; rpt. in E. Williams, *Poetry Renaissance*, 96.

54. Ezra Pound's enthusiasm for Chaucer would become only more extreme. In *ABC of Reading* (New Haven: Yale University Press, 1934), he proclaimed, "As for the relative merits of Chaucer and Shakespeare, English opinion has been bamboozled for centuries . . . Chaucer had a deeper knowledge of life than Shakespeare . . . No one will ever gauge or measure English poetry until they know how much of it, how full a gamut of its qualities, is already THERE ON THE PAGE of Chaucer," 87–90.

55. Paglia would dethrone Chaucer as the Father of English Poetry and install Edmund Spenser in his stead: "Chaucer's comic persona resembles that of Charlie Chaplin's Little Tramp, whom I seem to be alone in loathing . . . The hearty warmth of it all makes my skin crawl," *Sexual Personae* (New Haven: Yale University Press, 1990), 171.

56. Monroe, *Poetry*, VI 300. Pound subsequently approved Chaucer's dismissal of the Alliterative Revival: "He made fun of the hrimm hramm ruff, the decadence of Anglo-Saxon alliteration, the verse written by those who had forgotten the WHY of the Anglo-Saxon bardic narration," *ABC*, 89. Gerard Manley Hopkins had similarly considered William Langland's alliterative line to be only a diminished echo of Old English poetry and, as such, a false precedent for his own sprung rhythm; in 1882, Hopkins wrote Robert Bridges that he thought Anglo-Saxon verse was represented only "in a degraded and doggerel shape in *Piers Ploughman* (I am reading that famous poem and am coming to the conclusion that it is not worth

reading)" in Claude Colleer, ed., *The Letters of Gerard Manley Hopkins to Robert Bridges*, 2nd imp. (London: Oxford University Press, 1955), 156.

57. Hugh Kenner, *The Pound Era* (Berkeley: University of Calfornia Press, 1971), 108.

58. Fred C. Robinson, " 'The Might of the North': Pound's Anglo-Saxon Studies and 'The Seafarer'," *Yale Review* 71 (1981–1982): 199–224.

59. Monroe, "The Free Verse Movement," *Poets & Their Art*, 291–301 (291–2); a longer version of this essay originally appeared in the *English Journal*; a revised and expanded version of this collection of essays appeared in 1936.

60. Harriet Monroe and Alice Corbin Henderson, eds., *The New Poetry* (New York: Macmillan, [1917, 1923] 1932), xxxvii–xxxviii.

61. Monroe, *Poet's Life*, 404.

62. In her autobiography, Monroe reminisced that Pound continued to prod "*us* now and then in different moods of humor or impatience or violence. And if his stings and stabs should cease, it would mean for *me* the loss of [Pound]'s most deliciously acrid flavor," *Poet's Life*, 404 (italics mine). In this phrasing, Monroe's initial use of a plural first-person pronoun probably indicates her collaborative conception of editing *Poetry*, but it also may be termed an *editorial* or *royal* self-reference.

63. Craig Abbott, "Publishing," 104.

64. See reviews in Monroe, *Poetry*, XXI (March 1923), 325–30, and XXVI (May 1925), 90–97.

65. In actuality, the "certain person" who had commanded Chaucer to compose *Troilus and Criseyde* and the *Roman de la Rose* – "those two" offensive or, worse, insignificant poems – was putatively Queen Anne herself whom Chaucer certainly dared not deny.

66. Ezra Pound seems to have suspected some irony in Chaucer's confessions of prosodic incompetence: "Chaucer's self-criticism placed in the mouth of the Man of Law. He professes himself untaught in metre," *ABC*, 86n.

67. Monroe dedicated this poem "To. W.S.M." her brother, "builder of record-breaking power plants, whose talk about a dangerously injured generator inspired the poem," Monroe, *Poet's Life*, 191.

68. Monroe, "The Turbine," rpt. in *You and I* (New York: Macmillan, 1914), 15–20.

Zoë Oldenbourg, the Albigensian Crusade, and Terrorist Repression

Peter G. Christensen

Like the Knights Templar, the Cathars keep on returning from the dead to haunt the imagination of medievalism. Since 1870 when Napoléon Peyrat drew attention to a Cathar treasure taken away from Montségur at the time of its destruction, an incident briefly mentioned in a confession of Imbert de Salles to Inquisitors,[1] the Cathars have prompted the fantasies of a host of diverse groups, from mystics to Nazis. At the same time much serious research has illuminated the Cathars and their religion in a way almost unimaginable before World War II. The works of Zoë Oldenbourg (1916–2002), novelist, playwright, and historian, straddle the line between the Cathars of the imagination and the Cathars of history. In two long (almost 1000 pages in all), interlocking novels, *Les Brûlés* (1960) and *Les Cités charnelles* (1961), a play, *L'Évêque et la vieille dame, ou la belle-mère de Peytavi Borsier* (1983 [untranslated]), and a scholarly history of the Albigensian Crusade, *Le Bûcher de Monségur, 16 mars 1244* (1959) she has tried to give voice to those whom history has silenced.[2]

Although Oldenbourg's extensive literary *oeuvre* has been neglected by scholars and mostly limited to reviews of individual books, we can point out three different attitudes that have been taken to her work. First, and most positively, she has been accepted as a great historical novelist who has succeeded in creating believable characters from the High Middle Ages. Second, she has been considered a biased partisan of the Cathars, whose work is flawed by a failure adequately to consider a Catholic viewpoint.[3] Third, in the words of historian Krystel Maurin, Oldenbourg's novels represent a democratisation of the romantic myth of the Cathars inherited from the 19th century.[4] In this essay I will use recent research on the Cathars to show that the first of these three views is closest to the mark. I believe that Oldenbourg presents a credible view of the Bons Hommes and Bonnes

Femmes, generally known as Cathars, given the scarcity of documentation of their everyday lives in the early 1200s.

Oldenbourg makes it clear in *Massacre at Montségur* that the Albigensian Crusade was a turning point for the worse in the history of the Western Christian Church. Before this event abbots and bishops still protested against the burning of heretics, but after it the persecution of heretics by the Roman Catholic Church was a "repressive terrorism" continued by the Inquisition.[5] Oldenbourg's view of the Cathars and her understanding of the Albigensian Crusade hold up well today after forty years. There is no doubt that Oldenbourg did her homework. In presenting the Cathars as innocent victims of a terrorist war waged by the Catholic Church in conjunction with military forces and civil authority, she has not departed from what the historical record reveals. Nevertheless, it should be remembered that the Albigensian Crusade remains a controversial event in modern historiography, for at least two reasons. The role of the Roman Catholic Church in initiating the violent events and following up the military suppression with the Inquisition has been a hot issue, as has the question of whether or not a view such as Oldenbourg's, which reflects contemporary expectations about tolerance, is appropriate or not. After presentation of background information about Oldenbourg and about the Cathars, I will examine her depiction of terror in the two novels, the play, and then the history.

Background

Oldenbourg has published about twenty books since 1946. Through Gallimard she issued her novels, stories, and plays on the Middle Ages. These include three other novels about the Middle Ages: *Argile et cendres* (1946), *La Pierre angulaire* (1953) and *La Joie des Pauvres* (1970). The first two of these medieval novels deal with France at the time of the Third Crusade, and the last with the First Crusade. In her collection of three novellas, *Déguisements* (1989) one of the stories takes place during the Middle Ages, and concerns the so-called Bal des Ardents. Her most recent play *Aliénor* (1992) is about Eleanor of Aquitaine.[6] She has received little scholarly attention, although she has been the subject of a short book by Sophie Massalovitch.[7] For the last thirty years of her life most of Oldenbourg's novels have dealt with twentieth-century themes, often with Russian emigration to France, which she also treats in her two-volume autobiography.

Even before Oldenbourg wrote her works in the late 1950s, quite a few novels on the Cathars had appeared, including two which initiated the vogue for mythographic novels on the Albigensian Crusade: Maurice Magre's *Le*

Sang de Toulouse and *Le Trésor des albigeois*. They appeared shortly before Antoine Dondaine published important new sources of Cathar doctrine which he had uncovered.[8] Excavations at Montségur begun in the late 1940s revealed that the ruins on the spot today come from a structure made by Guy de Lévis later than the 1240s, and that the Montségur of the Cathars no longer remains.[9] Still, theology and archaeology could not stem the flood of pseudo-histories of the Cathars, and speculations on their treasure and fantastic stories of their relationship to the Templars and the Holy Grail continued to appear. In the 1980s there was a boom in novels about the Cathars, and today novels on the Cathars continue to be popular.[10]

Since the publication of *Destiny of Fire* and *Cities of the Flesh*, much progress has been made in the study of the Cathars and the Albigensian Crusade. In 1959, just before the publication of these two novels, René Nelli, later to become the founder of the Centre National d'Études Cathares in Carcassonne, published his collection of source materials, *Écritures Cathares*, which was updated in 1969 and revised again after his death by Anne Brenon in 1995. This volume brings together along with a few other items the three surviving rituals (the Occitan rituals in the Lyons and Dublin mss. and the Latin ritual in the Florence ms.), along with two Cathar treatises (*The Treatise of the Two Principles* and the *Anonymous Treatise*).[11] The availability of these documents helped promote a flood of research in the periodicals *Cahiers de Fanjeaux* (1966–) and *Herésis* (1983–). Since the 1970s the study of Catharism has been revolutionised by René Nelli's *La Philosophie du catharisme*, Jean Duvernoy's *La Religion des cathares*, and *L'Histoire des cathares*, and the multi-volume history of the Abigensian Crusade and its aftermath by Michel Roquebert, *L'Epopée cathare* and *Montségur: Les Cendres de la liberté*.[12] Since 1961 there have been several more histories of the Albigensian Crusade, such as Joseph Reese Strayer's *The Albigensian Crusades*, Walter Leggatt Wakefield's *Heresy, Crusade and Inquisition in Southern France, 1100–1250*, Jonathan Sumption's *The Albigensian Crusade*, M. D. Costen's *The Cathars and the Albigensian Crusade*, and Stephen O'Shea's *The Perfect Heresy*. The most recent major work in English on Cathar religion is Malcolm Lambert's *The Cathars*, and on Catharism in relation to dualism, Yuri Stoyanov's *The Other God* and Malcolm Barber's *The Cathars*.[13]

In her novels, Oldenbourg responded indirectly to earlier studies such as Stephen Runciman's *The Medieval Manichee*, Hans Söderberg's *La Religion des Cathares*, and Arno Borst's *Die Katharer*. Borst felt that no simple either/or answer could be given to the question of whether or not the Cathars were medieval Christians or inheritors of a Gnostic tradition that had been passed along through history.[14] Oldenbourg does not present the Cathars as heirs of a tradition of Manichean or Gnostic religion that has been continuous across the centuries. Rather for her, Catharism is a dualism springing from Christianity as practiced in Languedoc, and this opinion has become the new consensus since the 1970s. This view is shared by Anne Brenon, who now directs the C.N.E.C. in Carcassonne. As Brenon says in the Preface to the 3rd edition of *Écritures Cathares*, the Cathars did not use Manichean writings to come up with their beliefs. Instead they developed their ideas from their understanding of Christianity.[15] In addition, Brenon in *Les Cathares* stresses Cathar belief in universal salvation and denial of the concept of Christ's redemptive suffering on the Cross. Christ's suffering could not have been willed by God, so it was important to denounce the human cruelty that brought about his suffering.[16]

Unfortunately, we do not have any personal life-writing on the part of the Cathars to reveal their beliefs and their everyday life. Although we can get a picture of everyday life in the town of Montaillou from the testimonies recorded by Jacques Fournier published in three volumes by Jean Duvernoy, that is, the records used by Emmanuel Le Roy Ladurie for his classic study, *Montaillou*, this material dates to 1318–25, one hundred years after the events of Oldenbourg's novels. The Languedoc Cathars of the 13th century have been silenced.[17]

The main sources for the Albigensian Crusade itself as distinct from Catharism are (1) *La Chanson de la Croisade contre les Albigeois* in Occitan by William of Tudela, continued one third of the way through by an anonymous, pro-Languedoc but non-Cathar Occitan poet; (2) *The History of the Albigensian Crusade* by Peter of les Vaux-de-Cernay (Petrus Sarnensis), who came south with the invading army, written in Latin and strongly biased in favour of Simon de Montfort; and (3) *The Chronicle of the Albigensian War* in Latin by Guillaume de Puylaurens. Guillaume's work is much shorter than the other two, and it covers a much longer time period, as it was written later in the 13th century. It gives an overview of the events. In contrast, the *Chanson* and Pierre des Vaux-de-Cernay do not take us past 1219.[18] Other sources of information, such as the Catalan account of Pedro II at Muret in the *Libre dels fets*, the chronicle of the Dominican Inquisitor Guillaume Pelhisson, the brief discussion of the massacre at Béziers by the Cistercian Caesarius of Heisterbach, the correspondence of Innocent III, diplomatic correspondence from Toulouse and elsewhere, the Doat Archive of Catholic Church materials in the Bibliothèque Nationale, and troubadour lyrics all fail to offer a Cathar perspective. Thus here Oldenbourg as historical novelist fills in the gaps left by historians.[19]

Destiny of Fire

In *Destiny of Fire* Oldenbourg's main concern is to show local response to the invasion of Languedoc by the Crusading armies and persecution by the

Catholic Church. We see how they affect one family and the people who come into contact with them. By keeping historical events in the background, Oldenbourg does not take liberty with them. Nor does she move her characters around unrealistically so that they are at major conclaves such as the Fourth Lateran Conference or in major battles such as Muret. Oldenbourg has put the major military-political events except for Count Raymond VI's entry into Toulouse (September 13, 1217) in the background, but it is not out of a desire to be ahistorical that she does so. Rather her goal is to re-create the daily lives of those who have been lost to history.

In a Preface to *Destiny of Fire* of less than two pages, Oldenbourg begins by saying:

> Cet ouvrage est une oeuvre d'imagination. Aucun des personnages qui y apparaissent n'a réellement existé (à l'exception d'un seul: Bernard de Simorre, qui fut l'évêque cathare de Carcassonne au début du XIIIe siècle. L'auteur s'est efforcé de respecter l'esprit de la religion cathare, en se basant sur le peu de renseignements qui nous ont été conservés. De ces gens qui furent avant tout de grands prédicateurs aucun discours ni aucun écrit ne sont parvenus jusqu'à nous.) Les faits décrits sont conformes à la réalité historique.
>
> [This book is a product of the imagination. None of the characters portrayed in it actually existed, with the single exception of Bernard de Simorre, who was the Catharist Bishop of Carcassonne at the beginning of the thirteenth century. The author has endeavored, by basing her picture on such scanty evidence as has been preserved, to convey the spirit of the Catharist religion as it really was: though it must be made clear that the Cathars were, first and foremost great preachers – of whose discourses and sermons not one single word survives.][20]

Oldenbourg's assertion is no longer completely true, for three short sermons by Pierre and Jacques Authié from the Fournier records were later published, though they date from the 14th not the 13th century.

Oldenbourg takes a third-person point of view, yet she is not interested in presenting the "big picture" of the Albigensian Crusade and its leaders. She does not comment on the action, and the narrative features six characters who at various points become the chief focus of the story. Since we have access to the minds of those characters, and since they discuss their views in detail, the novel concentrates on their view of events. Her technique of keeping dates as non-obtrusive points of reference helps her to avoid an Olympian point of view of the Crusade.

Although Oldenbourg writes in the Preface to *Destiny of Fire* that it is "not my business to discuss the value of this creed,"[21] she admires the fact that Cathar "priests (with perhaps four or five exceptions, if we search the records closely) all preferred martyrdom to abjuration."[22] Although the Preface does not make the point, the novel is as much about a brutal colonialist war aimed at destroying Languedoc's culture and ending its independence as it is about religious persecution. In *Massacre at Monségur*, in contrast, Oldenbourg states directly what she thinks about the Albigensian Crusade: "The so-called Holy War, directed against a heresy about which the belligerents no longer appear to care, would be revealed as a war of conquest pure and simple, fought on Christian soil, led by an unscrupulous adventurer [Simon de Montfort], and backed by a handful of ambitious prelates."[23] Here she stresses the point that for the Catholic Church, might made right, whereas "we never find a *perfectus* playing even the most unobtrusive part in any of the countless rebellions that constantly flared up all over Languedoc."[24]

In *Destiny of Fire*, the protagonists are Cathars who accept martyrdom when it arrives, whereas the hero of *Cities of the Flesh* is a Catholic who eventually makes a false confession of being a Cathar in order to escape the Inquisition, and who dies at the Inquisition's hands after being recaptured. *Destiny of Fire* is in short a story of martyrdoms. It begins in early 1209. The army of Crusaders is awaited, but it has not arrived yet. We are introduced to a family of the Sault area of the northern Pyrenees in the southern part of the County of Foix, whose head is Ricord de Montgeil, age forty-five, married to Arsen de Cadéjac, age forty. They have four sons and a daughter, seventeen-year-old Gentian, who will be one of the chief characters of both novels, in fact, the one who links the two novels together. It is a staunch Cathar family, and they are visited by a very distinguished fifty-year-old Cathar deacon, Raymond de Ribeyre, and his companion in preaching, Aicart de la Cadière, age thirty.[25]

In the course of *Destiny of Fire*, Ricord leaves his estate to fight Simon de Montfort. He casts aside the non-violent teachings of the Cathar Church, and he dies under torture at Carcassonne in 1214, just before he is to be beheaded for his acts against the Crusaders. Aicart, tormeneted with desire for Gentian, tries to reach her father Ricord to bring him spiritual comfort, but he is captured, condemned by the Catholic Church as a heretic and killed in Carcassonne at the same time as Ricord. The man who replaced Raymond the deacon as Aicart's traveling companion, an ex-blacksmith named Renaud of Limoux, is burnt at the stake two years later. When her husband becomes a warrior, Arsen leaves Montgeil to lead the life of a Cathar non-cloistered nun, traveling about the countryside with another Cathar woman. Oldenbourg here illustrates a point also made by Anne

Brenon, namely that the Cathar convents were not shut off from the world like Catholic monasteries, which made them preferable to otherwise similar Catholic institutions. They opened on to the streets, and the public could see how they lived their lives without riches and free of hypocrisy.[26]

Gentian, after four years in a Cathar convent in Foix, marries the non-Cathar nobleman Bérenger d'Aspremont. Arsen is one of those killed in the Massacre at Montségur, March 16, 1244, and Gentian is burned at the stake in Toulouse in 1246 along with Bérenger, turned over to the secular authorities after being condemned by the Inquisition. Thus the time covered by the novel is 1209–1246, from the beginning of the Crusade to the aftermath of Montségur although there is a 25-year narrative gap between 1218 and 1243, when Arsen and Gentian are living independently of one another at Montségur.

After the Crusade begins, the narrator writes: "Longue, cette guerre ne le fut pas; mais elle fut telle que cent autres guerres n'eussent pas, en dix ans, causé autant de deuils, de dommage et de peur" [The war was not, indeed, lengthy; yet it was such that it caused more terror, destruction, and loss than a hundred ordinary wars could have done in ten years].[27] Although it is noted that "par la grande terreur de Béziers le ciel devint noir et le soleil couleur de sang" [When the Great Terror swept over Béziers the sky turned black and the sun shone red as blood],[28] it is not mentioned here that approximately 20,000 people were killed in a massacre planned by Innocent III's Papal Legate. Oldenbourg also avoids descriptions of the three worst episodes of burnings of heretics during the Crusade: Minerve (July 22, 1210 – 140 burned), Lavaur (May 3, 1211 – 94 burned), and Cassès (June 1211 – 94 burned), although these events are mentioned by the characters and the narrator. Thus Oldenbourg does not need descriptions of any of the four worst episodes of persecution to create sympathy for the Cathars. The main military event of the resistance, the Battle of Muret, in which Pedro II of Aragon was killed in a defeat in battle against Simon de Montfort (September 12, 1213) is another major event of the Crusade which is only mentioned briefly. She does, however, include the siege of Toulouse from 1217 to 1218 in which Simon de Montfort is eventually killed. She maintains her focus on individual fates not group slaughter.

Oldenbourg closes the introductory passage to Part Two of *Destiny of Fire* with words that reflect the apocalyptic outlook of her Cathar characters toward Simon de Montfort:

> Qui osera marcher contre cette Bête? Elle se nourrit de chair humaine, s'abreuve de sang, là où elle pose son pied la terre pourrit, son souffle empeste l'air à cent lieues alentour. Mais le jour

vient où l'on s'aperçoit que l'ennemi est aussi un homme, et qu'on peut le tuer.

[Who would dare to march against the Great Beast (Montfort)? His food was human flesh, and he slaked his thirst with blood. Where he set his foot the earth rotted away, and his breath poisoned the air for a hundred leagues around. Yet a day would come when men would see that the enemy was human, and could be slain.][29]

Gentian, one of the most dedicated believers in *Destiny of Fire*, says sarcastically to her husband Bérenger after the defeat of Montfort, that even if Count Raymond VI were to bow to the Catholic Church, she herself has no intention of prostrating herself in the haunts of Satan (Catholic churches) and telling her children to honour the Catholic bishops who have betrayed their country. At other points in the novel, conversations reveal that the Cathars looked upon the Catholic Church as Antichrist. For example, Raymond de Ribeyre tells Arsen when he visits her castle before the war starts that Antichrist is girding himself against Christ's Church.

Although it might at first seem that the presentation of such apocalyptic thoughts on the part of the Cathars might decrease sympathy for them, it really does the opposite. Each side thinks of the other as agents of Satan, but the Cathars, unlike the Catholics, did not translate these ideas into persecution. Oldenbourg gives no examples of Cathar *perfecti* resorting to violence. However, we should note that Jean Duvernoy mentions that, according to the *Chanson*, a man named Guiraud de Gourdon temporarily shed his status as a *perfectus* to fight for Raymond VI. Perhaps there were others as well.[30]

In *Destiny of Fire* Ricord de Montegeil furnishes a good example of a person who believes in Catharism for much of his life, but when Languedoc is invaded, he takes up arms. He realises with alarm that he is turning into a professional soldier whose major concern is to kill as many enemies as he can. He meets a traveling Cathar deacon and seems to expect that the deacon will condemn him for fighting, but instead the deacon tells him that the Kingdom of God is open to all kinds of labourers in the field and that death will be deliverance from this world. The deacon gives Ricord a blessing ("amelioration"), but it does him no good, since he feels that the deacon should have denounced violence. He thinks:

Quand donc, Seigneur, t'avons-nous vu sous le couteau des assassins? Quand donc? En vérité, ce moine que j'ai égorgé, c'était Toi, ce jeune homme au nez couvert de taches de rousseur auquel j'ai fracassé le crâne l'autre jour . . . c'était Toi, c'était Vous . . .

Assassins et assassins d'assassins jusqu'à la fin du monde, où vous chercher, Seigneur, sur quels visages? C'est Vous que l'on tue en Vous protégeant contre les assassins, Seigneur, je le sais, je l'ai toujours su, et je ne m'arrêterai pas. Car tout homme doit boire son calice jusqu'à la lie.

[When, O Lord, have we seen Thee under the assassin's knife? When was it? Lord it was *Thy* throat I slit, not the monk's. *Thy* skull I split the other day, and not the skull of that freckle-faced boy. Murderers, murderers of murderers, till the end of the world – where should we seek Thee, Lord? How can we recognize Thy face? O Lord, when we protect Thee against the murderers, it is Thee whom we kill, I know it. Lord. I have always known it, yet I cannot stop: every man must drink his cup to the bitter dregs.][31]

Although the chapter of the novel closes with this reflection by Ricord and there is no comment, Oldenbourg means for us to agree with Ricord and feel that the end does not justify the means and that the deacon should have told him so.[32]

Cities of the Flesh

Although the two novels can be read separately, *Cities of the Flesh* is better read in conjunction with *Destiny of Fire*. When we see Gentian and her husband Bérenger burned at the stake in Toulouse (1246) at the end of *Destiny of Fire*, we do not realise unless we go on to read *Cities of the Flesh*, that the greatest love of her life had been Roger de Montbrun, who had been her lover from 1219 to 1226. Because *Destiny of Fire* skips over twenty-five years in Gentian's life, until we read *Cities of the Flesh*, we do not see her come to the realisation that she should end her affair with Roger, a Catholic, who can not share her religious beliefs. She eventually looks upon Roger as the Devil in the Flesh, luring her away from the spiritual quest which eventually leads her to the Cathar community set up in Montségur in 1231.

Except for the first three pages (1219), when Gentian D'Aspremont first meets her lover Roger de Montbrun, the events of the first eleven chapters of *Destiny of Fire* (1209–18) take place during 1209–16 (the first chapter of *Cities of the Flesh*) and the next two years 1217–18 (which fall between the first and second chapter of *Cities of the Flesh*). Chronologically the middle four (of the six) chapters of *Cities of the Flesh* then follow (1219–38). Then come the two closing chapters of *Destiny of Fire* and then the last chapter of *Cities of the Flesh*. Although events in the first part of *Cities of the Flesh* transpire against a backdrop of Prince Louis's Crusade (1219), Amaury de Montfort's departure in defeat from Languedoc (1225),

Louis VIII's Crusade (1226), and the Treaty of Meaux (1229), the middle section of the novel is devoted in detail to the operations of the Languedoc Inquisition shortly after its establishment in 1233.

In the course of *Cities of the Flesh*, Roger de Montbrun continually tries to hold on to his own and his wife's feudal estates. In contrast, in *Destiny of Fire* we see the artisanal work performed by the Cathar characters in the communities frequented by Arsen and her missionary companion. Both Anne Brenon and René Nelli, one should note, associate the Catharist way of life with artisanry and bourgeois aspirations, and see it as a form of rejection of feudal society.[33]

Oldenbourg's novels do not give a sense of what percentage of punishments delivered by the Inquisition were mortal but rather treat individual characters and their destinies. In *Cities of the Flesh*, two major characters, Roger de Montbrun's brother Bertrand and Bertrand's wife Rachel are burned at the stake after the Inquisitors turn them over to secular punishment. Bertrand was also hideously tortured. Isaac Abrahamide, Rachel's father, although he refused to recant his Cathar faith, was sent to prison instead, where he died from a chest infection after two months. Roger is twice imprisoned and tortured by the Inquisition and seems at the point of death on the last page of the novel. Indeed, much of the second half of the novel is devoted to the Inquisition's attempt to destroy the Montbrun brothers. In these long episodes, the famous Inquisitors Peter Seila and Guillaume Arnaud appear in the background.[34]

Roger de Montbrun is imprisoned twice in the last half of the novel. After his first experiences at the hands of the Inquisition, he makes a false confession and says that he is a Cathar believer. Since the Inquisition was determined to get him to confess (1234–35), and he does not want to be executed like his brother, he makes a false confession. It enables him to have access to the monastery grounds from which he makes an escape. When he is captured again in 1247, he spends two more years in prison. After Raymond VII dies in 1249, he realises that he wants nothing more to do with Catholicism, and on the next-to-last page of the novel declares that he is a heretic and has always been a heretic. Then either he dies, is carried off to more torture, or faints with the name of "Rigueur," his poetic appellation for Gentian, on his lips. The last lines of the novel read:

> Un homme était là qui lui donnait des coups de pied, le tirait par les chaînes pour le faire rentrer dans la cellule. On le traînait, il lui semblait que cela durait des heures, qu'il était attaché pas les pieds à la queue d'un cheval.
>
> Des hommes criaient, le rouaient de coups, lui lançaient des pierres. Châtié comme traître, pourquoi? . . . Il avait le visage en

sang, il vomissait du sang. Pourquoi m'ont-ils fait cela? . . .
Rigueur. Douce Rigueur. Tendre Rigueur.

[A man was there, kicking him and dragging at the chains to get him back into the cell. He was being dragged along, and it seemed to go on for hours, he was fastened by the feet to a horse's tail.
Men were shouting, raining blows on him, hurling stones. Punished, like a traitor. Why? . . .There was blood on his face, he was vomiting blood. Why have they done this to me? . . . Rigueur, Sweet Rigueur. Gentle Rigueur.]35

As Anne Brenon writes in *Les Femmes cathares*, it would be wrong to think that *fin amors* and Catharism were directly connected, although these ideas flourished in Languedoc in the same period around 1200. However, it is fair to say, she continues, that the invasion of Languedoc wiped them out together, a fact to which the poetry of Raymond de Miraval bears witness.36 Early in *Cities of the Flesh*, Roger de Montbrun had written poetry to Gentian, and now the novel ends with her name on his lips. Oldenbourg demonstrates in the novel Brenon's association of the end of *fin amors* with the end of Catharism under Church persecution.

Malcolm Lambert indicates that the Languedoc Inquisition during its first two decades of interrogations was more concerned with asking questions about acts rather than theological beliefs.37 Questions about a person's contacts with the Cathar community were important here. Oldenbourg reflects this situation when she recounts the interrogation of Roger de Montbrun in the latter half of *Cities of the Flesh*.

The formal conscientiousness of some of the Dominicans at their Inquisitorial tasks seems irrelevant here since their goal is to eliminate freedom of conscience. Roger thinks of them during his first imprisonment as agents of terror: "Il se sentait encore plus effrayé que triste, comme si ces maudits avaient fait une alliance sacrilège avec les forces mauvaises, et possédaient le pouvoir de violer la nature elle-même et le cours du temps" [He was conscious of more terror even than sadness, as if these accursed devils had made a sacrilegious alliance with the forces of evil and possessed the power to violate even nature and the course of time].38 Since the Catholic Church is presented as so devoid of compassion, by the end of the novel the reader is made to feel that whereas Gentian lived her life and died for a viable, non-violent faith, Roger only found in the very last moments of his life the courage to identify with her Cathar beliefs. The irony of life, which of course, only comes across if the novels are read together, stems from the fact that Roger can no longer even reproach Rigueur for abandoning him. In fact, his years with her must be interpreted as a step on his progressive understanding of God.

In one of the conversations with Roger that marks the end of their relationship, Gentian tells him:

> Je ne cache mes pensées ni à ceux qui m'aiment ni à ceux qui ne m'aiment pas. Et si j'en parle, c'est pour vous dire que vos prêtres se trompent en croyant que le corps et la volonté de l'homme sont l'oeuvre de Dieu. Ils sont en vérité l'oeuvre d'un maître puissant et rusé qui ne les a pas formés pour le service de Dieu.

> [I do not hide my feelings from those who love me any more than from those who do not. The reason I mention it at all is to show you that your priests are mistaken in thinking that man's body and will were created by God. In reality they are the work of a cunning and powerful craftsman who did not form them for the service of God.] [39]

Gentian's belief reflects the absolute dualism that we find in the *Anonymous Treatise*, where it says, "The devil engendered the children of this world, who are born of the flesh of sin, who are born of blood and of the will of the flesh and of the pleasure of men."[40] It is for this reason that Gentian can think of Roger as the Devil.

L'Évêque et la vieille dame, ou la belle-mère de Peytavi Borsier

This play, unlike the two novels, is a dramatisation of a historical incident – one described on two pages of *Massacre at Montségur* (290–92), where Oldenbourg indicates that the original source material is the *Chronique* by William Pelhisson, a native of Toulouse. He joined the Dominican Order, and (in about twenty pages) he describes some incidents from 1230 to 1238, during at least part of which time he was an Inquisitor. He wrote after 1244 and died in 1268. Oldenbourg writes in *Massacre at Monségur* that the story is so disturbing that it "might well have passed for a piece of slander by those who disliked the Inquisition."[41] She states:

> Yet it cannot be doubted, for Pelhisson, as a Dominican, could have no possible motive for inventing it. All the same, it is so odd that it might have come from a madhouse. The harshness of contemporary ethics cannot wholly explain it, and in any case the principal actor was not a brigand-knight, but a bishop. Not even fanaticism can account for a whole group of monks and clergy behaving quite so savagely towards a helpless old woman.[42]

So what did he do, this Raymond de Falgar (Faura), the Catholic (Dominican)

Bishop of Toulouse who had earlier replaced the notorious Foulques of Marseilles, on this August 5, 1234, the feast day of St. Dominic?

Falgar went with a prior and several monks to the home of a dying old woman, the mother-in-law of Peytavi Borsier, a man known to be a Cathar *credens*. When the old woman, who must have had vision impairment or some other problem, heard that the "Bishop" was coming, she assumed that it was the heroic Cathar Bishop of Toulouse, Guilhabert of Castres, who was coming to offer her solace or the *consolamentum*. When Falgar arrived, instead of disabusing her of her confusion, he encouraged her to confess to her heretical beliefs and led her on in doing so before several witnesses. After he got her to confess, he tried to get her to abjure her faith, but she heroically clung to her belief. A magistrate was summoned to condemn her to death, and she was carried in her bed, since she could not walk, to the stake where she was burned.[43] Pelhisson concludes his story by indicating that Falgar and his companions had done their job well: "And after the bishop and the friars and their companions had seen the business completed, they returned to the refectory and giving thanks to God and the Blessed Dominic, ate with rejoicing what had been prepared for them."[44]

At the end of the play Oldenbourg includes a note, giving some other background details.[45] She mentions that she has relied on Guillaume de Puylaurens's statement that Foulques was so much hated by the people of Toulouse that he could not go out in the streets without attracting angry people, a situation dramatised at the beginning of the play. The Dominicans, such as Pelhisson himself, were so much hated that at one point (1235), the Count and the consuls expelled them from the city.

It is in Scene Six of the play that Raymond de Falgar tricks the old woman into going on with her confession. The tenth and last scene is performed in silence as the Old Woman is being burned at the stake. We see her face through the flames. Other characters are either watching from prison or elsewhere. The inquisitor Guillaume Arnaud is described as covered with blood and hardening himself with wild resolution. Falgar has a hard and triumphant look.[46] Perhaps even more chilling than the execution is the penultimate scene in which Falgar justifies his acts before Count Raymond VII, who maintains to him the need for freedom of conscience. Falgar answers by justifying the tactics of terror. When the Count asks him how he will be able to command respect, he responds:

> Par la peur. Car ils auront de plus en plus peur. Je vous le prédis. Le jour viendra où ils auront si peur la seule pensée de ne pas nous respecter leur paraîtra criminelle!
>
> Alors, si Dieu veut, ils trouveront moyen de nous aimer; ils n'auront pas le choix.

> L'amour n'est vrai et légitime que là où il n'y a pas de choix possible.[47]

> [By fear. For they will have more and more fear. To you I predict it. A day will come when they will have so much fear that even the thought of not respecting us will seem criminal to them.
> So, if God wishes, they will find a way to love us; they won't have a choice.
> Love is true and legitimate only where no choice is possible. (translation mine).]

These are the final words of the play before the final silent tableau. The confrontation of the Count and Folgar makes the point even more clear perhaps than in the two novels that it is not just heresy which is feared by the Dominicans but tolerance itself. Oldenbourg's note at the end of the play indicates that the incident also dramatises the Inquisitors' fear of women, particularly old women.[48]

Whereas Stephen O'Shea in *A Perfect Heresy* tells this story in full without any commentary, as though none were needed, Oldenbourg writes in *Massacre at Montségur* that events such as this one, "which provoked rather more terror than indignation in Toulouse" need further discussion.[49] She claims that the cheerfulness of the monks at their dinner after a job well done "suggests some sort of militant Brotherhood, or legal Ku Klux Klan, which was, nevertheless, itself hunted and persecuted, and determined to win at all costs."[50] She adds, "at least a proportion of the Dominicans in Languedoc must, at this period, have resembled such a Brotherhood."[51] For Oldenbourg the fact that Falgar acted as a spy and could not allow an old woman to die in peace can not be written off as simply an attitude of the time. Raymond VI of Toulouse (1156–1222) had shown himself to be a tolerant ruler. Although not a Cathar himself, he did not interfere with religious freedom, and in so doing he provoked a Crusade. Thus there is a political standard of tolerance by which to judge the civil and religious authorities of the time.

Massacre at Montségur

The strong denunciations of the Catholic Church we see in Oldenbourg's commentary on the events of her play in the earlier *Massacre at Montségur* stand in marked contrast to those of her predecessor, the distinguished historian Pierre Belperron, who makes it clear at the end of his 472-page *La Croisade contre les Albigeois* (1942) that he absolutely despises Catharism, and that he is glad that the Cathars lost to the Catholics. For him, the Cathars were really dangerous because they called for a return to the Bible and thus denounced the value of Church tradition, which enables Catholicism to adapt itself continually to new circumstances. For Belperron, from a human view Catharism is simply indefensible because it is arrogant. He says that whereas Saint Bernard could no more be sure of salvation than the most lamentable of sinners, a Cathar perfect considered himself alone worthy of approaching the throne of God. Furthermore for Belperron, Catharism generated social anarchy and supported mob rule. It was as tolerant as John Calvin. Its scorn for that which was not of the spirit kept people from loving each other and if Catharism had triumphed, the world would have become unlivable.[52] Belperron says all this in spite of events like the slaughter at Béziers.

In *Massacre at Montségur*, when Oldenbourg denounces the slaughter of 20,000 people at Béziers to launch the Albigensian Crusade she does so on good authority, and her view is shared by other distinguished historians. In *Cathares*, Yves Rouquette calls this event a rehearsal for Guernica and Hiroshima.[53] In their edition of the *Historia Albigensis* of Peter of les Vaux-de-Cernay, W. A. Sibly and M. D. Sibly state that although the *ribauds* were "largely if not solely responsible for carrying out the massacre," rather than the army proper, this was consistent with the intention of the leaders of the Crusade at this stage."[54]

Michel Roquebert in *L'Épopée Cathare; Vol. 1: 1198–1212: L'Invasion*, believes that the Catholic Legates' report to Pope Innocent that 20,000 people were massacred at Béziers is an accurate number and that this "effroyable saignée" and "hécatombe" were aimed at creating terror and that it succeeded.[55] Roquebert demonstrates that the premeditated intention of the Papal Legate, Arnaud-Amaury, who led the attack, was to kill all the inhabitants if the city did not surrender or if the heretics were not turned over. For Roquebert, both the *Chanson* and Pierre des Vaux-de-Cernay make this situation clear. Roquebert believes that Caesarius of Heisterbach may well have been right in claiming that the Legate actually did say the infamous words, "Tuez-les tous! Dieu reconnaîtra les siens."[56] Still there is no uniform agreement.[57] For example, Jonathan Sumption tries to avoid this conclusion.[58]

When we compare Oldenbourg's attitude to the Languedoc Inquisition with that of another prominent historian, Walter L. Wakefield, we see that she is considerably more outraged and judgmental. He indicates that we do not have enough surviving materials to permit an "accurate statement of how far [the Inquisition's] net was cast or how great a catch it made" in its first two decades, the 1230s to 1240s. However, it seems that in Toulouse, the city where it first operated in strength, in 1249–57, a period in which detailed sentencing records are available, of 306 severe sentences in eight years, no more than twenty-six, i.e. 8.5% led to execution.[59] Wakefield takes the view that "implacable as they seem to modern eyes, the inquisitors did act in a scrupulously legal manner, as they saw legality in those early years, did use discretion in fitting penance to the office, and were not without conscience."[60] Similarly the Catholic historian Elie Griffe in the fourth of his volumes on the Crusade stresses the fact that the Inquisitors were not strangers to compassion and injustice and that they often lessened the official sentences that they handed out.[61]

Wakefield is also less condemnatory of the Crusade itself. He writes, "Yet defeat of the heresies was not an unqualified triumph for the church, for, in part the victory was bought at the cost of centralising authority, loss of flexibility, unwillingness to absorb innovative movements but willingness to resort to force against dissent.[62] In contrast, for Oldenbourg, both the Crusade and the Inquisition are institutionalised forms of terror, and the Catholic Church defeated Catharism only "at the cost of a moral capitulation the consequences of which she is still suffering today."[63]

Oldenbourg's view stops short of the paradigm-shifting denunciation of the Catholic Church made by Robert Ian Moore in his *The Formation of a Persecuting Society: Power and Deviance in Western Europe, 950–1250*. He declares that 'if sympathy is a necessary condition of understanding, it is not a sufficient one.'[64] He criticises the view of Sir Richard Southern in *Western Society and the Church* that the appropriate attitude is to remember that "on the whole the holders of ecclesiastical authority were less prone to violence, even against unbelievers, than the people they ruled."[65] Moore says that it is just a "short and logical step" from Southern's view to Bernard Hamilton's in *The Medieval Inquisition* (1980) that the Inquisition "submitted the rule of law for mob violence in the persecution of heresy."[66] Moore feels, as Oldenbourg did before him, that the best way of understanding the Inquisition in Languedoc is not to look at the penalties that they gave but rather at the effect that they had on society in a more general way. For Moore, Christianity changed for the worse in the 1200s, and the Dominical Inquisition at Langedoc was part and parcel of the change. He describes how lepers, Jews, Cathars and sexual deviants became the objects of hate in the new persecuting society. In similar fashion, Oldenbourg notes that from the thirteenth century onwards the killing of heretics was accepted as a matter of course.[67]

Oldenbourg would strongly disagreed with Bernard Hamilton, who was to write in *The Albigensian Crusade* (1974) that it is easy to idealise the Cathars, who were mindful, as thirteenth century Popes were not, of Christ's words to Pilate: "My kingdom is not of this world," and who were burned alive for no other offense than that of holding and teaching religious opinions at variance with those of established orthodoxy. It should not be forgotten that they did not succeed in imposing their ethic of non-violent otherworldliness on the mass of their believers but only on those few who embraced the austere life of the perfect.[68] Hamilton claimed that ultimately

Catharism lost to Catholicism not because of the Inquisition but because of the "pastoral concern of the Mendicant Orders and new devotions such as the Rosary and the Stations of the Cross" which "tried to bring the life of perfection within the attainment of the people." In contrast, in his view, the Catharist faith left the "full Christian life" to the few *perfecti*, and so the friars enabled Catholicism to "fulfill a spiritual need which Catharism had never fully met."[69]

Oldenbourg's point is that, *pace* Hamilton, the Inquisition did play a major part in the Catholic victory over the Cathars. Like Joseph Reese Strayer in *The Albigensian Crusades*, she stresses the importance of the Inquisition in suppressing Catharism, although he pays more attention to a situation that Oldenbourg does not show in her novels, the fact that the King of France profited economically from a greater number of severe sentences against heretics.[70] Oldenbourg would have found Strayer obtuse when he writes, "It is unlikely that many innocent men were burned at the stake," since it rather implies that believing heretical thoughts makes you guilty.[71]

However, as Carol Lansing points out in her Epilogue to Strayer's *The Albigensian Crusades*, it is wrong to stress that the Cathars were perhaps "attracted to a church that did not meddle with their everyday lives" and that it was not an easy religion to follow because of the persecutions.[72] M. D. Costen adds, we should not think that people in Languedoc chose the Cathar Church "in default of the actions of the Church in the Midi." Instead, the people had a "very unusual opportunity to hear a new theology and choose for themselves as a result of the uncoupling of the powers of Church and secular authority."[73]

At the close of *Les Cathares: Vie et mort d'une Église chrétienne*, Anne Brenon writes passionately that whether or not we accept the idea of tolerance as a medieval concept, the fact remains that Catharism was, in the heart of the Middle Ages, against all crusades, all inquisitions. It was a Christianity that affirmed loudly that one cannot serve a good end with a bad means.[74] Zoë Oldenbourg is in agreement. Although Cathar theology is less of a concern to her than to Brenon, she feels we must not forget what happened to the Cathars. Because, as she says, it is the Catholic Church which survived, not the Cathar Church, then, we need to look at the Albigensian Crusade, the massacre at Béziers, the warfare, and the Inquisition, and analyze their effects. Since the Vatican still bears the weight of decisions made at the Fourth Lateran Council, called in part to further the Albigensian Crusade, perhaps the Crusade still haunts Catholicism as much as the Cathars haunt the imagination of medievalism.

Oldenbourg's approach to the historical novel remains distinctive because of her desire to place the common people in the foreground and reduce to very minor roles the few historical characters she lets on stage. She is not interested in a historical novel in which actions are caused by famous historical figures; rather she shows people reacting to forces much larger than themselves. However, she is not a determinist. She is trying to find in historical fiction a method which can run in tandem with some of the ideas which led to the Annales school of history and the publication of the first issue of their journal on 15 January 1929.[75] As we have seen, Oldenbourg departs from a straight story line and creates links between her two novels so that we can escape from the tyranny of a chronology of a political history dominated by figures such as Simon de Montfort and immerse ourselves in a sense of lived experience of persecution. It is not easy for a historical novelist to write a story that develops the idea of change over a long term and to try to see the "big picture," but Oldenbourg's novels succeed through her contribution to a change in the historical novel as a genre, avoiding the Scylla of romanticising the past and the Charybdis of superimposing current ideologies onto her characters.

NOTES

1. Yves Roquebert "Napoléon Peyrat, le trésor et le 'nouveau Montségur'," in Jacques Berlioz and Jean-Claude Hélas, eds. *Catharisme: L'Édifice imaginaire* (Carcassonne: Centre d'Etudes Cathares, 1998), 345–73. For a recent historiography of Catharism, see Philippe Martel, *Les cathares et l'histoire: le drame cathare devant ses historiens, 1820–1992* (Toulouse: Privat, 2002); Monique Zerner-Chardavoine, *La Croisade albigeoise* (Paris: Gallimard, 1979); and Suzanne Nelli, *Montségur: Mythe et histoire* (Monaco: Ed. Du Rocher, 1996).

2. Three translations will be used in this essay: Zoë Oldenbourg, *Destiny of Fire*, trans. Peter Green (London: Gollancz, 1961; rpt. New York: Carroll & Graf, 1999); Zoë Oldenbourg, *Cities of the Flesh*, trans. Anne Carter (New York: Pantheon, 1963); Zoë Oldenbourg, *Massacre at Montséur: A History of the Albigensian Crusade*, trans. Peter Green (London: Weidenfeld & Nicolson, 1961; rpt. London: Phoenix, 2000). The corresponding original editions are as follows: Zoë Oldenbourg, *Les Brûlés* (Paris: Gallimard, 1960); Zoë Oldenbourg, *Les Cités charnelles* (Paris: Gallimard, 1961) and Zoë Oldenbourg, *Le Bûcher de Monségur, 16 mars 1244* (Paris: Gallimard, 1959). Oldenbourg's play, *L'Évêque et la vieille dame, ou la belle-mère de Peytavi Borsier* (Paris: Gallimard, 1983) remains untranslated, so I have used my own translation here.

3. See reviews mentioned in Sophie Massalovitch, *Zoé Oldenbourg* (Monaco: Du Rocher, 1997), 133–34.

4. Krystel Maurin, *Les Esclarmonde: La Femme et la feminité dans l'imaginaire du catharisme* (Toulouse: Privat, 1995), 66, 69.

5. Oldenbourg, *Massacre at Montségur*, 367.

6. For translations, see Zoë Oldenbourg, *The World Is Not Enough*, trans. Willard Trask (New York: Pantheon, 1948); Zoë Oldenbourg, *The Cornerstone*, trans. Edward Hyams (New York: Pantheon, 1955); Zoë Oldenbourg, *Heirs of the*

Kingdom, trans. Anne Carter (New York: Pantheon, 1971). Oldenbourg has published a historical work *Les Croisades* (Paris: Gallimard, 1965 [*The Crusades*, trans. Anne Carter (London: Weidenfeld & Nicolson, 1966)], a long essay on Saint Bernard included in *Saint Bernard: Textes de Saint Bernard, Geoffroi de Clairvaux, Bérenger de Poitiers, Bossuet* (Paris: Albin Michel, 1982) and commentary for a book on medieval cathedrals, *L'épopée des cathédrales* (Paris: Hachette / Réalités, 1972).

7. Sophie Massalovitch, *Zoé Oldenbourg* (Monaco: Du Rocher, 1997).

8. Maurice Magre, *Le Sang de Toulouse: Histoire albigeoise du XIIIe siècle* (Paris: Fasquelle, 1931); Maurice Magre, *Le Trésor des albigeois: roman du XVIe siècle à Toulouse* (Paris: Fasquelle, 1938); Antoine Dondaine, *Un traité neo-manichéen du XIIIe siècle: le liber de duobus principiis, suivi d'un fragment de rituel cathare* (Rome: Istituto Storico Domenicano, 1939).

9. Rion Klawinski, *Chasing the Heretics: A Modern Journey through the Medieval Languedoc* (Saint Paul, MN: Hungry Mind, 1999), 210.

10. Other novels on the Cathars include the following: Charles Robert Maturin's *The Albigenses* (1824), Giuseppe La Farina's *Gli Albigesi* (1855), Coussou's *Mountségur* [sic] (1890), Hannah Priebsch Closs's "Tarn Trilogy," *High Are the Mountains* (1959), *Deep Are the Valleys* (1960) and *The Silent Tarn* (1963), Georges Bordonove's *Le Bûcher* (1957), Jacqueline Dumesnil's *Les Cavaliers de la nuit* (1964), Saint-Loup's *Nouveaux cathares pour Montségur* (1968), Gérard de Sède's *Du trésor de Delphes à la tragédie cathare* (1977), Michel Peyramaure's *La Passion cathare: 1. Les Fils de l'orgueil. – 2. Les Citadelles ardentes. – 3. La Tête du dragon* (1977), Roger de Cardelus's *Sous le signe cathare* (1977), Sissel-Lange Nielsen's *Bålet* (1982), Henri Gougaud's *Bélibaste* (1982), Jean Blum's *Guilhem Blasquo: Un fils du Languedoc cathare* (1985), Patrick Harper's *The Serpent's Circle* (1985), Jean Broutin's *Le Marteau de Saint Eloi* (1982) and *Les Cathares, ou, Le baiser de lumière* (1986), Philippe Randa's *Alaïs* (1989), Christian Pastre's *La Fleur de bûcher* (1992), Elizabeth Chadwick's *Children of Destiny* (1993) and *Daughters of the Grail* (1995), Jean-Yves Pahin's *Le Baptême d'esprit* (1993), Michael Baldwin's *The Rape of Oc* (1994), Jean-Jacques Bédu's *Les Terres du feu* (1994), Jan Arvid Hellstrom's *Änglarnas fall* (1995), Dominique Baudis's *Raimond, "le Cathare"* (1996), Jean-François Nahmias's *L'Illusion cathare* (1997), Susan Kelly's *The Ghosts of Albi* (1998), René-Victor Pilhes's *Le Christi* (1998), Florence Ferrari's *Le Dernier Comte Cathare* (1998), François M. Bluche's *La Vénus de Montségur* (1998), Hanny Alders's *De volmaakte Ketter* (1999), David Thomas's *The Fire* (1999), Georg Brun's *Das Vermächtnis der Katharer* (2000), Jerome V. Lofgren's *Love in the Time of the Inquisition* (2000), Sylvie Miller and Philippe Ward's *Le Chant de Montségur* (2001), Anne Brenon, *L'Hiver du catharisme* (2001), and Sophy Burnham's *The Treasure of Montségur* (2002).

11. Anne Brenon, "Préface à la Nouvelle Edition," in René Nelli and Anne Brenon, eds. *Écritures Cathares*, New [3rd] ed. (Monaco: Ed. Du Rocher, 1995), 9–17. The first edition was published as René Nelli, *Écritures cathares* (Paris: Denoël, 1959), and the second as René Nelli, *Écritures cathares: La Cène secrete, Le livre des deux principes, Traité cathare, Le Rituel occitan, Le Rituel latin; Textes précathares et cathares présentés, traduits et commentés avec une introduction sur les*

origines et l'esprit du catharisme, Nouvelle éd. revue et augmentée (Paris, Planète, 1968).

12. See René Nelli, *La Philosophie du catharisme: le dualisme radical au XIIIe siècle* (Paris: Payot, 1975); Jean Duvernoy, *Le Catharisme, 1: La Religion des cathares* (Toulouse: Privat, 1976) and *Le Catharisme, 2: L'Histoire des cathares* (Toulouse: Privat, 1979); Michel Roquebert, *L'Epopée cathare* (1971–89): *Vol. 1: 1198–1212: L'Invasion* (Toulouse: Privat, 1970); *Vol. 2: 1212–1217: Muret, ou la dispossession* (Toulouse: Privat, 1977); *Vol. 3: 1216–1229: Le Lys et la croix* (Toulouse: Privat, 1986); *Vol. 4: Mourir à Montségur* (Toulouse: Privat, 1989), as well as Roquebert, *Montségur: Les Cendres de la liberté* (Toulouse: Privat, 1992).

13. Joseph Reese Strayer, *The Albigensian Crusades* (1971; 2nd ed. Ann Arbor: University of Michigan Press, 1992); Walter L[eggatt] Wakefield's *Heresy, Crusade and Inquisition in Southern France, 1100–1250* (London: Allen & Unwin, 1974); Jonathan Sumption, *The Albigensian Crusade* (London: Faber & Faber, 1978); M. D. Costen, *The Cathars and the Albigensian Crusade* (Manchester: University of Manchester Press, 1997); Stephen O'Shea, *The Perfect Heresy: The Revolutionary Life and Death of the Medieval Cathars* (New York: Walker, 2001); Malcolm Lambert, *The Cathars* (London: Basil Blackwell, 1998); Yuri Stoyanov, *The Other God: Dualist Religions from Antiquity to the Cathar Heresy* (New Haven: Yale University Press, 2000); Malcolm Barber, *The Cathars: Dualist Heretics in Languedoc in the High Middle Ages* (New York: Longman, 2000). See "Further reading" in Barber and his excellent references to primary and secondary sources, 239–53.

14. Stephen Runciman, *The Medieval Manichee: A Study of the Christian Dualist Heresy* (Cambridge: Cambridge University Press, 1947); Hans Söderberg, *La Religion des Cathares: Étude sure le gnosticisme de la basse antiquité et du moyen âge* (Stockholm: Almqvist & Wiksell, 1949); Arno Borst, *Die Katharer* (Stuttgart: Hiersemann Verlag) 1953, v.

15. Anne Brenon, "Préface à la Nouvelle Edition," (12). Against Brenon, for the competing view of a dualism spread to the Cathars from the East, see Malcolm Barber, *The Cathars: Dualist Heretics in Languedoc in the High Middle Ages*, 6–33.

16. Anne Brenon, *Les Cathares: Vie et mort d'une Église chrétienne* (Paris: Jacques Grancher, 1996), 350–51.

17. Pope Benedict XII, *Le régistre d'inquisition de Jacques Fournier (Évêque de Pamiers), 1318–1325*, ed. and trans. Jean Duvernoy. 3 vols. (New York: Mouton. 1978); Emmanuel Le Roy Ladurie, *Montaillou, village occitan de 1294 à 1324* (Paris: Gallimard, 1975).

18. All three major sources were translated into English between 1996 and 2003: (1) William of Tudela and an Anonymous Successor, *The Song of the Cathar Wars: A History of the Albigensian Crusade*, trans. Janet Shirley (Aldershot: Scolar Press, 1996); (2) Petrus Sarnensis, *The History of the Albigensian Crusade: Peter of les-Vaux-de-Cernay's Historia Albigensis*, trans. W. A. Sibly and M. D. Sibly (Woodbridge: Boydell Press, 1998); (3) Guillaume de Puylaurens, *The Chronicle of William of Puylaurens: The Albigensian Crusade and its Aftermath*, trans. W. A. Sibly and M. D. Sibly (Woodbridge: Boydell Press, 2003).

19. James, King of Aragon, *The Book of Deeds of James I of Aragon: A Translation of the Medieval Catalan Llibre dels fets*, ed. and trans. Damian J. Smith and

Helena Buffery (Aldershot: Ashgate, 2003); Caesarius of Heisterbach, "A Northern View of the Crusade," in Wakefield, ed. *Heresy, Crusade, and Inquisition*, 195–99; William Pelhisson, "Chronicle," in Wakefield, ed., *Heresy, Crusade, and Inquisition*, 207–36. See also Guillaume Pelhisson, *Chronique, 1229–1244; suivie du Récit des troubles d'Albi, 1234*, ed. Jean Duvernoy (Paris: CNRS, 1994).

20. Oldenbourg, *Les Brûlés*, 5 and *Destiny of Fire*, 15. Note that Green's translation here is slightly impressionistic.

21. Oldenbourg, *Les Brûlés*, 6 and *Destiny of Fire*, 15.

22. Oldenbourg, *Les Brûlés*, 6 and *Destiny of Fire*, 15.

23. Oldenbourg, *Massacre at Montségur*, 163 and *Le Bûcher de Monségur*, 167.

24. Oldenbourg, *Massacre at Montségur*, 151 and *Le Bûcher de Monségur*, 155.

25. I have worked out the following chronology for the novels:

Destiny of Fire

		Chapter Title	
Part One	Chapter 1	Raymond de Ribeyre	early 1209
	Chapter 2	The Chosen	Lent 1209
Part Two	Chapter 3	First Temptations and Ordeals	1209–11
	Chapter 4	The Scarlet Crosses	1211–12
	Chapter 5	The Church Militant	1213
Part Three	Chapter 6	The Passion of Ricord	1213
	Chapter 7	Aicart	1214
	Chapter 8	Gentian	1215
	Chapter 9	Renaud of Limoux	1216
	Chapter 10	Love Defeated	1217
Part Four	Chapter 11	Toulouse	1217–18
	Chapter 12	Montségur (April 1243)	1243
	Chapter 13	The Faithful (1246)	1246

Cities of the Flesh

Part One	Chapter 1			1209–16
	Chapter 2			1219–22
	Chapter 3			1222–29
Part Two	Chapter 1			1229–34
	Chapter 2	Section I		1234–35
		Section II		1235–38
	Chapter 3	Section I	Brother Alberic of Montpellier	1247
		Section II	The Last Prison	1247–49

26. Anne Brenon, *Les Cathares: Pauvres du Christ ou Apôtres de Satan?* (Paris: Gallimard, 1997), 57.

27. Oldenbourg, *Les Brûlés*, 69 and *Destiny of Fire*, 73.

28. Oldenbourg, *Les Brûlés*, 69 and *Destiny of Fire*, 73.

29. Oldenbourg, *Les Brûlés*, 69 and *Destiny of Fire*. 73.

30. Jean Duvernoy, *Le Catharisme: Vol. 2: L'Histoire des cathares* (Toulouse: Privat, 1979; rpt. Toulouse: Privat, 1986), 260.

31. Oldenbourg, *Les Brûlés*, 153 and *Destiny of Fire* 147.

32. In *Destiny of Fire* the Cathars are never connected to any other dualistic group, and we find no mention of the Bogomils from Serbia, who may have influenced the growth of the movement in the previous century (See Malcolm Barber,

The Cathars: Dualist Heretics in Languedoc in the High Middle Ages (New York: Longman, 2000), 32–33). Also, little is made of the idea of the transmigration of souls. Oldenbourg presents the Cathars in terms of their rites, such as the *consolamentum* and the laying on of hands, rather than their theology except for some explication of their understanding of the Lord's Prayer. Wisely, she does not risk making mistakes on the more complex beliefs and aspects of Cathar faith. Jean-Pierre Cartier in his *Histoire de la Croisade contre les Albigeois* (Paris: Bernard Grasset, 1968) raises the hard-to-answer question of whether the "Parfaits" unlike the *croyants (credentes)* were initiated into a secret knowledge (39). In Oldenbourg's presentation, initiates appear to have no secret knowledge.

Oldenbourg presents her Cathars neither as intellectuals nor as scholars engaged in polemics. Perhaps this is an oversimplification. Yuri Stoyanov in *The Other God* has claimed that recent research confirms that Languedoc Cathars "participated in the broad theological and educational trends of the late twelfth and early thirteenth centuries, including the reception of Aristotle's *On Generation*" (261).

The recital of the Lord's Prayer appears twice in the novel (*Les Brûlés*, 192–93, 402; *Destiny of Fire* (185, 375). In the Florence (Latin) ritual, the Lord's Prayer is presented, and the phrase "superstantial bread" is explained as it also is in the Lyon (Occitan) text and Dublin (Latin) version (Walter L. Wakefield and Austin P. Evans, *Heresies of the High Middle Ages: Selected Sources Translated and Edited* (New York: Columbia University Press, 1969; rpt. New York: Columbia University Press, 1991, 469, 483, 618). It represents the Cathar understanding of the word, *epiousios*. The Florence ritual glosses the word as "the Law of Christ which was laid down upon the whole people" (469) and the Dublin ritual identifies it as "charity" (618). Aicart explains the first reference to it in the novel as "The True Bread which is the Spirit and the Life, Thy true teachings that are the soul's only bread; that food of Christ which is to do the Father's will" (*Destiny of Fire* 185; *Les Brûlés* 192–93).

The *consolamentum*, as Stephen O'Shea states in *The Perfect Heresy*, was the only Cathar sacrament. Through its agency the believer became one of the Perfect, who could then give the *consolamentum* to others. It consisted of the laying on of hands and was to be given only when the recipient wanted to take the final step of living a life of constant prayer and frequent fasting while abstaining from sexual intimacy. Fasting meant avoiding meat and dairy products. Those who failed to live up to the *consolamentum* had to receive it again (23). More information on Cathar beliefs can be found at www.cathares.org.

33. See Anne Brenon, "Préface à la Nouvelle Edition."

34. Oldenbourg admits in an article, "Le roman et l'histoire," *Nouvelle Revue Française* 238 (Oct. 1972): 130–55, explaining her views of the writing of historical novels, that in *Cities of the Flesh*, she uses more historical characters than in her other four novels set in the Middle Ages. (145). I would like to thank Oliva Schaff for bringing this article to my attention as well as another short article by Oldenbourg about historical fiction, "Histoire et Roman," *Perspectives Médiévales: Société de Langue et de Littérature* 9 (1983), 83–86, in which she stresses the need for historical novelists to avoid the trap of granting to their characters embroiled in events a greater historical perspective than they can reasonably have (86).

35. Oldenbourg, *Cities of the Flesh*, 569 and *Les Cités charnelles*, 503.

36. Anne Brenon, *Les Femmes cathares* (Paris: Perrin, 1992), 151.
37. Malcolm Lambert, *The Cathars* (London: Basil Blackwell, 1998).
38. Oldenbourg, *Cities of the Flesh*, 397 and *Les Cités charnelles*, 349.
39. Oldenbourg, *Cities of the Flesh*, 108–09 and *Les Cités charnelles*, 94.
40. Wakefield and Evans, *Heresies of the High Middle Ages*, 401.
41. Oldenbourg, *Massacre at Montségur*, 290–92 (291). In the French original, the episode can be found on 298–301.
42. Oldenbourg, *Massacre at Montségur*, 291.
43. Oldenbourg, *Massacre at Montségur*, 291; William Pelhisson, "Chronicle," 207–36 (215–16).
44. Pelhisson, "Chronicle" (216).
45. Oldenbourg, *L'Évêque et la vieille dame, ou la belle-mère de Peytavi Borsier* (Paris: Gallimard, 1983), 113–19.
46. Oldenbourg, *L'Évêque*, 111.
47. Oldenbourg, *L'Évêque*, 109–10.
48. Oldenbourg, *L'Évêque*, 117.
49. *The Perfect Heresy*; Oldenbourg, *Massacre at Montségur*, 292.
50. Oldenbourg, *Massacre at Montségur*, 292.
51. Oldenbourg, *Massacre at Montségur*, 292.
52. Pierre Belperron, *La Croisade contre les Albigeois et L'Union du Languedoc à la France (1209–1249)* (Paris: Plon, 1942; Paris: Librarie Académique Perrin, 1967), 469–70.
53. Yves Rouquette, *Cathares* (Portet-sur-Garonne: Loubatières, 1991), 86.
54. Peter of les Vaux-de-Cernay, *The History of the Albigensian Crusade (Historia Albigensis)*, trans. W. A. and M. D. Sibly, 293.
55. Michel Roquebert, *L'Epopée cathare* (1971–89), *Vol. 1: 1198–1212: L'Invasion* (Toulouse: Privat, 1970), 263.
56. Caesarius of Heisterbach, "A Northern View of the Crusade," 195–99; Michel Roquebert, *L'Epopée cathare* (1971–89), *Vol. 1: 1198–1212: L'Invasion* (Toulouse: Privat, 1970), 261.
57. Caesarius of Heisterbach, "Northern View," 197; William of Tudela and an Anonymous Succesor, *The Song of the Cathar Wars: A History of the Albigensian Crusade*, trans. Janet Shirley (Aldershot: Scolar Press, 1996), 21; Peter of les Vaux-de-Cernay, *The History of the Albigensian Crusade*, trans. W. A. and M. D. Sibly, 48–51; Guillaume de Puylaurens, *The Chronicle of William of Puylaurens*, trans. W. A. and M. D. Sibly, 33, 127–29.
58. Jonathan Sumption, *The Albigensian Crusade* (London: Faber & Faber, 1978), 93.
59. Wakefield, *Heresy, Crusade, and Inquisition*, 184.
60. Wakefield, *Heresy, Crusade, and Inquisition*, 185.
61. Elie Griffe, *Le Languedoc cathare et L'Inquisition (1229–1329)* (Paris: Letouzey et Ané, 1980), 30.
62. Wakefield, *Heresy, Crusade, and Inquisition*, 191.
63. Oldenbourg, *Massacre at Montségur*, 367.
64. R. I. Moore, *The Formation of a Persecuting Society: Power and Deviance in Western Europe, 950–1250* (New York: Blackwell, 1987), 3.

65. R. W. Southern, *Western Society and the Church* (Harmondsworth, Eng.: Penguin, 1970), 19 quoted in Moore 3.

66. Bernard Hamilton, *The Medieval Inquisition* (London: E. Arnold, 1981), 57, quoted in Moore 3.

67. Oldenbourg, *Massacre at Montségur*, 367.

68. Bernard Hamilton, *The Albigensian Crusade* (London: The Historical Association, 1974), 31–32.

69. Hamilton, *The Albigensian Crusade*, 32.

70. Joseph Reese Strayer, *The Albigensian Crusades*, 2nd ed. (Ann Arbor: University of Michigan P, 1992), 156–57.

71. Strayer, *The Albigensian Crusades*, 157.

72. Carol Lansing, "Epilogue" to Strayer, *The Albigensian Crusades*, 175–239 (211).

73. M. D. Costen, *The Cathars and the Albigensian Crusade* (Manchester; University of Manchester Press, 1997), 200.

74. Anne Brenon, *Les Cathares: Vie et mort d'une Église chrétienne*, 350.

75. The economist François Simiand had criticised historians' overemphasis on political history, the great individual, and chronology as far back as 1903, in his "Méthode historique et sciences sociales," *Revue de Synthèse Historique* 6 (1903), 1–22.

Contributors

MARK BURDE is currently Assistant Professor of French at Yale University. His primary areas of interest and research are the French literature and culture of the twelfth and thirteenth centuries, particularly the inter-related problems of satire, parody, the carnivalesque and figurations of the alimentary. His recent foray into French institutional medievalism began with an article published in the journal *Exemplaria* in 2004 and will likely continue with investigations into other aspects of the under-investigated period of 1830s and 1840s French medieval scholarship.

PETER G. CHRISTENSEN is an Assistant Professor of English at Cardinal Stritch University in Milwaukee, Wisconsin. He received a Ph.D. in Comarative Literature from SUNY-Binghamton, where he specialized in twentieth-century fiction. He has published articles on historical novels by such authors as Marguerite Yourcenar, John Hersey, Henrik Stangerup, Per Olaf Enquist, Nils Petersen, John Cowper Powys, and Johannes V. Jensen.

ALPITA DE JONG studied General Literature at the University of Leiden and is currently working on her thesis at the department of Modern European Literature of the University of Amsterdam; it will outline the European and political dimensions of Frisian cultural nationalism, and concentrates in particular on the exchange of ideas about the Frisian language between the Frisian philologist Joast Halbertsma (1789–1869) and his English, Danish, German and Italian colleagues. She has published on this subject in several Dutch periodicals, and has also published translations of Italian novels, literary essays, and an anthology of Frisian prose.

RACHEL DRESSLER is Associate Professor of Art History at the University at Albany, State University of New York, where she teaches courses on medieval art. She has published articles on the Royal Portal sculpture at Chartres Cathedral and, more recently, on English medieval knights' effigies. She is author of *Of Armor and Men in Medieval England: The Chivalric Rhetoric of Three English Knights' Effigies*.

MAGNÚS FJALLDAL trained as a medievalist at the University of Iceland, Yale and Harvard Universities, and completed a Ph.D. in Medieval English and Germanic Philology at Harvard. Since 1982 he has taught at the University of Iceland in Reykjavik, and is currently a Professor of Old and

Middle English there. For the last fifteen years he has been studying the proposed contact points between Anglo-Saxon literature and Icelandic medieval texts; in particular the so-called genetically related analogues between *Beowulf* and *Grettis saga*, and Anglo-Saxon history as related in Icelandic histories of kings, family sagas, *þættir* and saints' lives. He is also increasingly interested in the early interpretation of medieval texts.

KARL FUGELSO, an assistant professor of art history at Towson University, earned his Ph.D. from Columbia University in 1999 for a dissertation on illuminated manuscripts of the *Divine Comedy*. Since then, he has published numerous articles on modern and medieval illustrations of Dante's text, as well as articles on medieval architecture and on images of the Palaeologus in Renaissance art and modern art historiography. He is currently working on the intersection of neo-classicism and medievalism in nineteenth-century engravings of the *Commedia*.

ANNETTE KREUTZIGER-HERR studied musicology, Italian and Medieval German in Hamburg, Kiel and Bologna, finishing with a Ph.D. thesis on language and music in the fourteenth century. She has taught musicology since 1992 both at the College of Music and the University of Hamburg as well as at Smith College, Northampton, MA, and is currently Associate Professor of musicology at the University of Music and Drama in Hanover. She is editor and/or author of eight books on music and editor of the forthcoming series "European women composers". One of her most recent publications is *Dreaming the Middle Ages: The Rediscovery of Medieval Music in Modernity*, described in the *Neue Zürcher Zeitung*, as "an inspiring example of cultural history writing, which is of interest not only to the musicologist."

NILS HOLGER PETERSEN is Associate Professor of Church History at the University of Copenhagen. Since 2002, he has been the leader of the Centre for the Study of the Cultural Heritage of Medieval Rituals, a temporary research centre at the University of Copenhagen funded by the Danish National Research Foundation. He has mainly published in two academic areas: Latin music drama in the context of the public ceremonies of the medieval Latin church (the subject of his doctoral dissertation), and the reception of the Middle Ages in Early Modern and Modern European music drama. He is also a composer of modern classical music: his medievalistic opera, *A Vigil for Thomas Becket* (premiered in 1990 in Copenhagen) was presented at the *Studies in Medievalism* conference in Canterbury in 1997.

WILLIAM A. QUINN is a Professor of English as well as Director of the Medieval and Renaissance Studies Program at the University of Arkansas,

Fayetteville, where he has taught since 1979. His publications include *Chaucer's Dream Visions and Shorter Poems* (2000), *Chaucer's Janglerye: The Performability of The Legend of Good Women* (1994), and *Jongleur: A Modified Theory of Oral Improvisation and its Effects on the Performance and Transmission of Middle English Romance* (1982, with Audley S. Hall). He has also written more than a dozen articles appearing in *The Review of English Studies, Chaucer Review, Studies in the Age of Chaucer, Viator, Medium Aevum,* and *Studies in Scottish Literature* among other journals. He is currently completing a book on Chaucer's *Troilus and Criseyde*.